THE REGIME OF ANASTASIO SOMOZA, 1936–1956

THE REGIME OF
ANASTASIO SOMOZA
1936–1956

Knut Walter

The

University

of North

Carolina

Press

Chapel Hill

& London

The paper in this book meets the guidelines for
permanence and durability of the Committee on
Production Guidelines for Book Longevity of the Council
on Library Resources.

Knut Walter is professor of history at Universidad
Centroamerica in San Salvador.

Library of Congress Cataloging-in-Publication Data
Walter, Knut.
    The regime of Anastasio Somoza / Knut Walter.
      p. cm.
    Includes bibliographical references (p.   ) and index.
    ISBN 0-8078-2106-3 (cloth : alk. paper).—
    ISBN 0-8078-4427-6 (pbk. : alk. paper)
    1. Nicaragua—Politics and government—1937–
1979. 2. Somoza, Anastasio, 1896–1956. I. Title.
F1527.W34   1993
972.8505′2—dc20   93-12467
                                    CIP

97 96 95 94 93   5 4 3 2 1

CONTENTS

. . . .

Chapter 4

Chapter 5

Chapter 6

A section of illustrations follows page 117.

TABLES

· · · · · · · · · · · · · ·

ACKNOWLEDGMENTS

· · · · · · · · · · · · · · ·

A number of individuals and organizations shared in the writing of this book. I must thank the Ford Foundation and the Social Science Research Council, as well as my Universidad Centroamericana José Simeón Cañas in San Salvador, for providing the grants and loans that enabled me to complete this study. This book is a direct offspring of the work that I did on state formation in Nicaragua.

In Nicaragua I had unrestricted access to the holdings of the Instituto Histórico Centroamericano, whose director, Alvaro Argüello, S.J., took a personal interest in my work. At the Archivo Nacional de Nicaragua, Adilia Moncada, Alfredo González, and Liduvina Calatayud, as well as the rest of the staff, did everything possible to assist me in my work under conditions that were trying, to say the least. The Archivo Nacional, together with the Instituto de Historia de Nicaragua and its director, Margarita Vannini, allowed me to look through their extensive photographic archives and copy whatever material I found interesting; all the pictures included in the text come from these two sources. And last, but not least, Eugenio Arene plowed through mountains of pages filled with numbers to distill the data for some of the tables I have used to explain the growth of state institutions and functions. To all of these good friends, I extend my thanks and respect.

The writing itself benefited at different stages from abundant comments by Joseph S. Tulchin, Gilbert M. Joseph, and Rose Spalding. Their assistance and interest in this project gave me confidence to wrap the thing up. The editors at the University of North Carolina Press, particularly David Perry, as well as the anonymous readers of various drafts, were instrumental in turning this study into a book. Stevie Champion did an extraordinary job of copyediting a final draft that I thought was ready for the printer.

My parents supported my efforts at all times; if only they had lived to see the final product. Finally, Mely, Carlos, and Anna are the real authors of this book, although I alone am responsible for its shortcomings.

San Salvador, October 24, 1992

INTRODUCTION

. . . .

In July 1979, after a brief but bloody popular insurrection, the last member of the Somoza family to head the government of Nicaragua fled into exile. So ended a political system that seemed solidly entrenched since the mid-1930s when Anastasio Somoza García became president of the republic. How can the longevity and the strength of the Somocista regime be explained? To discount the regime as just another Latin American military dictatorship bent on familial enrichment through the corruption of the state's power misses a central point: that the figure of the dictator and his coterie were but the public face of a much wider and deeper network of economic and political domination. In general, dictatorships in Latin America have been viewed through the figures of the dictators themselves as representatives of a given tradition of political culture while little effort has been made to search out those characteristics of dictatorial political control that distinguish it from other types of political systems.[1]

The basic question of how we are to understand the Somoza regime has been rendered increasingly important by current events in Nicaragua. As it turns out, the Sandinista revolution sought not only to eliminate the most obvious vestiges of the old regime but also to overhaul the Nicaraguan state in an attempt to create a new social and economic order. In this endeavor, the greatest obstacle the revolution faced is what might be called the passive legacy of the Somoza era—that combination of public and private institutions and economic interests that together constituted the prerevolutionary state. In seeking to reorient government policies and the role of private producers to favor popular demands, the revolutionary regime tried to rebuild the Nicaraguan state, reform its institutions and laws, and purge its bureaucracy of disloyal and inefficient elements. Such a task could not be undertaken and completed from one day to the next; the old order, solidly entrenched and relatively impervious to change, combined the coercive power of its armed forces with an array of political and economic alliances that survived, albeit weakened and transformed, the policies implemented and planned by the revolutionary regime.

This study addresses the problem of Nicaragua's political development by focusing on the formation of the state under the first years of Somocista rule from 1936 to 1956. During this period, the Somocista regime and the modern Nicaraguan state acquired their fundamental characteristics and thereby laid the bases for Nicaragua's subsequent economic and political development, including, of course, the recent revolutionary outcome.

The use of the state as an object of study is especially relevant in this regard. In the first place, the state is a concept that explicitly involves the questions of political power and societal domination. This consideration is of particular importance in the case of Nicaragua with its antecedent of long-term dictatorial control and the triumph of a revolutionary movement in the late 1970s, when one form of political domination was replaced by a new one of a markedly different orientation. In the second place, the state can be construed as a political arena in which various social forces vie for control of the government. This approach is important to understand Nicaraguan political history since independence from Spain, with its profusion of civil wars and regional animosities, together with various attempts by political leaders and interest groups to create a strong state either through political accommodation or military force. And finally, Nicaragua's location made it the target of great power designs that subjected the local dominant classes to intense pressures, especially those involving the construction of a transisthmian canal. As a result, the Nicaraguan political system was determined to one extent or another by the actions of foreign states; that is, the Nicaraguan state was the product in important respects of the political and military decisions of stronger states.

In more general terms, the concept of the state, both as a theoretical and a practical consideration, has engaged the attention of Western thinkers since at least the late Renaissance. Some of the more recent scholarship on European political and economic development has placed the state in a central position in any explanation of the rise of capitalism.[2] Another contemporary approach has looked to explain the state more in political and institutional terms.[3] In fact, the current debate hinges precisely on the relationship between the role of the state and the attainment of a society's fundamental goals. More class-oriented interpretations insist, of course, on the primacy of class conflict in determining the form and orientation of the state. For example, Harold Laski suggests that within each state there is always a bias in favor of a specific group because the state's primary function is "to ensure the peaceful process of production of society" and, therefore, the basic struggles within the state are always those "between economic classes to secure control of the sovereign power."[4] Similarly, Guillermo O'Donnell defines the class basis of society as the "great differentiator" that allows some individuals greater access to the resources of power within the state.[5] In any case, control of the state is the ultimate objective of political activity. Therefore, any study of state formation and consolidation must identify those political actors, be they defined as groups, classes, or sectors of society, that participate in the struggle for control of the state and whose interests are reflected in the policy decisions that the state implements.

In sum, power, political conflict, and governmental policies are the parameters that define the state and within which it must be analyzed. To the extent that states are able to exercise power, defuse, channel, or repress political conflict, and formulate policies that guarantee the fundamental stability of the social system, they acquire strength and legitimacy, which are the ultimate objectives of any state. The first is a precondition for the permanence in office of the government of the state in the face of claims to power from rival groups. The strength of the state is synonymous with political and institutional stability and continuity and is closely dependent on the state's ability to extract and control the material resources needed for the exercise of effective political power; such resources would include, among others, a taxable economic base, an effective bureaucracy and armed force, and an infrastructure commensurate with the needs of the state itself.

The second objective, legitimacy, is expressed in practice by the state's ability to demand obedience from a population without recourse to violence or coercion and rests, therefore, on widely held beliefs about the desirability of peace and order and the attainment of the common good. Legitimacy is necessary for the government of a state because the costs, both economic and political, of societal domination can be lessened considerably if the state's population is willing to obey out of conviction or convenience and not out of fear of physical or judicial punishment. In order to instill the notion of legitimacy among a population, the state must keep a handle on the instruments of ideological control that reinforce the population's allegiance to the social and economic structure and the institutions of government; such instruments include the educational system, the communications media, and a religion and/or a political ideology that provide the ultimate moral sanction for the state.[6]

The legitimacy and the stability of a state are not achieved in a short time. They are the result of a process that may take centuries to play itself out and that arguably is never totally finished. Oscar Oszlak has suggested that what should be measured is precisely the level of "stateness" that a given society has achieved over time and that not only must include characteristics of stability and legitimacy but also must identify the issues around which political conflict occurs and the political actors so engaged. He indicates that stateness can be measured in terms of the state's capacity to extract and allocate societal resources, to impose collective identities and loyalties, to institutionalize its authority, and to externalize its power within an international system of states.[7]

In his measurement of stateness, however, Oszlak attributes particular importance to the development of the institutional apparatus of the state. He broadly defines the institutional apparatus of the state as that "heterogeneous and interdependent group of 'public' organizations," both private and public (governmental), in which "socially crucial issues are settled." As the level of involvement of these institutions increases, so does the level of state autonomy as the guarantor of the social order; the resolution of social issues is gradually transferred from the direct interactions between individuals and groups and is subsumed within a network of institutions that presumably act in the "general interest." In other words, the existence of state institutions not only reflects the contradictions and conflicts of a society; state institutions also are formed and evolve precisely out of the need to settle "socially crucial issues," which means that state institutions and social issues are inseparable. For Oszlak, therefore, the important social issues are those that contribute to the development of stateness.[8]

In Latin America, according to Oszlak, early state formation and increasing levels of stateness depended basically on the articulation of urban and rural interests connected with export economic activities, such as the cases of Chile and Costa Rica. In most other countries of Latin America, however, such unity did not materialize in the years after independence from Spain. In these, instead, "order and progress" became the basis of state formation: an order imposed by a central government on local and regional power holders, and progress as a consequence of eventual political stability and the opportunities offered by rapidly growing world markets for raw materials and food products. In these countries, the state became the axis around which new forms of political and economic domination were consolidated; around the issues of order and progress the state acquired stateness.[9]

In Central America, the development of the state generally followed the pattern described by Oszlak. Three of the Central American nations, El Salvador, Guatemala, and Costa Rica, developed dynamic export sectors in a relatively short period of time after independence. There, the years of anarchy and regional rivalries were substantially over by 1870, to be substituted by strong central governments under the control of local coffee-growing oligarchies. In the cases of Honduras and Nicaragua, what export sectors developed in the nineteenth century were under foreign control and operated as enclaves, so that the wider social and political systems were hardly affected. In these countries, economic activity and political life for most of the population during the nineteenth century still centered around the traditional hacienda, with its semiautarchic and labor-intensive agricultural production and caudillo domination.[10] In the particular case of Nicaragua, political developments were further complicated by various episodes of foreign intervention related directly or indirectly to Nicaragua's privileged position as a possible transisthmian canal route.

The research undertaken here will focus on these historical questions as they developed in Nicaragua, a "late starter" in the process of export production and state formation, concentrating on the period 1936–56 when Anastasio Somoza García was head of state and commanding officer of the Guardia Nacional of Nicaragua. It is my contention that the Somocista regime laid the foundations of the modern Nicaraguan state by implementing a number of important changes in the Nicaraguan political system. In the first place, it neutralized or co-opted the old caudillo leadership based on regional interest groups and replaced it with a broad coalition of agricultural entrepreneurs, government bureaucrats, and party and labor organizations favorable to the regime. In the second place, it strengthened and specialized the state's institutional framework as a result of the growing complexity of Nicaraguan society and the need to resolve the issues (social, financial, and legal) that accompanied export-oriented growth. And finally, it used coercion in moments of political crisis during which the basic contradictions and tensions within the state became evident, although the regime did aspire to a level of legitimacy that would allow it to function without constantly having to bring its coercive power into play.

Each one of these three main areas of study will require a distinct approach. The first involves identifying those political actors whose alliance with Somoza laid the foundations of the regime. The government bureaucracy, the official party, and other organized groups of society loyal to the regime can be studied through their public expressions of support during electoral processes or other critical instances of political mobilization, as well as by analyzing their development and growth.

Second, institutional development and differentiation were part and parcel of export-oriented growth. Not only was the state's involvement in the export sector vital in the creation of infrastructure and in administrative tasks, but also it had to respond to changes in Nicaraguan society resulting from export production: urbanization, incipient manufacturing, increased demands for social services, and the growth of the salaried labor force. Of importance in this respect will be the development of government ministries and departments (particularly in the fields of credit and finance, infrastructure, and political and labor control), private sector associations, and diverse craft and labor associations.

Finally, the nature of the Nicaraguan state will become all the more evident if the social and political cleavages of the export-oriented model of growth can be dissected and exposed in detail. Under the Somoza regime, the most vocal and persistent opposition came from the Conservative party, especially during the periodic reelections of Somoza to the presidency. However, the rhetoric and actions of this party generally fit the description of a "loyal" or co-opted opposition; that is, the regime usually was able to defuse the Conservatives' criticisms by some nominal power-sharing formula backed up with the threat of coercion. But there was also a political opposition that was not tamed so easily and whose rhetoric and actions called into question the Nicaraguan state itself. Somoza's anticommunism was aimed clearly at these: the radicalized labor and student groups and nationalist intellectuals who saw in Somoza the hand of U.S. imperialism and capitalist exploitation. They became the implacable enemies of the regime and sometimes were subjected to harsh forms of repression.

In conclusion, the research will show how increasing stateness was indispensable to the success of the Somoza regime and how an outwardly personalistic dictatorship was able to adapt to these changing levels of stateness. Although the period of revolutionary upheaval lies outside the scope of this research, the study seeks to explain how the more radical opposition eventually coalesced around the option of armed insurrection as the only viable means of challenging the regime.

The organization of the chapters generally follows a chronological sequence. This is necessary to provide a minimum narrative and to highlight the more important problems faced at different time periods in the consolidation of the regime and the organization of the state. The first chapter attempts to describe and analyze the Nicaraguan state prior to 1930. In general, it will show that the Nicaraguan state was weak, that there was no "national" social or economic policy, and that political conflict and competition were compounded by pervasive foreign pressures and occasional direct intervention. The second chapter will look at Somoza's rise to power beginning in 1933, when he was named commanding officer of the Guardia Nacional, and finishing in 1937, when he became president. The emphasis in this chapter will not be on events but on the issues and the political alliances involved in Somoza's grab for the presidency, as well as the use of force and the role of ideology. Above all, this period represented a watershed in Nicaragua's political development because a government came to office that claimed to speak for all Nicaraguans, that placed itself above party and factional politics, and that offered to get things done (which at the time meant undertaking measures to counter the Great Depression and restoring central government control to the entire national territory).

The third chapter will focus on the Somoza regime's first seven years in office (1937–43), during which a number of important legislative and institutional developments took place. These were years during which the regime defined its relationship with the private sector, organized labor, the traditional political parties, and opposition groups on the fringe. Among the aspects to be included are the financial and banking reforms of 1940, fiscal and monetary policies (including devaluation, tax increases, and exchange controls), incipient labor legislation, agreements between the ruling party and factions of the main opposition party, constitutional and municipal reform, and repressive measures against select opponents of the regime. In general, these were years when the new regime tried to organize everyone and everything in terms of a national effort to overcome the depression, eliminate "sterile" factional strife and social conflicts, and guarantee the efficient functioning of the state apparatus.

The fourth chapter will look at the regime's first serious crisis, which began during June and July 1944 when thousands marched through the streets of Managua and other cities demanding an end to the Somoza presidency. The crisis was resolved in the short term through repressive measures, but in the next three years the regime sought accommodation with opposition groups and extended a hand to organized labor and the political left. Contrary to the first period from 1937 to 1943, when the principal activity of the regime had to do with fiscal and economic measures, the period from 1944 to 1947 was one of political maneuvering in order to reconstruct a new political coalition favorable to the regime. When this attempt collapsed in 1947 after a particularly fraudulent election and after a handpicked successor in the presidency turned out to be too independent, Somoza staged a coup d'état and proceeded to work out a more long-lasting solution to provide stable government for the country.

This solution, as outlined in the fifth chapter, involved the co-optation of the opposition Conservative party and the creation of state institutions and policies favorable to producers for export. The more confrontational wing of the Conservative party finally came to terms with the regime, which together with the economic boom sparked by cotton cultivation after 1950 laid the basis for the fundamental political agreement among the main political actors in the country. However, opposition to the Somocista regime did not disappear by any means; it took on new forms and contents, seeking ways of overthrowing the regime by force of arms and by presenting new ideological and programmatic alternatives to Somocismo. As described in the sixth chapter, these opposition activities were failures on the whole; they did not produce any important increase in either elite or popular rejection of the Somoza government, but they did open the way for the birth and development in succeeding decades of a more radical opposition committed not only to the elimination of the Somoza government but also to the entire overhaul of the Nicaraguan state.

The conclusion will attempt to identify those peculiar characteristics of the Nicaraguan political system that explain the longevity of the old regime while at the same time throwing light on the origins of the revolutionary movement. Of importance in this respect will be the political spaces that the regime was unwilling or unable to close; the strength of the ruling political coalition in terms of shared interests, ideological affinities, and opposition to radical political alternatives; the regime's ability to deliver economic and political rewards to diverse social groups or classes; the repressive features of the regime in maintaining itself in power; and the nature of dynastic rule within a dictatorial political system. On a more general level, the conclusion will attempt some observations on the problem of democracy and dictatorship in an underdeveloped, capitalist society, and the stability and permanence of dictatorial regimes.

THE REGIME OF
ANASTASIO SOMOZA,
1936–1956

Republic of Nicaragua

Reprinted from *The Catholic Church and Politics in Nicaragua and Costa Rica*, by Philip J. Williams, by permission of the University of Pittsburgh Press. © 1989 by Philip J. Williams.

1

NICARAGUAN SOCIETY & POLITICS PRIOR TO 1930

· · · · · · · · · · · · ·

Even in a region proverbial for internal anarchy and foreign intromissions, Nicaragua stands out as an extreme case. From the days of the Spanish Conquest itself, Nicaragua was already a battleground of competing expeditions of discovery and conquest that set the basis for factional conflict during the centuries to come. One group of Spanish settlers made its home in the town of Granada, founded in 1524 by Hernández de Córdoba at the northwestern edge of Lake Nicaragua. Other Spanish conquerors, advancing south from Mexico and Guatemala, threatened Hernández de Córdoba's control over the territory, so he sent a group of his men north to found the town of León in a move to consolidate his hold over the territory and to repel groups of Spaniards that were moving about in Honduras.[1]

Colonial Society and Politics

Although León became the administrative center in the territory, Granada retained a privileged social and economic position. Most of the noblemen and hidalgos in the expedition of conquest settled there because the Indian population of the province was concentrated around Granada. Furthermore, its location on the lakeshore allowed for direct transportation by water upon the Great Lake. However, Granada remained landlocked until a river route from the Great Lake to the sea was discovered in 1539.

León had access to the sea through the port of Realejo, a few miles west on the Pacific coast, which during the first century of colonial rule was an important shipbuilding and repairing facility, as well as a trading port. León was able to control the exploitation of naval stores in the forests of the Northern Highlands (the departments of Nueva Segovia and Madriz in contemporary Nicaragua) and thus supply Realejo with wood, pine tar, and resins.

While León took an early lead in productive and commercial ventures within Nicaragua, Granada enjoyed little trade outside of its immediate area of influence. The Río San Juan eventually opened to traffic to the sea in the 1540s, although the river route always was troublesome and slow due to rapids, sandbars, and low water in the dry season. Nevertheless, trade through Granada increased, especially when Realejo and the Pacific coast of Central America in general came under increasing threat from pirates in the late sixteenth century. Exports from as far away as Guatemala and El Salvador (principally indigo) were carried on mule trains to Granada and there placed on ships for the slow trip to the Caribbean Sea. For more than a century, the merchant families of Granada prospered.

Yet Granada's long-term economic prosperity was not based on imperial trade within which it was only an intermediary; instead, the city became the major base for a considerable number of ranchers who owned land in the areas of Rivas, Carazo, Masaya, and, most important, Chontales, a strip of particularly rich and moist land on the eastern shore of the Great Lake. Beginning in the seventeenth century, a number of families obtained large tracts of land from the Crown and laid the basis of what eventually became the Granada oligarchy. Through their ownership of land and family ties, the Granada merchant-ranchers exercised control over most of the shoreline of the Great Lake.

The decline of Pacific navigation also fostered cattle and cereal production in the area of León and northwestern Nicaragua. However, there were practically no commercial exchanges or business links between León and Granada given the similarity of their material production and the different markets they each supplied. Granada's meat and hides were sent to Spain and Costa Rica, whereas León's cattle were exported on the hoof to markets in Salvador and even Guatemala City. By the end of the colonial period, therefore, Granada and León had no history of conflict, other than the usual administrative problems emanating from the provincial capital in León that might have caused resentment or disgust among the Granada oligarchy. But there was no history of social or political integration, either. Each city had gone its own way, extending its control into the corresponding sphere of influence by means of networks of trade, land ownership, and family connections under the aegis of cattle raising.

The impact of a cattle-raising economy and subsistence cereal production on the formation of government institutions proved decisive in colonial Nicaragua. The lack of an internal market of any size, the limited investment in infrastructure required for cattle export, and the importance of family and landownership patterns in determining power and influence all combined to restrict the growth of governmental institutions within the province itself. In fact, the strength of the colonial state in all of Central America was never great. Under the Hapsburgs, the main preoccupation of the authorities was tribute collection and political loyalty from Creoles and Indians. Under the Bourbons, attempts to centralize the state's apparatus in order to collect more taxes and strengthen defenses against foreign attack were unsuccessful on the whole, especially in the areas outside of the direct control of the captain general in Guatemala City. At most, some sort of cohesion was provided by the Crown's agents in the province and the Catholic church.[2] When these unifying factors were removed or weakened at the moment of independence from Spain, Central America entered into an era of divisiveness and civil conflict that lasted for the better part of half a century.

Independence and Factional Conflict

Independence from Spain came to Central America in September 1821 more as a reflection of the Mexican independence process than a locally determined step. In fact, Iturbide's imperial government tried to annex Central America, but Mexico's own internal problems prevented its armies in Guatemala and Salvador from consolidating their hold and they were forced to retreat in 1823. The same year, the Central American representatives meeting in Guatemala drafted and signed another declaration of independence that reaffirmed Central America's independence and created a new political entity, the United Provinces of Central America, organized under a constitution drafted the following year that provided for a weak federal government to handle foreign affairs, military security, and international trade.[3]

This Central American federation thus constituted had a fairly short and violent existence. The relative absence of civil conflict during the independence movement was followed by a period of near chronic civil war in the years after 1824. Liberals and Conservatives, each determined to impose their program of government and ideology, eventually tore the federation apart in 1839.[4] Within Nicaragua itself, León and Granada vied for control of the state of Nicaragua. In 1824, a war broke out between the two cities which Granada won after virtually destroying its enemy: nine hundred houses were demolished in León and some neighborhoods were reduced to ashes. An army of federal soldiers from Salvador had to be sent to Nicaragua to pacify the province.[5] Thereafter, in Nicaragua central government as such ceased to function. Nominally, government posts and offices and constitutions and laws existed, but in practice political power reverted to landed families that dominated their respective regions.

Nicaragua's fractious politics can be attributed to its tradition of decentralized power and regional conflict. But special conditions that affected the province's economy also must be considered. For one, civil strife meant that the peasant population was called upon frequently to render military service; as Miles Wortman states, "ranch hands and private armies became one and the same." Second, manpower was scarce and tended to become even more so as violence persuaded people to flee to the relative peace of salaried labor in Costa Rica or Salvador. Finally, abundant land meant that laborers could move on to fringe areas if conditions of employment were not satisfactory. As a result, many hacendados abandoned their estates during the first decades of the nineteenth century, thus contributing to a deterioration of the economic situation and a further reduction of government income.[6]

Political strife was accompanied by territorial dismemberment. By the mid-nineteenth century, the Mosquito Coast on Nicaragua's eastern shore had come fully under British control. Even before, the entire southern region of Nicaragua called Guanacaste had seceded and joined the new republic of Costa Rica. Political conflict was therefore limited to the northeastern axis connecting León and Granada with their respective outlying areas. Out of this rivalry emerged the two parties or factions that dominated Nicaraguan political life for the next century and a half: the Liberals, who were strongest in León, and the Conservatives with their base in Granada. At issue was not a national political or economic model or program that might favor one city over the other because, in fact, there was no national economic or political system in existence. What was at issue was control of the central government's limited finances and oligarchic control over each region's territory.

The national government's income came from very few sources, including customs duties and assorted excise taxes, as well as the duties charged to companies engaged in transisthmian traffic. All together, these did not amount to much, but they were the only source of liquid income available and control over them gave considerable advantage to one faction over the other.[7] Compounding the fiscal weaknesses of the government was the well-entrenched system of caudillo domination in the countryside and a network of political alliances based on personal or familial relationships. As Humberto Belli has pointed out, the formation of a national state, based on impersonal and rational bureaucracies and laws, was all but impossible. Instead, political conflicts and agreements boiled down to arrangements between individuals and thereby favored those that involved blood relations or friendship. The poor—those campesinos, peons, and artisans who made up the mass of the political factions and the private armies—came under the control of diverse local oligarchies whose protection and favor they sought, thereby strengthening patron-client relations.[8]

The nonnational character of this political confrontation is best illustrated by the William Walker episode of 1856, when the Liberal faction contracted with the U.S. filibuster to provide an army of mercenaries to defeat the Granada faction then in control of the government. Instead, Walker decided to make himself president of the republic after defeating the Conservatives and turning his back on the Liberals; he was expelled from Nicaragua only after a concerted military effort that brought together Liberals and Conservatives, as well as troops from Costa Rica, El Salvador, and Guatemala. Such was the first of a number of U.S. interventions that Nicaragua would experience in the next seventy-five years of its republican existence. Although Walker's was a private venture in comparison to U.S. government and military intervention later on, the immediate cause was the same: sectional antagonism that degenerated into open conflict with one of the parties requesting outside assistance to impose its will together with a disposition on the part of some outside group or government to provide such assistance.

The Walker episode at least served to bring the Granada and León oligarchies together, both to expel Walker and to seek some sort of political accommodation. This last was achieved by means of a pact signed by the two parties in 1856 and formally ratified in the Constitution of 1858. In its economic aspects, the agreement included a more equitable distribution between the two cities of customs duties and taxes on the transisthmian route, the elimination of certain commercial monopoly rights enjoyed by Granada and the reopening of the port of Corinto (the successor to Realejo), and fiscal concessions for export producers, including free import of capital goods and reduced taxes on exports. In its political aspects, the agreement ratified oligarchic control of the political process by limiting voting rights to property holders, recognizing caudillo political influence through the creation of local governorships called *prefecturas*, and allowing for the existence of informal armed groups under caudillo control.[9]

The Political Impact of Coffee Production

For the next thirty years, the interoligarchic pact kept Nicaragua free of civil war. From 1858 until 1893, leaders of the Granada faction occupied the presidency of the republic, but Liberals from León were included in the cabinet and in the National Congress. During these years, political peace and a growing demand on the world market for coffee set the basis for Nicaragua's modern export economy. However, the development of coffee production in Nicaragua eventually weakened the oligarchic pact for two reasons: first, new social and political actors, the coffee growers from the Managua and Carazo regions midway between León and Granada, upset the balance between the traditional power groups; and second, coffee growing tended to favor León more than Granada, as coffee exports and railway construction headed toward the port of Corinto, León's outlet to the sea. By 1890, the coffee growers of Managua and Carazo had made their political preference clear by joining the Liberal party and the León faction. Three years later they were strong enough to take advantage of a split within the Conservative party to overthrow President Roberto Sacasa in a coup d'état.

From 1893 to 1911 the national government of Nicaragua was in the hands of the Liberal party. More exactly, it was in the hands of the coffee grower faction within the Liberal party under the leadership of José Santos Zelaya, a coffee grower from Managua. Zelaya ruled Nicaragua as a dictator until 1910, when he resigned under pressure from the U.S. government. During the seventeen years of his regime, he was credited with orienting the policies of the state toward open support for export development and foreign investment. But his government was not the initiator of such measures. Already during the thirty years of Conservative rule, railroad construction had begun, coffee growing had expanded rapidly, bank credit had been established, and communal lands had been privatized.[10] Nevertheless, Zelaya's measures provoked extreme reactions from Conservative opponents such as had not been seen since the middle of the nineteenth century. The Conservatives tried once and again to overthrow Zelaya by force of arms. It was during these years that the perennial Conservative caudillo and conspirator, Emiliano Chamorro, gained his initial fame and following. The question, therefore, is, what did Zelaya do to provoke such active opposition?

Zelaya's policies and the opposition they generated were but the open expression of the regional and ideological cleavages that thirty years of Conservative rule had failed to bridge. Undoubtedly, Zelaya's anticlericalism was rejected outright by the Granada oligarchy with its close ties to the Catholic church; the 1893 Constitution secularized public education and removed church control over marriages, cemeteries, and birth records, as well as declaring Nicaragua a nonconfessional state. But the religious problem was not the fundamental one. What Zelaya tried to do was to engage the state even more strongly than the past Conservative regimes in the promotion of export development; that is, to devote as much of the·government's resources as possible to the extension of the railway system, a network of highways, and port improvements, as well as to modernize the apparatus of the state and extend education and literacy. Zelaya also was keen on promoting foreign capital flows into Nicaragua, through either direct foreign investment under a policy of exclusive concessions or government-contracted loans. All of this was perfectly in line with Zelaya's upbringing in European schools and universities of the time, but it defined clearly for the first time in Nicaragua's history a political and economic plan with national projections.[11]

Behind Zelaya's regime were most of the coffee growers of the Managua-Carazo region of central Nicaragua, a new economic group that included cattlemen and indigo planters who had been put out of business by synthetic dyes, as well as medium-sized farmers and a number of urban dwellers looking to make some money in coffee. In the north of Nicaragua, in the region of Matagalpa and Jinotega, there was also a foreign component, principally German immigrants, who began to plant coffee with great success but who needed state support to build infrastructure in order to get their coffee to the ports. Behind Zelaya, too, was the Liberal oligarchy with its base in León, which stood to gain as coffee exports increased and trade passing through León on the railroad stimulated the region's commerce.[12]

Those who stood to lose from the Zelaya government's policies (or who stood to gain the least) were the Granada oligarchs. They were not against export production itself; for centuries they had been involved in the export of cattle and hides. A group of prominent Granada businessmen had also invested in sugar production and refining in the region of Chinandega in northwestern Nicaragua; the San Antonio sugar mill that they founded in 1890 became in a short time the most important sugar refinery in all of Central America.[13] But most of the cattlemen and merchants of Granada and their allies in the departments of Chontales and Boaco had no interest in government financing of development infrastructure that favored coffee growers and others in the rest of the country. For years they had controlled the national government and kept its functions and taxing power at the barest minimum, preferring to run their affairs through the system of caudillo domination and family agreements. At most, they expressed great interest in the construction of a transisthmian canal across the southern part of the Great Lake. Such a canal would increase Granada's importance as a port of embarkation for diverse export products, as well as greatly increasing the competitiveness of the Granada merchants. Granada's cattlemen conceivably owned large amounts of land along the canal route itself, too.

Zelaya did not oppose the canal across Nicaragua. Quite the contrary; his government sought U.S. backing for the project but his demands were too high, apparently. The Panama lobby in Washington persuaded the U.S. Congress to finance a canal through that part of the isthmus and Zelaya was left with empty hands. Once returned to power, the Conservatives eagerly signed the Bryan-Chamorro Treaty in 1914, giving the United States perpetual canal rights across Nicaragua in return for a pittance. At that moment, of course, the United States had no interest in a canal across Nicaragua when the Panama Canal was just beginning to operate; the Bryan-Chamorro Treaty was simply a means to prevent any other country from building a canal across the isthmus then or thereafter.

The Years of Protectorate Status

The Zelaya era came to an end in the face of a revolt by the Conservative party allied with a number of disaffected Liberals and with the support of the U.S. government. Zelaya's independent foreign policy, which included overtures to build a canal without U.S. participation and the negotiation of substantial loans with European consortiums, as well as meddling in the internal affairs of Honduras, prompted Secretary of State Philander Knox to seek his ouster by supporting Zelaya's internal political enemies. Through a combination of international condemnations of the Zelaya regime and open military support for a rebel army that was organized on the Atlantic coast in the Bluefields area, the Taft administration was able to force Zelaya's resignation in December 1909 and that of his handpicked successor, José Madriz, in August of the following year. But the new government that came to power in Managua was unable to provide unified direction to the country as it bogged down in petty squabbling and the struggle for control of the presidency of the republic. Overthrowing Zelaya turned out to be the most easily achieved objective for the United States; maintaining internal political peace and order required successive military interventions, outright meddling in internal Nicaraguan politics, and the control of practically all of the the country's financial and fiscal institutions for the better part of a quarter of a century.[14]

The new government, headed by an unstable coalition of Conservative military caudillos, anti-Zelayista Liberals, and representatives of foreign business interests, realized that the support of the United States was vital for its permanence in power. From the beginning, the leaders of the anti-Zelayista movement consulted with the U.S. government representatives, including Thomas Dawson, U.S. minister to Panama, who was sent to Managua in October 1910 to help patch together a government. The so-called Dawson Agreements, signed on October 27 by the leaders of the rebel armies, established, among others, a mixed-claims commission of Nicaraguan and U.S. representatives to solve disputes involving contracts and concessions granted by Zelaya, a loan to the Nicaraguan government from private banks via "the good offices of the American government" under the guarantee of the customs' receipts, and the formal promise to exclude "the Zelayista element" from any future government.[15] The Dawson Agreements were only the beginning, however.

The new government was practically bankrupt and its leadership plagued by personal rivalries. During two years following the departure of President Madriz, the U.S. ministers in Managua moved their weight around seeking to achieve a semblance of political order and administrative efficiency. Eventually, however, the governing coalition flew apart and the United States, at the invitation of President Adolfo Díaz, intervened militarily to keep him in office and put down a rebellion headed by the minister of war. During August and September 1912, the United States landed 2,300 marines at the port of Corinto, forcibly occupied the city of León, and extended its control along the railway line all the way to Granada. The principal marine force abandoned Nicaragua in mid-November but left behind a legation guard of 100 marines, which remained in Nicaragua for the next fourteen years as a reminder that the United States could intervene again should the need arise.

More pervasive and prolonged was the U.S. fiscal and financial intervention in Nicaragua. Under the assumption that the United States's interests of preserving peace and order in the Central American region would be served best by promoting U.S. business ventures and avoiding financial entanglements between Central American governments and extracontinental powers, Washington engaged in attempts to clean up Nicaragua's finances and repay outstanding debt obligations. The Nicaraguan government also was desperate to negotiate loans with American banks in order to cover its operating expenses and pay off a number of claims presented by nationals and foreigners alike for damages sustained during the fighting and compensation for canceled concessions of the Zelaya years.

In order to obtain a loan of U.S.$1.5 million in the United States, the Nicaraguan government in 1911 relinquished the control of the customs houses to a North American administrator, the collector general of customs, to be appointed by the State Department. Subsequent loan agreements in 1912 and 1913 failed to improve Nicaragua's finances and in the process the national railway (Ferrocarril del Pacífico de Nicaragua) and the national bank, founded in 1912, were turned over to the U.S. banks as collateral under the terms of the loan agreements; both of these became U.S. corporations chartered in Maine and Connecticut, respectively. The fiscal mess reached such proportions in 1917 that the government was forced to take desperate measures to maintain its obligations with the foreign bankers and its commitment to the U.S. government. The Financial Plan of 1917, drafted under State Department pressure to keep Nicaragua solvent by disbursing the U.S.$3 million that the United States paid for the Bryan-Chamorro Treaty, sought to consolidate the floating debt of the national government. It also set up a High Commission to approve and supervise the national budget, to fix customs duties, and to see that all government bonds were paid on time. The High Commission was made up of two North Americans named by the State Department and one Nicaraguan appointed by the government in Managua. Finally, the plan required that all funds received by the collector general of customs be turned over to the national bank and allocated with top priority to payment of the public debt. As a result, the Nicaraguan government received only U.S. $500,000 of the Bryan-Chamorro monies, and that all went to pay back salaries. Most of the rest was handed over to the American bankers and to the British syndicate that had extended a loan to Zelaya in 1909.[16]

The consequences of these financial and fiscal policies for the country's economic development were anything but advantageous. During the period 1917–27, the Nicaraguan government spent over 43 percent of its total outlays to cover its public debt commitments and the expenses incurred in collecting taxes and duties. An additional 18.6 percent went for the army and police. Although it is true that Nicaragua was thus able to meet its financial obligations after 1920 with none of the problems of the previous decade, the emphasis given to maintaining a sound fiscal policy and the prompt payment of foreign and local debt obligations meant that there was little, if anything, left over for infrastructure, education, health, and government-supported incentives for production and exports. During the years 1910–30 there was no expansion of the railway network nor construction of roads north or east from the central departments. Nicaragua remained a country of disconnected regions and very limited means of communication. At most, it bought back some of its economic independence from the U.S. bankers when it purchased in 1924 a majority of shares in both the national railway and the national bank. However, both corporations remained chartered in the United States and their boards of directors continued to meet in New York City.[17]

That the Conservative governments under whom these measures were implemented were subservient to the interests of the United States does not mean that the measures in themselves were incompatible with the interests of the Granada Conservatives. Commercial concessions that had been canceled after the overthrow of Zelaya were granted frequently to Conservatives who had been active in the rebellion. In addition, the funds handed out by the mixed-claims commission for damages during the struggle against Zelaya ended up mostly in the hands of Conservatives.[18] More important, however, was the Conservatives' disinterest in a strong government that could extract and invest national resources in development projects. At most, they sought the dredging of the San Juan River to permit oceangoing vessels to reach the port of Granada directly, a project that by that time made little economic sense with a completed railway line from Granada to Corinto already in operation. Their interests in cattle raising and export were well served by the existing fleet of lake steamers and the land routes that allowed their herds to move on the hoof to Costa Rica. Granada merchants, in turn, catered to the demand for imported goods of a very reduced social group of high-income level; they had no interest, therefore, in any kind of redistributive income policy that would widen the size of the market or foster the production of local manufactures. On the contrary, the evidence suggests that the years of Conservative rule and U.S. fiscal intervention were most harmful to Nicaraguan artisans (hatters, shoemakers, carpenters) who were unprotected from competition by cheaper, industrially produced goods, chiefly from the United States.[19]

U.S. intervention in the political arena was as direct and forceful as it was in the economic and fiscal sphere. The U.S. minister in Managua was inevitably consulted about any possible presidential candidate, coalition of parties, or electoral procedure. The main concern of the State Department was that the issue of presidential succession should not bring upon the country another bout of armed resistance. Thus, the U.S. ministers in Managua constantly preached the need for fair and honest electoral practices that would result in an elected president of unquestionable legitimacy.[20] In 1921 Dr. Harold Dodds, a U.S. professor, was contracted by the government of Nicaragua (under strong pressure from Washington) to study Nicaragua's current electoral law and propose changes to make it more impartial. In April 1923, the Nicaraguan Congress passed an electoral law that was Dodds's project with some minor modifications. The electoral procedures that it established were fairly conventional, with the exception that voters would line up according to their party preference and that votes would be marked publicly in the presence of the electoral board. Furthermore, the appointment of the electoral boards was favorable to the party in power at the time of the election, making fraud and coercion as easy as before. Finally, the law recognized the existence of a limited number of parties: those that had participated in the last presidential election and had received more than 10 percent of the vote, and that had maintained a viable national organization in the interim. In fact, the electoral law of 1923 institutionalized a two-party system, since it made the formation and inscription of new parties very difficult.[21]

The Crisis of the Protectorate

In 1926 a new civil war broke out between insurgent Liberals and a Conservative government headed by Emiliano Chamorro. Fifteen years of protectorate status had not solved the internal political, economic, and social conditions that had precipitated the U.S. intervention in the first place. The simplistic and superficial argument put forward at the time by U.S. policy-makers pointed a finger at legalistic and cultural obstacles that inhibited the development of democracy and honest elections in Nicaragua.[22] That is, instability and undemocratic procedures were the product of years of educational backwardness and disrespect for law and decency. But that does not explain the root causes of political conflict. A more plausible explanation should concentrate on the issues involved in the conflicts of the period, and not just the superficial manifestations such as electoral fraud, civil war, and foreign intervention. After all, the Liberal party was active during all the years of Conservative rule, seeking to broaden its base of support. For what purpose, if not to achieve a takeover of the government?

The Nicaraguan political crisis of 1910–27, which corresponded to the years of U.S. protectorate status, was in reality a crisis of the state itself.

Although not expressed clearly in political platforms and programs, basic differences existed among the groups that competed for control of the government. The United States, in turn, which had more control over the government than any Nicaraguan political faction, was seeking to establish political stability in Nicaragua through institutional development and political procedures (both electoral and legislative) that would guarantee participation to both historic parties. U.S. policy did not favor one party over another because of ideological preference; what the United States wanted was a government that could establish effective control over the national territory, that would not create trouble among its neighbors, that would protect U.S. canal rights across Nicaragua, and that, in sum, would be subservient to Washington's interests in the region.[23]

From 1911 to 1927, the Nicaraguan faction that was willing to do whatever the United States required was the Conservative party because it knew that support from Washington was vital to maintain its hold on the government. But there was no fundamental quarrel between the Conservatives and U.S. interests in Nicaragua, either. That U.S. corporations took over control of the national railroad and the national bank and that U.S. officials collected customs duties and determined government expenditures was of no great concern to the Conservative oligarchy from Granada. Not even national sovereignty meant much to the Conservatives who signed the Bryan-Chamorro Treaty in exchange for three million dollars. The fact of the matter was that Conservative government policy, in line with U.S. interests, was geared fundamentally to ensuring fiscal solvency and public order. The Conservatives' vision of the state, therefore, was in line with that which they had preached since the days of independence from Spain: a strong role for regional power brokers (caudillos), minimum government participation in developing the country's infrastructure, and the defense of traditional values in the face of secular forces that threatened to abolish religious education and undermine the sanctity of the family through civil marriage and divorce. The government itself would serve primarily as a dispenser of limited public employment and as the medium for conciliation of political differences that could not be settled at lower levels.

The Liberals objected to the Conservative perspective because they espoused a stronger state in terms of greater government participation in the financing of infrastructure, the promotion of education and public health, and the establishment of closer financial and commercial ties with the industrialized countries. The Liberals needed a more dynamic banking system, if necessary with a strong state component that would channel more of the country's limited savings to productive investment, especially in the export sector and in local manufacturing. The coffee growers, the backbone of the Liberal party, remained the dominant economic force in the country, but they were deprived of direct access to state power by the Conservatives' stranglehold on the electoral machinery and their alliance with the United States. It was not surprising, therefore, that the Liberal party in its struggle to regain power took on an "anti-interventionist" stance in the face of the United States's presence. More specifically, the Liberals wanted the United States to give up its control of the state's financial institutions in order to commence a program of economic reactivation.[24] Even sectors of the Conservative party were willing to enter into alliances with Liberal politicians, as is evident in the 1924 elections, when José Solórzano, a progressive Conservative, ran for president with Juan Bautista Sacasa, a Liberal from León, as his vice-presidential candidate; this Conservative-Liberal ticket won by a wide margin over the Conservative candidate, the caudillo Emiliano Chamorro.

In general terms, the election results in 1924 suggest an incipient bridging of the ideological and regional gap that had kept Liberals and Conservatives apart. The stagnation of coffee production during the U.S. protectorate had affected coffee growers regardless of political faction. (In fact, there were quite a few Conservative coffee planters. Anastasio Somoza's father was such an individual.) The absence of another dynamic export product made it essential to revitalize coffee exports for the country's future economic health and, if possible, to encourage any other export products. In order to reach a political consensus along these lines, certain sectors of the Liberal and Conservative parties were willing to discuss the formation of bipartisan governments and power-sharing arrangements that had to do more with economic self-interest and national political peace than with ideology or sectionalism.

For the United States, by the 1920s there was no problem in the formation of governments that included Liberal elements. Washington recognized the results of the 1924 presidential election, which included the Liberal Sacasa as vice-president. The United States even withdrew the marine contingent that remained at the legation in Managua in August 1925, thus ending thirteen years of continued foreign military presence in Nicaragua. When Emiliano Chamorro launched a coup d'état in late October 1925 and exiled President Solórzano and Vice-President Sacasa, the United States denied diplomatic recognition to the new government until Chamorro was forced to resign and turn over the presidency to Adolfo Díaz, a stalwart of Washington's policy in Nicaragua. But the United States could not countenance losing control over events, as began to happen when the exiled Vice-President Sacasa landed in Puerto Cabezas in December 1926 and proclaimed himself constitutional president of Nicaragua. Sacasa received aid from the Calles government in Mexico and proceeded to organize an army to overthrow Díaz. When it became clear that the Díaz government could not hold off the Liberal forces, the United States returned the marines to Nicaragua to put an end to the fighting. It also sent Henry Stimson to Managua in April 1927 to arrange a political solution to the conflict.

The Stimson mission to Nicaragua was intended to convey the very highest level of U.S. presence and concern. Stimson was named President Calvin Coolidge's personal representative with ample powers to reach agreements on the spot. Upon arrival in Managua, he began to consult with representatives of both parties, who expressed to him that U.S. mediation was indispensable and that the formula most likely to appeal to both parties was an election in 1928 supervised by Washington. As preconditions for a free election, which Stimson considered the only solution to Nicaragua's perennial political strife, there was need for complete disarmament, a general amnesty, and the establishment of peace and order in the country. The Díaz government, beholden to U.S. interests, completely agreed with Stimson's proposals and added on a few more of its own, including the participation of selected Liberals in the Díaz cabinet and the organization of a nonpartisan constabulary commanded by U.S. officers.[25]

On 27 April, Stimson met a delegation of three prominent Liberals: Rodolfo Espinoza, a future vice-president, Leonardo Argüello, a future president (for all of twenty-seven days), and Manuel Cordero Reyes, a future foreign minister. The three men generally approved of Stimson's diagnosis of the situation and "vigorously disclaimed any anti-American feeling on the part of Liberals or any hostile understanding with Mexico. They asserted that their party recognized that the United States had a legitimate zone of interest and influence extending as far south as Panama and that they considered this fact natural and beneficial in its results to Nicaragua." Shortly afterward, on 4 May, at the small town of Tipitapa just to the north of Managua, Stimson met with the principal Liberal general, José María Moncada, who accepted the Díaz government's terms in return for firm U.S. guarantees of a supervised election in 1928. Stimson produced such a document, stressing that a general disarmament was absolutely necessary for such an election and that U.S. forces would accept custody of all weapons and would proceed "to disarm forcibly those who will not do so."[26]

One week after the Tipitapa agreement, Moncada issued a manifesto stating that the Liberals accepted the word of the Washington government and placed their confidence in the United States. In the next few days, the contending forces turned over 9,000 rifles, 296 machine guns, and nearly 6 million rounds of ammunition. Only the Liberal general Augusto C. Sandino did not agree with the Tipitapa agreement; he took 150 of his men and proceeded north to begin armed resistance to U.S. military intervention in the country. But the principal political forces in the country had come to accept the inevitable: the presence of the United States in Nicaragua was determinant, both as an instrument to seek political conciliation between Liberals and Conservatives and as a force unto itself with its own strategic and political agenda. To come to understand the United States and to seek its blessing therefore became part of Nicaraguan politics, just as Nicaraguan politicians were forced to reconcile themselves with a new political system that was emerging under U.S. tutelage.

The new political system was not completely defined by 1930, of course, but some of its major components were already in place and functioning. First of all, Nicaragua got a national army under the guise of the Guardia Nacional according to the terms of a treaty signed in December 1928 by Dana C. Munro, Washington's minister to Nicaragua, and Carlos Cuadra Pasos, then Nicaraguan foreign minister in the Conservative government of Adolfo Díaz. The treaty provided for an armed force of nearly 100 officers and over 1,100 soldiers to be the sole military and police force of the republic. Until Nicaraguan officers had been trained to take over command, the treaty stipulated that U.S. Marine Corp officers would run the Guardia, such officers being exempt from the jurisdiction of Nicaraguan courts.[27] The U.S. government believed that the creation of a national, apolitical armed force would end Nicaragua's long history of private and factional armies and the civil wars they spawned. Such a force was also needed to help in the fight against Sandino, who was making things difficult for the U.S. occupation forces.

In the second place, by 1930 the financial institutions set up by U.S. interventors were in place, albeit under foreign control. The National Bank of Nicaragua, Limited, combined the functions of a central reserve bank, a bank of issue, and a commercial bank, making it the most powerful institution in the country's financial system. Its board of directors, with a majority of U.S. citizens, met in New York City, although its general manager ran the operation in Managua. The collector general of customs was similarly under the direction of a U.S. citizen (and would continue so until the early 1950s).

In the third place, the Dodds law governing electoral practices and the activities of political parties was to remain on the books with only minor changes until the 1960s. The Dodds law set the rules of the game for a nominally two-party system, although the Somoza dictatorship in the future prevented all but some minimal power-sharing with the Conservatives. Nor was the law a guarantee against electoral fraud; the Nicaraguan saying "Quien escruta, gana" (he who counts the ballots wins) held true for the next half century, although the two supervised elections for president in 1928 and 1932 were considered fairly honest at the time.

By 1930, then, the United States had saddled Nicaragua with the trappings of a modern democracy and hopefully, so Washington thought, the old causes of civil strife had been eradicated for good. Undoubtedly, a simple logic that analyzed the roots of political instability in terms of partisan armies, fraudulent elections, and financial mismanagement would approve of U.S. initiatives in Nicaragua and foresee a better future for that country. However, the existence of the important financial, electoral, and coercive institutions set up under the U.S. protectorate was no guarantee of a powerful state. During the time these institutions had been imposed and/or consolidated under direct U.S. tutelage, political and economic forces within Nicaragua could either agree with the United States's objectives or they could keep their mouths shut. But once the direct foreign presence was removed in 1925 with the departure of the marine legation guard, dissenting positions on the future of the Nicaraguan nation came to the surface once more with such virulence that the U.S. intervention of 1927 required much greater force until a new political settlement could be imposed.

That is, U.S. intervention in 1911–12 to resolve the succession question after Zelaya proved far simpler in its basic issues than the national crisis that erupted in 1927. The reason for this difference must be sought in changes that had occurred in Nicaraguan society and politics in the first quarter of the twentieth century. From a situation of purely oligarchic control under the thirty years of Conservative governments and the seventeen years of Zelaya, new political actors (in addition to the United States, of course) had been drawn into the political process and were claiming a voice and a share of things.

Political and Social Forces under the Protectorate

The political grouping that dominated Nicaraguan politics from 1911 to 1927 was the Conservative party. Soon after the overthrow of Zelaya, the party came under the growing control of Nicaragua's eternal caudillo, Emiliano Chamorro. By 1916, the year he was elected president, Chamorro was the undisputed leader of the Conservatives and would continue to be so until the 1950s. However, his lack of a clear political program for Nicaragua on occasion led him to quarrel openly with sectors of his own party, as was most evident in his coup d'état in 1925 against the Solórzano government. In opposition to Chamorro and his followers within the party, there emerged another group, weaker in numbers and strength, which sought political accommodation through negotiations with the Liberals, while attempting to formulate a more concise Conservative ideology as an alternative to the Liberal party. This group was headed by Carlos Cuadra Pasos, a lawyer from Granada, whose political activity within the party coincided with Chamorro's all the way until mid-century. Cuadra Pasos eventually came to lead the so-called Civilista faction within the party, a group generally opposed to violent confrontation with the Liberals but very vocal in its defense of traditional Catholic values of family, property, and harmonious church-state relations. Over the years, Chamorristas and Civilistas vied for control of the Conservative party, with Chamorro undoubtedly the clear favorite with the rank and file, while Cuadra Pasos appealed more to the intellectual and professional elements.

Conservative ideology in Nicaragua in the period 1911–30 is easier to define for what it was not than otherwise. The party's slogan of *Dios, orden, justicia* says something, but it is hardly sufficient. Another important slogan, *Viva el general Chamorro!*, says even less about ideology, although its political appeal among the people was most likely stronger. The fact is that few Conservatives took the time and trouble to write about Nicaragua's political past and future; most were engaged in the give-and-take of everyday politics. The most consistent stream of writing and analysis from the Conservative party came from the pen of Cuadra Pasos, the intellectual eminence of the party, whose published works appeared generally after the mid-1930s.

As could be expected, Cuadra Pasos was concerned primarily with the weakening of traditional values in Nicaragua in the face of modernizing and progressive secular tendencies. The strength of a society, he believed, rested on the strength of its basic institutions, which in the case of Nicaragua he defined as family, property, and church. The family in Nicaragua was strong only among the elite (defined by him as the *familias principales*, the middle class, and the artisans); among the proletariat it was very weak or nonexistent. Property also had suffered, especially because there existed no desire or respect for property among the lower classes, adding to the destruction and appropriation of property during the frequent civil wars which had benefited only the military leaders of the diverse factions. Worse still, Cuadra Pasos believed, the backbone of the Nicaraguan social order, the landowners, were less and less interested in managing their rural estates; their love for the land had declined, and they preferred to live in the cities and visit their properties only occasionally. Finally, the presence of the church among the people had declined due to the scarcity of priests. The life of the parishes, so important to the maintenance of social harmony and the resolution of private quarrels, had deteriorated.[28] In general, Cuadra Pasos thought that the Liberal reforms had destroyed the old patrician order, that ancestral bond between the caudillo/landowner and the people, and replaced it with a relationship between a nouveau-riche bourgeoisie and salaried workers. The generous, charitable relationship between the upper and lower classes had given way to a "plutocratic" attitude on the part of the employers toward their employees.[29] In sum, the mass of the people no longer expressed respect for the upper class, while the upper class held neither respect nor compassion for the people.[30]

Cuadra Pasos's position was one of looking back with nostalgia on a past that presumably was crumbling in the face of secular and urban forces. At most, the role of the Conservative party was that of keeping alive that nostalgia and pressing to limit or contain change in Nicaraguan society. But other thinkers within the Conservative party developed an alternative viewpoint, one that, as might be expected in the 1920s and 1930s, looked to fascism and corporatism for answers to the problems of the day. Such a perspective was developed in the writings of José Coronel Urtecho and Pablo Antonio Cuadra in the 1930s, but the roots of this school of thought must be traced to the civil wars of the 1920s. The destruction resulting from the Liberal-Conservative confrontation of 1926–27 and the war in the north against Sandino in the succeeding years impressed on some that Nicaragua could progress only under a strong regime that by force, if necessary, might control the centrifugal tendencies of Nicaraguan politics. Social and political peace was, therefore, the paramount objective; the means to achieve it were associated precisely with the elimination of those causes of civil war that had plagued Nicaragua, such as the struggle for power for its own sake among different political factions. What Nicaragua needed was a strong government backed by a strong army, which the United States was already preparing in the form of the Guardia Nacional. Some of these essayists even flirted with the idea of a monarchy for Nicaragua, but in the end they sided with Somoza, in whom they perceived the guarantor of order and progress.[31]

By 1930, then, the Conservative party was a mix of traditional caudillos without any specific ideology or political program and a couple of ideological tendencies, one that looked to a concrete past that had little possibility of reproducing itself in the future and another that looked to a future with uncritical confidence but that lacked a concrete program of action save its calls for a strong government. Possessing a weaker electoral base than that of the Liberals, the Conservatives faced the dilemma of either opposing through the use of force the Liberal governments that returned to office after 1928 or of seeking such accommodation that would allow at least some Conservative participation in governmental decisions. This contradictory position would be exploited by Somoza beginning in the early 1930s, when he promised to lead a government of national unity, above and beyond party factions and disputes.

The Liberal party, out of power since 1910, was not exempted from the infighting that characterized the Conservative party. For the Liberals, however, the main problem after 1911 was how to regain power, and, especially, how to regain the confidence of the United States, which perceived Liberalism and Zelayismo to be one and the same. The use of force, by which Zelaya came to power in 1893, was out of the question: the United States would not tolerate the violent overthrow of the government. What was left, then? The only alternative was political organization, that is, the expansion of the political base through measures that sought to mobilize a number of social groups up to then excluded from the political process. While the Conservatives remained in power with the backing of the United States and paid little attention to popular demands, the Liberals set to work among urban artisans, middle-class professionals, and rural workers (particularly in the areas where small farmers and salaried labor prevailed).

As a party that was excluded from government and that experienced varying degrees of persecution, the Liberals first had to look after their own. It is not surprising, therefore, that the party's convention held in Managua on 22 August 1913 approved a series of measures that sought to strengthen the bonds among Liberals. The party called upon its members to help others who might be suffering from political repression ("ataques del Poder Público") as if they were brothers in need. Party members also were enjoined to create mutual aid societies to care for invalid party members (most likely those injured during the confrontations of the Zelaya years) and for the widows and orphaned children of those deceased. Similarly, the party should help in the establishment of cooperatives, paying special attention to Liberal artisans and workers, as well as creating schools for artisans where Liberal principles could be taught.[32] The most active area of Liberal organization efforts seems to have been León, where as early as 1913 a group of Liberals founded a labor union; thereafter, other unions were organized in Granada, Managua, and Chinandega. In part, the Liberals generated sympathy among laborers to the extent that the party maintained its nationalistic line by repudiating U.S. intervention.[33]

Not all laborers were attracted to the Liberal party. The Federación Obrera Nicaragüense (FON), founded in 1918, sought the support of artisans in particular. It was a composite of diverse unions and mutual aid societies. In the following years, the FON established international contacts with the AFL in the United States and the CROM of Mexico, leading to a split with the more radical elements who founded the Grupo Socialista, which demanded a more independent posture in terms of both international and national alliances. Still other laborers and artisans gravitated toward a movement called Obrerismo Organizado, formed by Sofonías Salvatierra in 1923. Salvatierra, a member of the Liberal party, had begun his activities in the labor movement years before, when he established a school for workers in Managua. Obrerismo's position was clearly nationalist (it consistently opposed U.S. intervention in Nicaragua) but its platform for social reform was quite modest. Obrerismo called for greater worker unity around mutual aid societies, workers' schools, and savings and loan cooperatives. That is, Salvatierra and his organization sought to improve the social structure, not change it. He was openly anti-Marxist, rejecting class struggle and international worker solidarity, as well as mixing politics with the union's activities; for example, he opposed the celebration of Labor Day on the first of May.[34]

The links between the Liberal party and labor should not be exaggerated. Not only were organized laborers a very small fraction of the population, but also the Liberal party in its official stance remained fairly conventional. As one would expect, the party endorsed the right of habeas corpus, guarantees to private property, freedom of expression, association, movement, and business, public secular education, separation of church and state, direct and secret balloting, civil marriage and divorce, and independence among the branches of government. The party's declaration of principles also underlined a number of political issues that for the Liberals had priority, including the enactment of an electoral law that would eliminate fraud at the ballot boxes, the extension of political rights for women, and a strict separation of the military from party politics. Moreover, the declaration called for measures in the field of social security that would improve the lives of laborers and white-collar workers, including the creation of a national pawnshop, retirement plans, and laws governing worker benefits and industrial safety.[35]

The most significant obstacle to an expansion of the Liberal party popular base was not its ideology or its platform but the structural characteristics of Nicaraguan society; of course, these affected the Liberal and Conservative parties alike, but for the Liberals, the underdogs in the political struggle, the constraints imposed by the social structure weighed more heavily. A review of some demographic statistics should make it clear that the Nicaragua of the 1910s and 1920s was still very much under the influence of traditional patterns of political control and domination. The census of 1920, despite its inadequacies, gives some idea of population distribution and employment that suggest an overwhelming proportion of rural population and a labor force under the control of caudillo landowners. In 1920 about 79 percent of the Nicaraguan labor force was engaged in agriculture, be it as owners (32 percent) or as salaried labor (47 percent). Conversely, only 9.6 percent of the total labor force was classified as artisan or as industrial labor.[36] The remaining 11 percent of the labor force was engaged in various professions, trade, mining (only 0.5 percent), and office work.

A more detailed breakdown of the labor force by department will help explain some regional diversities that influenced political developments (see Table 1.1). A number of aspects stand out. In the first place, the highest proportion of farmers, cattlemen, and others who owned or rented their land was found in the northern departments of Jinotega and Nueva Segovia; consequently, these departments had the lowest proportions of salaried rural labor (jornaleros), as well as some of the lowest proportions of artisans and industrial workers. It was in this area that Sandino operated most successfully in the period 1927–33. The peculiar nature of these departments can be explained in part by their position as frontier areas; workers and their families displaced by the expansion of coffee in the central areas and by cereal and cattle haciendas in León and Chinandega migrated in search of land to Nueva Segovia and Jinotega. Matagalpa, which is also part of the northern tier of departments, shows a much higher incidence of salaried labor due to the early beginnings of coffee cultivation there.

Second, the highest proportion of salaried labor in agriculture was found in Estelí and Chinandega; both of these departments, located within León's sphere of influence, must have furnished considerable support and votes for the Liberal caudillos of that area what with their high proportion of peons and the considerable concentration of landed wealth. (Chinandega had the lowest

Table 1.1 Regional Distribution of Select Types of Employment, 1920

Department	Farmers, Cattlemen, and Others		Rural Laborers ("Jornaleros")		Artisans and Industrial Labor	
	N	%	N	%	N	%
Bluefields	2,907	(23.4)	7,250	(58.3)	719	(5.8)
Carazo	3,058	(27.4)	6,179	(55.4)	926	(8.3)
Chinandega	3,334	(19.0)	10,426	(59.3)	2,161	(12.3)
Chontales	8,490	(34.9)	13,100	(53.9)	1,547	(6.4)
Estelí	3,410	(30.9)	7,102	(64.3)	289	(2.6)
Granada	2,040	(16.4)	4,120	(33.1)	2,320	(18.6)
Jinotega	5,768	(62.9)	2,695	(29.4)	441	(4.8)
León	7,125	(26.7)	11,114	(31.7)	3,333	(12.5)
Managua	5,302	(21.6)	10,179	(41.5)	4,636	(18.9)
Masaya	5,929	(44.4)	4,172	(31.2)	1,441	(10.8)
Matagalpa	9,575	(39.7)	12,854	(53.3)	692	(2.9)
Nva. Segovia	9,074	(62.3)	4,002	(27.5)	1,160	(8.0)
Rivas	2,397	(21.4)	6,288	(56.1)	939	(8.4)

Source: Oficina Central del Censo, *Censo general de 1920* (Managua: Tipografía Nacional, 1920). Not included are two small political subdivisions on the Atlantic coast: Comarca Gracias a Dios and Comarca San Juan del Norte. Percentages do not add up to one hundred because various categories of the work force are not included in this table.

proportion of landowners to rural workers in the country.) A situation similar to that of Chinandega and Estelí was found in the areas of Granada's sphere of influence, Chontales and Rivas, which also show relatively high concentrations of land ownership and a large proportion of rural salaried labor.

Third, the highest proportion of artisans and industrial labor was found in those departments where the principal cities are located: Granada, Managua, Chinandega, and León. Masaya stands out as well, due to its long tradition of artisanal production. To the extent that all but Granada lie in areas of Liberal preeminence, it is not surprising that the labor movement in its origins was identified largely with the Liberal party.

In general, therefore, we can assume that a large part of the population was under the influence of caudillos and regional power brokers, be they Liberal or Conservative. Only a few members of the labor force could be classified as unencumbered by prior political obligations or sufficiently independent economically to make a choice for themselves. Within this limited population, the

Liberal party sought to expand its political base. By 1928 the Liberal party was clearly stronger in numerical terms than its Conservative rival. The election results for that year gave the Liberal candidate, José María Moncada, a total of 76,676 votes as against 56,987 for his rival Conservative candidate, Adolfo Benard. This was the first election supervised by U.S. electoral officials, the fairness of which appears to have satisfied both candidates. The next presidential election in 1932 also was supervised by the United States and the results were surprisingly similar to those of 1928: 76,269 for the Liberal Juan Bautista Sacasa and 53,845 for the Conservative Adolfo Díaz.[37]

This last supervised election in 1932 coincided with the decision of the United States to withdraw its marine force, turn over the control of the Guardia Nacional to Nicaraguan officers, and let Nicaraguan politics proceed without a direct and visible U.S. presence. Just as important for the future of Nicaraguan politics was Sandino's decision to come to terms with the Nicaraguan government, including holding talks with the new head of the Guardia, Anastasio Somoza. Also important for the outcome of events was the depression, which by 1932 had seriously affected Nicaraguan exports and was producing strong demands from diverse social groups that something be done to remedy the situation. At this critical juncture, the Nicaraguan state, molded and overseen by the U.S. protectorate, was left to fend for itself. Presumably, everything had been done correctly: a constitutionally elected president was in place, a national armed force beholden to neither party had fought Sandino to a draw, two succeeding elections had demonstrated that Nicaraguans were not inherently incompatible with basic liberal democratic practices, and the country's finances were under the management of well-established institutions. What, therefore, could go wrong?

2

THE ROOTS
OF THE
DICTATORSHIP

. . . .

The two successive electoral victories of the Liberals in 1928 and 1932, supervised by the U.S. electoral missions, demonstrated support for the party in most of the country. Sacasa's election in 1932 was particularly rewarding for Liberals, because it installed in the presidency a man whose rights to that office had been violated by the Chamorro coup of 1925 when Sacasa was vice-president of the republic. But the Liberal vote for Sacasa was hardly a measure of the strength of the regime itself. Instead, Sacasa came to office at the worst imaginable moment, with Nicaragua suffering the effects of the depression and the protracted war against Sandino. In addition, the Sacasa presidency was the product, to some extent, of prior dealings and negotiations between the Conservatives and the Liberals.

Political Reconciliation and Armed Confrontation

Beginning in April 1932, a group of political leaders from both parties met to discuss ways to guarantee a smooth transition in the Nicaraguan government once the U.S. Marines had departed in January 1933. Most of the debate centered on the issue of minority representation in the government's various branches. At stake was the losing party's number of deputies and senators in the legislature, the distribution of positions in the municipal councils, party affiliation of judges on the Supreme Court and various appellate courts, as well as sundry positions held in the government bureaucracy by Liberals and Conservatives. On 30 June 1932, after a number of meetings, all presidential and vice-presidential candidates signed a general agreement by which they accepted minority representation as a fundamental principle of the political system and consented to include this principle in the country's Constitution. They agreed, furthermore, that after the election the members of the defeated party would be accorded a "just and amicable" treatment in order to promote national reconciliation. Finally, those that ended up in the minority would exert all their influence to persuade those not in accord with the results to support the national government and cooperate in maintaining peace.

A second agreement, signed on 3 October 1932 by presidential candidates Sacasa and the Conservative Adolfo Díaz, set down specific measures to follow in the wake of the election. The most important included, among others, the "immediate" formation of a bipartisan commission to negotiate a peace with Sandino, a Supreme Court with a majority representing the winning party and appellate courts with Liberal majorities in León and Bluefields and Conservative majorities in Granada and Matagalpa, minority party representation within the executive branch in two special bipartisan commissions organized to supervise the workings of the Ministries of Foreign Affairs and Finance, candidate lists for municipal office of one party to include one-third from the other party's members, and a future constitutional reform to include the above minority representation schemes. Subsequent discussions led to additional agreements, including one stating that the losing presidential candidate would automatically become a senator and that the electoral authorities should constitute an independent branch of government with minority representation guaranteed.[1]

Later Anastasio Somoza considerably refined these preelection agreements when they served to strengthen his hand in dealing with the opposition. In the case of Sacasa's election in December 1932, the agreements reflected instead the weakness of the political institutions by which the government was chosen and the need to achieve political accommodation through extrainstitutional means. For the Liberal party, in control of the government and reasonably certain of electing its candidate in 1932, the agreements were a means of assuring that the Conservatives would not cry fraud too loudly or attempt to overthrow a government in which they would have a direct participation. For the Conservatives, the agreements allowed them to check the implementation of Liberal principles to which they objected and to maintain some of their members on the public payroll; furthermore, if the system of elections held over time, the Conservatives might hope for a return to majority control of the government without the recourse to armed revolt. But the agreements suffered from two errors of omission: neither Sandino nor Somoza, by then assistant director of the Guardia Nacional, was consulted nor were their respective armed bodies taken into consideration when the agreements were discussed and signed. Without their support the agreements were in the end meaningless because only Sandino and Somoza had control over the elements of coercion required to guarantee obedience. It was left precisely to Sacasa, once sworn into office on 1 January 1933, to tackle the problem of two armies in his country headed by two men with very different ideas about what to do in Nicaragua.

The strongest of these two forces was undoubtedly the Guardia Nacional. Organized in 1927 under the direction of marine officers, it was conceived initially by the United States as a constabulary that would have no relation at all with either political party. But the difficulty of training an officer corps to include only nonpartisan individuals led to an agreement signed by both parties in November 1932 whereby each presidential candidate (that is, Sacasa and Díaz) would draw up a list of names for the Guardia's upper posts chosen equally from both Liberal and Conservative parties, with the president-elect then appointing those officers that appeared on his list. However, the agreement specifically exempted the *Jefe Director*, the commanding officer, who would be chosen at will by the president-elect. Thus, the national army then in formation would continue in the tradition of the partisan armed forces that had characterized Nicaragua for so long.

An additional agreement signed in the presence of U.S. Minister Matthew Hanna by Sacasa and Díaz, as well as by Anastasio Somoza, then foreign minister and representing the Moncada government, committed the new government to maintain the Guardia as the country's only armed force and to observe the nonpartisan character of the Guardia's officer corp (a provision already vitiated by the bipartisan selection of officers), and empowered the president to name the General Staff in agreement with the Jefe Director. But the initial and most important decision was the selection of the new Jefe Director to replace General Calvin B. Matthews, the marine officer who headed the Guardia at the moment. Although in principle President-Elect Sacasa had a free hand in choosing the Jefe Director that best suited his government, in fact the appointment was the end result of a complex process involving President Moncada, General Matthews himself, and U.S. Minister Hanna, all of whom backed Anastasio Somoza. Thus, Sacasa apparently had little say in the matter; he probably accepted Somoza because he was related to Somoza's wife, Salvadora Debayle Sacasa, but it seems certain that Somoza was not Sacasa's first choice for the job.

Whatever the procedure employed to choose Somoza as Jefe Director of the Guardia, Sacasa had no qualms about appointing a majority of Liberals to field-grade positions, when the November 1932 agreement provided for equal appointments of Liberals and Conservatives. As it turned out, three of the five colonels and six of the eight majors appointed by Sacasa were Liberals, in addition to Jefe Director Somoza. The Guardia, from its first moments under Nicaraguan control, was very much in the Liberal camp. The problem for Sacasa, however, was that he had little control over the Guardia (and even less as time passed), while that of Somoza would grow continuously. Moreover, the Guardia was a potent force in a country that had been largely disarmed by the Tipitapa agreement of 1927: in February 1933 it had over 4,000 men and possessed 259 machine guns, 54 submachine guns, 23 automatic rifles, and 4,474 standard rifles. The cost of maintaining such a standing army even produced debate and criticism in the legislative branch and in the media.[2]

On the other side stood Sandino. By 1932 his forces were much better organized and operated at times on the northern side of Lake Managua. The year before, Sandinista columns had carried out successful raids along the Atlantic coast, destroying U.S.-owned mines and banana operations. In Washington, the Hoover administration had made it clear that the marines would be pulled out of Nicaragua without fail on 1 January 1933. Thus, in Managua the leaders of both the Conservative and Liberal parties were mindful of the need to end the war through negotiations. Sandino himself had never refused to negotiate; his only precondition was that the U.S. forces withdraw prior to any political solution of the conflict. It therefore was not surprising that Sandinista forces curtailed their activities by November 1932, at the same time that the Liberal candidate for president, Juan Bautista Sacasa, was duly elected.[3] Almost immediately, correspondence was established between Sandino and Sacasa's representatives to seek a peace conference as soon as possible.

Sandino's willingness to negotiate at a moment when his military strength was at its height and that of the government was presumably at a low point with the withdrawal of the marines has led to debate over what Sandino in fact wanted. Without doubt, Sandino was principally concerned with the foreign presence in his country; once that presence was removed, the reason for his struggle lost considerable force. In addition, he objected particularly to the Moncada government, because it had been Moncada who signed the Tipitapa agreement that provided for U.S. intervention; in Sandino's eyes, Moncada was a traitor. With Sacasa in office, Sandino could justify more easily his decision to negotiate with a man not tainted directly by the events of 1927, even though Sacasa had been Nicaraguan minister in Washington during all the years of Moncada's presidency.[4]

But there were practical considerations as well in his decision to negotiate. In the first place, Sandino's appeals for assistance from Latin American governments had not been answered. Not even Mexico, which Sandino visited in 1930, was willing to send material assistance as it had done for the Liberal revolt of 1926. U.S. pressure on the government of Portes Gil allowed Sandino to take up residence in Yucatan but as an "exile"; his only visit to Mexico City in January 1930 led to nothing and he was back in Nicaragua by May of that year. Second, Sandino's army was undoubtedly exhausted and its supply of ammunition and arms low. Among his soldiers, a lack of a clear understanding of the objectives of the movement "too easily associated the withdrawal of the Marines with the total victory of their cause."[5] Third, negotiations were not a bad alternative because Sandino knew that an end to the war was a pressing concern for President-Elect Sacasa. The depression was hitting with particular strength and Sacasa needed to take urgent measures both to strengthen his future government and to combat the economic crisis. Sacasa also must have realized that Sandino did not present a truly national threat in the sense that his forces did not roam at will over the entire country; nor did Sandino count on widespread political support outside of the northern departments of Nicaragua. In purely military and political terms, Sandino was a regional phenomenon, even though during the latter years of his struggle his columns operated well beyond the Segovias. In fact, the outcome of the negotiations between Sacasa and Sandino confirmed Sandino's position within the Nicaraguan state: that of a regional caudillo with which the central government came to terms.

The agreement reached between Sacasa and his national government and Sandino and his Ejército Defensor de la Soberanía Nacional accorded Sandino control over a region of the northern departments of Nicaragua, along the Río Coco, where he could establish agricultural cooperatives for his followers. He would be allowed to maintain an armed force of 100 men for one year, at which time the national government would decide whether to disband it, reduce it, or place it under new officers. The rest of Sandino's troops would turn in all their weapons to Sofonías Salvatierra, by then minister of agriculture and labor who acted also as presidential delegate for the northern departments. Salvatierra had been very active in setting up the contacts between Sacasa and Sandino and he was trusted by the guerrilla leader. On 22 February 1933, Sandino disbanded his army at San Rafael del Norte; Salvatierra received a total of 337 rifles, 2 machine guns, and 16 automatic rifles, as well as some 3,000 rounds of ammunition, part of which was returned to Sandino for the hundred-man force under his command. The fact that about 1,800 Sandinista soldiers were demobilized the same day led some to question whether Sandino had really turned in all his weapons.[6]

The prior cessation of hostilities and Sandino's arrival in Managua on 2 February 1933 were received with jubilation in Nicaragua. Sandino's ride from the Managua airport to the presidential palace in a car accompanied by Jefe Director Somoza turned into an emotional experience as thousands lined the streets and cheered. The Conservative and Liberal parties issued proclamations applauding General Sandino's "noble and patriotic attitude."[7] The private sector's position was also one of optimism. The León Chamber of Commerce in its monthly publication, *Mercurio*, sent warm congratulations to Sacasa on his election victory and underlined the need to achieve peace at whatever cost. (Just one year before, *Mercurio* had urged that the U.S. government provide the Nicaraguan armed forces with abundant weapons to get rid of the *bandoleros* who had affected so seriously the coffee harvests in the north.)[8]

To give the peace settlement additional legality, Sacasa sent a bill to the Congress that provided a blanket amnesty to all participants in the war. In addition to the soldiers of the Guardia Nacional and of the Ejército Defensor, the proposed amnesty also covered those jailed or exiled for supporting the Sandinista cause. Debate in the Chamber of Deputies centered on how to distinguish crimes of common banditry from those committed in the course of the war itself; other deputies saw the problem as one of expediency, realizing that in the absence of an amnesty, violence might continue in the north. In the Senate, various members expressed doubts about leaving an armed force with Sandino that was outside of the control of the Guardia, while some were concerned about the precedent established by the distribution of land to Sandino's people. However, these considerations proved less important than the need to get the fighting over with and both chambers approved the amnesty as presented by the president.[9]

And so peace came to Nicaragua after six years of civil war and foreign intervention that took the lives of 136 marines (including 47 combat deaths) and 75 Guardias, as well as 1,115 Sandinistas.[10] But peace was not the proper description for the period following the formal cessation of hostilities. Guardia patrols in the northern departments on occasion bumped into Sandinista columns which led to shooting and some casualties. Guardia intelligence reports always referred to Sandinista positions as "posiciones de elementos enemigos" and to Sandino's followers as "bandoleros."[11] For Somoza and the Guardia, the war was not over; for Sandino, the Guardia represented a constant threat. By early 1934 Sandino had declared that the Guardia was "unconstitutional" and needed restructuring, while Somoza demanded that Sandino turn in all his weapons, as contemplated in the peace agreement of the year before. Between the two stood President Sacasa.

The situation had developed into a confrontation between two armed groups, one claiming a monopoly on the coercive power of the state and the other a monopoly on the control over part of the national territory. Sacasa attempted to mediate between the two, providing Sandino with the ammunition and weapons he needed to maintain his force of men, and placating Somoza and the Guardia with a considerable chunk of the national budget. In a very clear sense, Sacasa took advantage of the situation to guarantee his own position: by playing Somoza off against Sandino he was able to neutralize the Jefe Director of the Guardia, whose political aspirations were never well disguised. Eventually, the sentiment against Sandino within the officer corps of the Guardia led to an attempt on Sandino's life. On a visit to Managua to confer with Sacasa, Sandino was hauled off by a detail of Guardias and shot on the grounds of the Managua airport on the evening of 21 February 1934. In the succeeding days, details of Guardia troops invaded the Sandinista settlements along the Río Coco, killing Sandino's followers and destroying houses and agricultural installations. For the moment Sandino and Sandinismo had been eliminated from Nicaragua.[12]

The Decline of Civilian Political Control

The elimination of Sandino placed Sacasa face-to-face with Somoza. During the next two years, Sacasa and Somoza would play politics by attempting to influence the U.S. minister, ordering changes in the officer corps of the Guardia, and fortifying their respective places of residence.[13] But the most visible evidence of the Sacasa-Somoza power struggle involved the control of the National Congress; each had his own followers in both chambers, with those beholden to Somoza gaining the upper hand over time. Two votes in the Congress illustrate this tendency. The first took place on 23 May 1934, when a Conservative deputy stated in the Chamber that the country was perfectly tranquil and that the Guardia was clearly in control. He requested, therefore, that the Chamber enact a bill rejecting Sacasa's extension of the state of siege. He stated, furthermore, that he had been with General Somoza, who similarly believed that the state of siege was unnecessary. A number of Liberal deputies then replied that the president's opinion was more important than Somoza's, who as an active military officer had no right to involve himself in politics. The proposal for a bill was finally rejected 27 to 15. The following day the debate continued in a heated atmosphere, with certain Liberals accusing the Conservatives of trying to turn Somoza into the head of a military dictatorship.[14] In sum, it seems that Somoza was working with Conservative politicians to gain their support without breaking his formal loyalty to the Liberal party.

In the next vote of this sort, which came to the floor in August, Somoza's allies did much better. At issue on this occasion was a blanket amnesty for all those involved in the "events of February," a euphemism for the assassination of Sandino. The amnesty bill was submitted by a group of deputies against the wishes of President Sacasa, who wanted to prosecute those involved in the killing. Support for the bill was expressed by the Conservative party and by a number of Liberals who argued that it was in the interest of the country that the whole affair be buried and forgotten. For example, Liberal deputy Carlos Pasos argued that if an amnesty had been granted to the "bandits" in February 1933, it was not possible to deny the killers of the bandits a similar amnesty now. Only a few defended President Sacasa's position by arguing that it was incorrect to decree an amnesty when investigations were still in process to determine who was responsible for Sandino's death. The final vote in the Chamber of Deputies was 33 in favor and 4 against.

The Conservative party justified its vote in favor by stating that the very peace agreement with Sandino was the first evidence of the "moral decomposition" of Nicaragua because it undermined the political institutions of the country by placing the Guardia in opposition to the executive branch. It added that it was a mistake to have provided the "bandit" Sandino with lands and an armed force of his own in "feudal style." More important, however, was the inconvenience of an exhaustive investigation into the crime: it was unquestionable that the Guardia had a collective responsibility in the death of Sandino, said the Conservatives, but its internal order might collapse if it was threatened by judicial proceedings. Thus, the Conservative party was in favor of an absolute pardon because it preferred order over justice.

Whereas the Conservative party's position was one of momentary expediency, one Liberal who voted against the pardon looked into the future. Ildefonso Palma Martínez drafted an argument to back his negative vote by underlining the fact that Sandino had been killed in total contravention of the protection extended him by President Sacasa. He stated: "Those individuals who thus acted [in killing Sandino], either on their own or under orders, violated the amnesty decree that protected General Sandino from all aggression and placed in doubt the morality and civic-mindedness of the Nicaraguan people. If those [who killed Sandino] did not respect an amnesty decree that the Congress promulgated, we would be jeopardizing our own prestige if we now favor them with a law identical to the one they violated deliberately. . . . If we commit the mistake of pardoning them, we set precedents of the most dangerous consequences."[15]

In the Senate, the bill was approved by a large majority, including the support of the Conservatives, who explained their vote in a document that is especially revealing of the crisis within the Nicaraguan state. They suggested that the agreement signed by Sandino and Sacasa in 1933 was a truce and not the definitive conclusion of the war. That was so because the government did not assume complete control of the situation in the country to the extent that General Sandino, outside of the law, constituted "a state within a state." This situation became particularly evident when Sandino questioned the constitutionality of the Guardia Nacional, the only army in Nicaragua. They also expressed their concern that if this army was subjected to a judicial inquiry, the peace of the republic could be threatened because the army was the most powerful institution in the country and it might reject "violently" any decision unfavorable to its interests. In any case, they concluded, the murder of Sandino was not a personal act but a collective endeavor that had a "merely political" motivation that the law was incapable of punishing. Therefore, an amnesty was the best form of resolving the problem and closing, once and for all, "this period of agitation, stained by crime, that was most painful for the Fatherland."[16]

What the Conservatives really were saying was that the Guardia Nacional was beyond the reach of the law or, more precisely, that it was a law unto itself. Furthermore, it was the only guarantee of public order, but its own internal order might collapse if it were threatened as an institution; presumably, its officers and men might stage a coup or go on the rampage. For the Conservatives, therefore, nothing should be done to indispose this powerful body.

The amnesty bill was vetoed by Sacasa and his council of ministers, but the Congress overrode their veto and the bill became law. At this moment, Sacasa's authority began to decline. His own party had rebuffed him in the Congress and supported the position of Somoza and the Guardia. His attempts to control Somoza had done nothing but increase the animosity and distrust between the two.

The Political Impact of the Depression

Compounding his strictly political problems, Sacasa was pressured constantly by the enormous weight of the depression on the Nicaraguan economy. Coffee exports, the principal source of foreign exchange, had dropped in value from U.S.$5.9 million in 1929 to just under U.S.$2.4 million in 1934, even though Nicaragua exported *more* coffee in the latter year. As the value of exports declined, imports were cut back drastically in order to maintain a favorable balance of trade. Previously, under the government of Moncada, exchange controls had been set up under a special government commission formed by the minister of finance, the general manager of the national bank, and the collector general of customs. This commission was empowered to authorize the export of only those products that guaranteed the country the return of the exchange earned in the sale abroad. Similarly, it was ordered to prohibit all exchange operations involving speculative ventures or unnecessary purchases.[17] In September 1932 the commission's authority was extended to include a direct control of imports, whereby it would give preference to essential goods and raw materials required by the export sector.[18] In general, the government was struggling to maintain the parity of the Nicaraguan córdoba with the U.S. dollar in the face of a strong demand for limited amounts of foreign exchange.

At the same time, government income had declined sharply, in good measure reflecting the decline in imports and of import duties. Import duties had always covered a considerable proportion of government revenues. (See Table 2.1.) In the absence of new taxes or of additional internal revenue, the government was forced to reduce its expenditures drastically. Some public services were cut back to the extent that they did not function at all (as was the case with the public school system, which closed down entirely in 1932). On top of this economic and fiscal crisis, Managua was hit by an earthquake in 1931; the shock wave and the ensuing fires destroyed a good part of the houses and buildings in the city, requiring the government to spend money on the construction of a new national palace and a new cathedral at the least propitious moment.

The fiscal plight of the government was only part of the country's economic crisis. Merchants, landlords, coffee growers, cattlemen, and salaried labor all felt the pinch, albeit in varying degrees. The government took some measures to help but these were generally too late and too few. In 1930 a national mortgage bank, the Banco Hipotecario de Nicaragua, was created by con-

Table 2.1 Import Duties and Total Government Income, 1925–1935 (in C$)

Year	Import Duties	Government Income	% of Duties/Income
1925	2,621,595	3,860,000	67.9
1926	2,592,203	4,443,630	58.3
1927	3,118,091	4,871,427	64.0
1928	4,146,066	5,987,583	69.2
1929	3,917,553	6,553,094	59.8
1930	2,771,799	4,975,928	55.7
1931	2,330,542	3,934,185	79.1
1932	1,681,365	4,666,000	36.0
1933	1,772,359	2,771,000	64.0
1934	1,915,003	2,844,000	67.3
1935	2,213,862	5,044,000	43.9

Sources: Import duties for 1925–35 and government income for 1925–31 are from Recaudación General de Aduanas, *Memoria para 1931*, pp. 62, 95. Government income for 1925 and 1932–35 are from Luis Augusto Cantarero, "The Economic Development of Nicaragua, 1920–1947," Ph.D. dissertation, State University of Iowa, 1948, p. 262.

gressional resolution. The bank was authorized to grant long-term loans with up to thirty years for repayment; of these, at least half had to be allocated to the agricultural sector and no more than 25 percent for urban construction. The bank functioned for a short while and then closed for lack of funds, but it was reopened in late 1934 with a fresh injection of government monies and with the stipulation that at least 70 percent of its loans go to agriculture.[19] The government also decreed the creation of a national pawnshop, known formally as the Caja Nacional de Crédito Popular; this pawnshop was designed to provide small loans of up to one hundred córdobas (then equal to one hundred dollars) guaranteed by some personal effect and for up to six months at 2 percent interest. But the amount of capital provided by the government was very small, while the loans probably got people out of scrapes involving paying the rent or the grocer and not much else.[20] Another measure that sought to help debtors established a limit of 9 percent yearly on the interest that private lenders could charge. It stated furthermore that the salaries of all employees, governmental or private sector, could not be embargoed for any pending debts.[21] But one must ask what powers the government had to enforce this law.

That these measures were not considered sufficient is evidenced in a number of suggestions offered by private individuals and organizations. One proposed approach to the problem involved seeking loans in the United States while increasing the money supply within the country.[22] Others demanded redress on specific issues such as excessively high customs duties, the unavailability of dollars with which to pay for imports, and the need to protect national industries through tariff barriers.[23] A more general critique appeared in an editorial of the Managua Chamber of Commerce's *Boletín*, which described Nicaraguan business as still operating as if the country were living in a boom period and not in a crisis. It was no longer possible, the *Boletín* argued, to allow for complete laissez-faire in which the stronger gained total control over the weaker. Thus, the entire system required an overhaul according to a general plan of reconstruction, which the chamber believed should include a suspension of all embargoes until a just and lawful solution was provided for debtors, an increase in the money supply as a fundamental aspect of economic reactivation, the cancellation of mortgage loans through an increased issue of córdobas, and the reorganization of the banking system and of the exchange control commission so as to give priority to national interests.[24]

The main issue in this debate, however, had to do with something more fundamental: control over the national bank and its dollar reserves. The bank, with its majority of North Americans on the board of directors, had followed a very conservative policy of placing its dollar holdings on the short-term bond market in New York as a means of both earning a profit and maintaining its credit rating. Thus, few dollars were available to the Nicaraguan merchants who were desperate to cancel their import receipts. By December 1935, the Managua Chamber of Commerce was openly criticizing the bank's insistence on maintaining parity, a policy that, according to the chamber, was leading the country to disaster. The chamber's president, José Benito Ramirez, demanded that the bank's dollar reserves be made available to merchants immediately and that the exchange control commission be restructured to eliminate the bank's influence over it.[25]

The bank's role in furthering economic reactivation was hindered additionally by the demands placed on it by the government to cover budget deficits. Since the beginning of the economic crisis, the national budget had not been balanced and the deficit had been made up by loans from the national bank. However, by draining the bank of funds to cover government expenses, little was left over for the bank's private customers. A more conventional solution to the budget problem entailed raising taxes, but the Sacasa government never did this, either out of fear of the political consequences or because it thought that the depression would not last much longer.[26]

In summary, the government's handling of the economic and fiscal crisis compounded its political problems and divided the Liberal party. Sacasa's personality did not help, either; he is often characterized as an elegant and urbane gentleman, a medical doctor belonging to one of the principal families of León, who felt more at ease in the company of his aristocratic peers at cocktail time than in the mundane world of politics and public administration. An objective evaluation of Sacasa must consider that there was not much he could do; the depth of the crisis was far more than the country's underdeveloped economy could handle. At most, the government was able to negotiate an agreement with the British bondholders of the 1909 loan, the largest foreign loan then owed, to pay interest only during 1935 and 1936, as well as keeping expenses as low as possible in all government spending and calling for frugality in the everyday lives of the people.[27]

The impact of the economic crisis seems to have produced surprisingly little political ferment among the people. Most likely, the rural population living on haciendas and small and medium farmers who owned or rented their land cut back their purchases of imported goods (probably never very great, anyway) and continued to live at the near-subsistence levels to which they had been accustomed for ages. Among the urban population, unemployment and a decline in real wages were felt more acutely but still not in the magnitude to produce open discontent. Evidence of some repression of the popular sector was discussed in the National Congress in January 1933, when a number of deputies demanded an investigation of the Guardia and local police implicated in torture and summary executions of campesinos and urban laborers. In León, three prisoners had been removed from the jail and then killed along a highway "while trying to escape." Another prisoner, accused of contacts with the Sandinistas, had been tortured by the prison authorities until nearly dead. One deputy reported having received telegrams from various parts of the country recounting arbitrary arrests and executions. A Managua newspaper carried the story of various workers accused of communist activities who had been tortured in jail. The under secretary of the interior eventually appeared in the Chamber of Deputies for questioning; he said that the reports of alleged violations of individual rights were being investigated. He was questioned again in May 1933 but refused to accept that the authorities had committed any wrongdoing, claiming that the reports were unfounded or still confused as to the events described. The matter was dropped at this point and not taken up again.[28]

That is not to say that the government allowed open political expression and debate. On numerous occasions Sacasa decreed states of siege that limited the freedoms of the press and of association: in January 1933 (after a plot was discovered among some Guardia officers protesting politically motivated appointments), in May of the same year (after the Managua ammunition depot exploded), in February 1934 (in response to Sandino's death), and the following September (when the Managua ammunition depot blew up again).[29] In most of these cases, the state of siege was aimed at the Conservatives, who were suspected of constantly attempting to overthrow the government, especially in view of the fact that the Liberals were formally in control of the apparatus of the state and gave little indication of a desire to turn over or share control of the government.

Civilian Politicians and the Guardia Nacional

A greater threat to the Liberals was the problem of presidential succession, which threw the party into a crisis as various candidates for Sacasa's job maneuvered to gain the candidacy for the 1936 presidential election. Within the Liberal party, three candidates seeking the presidential nomination emerged: Rodolfo Espinoza (Sacasa's vice-president), Leonardo Argüello, and Enoc Aguado. All three were longtime Liberals whose activities in the party had begun in the 1910s; their credentials consisted mainly of their loyalty and dedication to the party's cause. For the Conservatives, on the other hand, the problem of presidential succession took on a different meaning: it was highly unlikely that the Conservatives could win an election outright on the basis of their previous electoral showing and even more unlikely in the absence of U.S. supervision aimed at preventing large-scale fraud. Furthermore, in July 1934 the Congress had approved a modification of the 1923 electoral law whereby the president now named the head of the National Electoral Council, a post previously determined by the Supreme Court. According to this reform, the Liberal party's authorities would draw up a list of six Liberal candidates for the job; the list would then go to the Conservatives, who would pick three candidates for consideration by the president, who would then select one for the post.[30] In the end, a Liberal got the post and thereby put the Conservatives at a disadvantage on the three-person board. The Conservatives, therefore, decided to work for a compromise presidential candidate with the backing of both parties and with a prior agreement on the distribution of posts in the legislative, executive, and judicial branches of government, an agreement somewhat similar to that of 1932.

The Conservatives were generally unhappy with the results of the 1932 agreements. In September 1934, in a letter to the Liberal party, the Conservative party's secretary, David Stadthagen, had complained that many municipal councils lacked a truly bipartisan representation and that Conservative party members continued to be persecuted and imprisoned while carrying out party activities. In December of the same year, he wrote again to insist that the object of the 1932 agreements was to achieve an overall equilibrium between the two parties "that currently divide up the country's public opinion." However, he said, the Conservatives had had to resign themselves to a small share of power within the legislative branch and not much else. As a result, the two-party system had fallen into disgrace among members of the electorate. In March 1935, Stadthagen wrote to Sacasa to inform him that the Conservative party deemed the 1932 agreements a "dead letter." Sacasa answered by deploring the Conservative party's attitude but declared that he considered the agreements still valid and would continue to appoint Conservative individuals to the posts they were entitled to.[31]

While Conservative and Liberal parties bickered over the conditions and the concessions to run a common candidate for president, Anastasio Somoza busily pursued his own political ambitions, which by then were an open secret. In November 1934 Somocista groups were being organized in several localities. For example, in Casa Colorada, a small town to the south of Managua, about 140 men met on 16 November and formally pledged their support for Somoza both in terms of their votes and their active involvement in his campaign, but in the meantime they would promote his candidacy "en privado" (in private) so as not to interrupt the work of the Sacasa administration with "premature activities of political propaganda." (A more likely reason was that Sacasa had forbidden all political campaigning until eight months before the election.) In León, a group of 27 supporters belonging to the Liberal party decided to begin to work in the open but under the name of Grupo de Unificación Liberal whose objective was to overcome the factionalism that weakened the party and bring everyone together to support one candidate. In Chinandega, a number of activists organized the Comité Departamental de Propanda Pro-Somoza and the Club Juventud Somocista. Similar committees appeared in various towns in Masaya, Estelí, and Matagalpa, and in Bluefields on the Atlantic coast. By early 1935, the U.S. minister, who was privy to everyone's opinions in Nicaragua, could report to Washington that "from many friends close to General Somoza I am informed that he is definitely determined to be the next President."[32]

In addition to the committees that supported him, Somoza was sending and receiving letters concerning his candidacy for the presidency. On the basis of this information, three types of Somoza supporters were evident. The first included Liberal party members who perceived the convenience of working for Somoza as the most likely candidate of the Liberal party; some of them were acquaintances that Somoza had made over the years before and during his tenure as Jefe Director of the Guardia. For example, Somoza addressed an acquaintance in Matagalpa, Leonardo Somarriba, to inform him that there existed strong backing for his candidacy and that, on the basis of their old friendship, he hoped that Somarriba would join up in this "crusade for the party."[33] In a similar vein, Baltasar López wrote to Somoza from Chichigalpa encouraging him to accept the presidential nomination because "most of the *pueblos* [townships]" supported him.[34]

A more elaborate mechanism of support appeared in early 1935, when a form letter was sent out from Managua to diverse Somoza backers requesting that they solicit as many signatures as possible from people in their communities. The letter itself was an apotheosis of Somoza and the Guardia. Among other aspects, it stressed Somoza's role in ridding the country of banditry and allowing the Sacasa government to concentrate on national reconstruction and administrative reorganization. In return, the letter said, the people everywhere had "spontaneously" identified Somoza as the embodiment of the popular desire for concord and national renovation. In particular, the working classes expected from Somoza great results in furthering the collective well-being, while all those who opposed Somoza's candidacy on legalistic grounds were nothing but jealous politicians who had no right to contravene the popular will, which was the final arbiter in the choice of a country's leader.[35] It seems that this exercise was an attempt to gauge the level of support for Somoza among Liberals in the entire country, but the evidence available does not allow us to draw any conclusions.[36] What is clear is that a cadre of supporters existed, willing to seek out others through either personal acquaintance or promises of a better future.

A second group of supporters of the Somocista cause included members of the Conservative party who saw in Somoza a chance to obtain a government post or some political favor. Such was the case of an old schoolmate of

Somoza's in Jinotepe, Agustín Sánchez Vijil, who offered Somoza the support of the Conservatives in that town if the Conservative party did not run a candidate of its own. He thought Somoza enjoyed considerable backing (*simpatía*) among the Conservatives as long as he did not commit any rash action and was willing to comply with requests for favors.[37] Even Emiliano Chamorro reportedly believed in early 1934 that Somoza's candidacy was in the best interests of the country.[38]

The most important group in promoting Somoza's candidacy was the Guardia itself, particularly those officers who were beholden to him through either their Liberalism or their personal friendship. Guardia officers were useful to Somoza as a source of information on the political sentiment in their regions and the effectiveness of Somoza's campaign, as well as on the political preference of other Guardia officers. On other occasions, Guardia officers became involved in handling campaign funds, giving speeches, and organizing the lists of Somoza sympathizers. Already in December 1934, Somoza had appointed Captain Ambrosio Parodi as his campaign coordinator in the department of Matagalpa, which had traditionally voted for the Conservatives.[39] As his campaign picked up steam, more and more responsibilities were turned over to the Guardia in different parts of the country. By early 1936, Somoza was receiving a stream of letters and telegrams reporting on political activities: Lieutenant J. E. Rourk from Ciudad Darío evaluated the work of the Somocista activists, Captain L. Delgadillo from Ocotal analyzed the overall support for Somoza (which he thought was widespread), Major A. M. Baca from Bluefields recommended that a prominent Somocista activist receive a bank loan, Captain R. Meza from Siuna suggested that income from the local gambling operations (which were controlled by a Major Balladares) be channeled into the campaign chest, Captain Francisco Gaitán in Puerto Cabezas sent a list of loyal and unreliable Guardia officers on the basis of intercepted letters, and so on.[40]

This Guardia political activity was conducted in the open, which was one of its objectives: to persuade the people that Somoza's support within the Guardia was complete and unchallenged. Sargeant Gámez in Boaco reported that he was active in the campaign and that he even went to church to take communion so that the people would see him. (Boaco was traditionally Conservative and Catholic.)[41] Similarly, Captain Hermógenes Prado wrote to Somoza from Estelí requesting that Guardia officers be posted in Pueblo Nuevo and Ocotal to work directly for the Somoza campaign.[42]

The Guardia's participation in the campaign was observed by President

Sacasa and his followers, too. The president received telegrams from various *jefes políticos* (the departmental governors) regarding unauthorized rallies in which Guardia officers even gave speeches and where the use of force was threatened if the popular will (presumably favorable to Somoza) was not respected.[43] On other occasions, the Guardia imprisoned Sacasista Liberals when they distributed fliers and, in general, threatened all Liberals not in favor of Somoza.[44] This repressive climate reached such a point that Rodolfo Espinoza, the vice-president and a candidate for the presidential nomination, complained bitterly to Sacasa in February 1936 that the Somocistas were intimidating people into signing the letters of support (*actas de adhesión*) for Somoza. He repeated "for the hundredth time" that Somoza legally could not be a candidate and that Sacasa's protestations of impartiality and due respect for the laws of the country were therefore null. He rejected Sacasa's affirmation that Somoza was not using his post to further his candidacy when he, Espinoza, had placed abundant documents in Sacasa's hands that demonstrated otherwise. He closed by threatening to withdraw from the race if this situation was not corrected.[45]

The Ideology of Somocismo

That Somoza controlled the Guardia Nacional should not be interpreted as if his eventual accession to power was purely by means of force. Somoza had a message for Nicaragua and for different groups within the society. At times the message seemed contradictory and, more frequently, it was couched in grandiloquent terms and phrases that could be interpreted in a number of ways. Still, there is no doubt that Somocismo represented a break with traditional Nicaraguan politics, especially in its attempt to incorporate workers and campesinos into a national political movement. Furthermore, his candidacy was projected as an alternative to the two traditional parties, which some identified with the national disasters that had befallen Nicaragua. What was the message of Somocismo in the mid-1930s?

It is not possible to point to some basic document from which the Somoza campaign took its program and its political philosophy. Undoubtedly, events in other parts of the world also influenced political thought in Nicaragua. Roosevelt's New Deal, Hitler's new Germany, and Mussolini's fascist Italy were mentioned as models by different Liberals at different moments, but their application to Nicaraguan reality did not go beyond some fuzzy suggestions for action. Somoza's own trilogy of heroes, according to the photographs he kept in his office, included Zelaya, Moncada, and the Duce.[46] (Later on he got rid of Mussolini and replaced him with Roosevelt.) In fact, Somocismo evolved over time in a manner more consonant with political opportunities than with a predetermined blueprint. Nonetheless, some of its basic postulates were already in place by 1935.

A general appraisal of the new Somocista version of Nicaraguan liberalism was presented by Horacio Espinoza in a speech delivered at the Ateneo Militar (military club) of Managua in July 1935. He recounted the evolution of classical liberalism in the Old World beginning with the French Revolution and finishing with the liberal reforms in Central America undertaken by Barrios in Guatemala and Zelaya in Nicaragua. But this liberalism, which stressed economic individualism and individual rights, was out of place in the contemporary world, where collectivism was the driving force. Thus, if the French Revolution proclaimed the rights of man in the face of autocratic despotism, today the peoples of the world proclaimed their collective rights in the face of the rights of man as an individual. If liberalism wished to maintain its role of leadership in the development of new political ideals, Espinoza said, it must break with the past, casting aside abstract concepts and replacing them with concrete programs aimed at obtaining tangible results, social justice, and equity. To achieve these goals, new social and economic organizations must be developed by complementing aspects of the existing capitalist system ("which we cannot and should not discard") with those aspects of collectivism that sought to distribute more evenly the opportunities for social and economic advancement to each individual. That is, Nicaragua needed a system of "moderate state socialism," such as that implemented by Roosevelt in the United States. This entailed the formation of cooperatives of all sorts, the distribution of small plots to campesinos on state-owned lands (especially in the Atlantic and northern regions of the country), and the promotion of artisanal forms of production.[47]

A more specific outline of Somocismo's goals appeared on a small card distributed to campaign workers in mid-1935 in the department of Chinandega; it was entitled *¿Por qué soy somocista?* In addition to emphasizing Somoza's role in achieving and maintaining peace and order in the country, the card summarized a future Somoza government's policies in terms of land for the peasants who had none, special consideration for the working class, economic growth through government support for trade and industry, and highway and school construction, especially in outlying areas.[48] None of these promises included a timetable or explanations of how these objectives would be reached. They were promises and nothing more, but those relating to land and labor did reflect a departure, especially coming from a politician seeking office in a department where latifundia were so prevalent.

Somocismo harped on the past, too, by criticizing the traditional parties and their leaders and by comparing them with a future Somoza government that would be above and beyond the old parties and their ineffective governments. A broadside that circulated in Jinotega in January 1936 claimed that although Nicaragua was a democratic republic in form, its people had the least say in the government because "the aristocracy had kept them in ignorance and misery" in order to dominate and exploit them more easily. And when civil strife erupted, the people were thrown against each other "without the unhappy soldier, that humble man of the soil, knowing why he dies nor for whom he dies." The Constitution was a dead letter pulled out at election time and then thrown away so the aristocracy could govern at will. Another broadside from the same month in Chinandega stated that Somoza would change all this, beginning with the national Constitution itself, which would be totally over-hauled to update it according to the requirements of the "new Nicaragua."[49]

In general, Somoza sought to distance himself from the traditional Nic-araguan party system, to present himself as a new type of leader. He even denied that he was a politician and he denied that he made worthless prom-ises.[50] Nevertheless, he obviously relied on the old caudillo system to further his candidacy. The organization of the pro-Somoza committee in La Concep-ción in the department of Masaya resulted from a meeting attended by a number of caudillos "with well-known popular credentials."[51] In León, the Somocistas sought out Marcial Rios Jerez, who had 979 compadres in the city and surrounding areas whose votes he controlled. In Corinto, Rufino Guerrero was approached because he had influence ("tiene ascendencia") over the approximately 400 voters in the town where he lived.[52]

Somoza himself projected an image of the strong caudillo, the redeemer of Nicaragua, the man who would take care of everyone's problems and especially those of his friends and supporters. In a form letter he sent out in February 1936 to his principal adherents in the country, he stressed the need to work hard in order to guarantee the coming electoral triumph "for the good of the motherland and of my friends."[53] His character was similarly extolled in speeches and fliers. The card distributed to campaign workers in Chinandega described Somoza in terms of valor, impetuousness, and strength. Julio César Saenz admired Somoza's "energetic and decisive move" that rid the country of

Sandinismo once and for all; this was the man Nicaragua needed to be saved "from the destruction and extermination, the smoke and the blood, that have been our shame in the eyes of all the countries of the world." On the other hand, he said, Somoza was a popular caudillo, generous and tolerant, but with an iron fist for those who attempted to break the peace of the country.[54]

Somoza and the Old Party Leadership

At the beginning of 1936, Somoza's campaign was proceeding at full steam even though Sacasa had persuaded the U.S. minister to pressure Somoza to withdraw his candidacy. For a time it seemed that Somoza would do as Sacasa asked. Sacasa even suggested that Somoza could participate together with the Liberals and the Conservatives in the selection of a candidate of national unity, which would guarantee his post in the Guardia. But the Conservatives made it known that they would support a Liberal candidate only if Somoza were the one chosen.[55] This should not be interpreted to mean that the Conservatives liked Somoza in particular. What they wanted was to drive the best preelectoral deal with the Liberals, and Somoza, at that moment, most likely offered them the most favorable conditions. Support for Somoza also weakened the unity of the Liberal party by strengthening the Somocistas at the expense of the Sacasistas. In any case, Somoza did not reach any agreement with the Conservatives on this occasion, so they turned to the established Liberal leadership and proposed an overall pact to get them through the election crisis. A detailed analysis of this proposal is very illustrative of the traditional style of party politics in Nicaragua.

In April 1936 Horacio Argüello B. and two other Conservatives presented a memorandum to the Liberal party in which they stressed the importance of cooperation between the two parties in the face of the serious general crisis affecting the country. The most pressing issue, therefore, was not the electoral process itself but the formation of a national government that with strong support from both parties could concentrate on the solution of the crisis in its various aspects. That is, the country needed "time out" from the political struggle through the formation of a government of national unity (*gobierno de concentración*). However, the Conservatives addressed this problem in terms not of a program of government but of the distribution of government posts.

First of all, a common presidential candidate must be selected, a man sufficiently prestigious so that the people would not feel defrauded and would go to the polls en masse. To this end, the Liberal party would send a list of fifteen possible candidates to the Conservatives, who would then pick one to head the ticket. Along similar lines, the matter of selecting deputies and senators to the National Congress would be settled before the election: the Conservatives would get 40 percent of the seats outright. The Liberals apparently had offered to repeat the distribution of legislative seats on the basis of the 1932 election, when the Conservatives got 40 percent of the votes but less than that proportion of congressional seats.

In the second place, in order to reform the Constitution, a Constituent Assembly would be elected with three deputies from each department, one from the minority party and two from the majority party according to the electoral results in each department. But even before the election of the Constituent Assembly, both parties would agree on a number of basic constitutional principles; for the Conservatives, these included religious freedom, respect for the family, prohibition of usury, and "the organization of property and labor on the basis of social justice."[56]

In the third place, the cabinet in a bipartisan government would include Conservative ministers selected by the Liberal president on the basis of lists presented to him by the Conservative party in order to ensure that only *real* Conservatives were chosen; in addition, all diplomatic and consular posts would be distributed evenly between Liberals and Conservatives (with the Washington embassy in the hands of a Liberal) and the Supreme Court would have three Liberal and two Conservative judges. Finally, employment in public works was to be determined on the basis of merit and competence and not party affiliation, but to begin to implement this system, 40 percent of all employed in these activities would be selected from the Conservative party.

The emphasis in this proposal was eminently clientelistic and bureaucratic. There was no attempt to diagnose the country's problems or to propose specific policies to face the economic and social crises. The authors believed that by reaching an agreement with the other party, everyone would be satisfied, as if everyone in Nicaragua were either unconditionally Liberal or Conservative. In other words, they perceived politics in terms of patronage and caudillo-client relations. There was no fundamental discrepancy with the Liberals on ideological grounds, except the insistence on a number of general principles with which nobody could quarrel.

On 14 May, the Liberals and the Conservatives did come to an agreement. In the presence of Sacasa, two representatives each of the Conservatives and Liberals signed a bipartisan pact in which they pledged to run a common candidate for the presidency and to undertake a reform of the Constitution as soon as possible. The choice of the presidential candidate would fall to the leadership of both parties, although he would be picked from the Liberal party with the consent of both Sacasa and Somoza. The seats in the Congress and the Supreme Court also would be determined beforehand, with the Liberals receiving the majority in both cases. Finally, the Conservatives would have two cabinet posts and jefes políticos in the departments of Matagalpa, Chontales, Boaco, Rivas, and Granada, the historical sphere of influence of Granada. Two of the signers of the agreement, Emiliano Chamorro, the Conservative caudillo, and Crisanto Sacasa, a Liberal from León, were instructed to meet Somoza at once to get his support for the pact.[57]

But Somoza had his own proposal, which he made known at the same time that the Liberals and Conservatives signed their agreement. According to his version, Somoza would name the presidential candidate from within the Liberal party because he claimed to have the greatest base of popular support in the country ("el mayor volumen de opinión pública"); furthermore, this was only correct since he was setting aside his own candidacy. In regard to the congressional elections, Somoza proposed that they replicate the results of 1932: single candidates would run in each district, Conservatives in those won by them in 1932 and Liberals in the rest. Somoza himself would choose the members of the Supreme Court, again in proportion to each party's electoral strength. To complete his control over the Guardia, he demanded complete and exclusive authority to appoint all officers, including those of the garrison in León, the Fortín de Acosasco. At that moment, its commander was Ramiro Sacasa, a nephew of the president, who was not under Somoza's influence. In addition, Somoza demanded that the government immediately approve the purchase of cloth and shoes for the Guardia, as well as all other requests for equipment then under consideration. The government would also seek to raise the salaries of officers and enlisted men, and the next government would undertake the creation of a military academy and a school of military aviation. Finally, the government would cease to collect the arbitrary contribution of 5 percent that was discounted from public employees' salaries, an old practice that gave the party in power a regular source of income.[58]

It was in these terms, then, that Somoza offered to give up his presidential candidacy, but the implementation of his proposal would have made him much more than a president. He would become Nicaragua's strongman to a much greater degree than he was already: the presidency of the republic would be a figurehead, the Congress and the Supreme Court would follow his orders, the Guardia would be beholden totally to him as its commanding officer and benefactor, and the bureaucracy would look to him for the solution of all types of problems. This was nothing less than a Somocista blueprint for government. Sacasa rejected it outright, but that did not solve the problem. Nor did a meeting on 22 May that brought together the executive committees of both parties, together with Sacasa and Somoza. The Conservatives were particularly impressed by the confrontation between these two, especially on the issue of the presidential nomination.[59] A week later the two parties met again with Sacasa and agreed to name Leonardo Argüello as sole presidential candidate.[60] Somoza was not present on this occasion; he was attending to more pressing matters, namely the organization and control of the coup d'état then in progress.

The Somoza Coup d'état

Once Somoza realized that neither party would countenance his own candidacy or a candidate picked by him, there was only one road for him to take if he wished to retain control of the Guardia and keep alive his own presidential ambitions: Sacasa had to go or be neutralized and the parties' hierarchies sidelined from the selection of a candidate. That is, he had to gain total control of the political process while not destroying it, if at all possible. In the previous months he had demonstrated the extent of his power and influence in the country: he had resolved (and perhaps even encouraged) a strike of taxi drivers complaining about the shortage of gasoline, he had pretty much replaced all pro-Sacasa officers in the Guardia with his own men, and he had become nothing less than the grand elector in everyone's eyes.[61]

Such was Somoza's control of events that he was able to ease Sacasa out of the presidency and replace him with a puppet with a minimum of violence and just a little bending of the law. Nor did he have to worry much about the United States, which after the withdrawal of the marines moved toward a position of nonintervention in Nicaraguan internal politics. Coming after years of blatant political interference, this new U.S. role in Nicaragua proved most disconcerting to the political establishment. President Sacasa, for one, desperately tried to get the U.S. government to express at least some words of support or advice regarding the best course of action to take in order to stall Somoza's ambitions. He sent his brother and confidant, Federico Sacasa, to Washington to talk things over with the State Department; Sacasa made the point that since the United States had created the Guardia Nacional, it had a measure of responsibility for its actions. But the State Department, in the person of Sumner Welles, made it very clear to Sacasa that the era of intervention and interference was definitely over and that the Nicaraguans would have to work things out by themselves.

In Managua, Minister Arthur Bliss Lane and his replacement, Boaz Long, who arrived in Nicaragua in March 1936, went to great lengths to explain that they could not say anything in favor of one or another candidate, nor could they answer hypothetical questions about U.S. recognition of a government that came to power through unconstitutional means. At most, the U.S. diplomats claimed to be opposed to any government that came to power through violence but refrained from explaining if "violence" meant only the use of force or if it included overstepping constitutional provisions. What the United States did not want was a crisis, a breakdown of law and order that would make a mockery of its efforts to set Nicaragua on the road to stability and solvency or, worse still, that might require another military intervention.[62] In the end, then, Sacasa's pleas for help and Somoza's maneuvering went unheeded and unchecked by the United States.

In his march to the presidency Somoza's first objective was to gain control over all the Guardia forces in the country. Two of its units were still loyal to Sacasa: the Presidential Guard and the Fortín de Acosasco in León, which had been reinforced by a number of civilian volunteers from the Sacasa wing of the Liberal party. Somoza began by moving a trainload of soldiers to León, where he demanded that the commander of the fort turn over its control to a Somoza appointee. When this petition was rejected, Somoza threatened to use force to take control of the garrison. On 31 May, his forces began firing at both the fort in León and the presidential palace in Managua. After three days of shooting, cease-fires, and conversations, the León fort surrendered and Sacasa began to pay off his soldiers at the palace.[63]

While the armed uprising proceeded, Somoza sympathizers took over the municipal governments in the major cities. They simply evicted the mayors and their staffs, with the Guardia standing by or intervening on behalf of public order, but the results were the same. Sacasa could do nothing about this, just as he had been unable to control the appointments of pro-Somoza officers to key posts in the Guardia. He had lost control of the country's political institutions and he could appeal to no one for help. On 6 June Sacasa resigned and left immediately for El Salvador; he never returned to Nicaragua.

On 9 June, the Congress selected a new president to finish out Sacasa's term.

The official turned out to be Carlos Brenes Jarquín, who had been suggested previously by Somoza as a compromise candidate. The two houses of the Congress had previously received Sacasa's letter of resignation and that of his vice-president, Rodolfo Espinoza. Both letters were accepted unanimously without debate. The selection of Brenes Jarquín proved a little more difficult, if only because there was some debate. The Conservative bench, led by Carlos Cuadra Pasos, announced its willingness to vote for a "distinguished" Liberal but cautioned that its vote did not carry or imply any political obligations in the future. In the end Brenes Jarquín was elected by acclamation.[64]

Two days after Brenes Jarquín's election, the State Department cabled the U.S. minister in Managua that "there appears to be no reason why you should not treat with the present Government which seems to be in control of the country and all governmental machinery and to be performing the regular functions of government as the Government of Nicaragua." Thus did Washington recognize Somoza's puppet. For Somoza, the rest of the way was downhill.[65]

Putting Together an Electoral Coalition

On 16 June the Liberal party met in León to hold its convention and name its candidate for the presidency. The nomination of Somoza was totally uneventful. But the significance of this event must not be underestimated. As the reporter for *La Prensa* wrote afterward, the events at the Liberal convention meant the cancellation of an entire political generation within the party.[66] The old party leadership was swept aside in favor of a new group of younger, more dynamic and ambitious men. Such was the style of Somoza's speech in accepting the nomination. He promised peace, orderly democracy (*democracia ordenada*), nationalism, social justice, education, and work for all through a government of institutional and constitutional renovation.

What did these concepts mean? "Peace" meant the normal functioning of the country's activities, including, of course, all national and foreign businesses; that is, peace was the necessary precondition for private enterprise. "Orderly democracy" meant the prevalence of the opinion of the majority, without the presence of demagogical or anarchical tendencies and extremist ideologies. Under "nationalism" all Nicaraguans, regardless of their political preferences (such as the Conservatives, for example), would have opportunities to serve their country. "Social justice" stood for the harmonious conciliation of the working classes' interests with those of businessmen through the appropriate legislation. "Education" implied the extension of the school system in order to elevate the cultural level of the masses. And "work for all" included the creation of new job openings and greater efficiency among public employees.[67]

During the next four and a half months, Somoza would campaign for the presidency calling for change and renewal without spelling out in detail what and how this was to be. Nor did he have much need to campaign, to begin with. The coup against Sacasa disbanded the Liberal party's old hierarchy; Argüello and Espinoza both left the country, the latter after reportedly receiving U.S.$20,000 for his cooperation. Leadership of the party fell into Somoza's hands, with a few loyalists of the old guard trying to organize a Liberal splinter group. The Conservatives were similarly in confusion. Emiliano Chamorro left for Costa Rica on 23 June 1936 claiming that his life was in danger; he remained abroad for the next ten years.[68] During this time, the divisions within the Conservative party became even more evident: the Chamorristas who attempted to control the party in the caudillo's name and the Civilistas who looked to Cuadra Pasos for leadership.

Although Somoza was running without any significant opposition, the campaign allowed him to begin to put together the political coalition that, with some exceptions, supported him for the next two decades. Some components of the coalition, such as urban labor, were still very weak and unimportant. Other groups made their presence felt from the moment that Sacasa resigned the presidency, especially those with complaints associated with the economic crisis. Such was the case of the business community, which lost no time in addressing Provisional President Brenes Jarquín to explain its problems and suggest solutions. In a letter to Brenes Jarquín at the end of June, the Managua Chamber of Commerce complained that Sacasa had been deaf to its problems; the chamber had asked for a meeting with Sacasa time and time again but its request had never been granted. Its discussions with Dr. Vicente Vita, the manager of the Banco Nacional, had not produced any results either; Dr. Vita one day promised currency conversion, on another devaluation, and then free convertibility, but in the end he did nothing. The Managua Chamber added that the coffee growers had been particularly hurt by the bank's policies because they were paid for their coffee in córdobas, which were now worth much less in relation to the dollar. In general, the letter said, the directors of the bank had not paid attention to the country's problems, while the exchange control commission was powerless to influence or determine the rate of exchange. Even worse, the bank had sold dollars to individuals without the approval of the exchange control commission, which encouraged black market operations and contraband. In general, then, the Banco Nacional under the leadership of the "financial wizards" on its board had thought it best to hoard the gold it owned in order to maintain the illusion of the gold standard instead of proceeding to pay off the outstanding commercial debt.

The Managua Chamber of Commerce requested that the bank proceed to sell dollars to the merchants to pay off their commercial debts and to sell such dollars at the exchange rate in effect when the goods were purchased. The bank must also provide farmers with additional credits because they had had to bear the heaviest burden of the bank's misguided policies. The letter listed a number of specific requests concerning the government's future economic policy: formulation of a national financial plan that "truly responded" to the country's needs, including free convertibility and abolition of the gold standard; elimination of the exchange control commission and of all restrictions on freedom to export and import; sale of the gold reserves to pay off the commercial debt; reduction of interest on agricultural credit to 4 percent; and proper supervision of the Banco Nacional's operations and transfer of its board of directors to Managua. The chamber also insisted that it and the Asociación Agrícola de Nicaragua should be informed beforehand of any government policy initiative "that affects the economic life of the country in those activities which they represent," which meant that their own interests should receive special consideration. The letter closed with praise for the new government's "genuine economic nationalism."[69]

The Asociación Agrícola followed with its own letter to Brenes Jarquín a few days later. The letter deplored the past government's credit and exchange policies, which had hurt the coffee growers especially. The association then proceeded to request the same things as the Managua Chamber of Commerce, in particular free convertibility of the córdoba and the reduction of interest rates.[70] Foreign business similarly pressed for greater concessions. The general manager of the Bragmans Bluff Lumber Company, Inc., a subsidiary of the Standard Fruit Company with operations on the Atlantic coast, wrote to Somoza requesting that he intercede with the authorities of the Banco Nacional to assure the company sufficient dollars to import those goods required for its operations. He stated that the company was operating at the lowest profit margin possible and that any measure inimical to foreign business might lead to its closing. In conclusion, he said: "Please do all you can to prevent any rulings which will seriously affect the business."[71]

The government responded to these requests in October 1936 by liberalizing exchange controls. The president issued a decree that recognized the need to "grant justly requested support to all national activities and groups that are involved in export production." The decree authorized exporters to receive 70 percent of the value of their exports in dollars so that they might sell them at the free rate to importers duly authorized by the exchange control commission. The remaining 30 percent would be purchased by the Banco Nacional at the official rate of 1.1:1 to cover the government's foreign exchange needs and the service of the foreign debt.[72] Because the free (that is, black market) rate at that moment was of the order of 1.75:1, the exporters began to receive about 60 percent more for each of their export dollars than previously.

Importers seem to have been generally pleased with this measure, although they suggested a number of changes. In the first place, they proposed that, of the 30 percent that the government purchased at the official rate, two-thirds be set aside for the payment of the unpaid commercial debt (*deuda comercial congelada*) at the official rate of 1.1:1. That is, they repeated their request to buy dollars at the lower rate in effect when they made their purchases in the years past. Because the unpaid commercial debt was somewhat in excess of U.S.$2.5 million, the merchants were asking for a considerable concession. They also asked that the export producers be forced to sell their dollars at the free rate within three months after receiving them so as to avoid hoarding and speculation. A similar request was made by the León Chamber of Commerce.[73] The government did not respond to these appeals until the next year, when the exchange control commission was overhauled again. Meanwhile, however, export producers were given considerable relief, while importers faced the prospect of a lower demand for their goods (as prices were bound to increase) but with a greater facility for purchasing dollars.

Other fundamental aspects of the economic crisis were not resolved immediately, although some obvious steps needed to be taken. As the collector general of customs and member of the High Commission pointed out, the national budget was still out of balance and more income was required to solve this problem. The collection of taxes also could do with considerable improvements, as there was much corruption and favoritism in this activity. The collector figured that government revenues could easily double if more reliable collection procedures were established.[74] In fact, Somoza put these recommendations into effect once he was president and had better control of the situation.

In 1936 Somoza approached organized labor in a very tentative fashion. To begin with, there was not much organized labor around. The efforts of Obrerismo Organizado and the Federación Obrera Nicaragüense to promote labor unions in the 1920s had not met with much success, given the limited size of the urban labor class and the prevalence of the artisanal form of production. At most, a small number of labor leaders gained experience in this kind of activity and prepared themselves for the next step, which came in 1931 with the founding of the Partido Trabajador Nicaragüense (PTN). The PTN's objectives were drafted in vague terms, with no reference whatsoever to Marxist or Leninist principles and with only some references to justice and the rights of man. Nonetheless, as early as 1932 the government expelled some of its leaders for engaging in labor organizing. The following year, the PTN had just sixteen members in Managua and the leadership was scattered. An attempt to reach some kind of contact with Sandino (which he rejected) only split the party along two lines: those who favored a more expedient kind of approach to the party's participation in politics and those who leaned toward more revolutionary approaches. The formation of labor unions was not successful, either. Most unions were small and were formed largely by artisans and their helpers, while the government saw no difference between *sindicato* and *bolchevismo* and continued to repress them.

By early 1935, the more progressive faction within the PTN took control of the leadership and set down a line more in accord with Marxist-Leninist principles. The party's newspaper, *Causa Obrera*, reflected this view until it was closed down by order of Somoza at the beginning of May and its editors were jailed. Still the party's leadership insisted on a radical line; in June 1935, the central committee of the PTN approved a program that proposed, among other things, a labor code with provisions on minimum wages and the right to strike, abolition of all liens on debts, a capital tax, socialization of all industrial and agricultural enterprises, nationalization of banks, state ownership of all lands, repudiation of all outstanding foreign debts, and an overhaul of the educational system to promote socialism. In addition to being very ambitious, the program was also contradictory, because some objectives could be achieved within a capitalist system whereas others would require a prior proletarian revolution. For Somoza at this moment, the PTN was nothing but a minor nuisance to be handled through the use of selective repression; after the overthrow of Sacasa, various PTN leaders were confined to Corn Island under the label of "communists."[75]

Somoza was interested in labor's support, but he wanted it on his own terms. He was willing to intervene in the taxi strike in February 1936 on behalf of the strikers, which included up to eight thousand construction workers, railroad employees, and artisans who joined in sympathy, but he repressed the PTN when it announced that the strike should continue.[76] More to his liking were organizations like Juventud Obrera, which invited him to a workers' dance to thank him for all his help to the working class; such groups claimed that they wanted to organize their activities along strictly legal lines and not allow any incident to incommode Somoza "in the very least."[77] It was this type of labor organization that Somoza had in mind when the government decreed an extra tax on liquor sales in August 1936, the proceeds of which would go to the construction of Casas del Obrero in Managua and in each of the principal departmental cities. The government would hand out these funds to previously approved committees for the construction of the Casa itself, within which workers would have a place to engage in diverse recreational and educational activities.[78]

Support for Somoza among the rural laborers most likely was determined by the presence of landowners who exerted political control within caudillo-client relationships. Where Liberal caudillos prevailed, the rural vote was for Somoza. In some areas, where traditional patterns of landholding were not prevalent, Somoza's candidacy was able to make inroads under the direction of Guardia officers and Somocista political activists. Along the Atlantic coast, workers engaged in banana production were approached by Somocistas and responded favorably. In the Siquía district of southern Zelaya department, some three thousand small banana growers looked to Somoza for redress of their grievances in the face of the low prices paid for their production by the North American banana company.[79] In addition, the distribution of fliers containing Somocista pledges to distribute land and improve living conditions for the campesinos would indicate an attempt to bypass caudillo control over the rural masses in some areas. But on the whole, it would seem that the Somocistas sought out the rural vote by working through the established political system, namely that controlled by the rural caudillos.[80]

A third group that Somoza incorporated into his coalition was the extreme right, whose most visible organizations were the Blue Shirts (Camisas Azules). The Blue Shirts took their role models from the European fascist movements and proceeded to organize a number of groups in cities like Granada, Managua, and León and in small towns near the capital. They seem to have been largely middle-class youths, some of them belonging to old families of Granada whose economic situation had deteriorated over the years. But the number they recruited was quite small; in Managua, they numbered about eighty.[81] The Blue Shirts were closely linked to the Guardia, from which they received military training. Somoza received a monthly report on their activities and issued identification papers to their organizers; he also gave them money for their expenses.[82] In addition to participating in parades in support of Somoza's candidacy and plastering walls with their propaganda, the Blue Shirts engaged in some shock troop tactics, including an attack on the small opposition newspaper, La Tribuna, which they vandalized in an operation in May 1936.[83] But their overall weight in the Somoza campaign was undoubtedly very limited; after Somoza's election they pretty much disbanded.

Of considerable importance in electoral terms was the Conservative vote itself, which Somoza sought earnestly. After Chamorro's departure from the country, the Conservatives were divided as to what to do in the coming elections. One faction, headed by Chamorro, decided to carry on with the candidacy of Argüello according to the Liberal-Conservative pact signed just before Sacasa was removed from office. A dissident faction of anti-Somoza Liberals formed the Liberal Constitutionalist party, which joined up with the Chamorrista Conservatives to support Argüello and Espinoza as his vice-presidential candidate.[84] Somoza's response was to promote the formation of a rival Conservative party that would support his candidacy. Thus in the end there were two Liberal candidates, Somoza and Argüello, each supported by a coalition of Liberals and Conservatives.

Somoza's Conservatives organized the so-called Partido Conservador Nacionalista. Although these Conservatives no doubt were genuine in the sense that they had voted Conservative in the past, their leadership probably belonged to the middle echelons of the party. None of the big names of the Conservative party joined this new group nor were they able to tap rich Conservatives for funds. Somoza had to bankroll practically all their activities, from campaign expenses to voter registration to getting the vote out on election day.[85] That is not to say that Somoza himself paid for these. His control of the state apparatus was already sufficiently complete to enable him to drain state funds for partisan political activities.[86]

The Partido Conservador Nacionalista campaigned fundamentally on the issue of Somoza's candidacy. It did not seek any type of concession or accommodation on the ideological level. What was in the minds of the leadership of the party was the opportunity to share in the spoils of office; the party's leaders were offered a number of seats in the National Congress and no doubt were promised a certain number of government posts for the less important members of the party. Their showing at the polls presumably would be the yardstick whereby their rewards would be determined.[87] For Somoza, the support of these Conservatives allowed him to project his candidacy in terms of a national coalition, in which the two historic political parties came together to support one man and one program of government. When the opposition decided to withdraw from the race in November claiming that the popular will would be flouted at the polls, Somoza was left as the only candidate, but he could still claim that he had bipartisan support.[88]

The 1936 Electoral Campaign

That Somoza represented a novel political program or political alternative was probably important to a relatively small proportion of the voting population. For the majority, the 1936 campaign differed little from previous exercises in Nicaraguan politics in which the mass of voters was led to support a given candidate and led to vote for him at the polls. Political rallies were festive events where liquor and tamales were distributed in order to guarantee attendance. Carlos D. García reported to Somoza that the rural population along the Río Coco received gifts of gunpowder, salt, tobacco, and food from campaign workers (mostly Guardia officers). On election day, he said, the voters must be promised much food, especially the Indians, because "they eat a lot and it is food which principally draws their attention and they will come from afar in order to have a good meal."[89] In areas with poor roads, it was necessary to assemble the voters at a given point a few days before the election to ensure that everyone was present to vote; during that time they had to be fed and provided with liquor and tobacco.[90] The distribution of *aguardiente* was so widespread that the minister of finance complained to Somoza that the tax-free liquor provided by the government's distillery to the Somoza campaign was being resold improperly by campaign workers at a low price and thus decreasing the government's income from the tax on legally sold alcohol. The minister suggested that the liquor used for the campaign be of a lower grade than the one sold commercially; that way there would be a greater volume of booze to give away and the cheaters might be caught.[91]

In the department of León, one of the Liberal strongholds, the Liberal party made a strong and coordinated effort to assure a massive Somoza victory. To begin with, all the party departmental committees were reorganized so that only Somocistas were left on them. Then the executive departmental committee put into place 115 committees at the local level and set up a number of more specialized committees, such as a medical committee that offered free medical consultations and medicines to sick party members and a food committee that provided meals and drinks at party rallies and meetings. A press committee worked with the newspapers to print articles favorable to Somoza as well as distributing broadsides of all sorts. Financing the campaign occupied the attention of another committee, which sought donations of beef, rice, and lard for food and sold bonds to finance other campaign expenses.[92]

Although other campaign machines were not as efficient as that of León, in all departments Somoza could count on the support of the Guardia and, in general, had the advantage provided by control of the state apparatus. And yet the results were not as gratifying as Somoza would have liked. Abstentionism seems to have been very high, even according to the official election figures released by the Consejo Nacional de Elecciones. In the two presidential elections supervised by the U.S. missions in 1928 and 1932, the proportion of registered voters to votes cast was 88.3 and 84.3 percent respectively; in 1936 it was only 49.8 percent.[93] This abstentionism of over 50 percent could be attributed mostly to the decision of the Conservatives to withdraw from the race; the Argüello-Espinoza ticket they supported together with the dissident Constitutionalist Liberals got all of 189 votes in the entire country. But that explains only part of the problem, because even in Liberal strongholds like León and Chinandega the level of abstention was high. (See Table 2.2.)

The levels of abstention in strongly Conservative departments, such as Chontales, Rivas, Boaco (split off from Chontales in 1935), and Granada suggest that the caudillo network of political control still operated efficiently. In Chontales, perhaps the most Conservative department with its large landholdings and rural caudillos, abstention in 1936 was above 70 percent, whereas in 1932 it was only a little under 15 percent. In general, the Conservatives' call to boycott the election was heeded by the party's regional leadership and the mass of its voters.

In strongly Liberal departments, such as León, Chinandega, Estelí, and Nueva Segovia, abstention most likely reflected the displeasure of many Liberals with Somoza's procedure to take over the government or the fact that they belonged to rival factions within the party itself, such as the Sacasistas or Argüellistas. In León, Sacasa's own department, abstentionism was just under 50 percent, and Chinandega did not perform much better. Managua's abstention of 57 percent probably reflected the strength of Argüello's faction there together with a good number of Conservative voters in that department. Estelí's abstention of 60 percent, the highest after Chontales, follows a pattern

Table 2.2 Registered Voters and Votes Cast, 1932 and 1936

	1932			1936		
Department	Regist. Voters	Votes Cast	%	Regist. Voters	Votes Cast	%
Bluefields	9,972	8,373	(84.0)			
Carazo	9,615	8,522	(88.6)	11,189	5,875	(52.5)
Chinandega	12,353	10,733	(86.9)	14,974	8,048	(53.8)
Chontales	17,923	15,391	(85.9)	20,387	5,605	(27.5)
Estelí	7,169	5,107	(71.2)	15,994	6,237	(40.0)
Granada	9,894	8,583	(86.8)	11,041	4,836	(43.8)
Jinotega	5,600	2,846	(50.8)	8,923	4,435	(49.7)
León	16,183	13,058	(80.8)	24,215	12,248	(50.6)
Managua	22,055	19,809	(89.8)	30,596	13,230	(43.2)
Matagalpa	17,104	14,717	(86.0)	22,008	12,778	(58.1)
Masaya	11,878	10,656	(89.7)	14,998	6,900	(46.0)
Nva. Segovia	6,659	5,388	(80.9)	4,765	3,202	(67.2)
Rivas	7,926	6,921	(87.3)	8,797	4,139	(47.1)
Boaco				9,250	4,161	(45.0)
Madriz				7,081	4,490	(63.4)
Zelaya				15,450	13,235	(85.7)
Total	154,331	130,114	(84.3)	219,668	109,419	(49.8)

Sources: Consejo Nacional de Elecciones, *La verdad electoral de 1936* (Managua: Talleres Nacionales, 1937); Recaudación General de Aduanas, *Memoria para 1932*. Bluefields was renamed Zelaya in 1935.

consistent with the experience in 1932, when its abstention was second highest in the country after Jinotega (then in the throes of Sandino's struggle).

With all the votes counted, Somoza ended up with 80.1 percent of the total and the Nationalist Conservatives with nearly all of the rest. (See Table 2.3.) In absolute terms, therefore, Somoza could say that he had a clear mandate to govern. However, in five of the departments the Liberals got less votes than in 1932 (Carazo, Chinandega, Granada, León, and Rivas) whereas in two they won slightly more (Managua and Masaya). Chontales and Boaco together gave the Liberals only about 600 more votes than they got in Chontales before its partition in 1932. The biggest gains for the Liberals were in Bluefields (which became Zelaya in 1935), Nueva Segovia (split into Madriz and Nueva Segovia

Table 2.3 Election Results, 1932 and 1936
(percentage of total vote in parentheses)

| Department | 1932 | | 1936 | |
	Lib.	Cons.	Lib.	Natl. Con.
Bluefields	6,569 (68.5)	1,804 (21.5)		
Carazo	4,718 (55.4)	3,804 (44.6)	4,403 (74.9)	1,465 (24.9)
Chinandega	8,799 (82.0)	1,934 (18.0)	7,144 (88.8)	902 (11.2)
Chontales	5,182 (33.7)	10,209 (66.3)	3,006 (53.6)	2,599 (46.4)
Estelí	3,356 (65.7)	1,751 (34.3)	4,741 (76.0)	1,482 (23.8)
Granada	3,961 (43.0)	4,892 (57.0)	3,296 (68.2)	1,539 (31.8)
Jinotega	1,767 (62.1)	1,079 (37.9)	3,433 (77.4)	1,002 (22.6)
León	11,913 (91.2)	1,155 (8.8)	11,437 (93.4)	802 (6.6)
Managua	11,398 (57.5)	8,411 (42.5)	11,541 (87.2)	1,663 (12.6)
Matagalpa	6,496 (44.1)	8,221 (71.4)	9,122 (71.4)	3,642 (28.5)
Masaya	5,696 (53.5)	4,960 (46.5)	6,050 (87.7)	821 (11.9)
Nva. Segovia	3,513 (65.2)	1,875 (34.8)	2,488 (77.7)	714 (22.3)
Rivas	3,171 (45.8)	3,750 (54.2)	2,885 (69.7)	1,182 (28.6)
Boaco			2,811 (67.6)	1,349 (32.4)
Madriz			3,481 (77.5)	1,009 (22.5)
Zelaya			11,810 (89.2)	1,411 (10.7)
Total	76,269 (58.5)	53,845 (41.4)	87,648 (80.1)	21,582 (19.7)

Sources: Consejo Nacional de Elecciones, *La verdad electoral de 1936* (Managua: Talleres Nacionales, 1937); Recaudación General de Aduanas, *Memoria para 1932.*

in 1935), and Jinotega. In all of these departments the influence of the Guardia Nacional was strong: in Jinotega, Nueva Segovia, and Madriz as a result of the military presence following the war against Sandino and in Bluefields/Zelaya given the extremely dispersed nature of the population, including many indigenous groups and English-speaking creoles, which the Guardia could control easily. These departments provided the Liberals with a total of 21,212 votes in 1936 compared to 11,849 in 1932, a difference of over 9,000 votes; this explains in great measure the gains in total votes made by the Liberals, from 76,269 in 1932 to 87,648 in 1936. Of course, the 21,000-odd votes of the Nationalist Conservatives were for Somoza, too; on that basis, he could claim that he got nearly 33,000 more votes than Sacasa in 1932. But even those votes fell far short of the 40,000 offered to him by the Nationalist Conservatives' leadership.[94] The election results must have indicated to Somoza that a considerable number of Nicaraguans of all political persuasions were not convinced by his methods or his call to national unity. In the future, therefore, there was need to strengthen the Somocista coalition.

For the moment, Somoza's strength was also the opposition's weakness. Once the votes were counted and Somoza was proclaimed the winner, the opposition of anti-Somoza Liberals and Conservatives could do little more than complain to the U.S. government. Sacasa, Adolfo Díaz, and Emiliano Chamorro had previously visited the State Department to request that the United States supervise the upcoming elections, but they were turned down.[95] After the elections, they hired two Washington lawyers, Charles A. Douglas and Joseph V. Morgan, to prepare a written argument against the recognition of the future Somoza government by the United States. They stated that Somoza's government would be unconstitutional (because Somoza was related to Sacasa and because he was a military officer) and that it was the product of a coup d'état. Thus, recognizing Somoza would go against the U.S. policy of non-recognition of governments that came to power by force. Such recognition also would violate the agreement whereby the United States helped create the Guardia Nacional as a nonpartisan military force.[96] But the U.S. government already had recognized the administration of Hernández Martínez in El Salvador, which came to power through a coup d'état, and it was not going to get involved in the legal debate concerning Somoza's qualifications for the presidency (which hinged, incidentally, on the importance of the position of a comma in the constitutional article on presidential succession). With the acquiescence of Washington, the support of the Guardia Nacional, and the political coalition he had put together in Nicaragua, Somoza had no effective opposition. He was duly installed as president on 1 January 1937 for a four-year term.

Conclusion

Somoza's rise to power was due to a number of fundamental political circumstances. Undoubtedly the most important was his control of the instruments of coercion. Both the Tipitapa agreement of 1927, which disarmed the contending partisan armies of Liberals and Conservatives, and the creation of the Guardia Nacional in the same year as the sole armed force of the country effectively eliminated any real possibility for caudillos to mount assaults on the state through the use of their private forces. In fact, Chamorro's overthrow of the government in 1926 in typical caudillo fashion would be the last in Nicaraguan history. After the formation of the Guardia, with its great superiority in firepower and manpower, it would have been impossible to challenge the central government on the battlefield. Sandino must have come to this realization, too; his decision to negotiate with the central government once the last U.S. Marines had left the country coincided with a shift toward a political role for himself and his following.

The assassination of Sandino and the destruction of his movement by the Guardia constitute a second important element in Somoza's rise to power. Although Sandino's forces at the beginning of 1934 had been reduced to the barest minimum after the peace agreement of 1933, it is conceivable that he could have reorganized and fielded his armies again either to come to the aid of the Sacasa regime or to undertake, in a wider political movement, a direct capture of the government. In any case, Sandino was the only political leader in 1933 and 1934 who was openly calling for a renovation of the Guardia in order to bring it into line with the constitutional authority of the president.[97] Somoza must have realized that such a measure would have involved his own head as Jefe Director or a reduction in the Guardia's strength and, thereby, in its political weight. Sandino, in turn, realized that the survival of his political and social experiment along the Río Coco required that the Guardia cease harassing his people. In the end, Somoza defused the confrontation by ordering the killing of Sandino, a move that simultaneously reduced Sacasa's room for maneuver and cleared the way for Somoza's ambitions.

In the third place, the foreign power that had intervened so forcefully during the two previous decades now turned into a political sphinx whose Good Neighbor policy toward Nicaragua really should have been called the Unconcerned Neighbor policy. In addition to Washington's decision to reduce U.S. interventionism in the hemisphere, after 1934 there was no danger of a situation arising that would have warranted direct intervention in Nicaragua. Both the Liberal and Conservative parties were beholden to Washington after years of negotiating with U.S. ministers and emissaries and submitting to electoral supervision. The Guardia Nacional was a direct creation of the United States and its Jefe Director was undoubtedly the most subservient of the Nicaraguan political leadership. Thus, the United States had no objective need to support anyone openly in order to protect its interests in Nicaragua; that is, it could position itself on the sidelines and allow the Nicaraguan political system to reach a state of equilibrium without its direct intercession. At most, Washington made it clear that it would not contemplate the violent breakdown of the system it had worked so carefully to put in place. Somoza knew this and therefore applied only the minimum amount of force necessary to achieve Sacasa's resignation, while conserving the outward appearance of constitutional legality needed to propel himself into the presidency. If anyone at this time had mastered the art of reading United States's intentions and acting accordingly, it was Somoza; over the years he would continue to perfect this ability.

Finally, Somoza promoted his ambitions for the presidency in a political campaign initiated long before his putsch against Sacasa. In this respect, Somoza did not take advantage of a given circumstance but created one. He projected his figure, enveloped in a program of government, as the necessary political alternative for Nicaragua at the moment. By offering something to nearly everyone who would listen, by promising to put the past behind, and by placing himself above the traditional divisiveness of the Nicaraguan polity, he presented himself as the successor of Zelaya, as the leader of a movement of national renovation, reconciliation, and reconstruction. Though formally a Liberal, he had no qualms about approaching the Conservatives, the extreme right, organized labor, or diverse agrarian and commercial interests. If anything, he was a consummate opportunist, but in the world of politics that is an important asset.

Within the Central American context of the time, it is impossible to find a comparable political phenomenon, even discounting the unique presence of the United States. Nor does Somoza's admiration for Mussolini and Roosevelt permit comparisons with the New Deal or Italian fascism. Perhaps Somoza's role model, if any, can be traced to Lazaro Cárdenas and Getulio Vargas, as subsequent Somocista policies would indicate, particularly in regard to the organization and mobilization of labor and the popular sectors and the role of the state in economic development. What was not clear at the time was Somoza's intention of becoming an economic power himself, of using the state's resources to bankroll an extensive business empire. In this respect, the appropriate role model perhaps is the entrepreneur-general of the *Maximato* in Mexico who combined a lip service to social reform with a practical dedication to capitalist development.

3 REVAMPING THE STATE

. . . .

Upon receiving the presidential sash on 1 January 1937, Somoza proceeded to deliver his first message to the Congress and the nation in terms that generally repeated his campaign platform of the preceeding months: internal peace, orderly democracy, social justice, education, and work. He expanded on some of these, thus giving a clearer picture of his government's policies. The maintenance of peace would be guaranteed through a strong government willing to take quick and decisive measures with the backing of a "disciplined and efficient army, which is the guarantor of the institutions of the state and the rights of the citizen." If this peace was not upheld, he said, the country would slip into "the chaotic madness of demagoguery or the oppression of more or less despotic regimes."[1]

A strong government, however, was not sufficient in itself to face the important questions of the day; there was also need for constitutional reform that would take into account the broader interests of the society and not just protect the rights of the individual. Social justice was the practical expression of this concern, which Somoza defined as "an equitable protection of the interests of workers and campesinos, without forgetting those of the entrepreneur, the industrialist or the capitalist, because true justice is defined as a balanced concept of equilibrium." Because this concept of social justice was based on principles of solidarity among men, the new government would prohibit the expression of *ideas exóticas* that tend to divide the social classes.

The principal immediate concern of the government would be the solution of the country's economic and financial problems, because the solution of all the other problems was subordinate to these. To that end, the government would strive for administrative honesty, fiscal solvency, equitable distribution of the tax burden, and efficient investment of public funds. In the short term, the government would seek a balanced budget, the consolidation of the internal debt, tax reform, monetary stability, and a careful selection of all public employees. In the longer term, the agricultural potential of the country would be stimulated through the state's promotion of highway construction, agricultural credit, education, and new markets. In general, the policies enunciated reflected the heavy weight of the depression still affecting the Nicaraguan economy and the new government's determination to do something about it. Somoza's challenge was to put together a package of measures that would not generate excessive popular opposition or, at the least, would minimally satisfy the more powerful economic groups.

The challenge was not an easy one. The price of coffee, Nicaragua's major export product, remained at a low level of around U.S.$0.07 per pound, the same price as in 1932 and 1933, while the volume of coffee exports had not increased. The production of bananas was in clear decline as the U.S. companies on the Atlantic coast reduced their purchases from the local producers. The production and export of gold was the only bright spot, but the nature of gold mining in Nicaragua greatly reduced its impact on the overall economy: the gold mines were mostly wholly foreign owned and operated as virtual enclaves. Furthermore, they paid practically no taxes on their operations. At most, the Banco Nacional purchased in córdobas some of the gold produced while the rest left the country unnoticed. Coffee thus remained the most important export product, both because it provided the largest portion of the nation's foreign exchange and because its cultivation employed the largest number of rural workers.[2] Once the United States entered World War II, Nicaraguan exports of other products, such as rubber and sesame seed, would increase dramatically. But in 1937, the economy still was in a very depressed situation.

The Regulation of Foreign Currency and Trade

As was the case of all the Latin American export economies at the time, the most pressing problem was that of the international trade imbalance. In 1936 Nicaragua still was running a negative balance of trade that put great strains on the ability to import and complicated the payment of foreign debt obligations. The government's prime concern was to assure a positive balance of trade, which could be achieved only by reducing imports. A number of alternative policies might be employed, including devaluation, exchange and import controls, and monetary inflation to cut back on purchasing power. In fact, all three were implemented at different times with varying degrees of success.

Two weeks after assuming office, Somoza addressed the nation to describe the seriousness of the economic situation. As a partial remedy, he announced that the Banco Nacional would henceforth sell dollars for the import of staples and raw materials at a rate of 1.9:1, instead of 1.1:1, thereby officially devaluing the córdoba by 80 percent. This announcement lowered the black market rate somewhat from where it stood at 2.6:1.[3] But it soon went up again and prompted import merchants to complain that the availability of dollars at the banks was still very much below the demand and that they were forced to purchase dollars on the black market. Without access to cheaper dollars to pay their debts, they argued, it was impossible to keep prices at the same level, as the government had been pressuring them to do. They again insisted that the Banco Nacional should sell its gold reserves and make the dollars available to the merchants to pay off the commercial debt.[4]

By mid-1937 the importers had seen no improvement. The Managua Chamber of Commerce wrote again to Somoza complaining that the October 1936 measure that sought to place 70 percent of export income in the hands of the merchants to pay for imports had never been put into effect by the Banco Nacional, while Somoza's plan to sell dollars at the rate of 1.9:1 had been implemented so slowly that its impact was nil. Thus, the laws and regulations that the state itself had decreed were not being carried out by the state's own institutions, while the importers still had to purchase dollars on the black market to the detriment of the consumer.[5]

In the face of the criticism, the government contracted the services of a U.S. financial expert, Dr. James H. Edwards, to analyze the Nicaraguan fiscal and financial situation and draw up a plan to put things right. After some months of discussions and study, Edwards recommended that the government return to a strict control of exports, imports, and exchange procedures. Following his suggestions, the Congress passed a bill in August 1937 that authorized the exchange commission to control all exports and imports and to establish an exchange rate that could not be higher than 2:1.[6] But the problem could not be solved by increasing government control of international trade and exchange. The problem was one of insufficient foreign trade earnings and an excessive demand for imports. Because foreign trade earnings could not be increased in the short term given the depressed conditions of the world market, the only practical alternative was to restrict the consumption of imports. What had to be defined was whether the allocation of the scarce foreign exchange for imports would be accomplished by the unfettered operation of the market forces or whether the government would ration out the dollars and pounds and try to keep the exchange rate from climbing too fast. Edwards's recommendations as implemented took the latter approach.

By December 1937 both the Managua Chamber of Commerce and the Asociación Agrícola de Nicaragua were expressing their wholehearted opposition to the so-called Edwards Plan. The chamber of commerce insisted that it opposed any type of exchange control, which had been its position ever since the exchange control commission was established in 1931. Now, the chamber argued, it was clear to all that the system had failed in every respect: it had not stabilized the currency, it had not avoided the flight of capital ("the only plausible reason to keep the system in operation"), nor had it eliminated the black market, which continued to thrive. The subsequent reforms had not led to any improvements, either. In sum, the chamber said, the whole system should be scrapped.[7]

The Asociación Agrícola complained that in the face of the depressed prices for coffee, the growers had to struggle with taxes and high freight rates on the national railway and, to top it all, with the exchange control commission, "an institution which has exercised the most nefarious influence over producers in general and coffee growers in particular." The Asociación claimed that the commission only favored the merchants, who sold their imported wares at black market prices while purchasing foreign exchange at the official rate. Further, while no farmer had been able to pay his debt obligations on time, not a single merchant had ever gone bankrupt because the commission's measures gave the merchants preferential treatment. As the Asociación put it, the merchants enjoyed "an enviable level of well-being thanks to the generosity of the Comisión de Control." Therefore, it concluded, the commission should be eliminated, the córdoba allowed to float, export taxes reduced, and the payment of the commercial debt suspended.[8]

Although the merchants and the coffee growers had very different interests to defend and different perceptions of the situation, they thus both agreed on the need to eliminate exchange controls and to devalue the córdoba. With these two powerful associations opposing the established policy, Somoza had to accept the fact that the commission had been a failure. At his weekly press conference on 10 December, he acknowledged that the Edwards Plan had not worked because Edwards supposedly had been given "incorrect data" on Nicaragua's gold reserves. Somoza now was proposing a new plan that would give exporters up to 80 percent of their foreign currency earnings to dispose of at will, while the commission would limit its functions to prevent capital flight. The Congress quickly ratified this proposal. The plan stipulated that all foreign currency could be exchanged freely in Nicaragua except for those monies received from the export of Nicaraguan goods, which would be handled by the Banco Nacional. But in all cases the exchange rate would be allowed to float, so that coffee exporters would get, and the merchants would have to pay, that much more for their dollars. At most, the bank would charge a 10 percent tax on each export and exchange operation.[9] The exchange control commission became at this moment a sort of clearinghouse where foreign exchange operations were handled.

The impact of these measures and the demand for dollars produced the result desired by exporters: the córdoba fell in value to settle in June 1938 at 5:1 at the official rate and somewhat lower at the free rate. (See Table 3.1.) But the merchants were not entirely convinced. In his year-end report to members of the Managua Chamber of Commerce, President Eduardo Mendoza stated that little had been achieved in 1937 and that government officials were difficult to reach. He added that the latest plan enacted by the government was a slight improvement but its effects were still to be seen. In general, he believed that the economic situation at the end of 1937 was worse than it had been at the beginning of the year, especially in the export sector, without which the import merchants could not prosper.[10]

Meanwhile, a group of businessmen got together on their own and came up with an informal agreement not to pay more than 4.5:1 for the dollars they purchased from the exporters. They also tried to work out an arrangement with the Asociación Agrícola to stabilize the rate at 4.5:1, but the Asociación maintained that at that rate the farmers barely made a profit and that it did not understand how the chamber of commerce could first seek a totally free rate and now propose a maximum rate. As it turned out, no agreement was reached.[11] What seems to have happened is that the Managua Chamber of Commerce came under the control of businessmen who identified more closely with the regime and who objected to a free-floating córdoba. As of January 1938, the president of the board of the chamber was Constantino Pereira, who in the following months would take every occasion to praise Somoza; furthermore, Somoza had named José Benito Ramírez, a previous president of the chamber, to the post of minister of finance. Both Pereira and Ramírez had signed the informal agreement on the exchange rate, too. The new board, then, tried to back the government in its attempt to keep the exchange rate as low as possible, while the exporters sought to raise it as much as possible.

In dealing with this issue, Somoza tried to act evenhandedly, although in

Table 3.1 Value of the Córdoba to the U.S. Dollar

Official Rate		Free Rate	
Prior to Nov. 1934	C$1.00		
26 November 1934	1.10	31 December 1934	C$1.25
16 March 1937	2.00	30 June 1937	3.20
23 December 1937	4.00	31 December 1937	4.30
9 June 1938	5.00	30 June 1938	5.90

Source: "Cost of Living in Managua, Nicaragua," a document prepared by the U.S. Embassy staff in Managua, 1944, based on data from the Banco Nacional and the Dirección General de Estadística, box 269, AN.

political terms the regime would benefit from a lower exchange rate to the extent that the price of imports would not climb as much. In a decree he signed in January 1938, Somoza set down the guidelines for the implementation of the latest exchange control system. Under its terms, all exporters first had to get the authorization of the exchange commission before they could ship their goods abroad. The foreign exchange received in payment by the exporters would then be channeled to the Banco Nacional, from which those authorized by the commission could draw dollars to pay for imports and other foreign obligations. The commission would assign first priority on the exchange available to merchants for their import requirements, while export producers would be allocated the foreign exchange they needed "in reasonable amounts." On the other hand, those authorized to purchase foreign exchange then had to go to the owners of foreign exchange in Banco Nacional accounts (that is, the exporters) and haggle with them over the purchase price.[12] The government thus withdrew from setting exchange rates but kept a hand on the exchange itself by controlling the administrative procedures that enabled it to grant authorizations to some and not to others.

Once the exchange rate had settled in the neighborhood of 5:1, the government tried again to control more strictly the purchase and sale of dollars. In June 1938 the Congress passed another exchange control measure that allowed the government to fix the official exchange rate weekly, in addition to keeping full control of the administrative procedures (that is, the private purchase and sale of dollars would be prohibited).[13] Because the exchange rate did not continue to fall, this procedure really did not increase the government's role in exchange operations. What the government had done was to remove itself from fixing the level of exchange while the córdoba was devalued in a free market environment. It returned to "fixing" the exchange rate once a stable córdoba had been achieved.

Price Controls and Financial Reform

As the value of the córdoba fell, Somoza had to address the political costs of a rise in prices that followed in its wake. His campaign promises to protect the workers, campesinos, and urban middle class would seem nothing in the face of an inflationary spiral. Price controls seemed to be the most effective measure at the time and more in line with the government's policy of active participation in the economy. The government had undertaken the first cautious steps in this direction in March 1937. Somoza, under his own initiative and "in the interests of the popular sectors," issued a decree ordering shopkeepers to display their prices in visible places so that agents of the exchange control commission could check them easily. These inspectors were also empowered to inspect the shopkeepers' books in order to compare costs with resale price. On the basis of this information, the commission would authorize the sale of foreign exchange with priority to those merchants who sold at the lowest prices.[14] This was not a system of price controls, strictly speaking, but a carrot-and-stick approach that was probably inconsequential; at least, there is no evidence that the merchants objected to its implementation.

By the end of 1937, however, the rise in prices had become a matter of concern to the government, and in January 1938 the regime made its first attempt to control prices under the guise of a law limiting profits. This law established a maximum of 20 percent profit that a merchant, either wholesale or retail, could make on the sale of basic staples, such as ordinary cloth, thread, tools, machetes, plows, shovels, medicines, flour, and, in general, all other articles considered necessary for the livelihood of the Nicaraguan people. To monitor the effects of this law, a new body called the Comisión Ajustadora Nacional was created; the president appointed to this commission representatives of the exchange control commission, the collector general of customs, and the Banco Nacional, as well as a representative of the merchants' associations and of labor. All complaints from consumers were to be addressed to the Comisión Ajustadora, which could levy fines and even close down businesses caught violating the 20 percent maximum profit.[15]

Passage of this law through the Congress was fairly uneventful. Some deputies inquired whether a retailer could make a 20 percent profit on top of the profit of the wholesaler. Others wondered if there would be sufficient administrative muscle to enforce the law.[16] The chamber of commerce did not object much, either. In a note to Somoza, it said that the reason for high prices in the stores was the uncertainty surrounding the declining exchange rate, which forced merchants to sell at a price that would compensate for a possible fall in the value of the córdoba.[17] Somoza subsequently met with a delegation of merchants to discuss the profits law; he mentioned to them that the law did not seek to harm anyone but to benefit the people as a whole. The president of the Managua Chamber of Commerce then sent a note to the membership asking that it comply with the law and pointing out that any injustice to the merchants would be resolved by the Comisión Ajustadora.[18] That this measure did not produce much of a backlash among the merchants was an indication of its minimum impact. A 20 percent profit probably was sufficient to compensate for the fall of the córdoba, while the enforcement capability of the government was not likely up to the level where every transaction could be monitored.

A few other measures to check the rise in prices were announced in the course of 1937. In June, Somoza decreed a five-year ban on the export of cattle, supposedly to keep the price of meat low in the internal market. Both the Asociación Nacional de Ganaderos and the Managua Chamber of Commerce objected to the measure, claiming that high taxes—not insufficient supply—raised the price of meat.[19] In any case, the opportunities for contraband along the border with Costa Rica made it very difficult to police such a measure, not to mention the fact that Somoza himself may have become involved with smuggling cattle by this time.[20] Later, in February 1938, Somoza unveiled a plan to create a national commissariat that would sell basic staples at cost to workers and peasants; it would be started up with small contributions from the workers themselves. But nothing came of this, nor of a proposal to establish rent controls.[21] In general, more stringent price controls would appear once World War II had broken out in Europe and the government acquired wider authority to intervene in diverse aspects of the economy. For the time being, Somoza had achieved what export producers and merchants had been demanding for some time: devaluation of the córdoba and a more stable exchange rate.

The regime's intervention in settling the exchange problem through devaluation was only the most visible of a number of economic measures that Somoza's government undertook during his first years in office. All of them sought to strengthen the state's institutions and none was more important in the long run than the reform of the banking and fiscal systems. Already in June 1937, just six months after assuming office, Somoza received from financial adviser Edwards a comprehensive report on the country's major economic problems based on conversations with diverse bankers, businessmen, merchants, farmers, and bureaucrats. Edwards's recommendations were fairly conventional: balance the budget, stabilize the exchange rate, increase government income by creating new taxes, and consolidate the floating debt, among others. He also suggested that the entire banking and financial system be overhauled to permit the effective implementation of fiscal and banking policies.[22] As it happened, Edwards fell from grace at the end of the year when his plan to stabilize the córdoba did not work. But his recommendations to balance the budget and increase tax revenue were implemented to some extent.

During Sacasa's last year in office, the budget finally had shown a small surplus. Somoza, however, endeavored to make the surplus even bigger and proceeded accordingly. Collection procedures were tightened, especially in the case of stamp and liquor taxes and user fees on the national railroad. Taxes were raised on gasoline, alcohol, tobacco, and sugar. A property tax was created for the first time in December 1939 (at a rate of 0.5 percent of assessed value) as well as a sales and inheritance tax on all real estate transactions (0.5 percent for a sale and a sliding scale from 0.5 to 15 percent for an inheritance).[23] But the amounts levied for property were minimal and the tax was collected only as of 1944, and the sales and inheritance taxes were frequently avoided. That is, the weight of the tax increases fell on the consumer, regardless of the government's statements to the contrary. At a press conference in December 1937 Somoza himself said that the tax increases and the new taxes to be levied would not fall on the common folk but on the rich "who want to enjoy certain luxuries." His minister of finance followed with a speech in which he criticized the weight of indirect taxation in Nicaragua and the need to redistribute the tax burden by means of direct taxation.[24] But the only important direct tax collected at that time was on coffee exports and that was *reduced* by 20 percent to favor producers.[25]

Whatever the regressive aspects of the tax structure, government income rose considerably beginning in 1937. (See Table 3.2.) The rapid rise was due in large part to the devaluation of the córdoba; if income figures are converted into dollars at the official rate in effect at the time, the increase in revenue was hardly as spectacular. Furthermore, the biggest increases occurred after 1940

Table 3.2 Government Income and Expenditures, 1935–1945

Year	Income in C$	Income in U.S.$	Expenditures in C$	Surplus/ Deficit
1935–36	5,302,486	4,820,442	4,945,823	356,663
1936–37	7,493,825	5,790,682	6,850,020	643,805
1937–38	10,416,000	3,645,600	na	na
1938–39	16,746,156	3,349,231	14,386,323	2,358,833
1939–40	28,147,895	5,629,579	23,388,784	4,759,111
1940–41	32,973,443	6,594,688	28,066,642	4,906,801
1941–42	40,724,658	8,144,931	38,053,185	2,671,473
1942–43	41,141,255	8,228,251	41,308,462	(–) 167,207
1943–44	48,893,683	9,778,736	43,247,971	5,645,712
1944–45	47,782,397	9,556,479	59,801,240	(–) 12,018,943

Source: Ministerio de Hacienda y Crédito Público, *Memorias.*

when the world war stimulated Nicaragua's exports. In any case, the budget consistently produced a surplus except for two fiscal years (1942–43 and 1944–45), clear evidence of the government's resolve and success in overcoming the fiscal imbalance.

Increased taxes and a balanced budget were two important aspects of the regime's economic policy that were complemented by the overhaul of the banking system. Ever since the creation of the Banco Nacional in 1912, the state banking system had completely dominated the country's credit operations. With the founding of the Banco Hipotecario in 1931, these two state banks acquired a near monopoly on all banking operations. However, for some time these institutions had been criticized for not operating in a more coordinated fashion. For example, the Banco Nacional had been involved in rural credit operations that coincided with the Banco Hipotecario's stated objectives or, as happened after 1935, the exchange control commission authorized the sale of dollars that the Banco Nacional did not have available. Also at issue were concerns regarding U.S. domination of the Banco Nacional and the conflict over the use of its gold reserves.

As a first step toward greater state control of the banking system, Somoza brought the board of directors of the Banco Nacional back to Managua in May 1938. Most of the bank's shares were already in the hands of the government, but the fact that the board was to function in Managua allowed greater pressure to be brought to bear on its members. Now the bank would be more responsive to the demands of exporters and merchants, while the national government would increase its influence over fiscal policy.

The second step involved the comprehensive overhaul of the entire banking system. To this end, Somoza contracted with Dr. Herman Max, a Chilean economist associated with the Banco Central de Chile, who arrived in Managua in May 1940. Max remained in Nicaragua for the rest of the year, beginning his work with a study of the banking system and finishing with a set of proposals for new laws governing monetary and credit policies. These were presented to the president as a package and were issued as an executive decree with only minor modifications on 26 October 1940.[26] In the preamble, a number of reasons were given to justify reform of the banking system, including the need to achieve price stability, to adapt the monetary and banking system to the new realities of a world at war, and to increase the number and amount of credit operations.[27] One objective it did not mention, however, was to bring the entire banking system under direct presidential control.

The first of these laws, and the most important, made the Banco Nacional an "autonomous entity" of the republic; that is, as of October 1940 it ceased to be a corporation of the state of Connecticut. Its basic functions were handled by a banking department, which operated as a commercial bank, and a department of issue, which operated as a central bank. Both departments functioned independently but were under one board of directors. The board would be picked by the president, with one representative each from the Managua Chamber of Commerce, the Asociación Agrícola (representing the coffee growers), and the Asociación de Ganaderos and four chosen at large. In this manner, the board always had a majority of directors beholden directly to the president. Because the bank's functions were in themselves very wide, presidential influence and authority would be felt in many aspects of the country's economic life. For example, the banking department with its sections of commercial, agricultural, and industrial credit could handle both small and large credit requests, particularly in the area of coffee and sugar production for export (créditos de avío). The department of issue, in turn, was empowered to fix the bank discount rate, the foreign currency exchange rate, and the maximum bank loan rate, as well as issuing currency and buying and selling all gold and foreign currencies.[28]

A second law covered the functioning of banking institutions, both foreign and national. The president of the republic had to authorize the creation of all banks and credit institutions. Once established, every bank came under the oversight of the Superintendencia de Bancos, which could audit books to determine whether the bank was complying with the regulations pertaining to deposits, credits, and exchange operations. The head of the Superintendencia was named by the president, although this office was attached to the Ministry of Finance.[29]

Other laws fixed the maximum interest rate for all credit operations at one and a half times the bank discount rate and empowered the department of issue of the Banco Nacional to determine the exchange rate of the córdoba. Foreign exchange operations were put under the Comisión de Cambios, formerly known as the Comisión de Control de Operaciones de Cambio. This renamed commission, formed by three individuals appointed by the president of the republic (who were to be knowledgeable about the world of trade and finance "without having any direct interest in such activities"), was to control all exports to make sure that the foreign exchange earned abroad returned to Nicaragua. It also would distribute this foreign exchange among individuals to satisfy "legitimate" needs defined as imports, payments on foreign debts, profit remittances by foreign concerns, and business and study trips abroad.[30]

The Banco Hipotecario was reorganized so that its credit policy did not overlap with that of the Banco Nacional. That is, it was limited exclusively to long-term loans for agricultural improvements, land purchases, and building construction for commercial, housing, and industrial purposes. Its board of directors was reduced from nine to five, all named by the president, three at large and one each from lists presented by the Banco Nacional and the Asociación Agrícola de Nicaragua. As with the private banks, the Banco Hipotecario's operations came under the audit of the Superintendencia de Bancos.[31]

The national pawnshop, the Caja Nacional de Crédito Popular, also came under the banking reform laws. The government's contribution to its capital was increased from C$50,000 to C$150,000, and the loan limit was raised from C$100 to C$3,000. Its board of directors of three and its general manager continued to be named by the president.[32]

A final law, passed in October 1940, reorganized the so-called Compañía Mercantil de Ultramar. The Compañía was founded in 1919 as a private trading company registered in New York State, the property of a North American and an Englishman. Later its shares were bought up by the Banco Nacional, and the Compañía Mercantil became the bank's commercial agent. According to the 1940 law, the Compañía ceased to exist as an independent corporation and became a part of the Banco Nacional under the name of Compañía Mercantil de Ultramar, Oficina de Exportación e Importación del

Table 3.3 Public and Private Bank Credit Operations,
1941–1945 (in thousand C$)

	1941	1942	1943	1944	1945
Private Banks					
JRE Tefel	76	139	235	397	453
Caley Dagnall	229	562	941	878	943
Banco de Londres	2,369	3,527	4,124	3,960	5,653
Total	2,674	4,228	5,300	5,235	7,049
State Banks					
Caja Cred. Pop.	638	758	842	962	1,162
Banco Hipotecario	5,069	5,851	6,167	7,339	7,873
Banco Nacional	16,516	21,664	26,466	36,408	45,861
Total	22,223	28,273	33,475	44,709	54,896
Total, All Banks	24,897	32,501	38,775	49,944	61,945

Source: Juan María Castro Silva, *Nicaragua económica* (Managua: Talleres Nacionales,
1949), pp. 103–10. JRE Tefel and Caley Dagnall were not, strictly speaking, banks but
casas de cambios autorizadas; both were involved primarily in the export of coffee and
loans to coffee growers. Caley Dagnall was owned by two Englishmen whereas JRE Tefel
was a Nicaraguan concern.

Banco Nacional de Nicaragua. Its principal activities involved coffee exporting
and the establishment of quality control standards, but it also could purchase
and export any agricultural product and import and sell at low prices all kinds
of goods required by the agricultural sector. Its three-person board of directors
included representatives of the Banco Nacional, the Banco Hipotecario, and
the Asociación Agrícola de Nicaragua.[33]

With the banking legislation in place, the new system began to function on 1
January 1941 when the Banco Nacional opened its doors as a strictly national
bank. The most striking feature of the new system was the enormous weight of
the public banks in the country's credit operations. (See Table 3.3.) At no time
in the period 1941–45 did private banks account for more that 14 percent of
all credit extended in the country. The Banco Nacional alone handled between
two-thirds and three-quarters of the value of all loans.

Undoubtedly, the political influence exercised through control of credit in
the country was considerable. Somoza received monthly copies of all credit
operations undertaken by the Banco Nacional and the Banco Hipotecario, and
he frequently wrote letters of recommendation to its presidents to back specific

loan requests.[34] Most likely, a letter from Somoza was a virtual guarantee for the successful resolution of a loan request, and letters of recommendation were extended only to those who Somoza thought worthy of his support.

Between 1941 and 1945, credit operations accelerated, with most loans going to agriculture and ranching. About half of the Banco Nacional's loan portfolio was in agriculture and cattle raising. The commercial sector also was an important client of the bank; it usually represented between one-third and one-quarter of the outstanding loans. Part of this increase in the volume of credit operations reflects the falling value of the córdoba and the inflationary spiral that began in 1938, which government measures were incapable of controlling. After the measures taken in 1937 and 1938 to limit profits and control the exchange rate, another set of measures was implemented at the beginning of World War II, including both import restrictions and an attempt to fix the maximum profit rate at 5 percent for those articles considered essential, as well as establishing maximum prices for some of them. Rents were frozen at the rate paid on 1 August 1939, a government monopoly was created for the importation of drugs to combat certain endemic diseases, and, when the United States entered the war in December 1941, a Junta de Control de Precios y Comercio was set up to tighten control over prices. In 1944 the authority of the Junta was expanded to include the control of all imports.[35]

The result of all these measures was, in fact, a system of rationing, especially of imported goods mainly from the United States, but the rise in prices continued unabated. (See Table 3.4.) The explanation for the continued inflation in the face of the new laws and regulations is that the government had increased greatly the money supply to coincide with the rapid devaluation of the córdoba and to cover budget deficits. (Between 1938 and 1945 the money supply grew fivefold.) The price of food experienced the steepest rise, probably due to the fact that locally produced food never came under the list of controlled or rationed goods and its price was fixed by the supply and demand in the country's market places. The other categories of goods and services did not experience such a rapid increase, but for people on low or fixed incomes the rise in food prices probably left very little for other expenditures.

By 1943 the country's finances were pretty much in order thanks in part to the world war and a rise in Nicaragua's exports, as well as to the government's economic measures. The budget and foreign trade had been balanced, the foreign commercial debt had been paid off, and the 1917 bond issue had been redeemed ahead of schedule, thus eliminating the High Commission.[36] The Banco Nacional was now totally under the control of the Nicaraguan govern-

Table 3.4 Cost of Living Index for Managua, 1940–1945 (1939 = 100)

Year	Food	Rents and Services	Drugs and Health Supplies	Dry Goods and Clothing	Combined Index
1940	123.6	113.6	97.2	110.2	115.9
1941	135.1	124.5	119.6	130.8	128.9
1942	185.1	145.7	190.8	162.8	164.1
1943	243.2	196.8	278.5	188.0	214.3
1944	352.5	300.4	321.4*	210.8*	271.9*
1945	433.4	na	na	na	na

Sources: U.S. Embassy at Managua, "Cost of Living in Managua, Nicaragua" (typed paper), box 269, AN; Recaudación General de Aduanas, Memoria de 1949, p. 80; Jeffrey Gould, "The Nicaraguan Labor Movement and the Somoza Regime, 1944–1946" (unpublished paper), app. D; U.S. Department of Commerce Yearbook Series, "Nicaragua" (August 1946), 3:8.

*First eight months only.

ment, as were all other banking institutions, both public and private, directly or indirectly. The price paid for these policies was a reduction of the levels of consumption achieved through a rise in prices and taxes and a cutback in imports. In a very real sense, these measures defined the regime's political orientation to a much greater degree than Somoza's public statements and political promises. The main beneficiaries were the producers for export and, to a lesser extent, the import merchants, whose differences concerning exchange rates and controls were minor compared with what they stood to gain from devaluation. Lower-income groups bore the brunt of the retraction.

The Reorganization of National and Municipal Government

As Somoza had mentioned in his inaugural address, economic recovery was his government's immediate and main concern. But his promises of greater social justice and material development, as well as the preservation of political peace, required the strengthening of the state's apparatus: the bureaucracy, the coercive authority, and administrative procedures in general. The underlying objective was to make the state's apparatus more responsive to presidential authority and to assure increased efficiency of its operations. Because the well-being and strength of that apparatus directly depended on the level of material support it received, one of Somoza's major concerns was to improve the level and efficiency of tax collection. As seen in Table 3.2, government income increased noticeably in real terms after 1939, the result of a hike in tax rates as well as improvements in the efficiency of tax collection through the creation of the Dirección de Ingresos.

Prior to the establishment of this Dirección, taxes were collected by a number of administrative units: the Dirección General de Rentas (primarily engaged in collecting alcohol taxes); the Negociado del Impuesto Directo sobre el Capital; the Estanco de Fósforos; the Inspección General de la Renta de Papel Sellado y Timbres; the Sección de Timbres para Cigarillos; the Inspectoría de los Impuestos sobre Cerveza, Destace de Ganado y Producción de Azúcar; and the Recaudación General de Aduanas. All of these units (except for the Recaudación General de Aduanas) were under the Ministry of Finance, but their administrative procedures were so dissimilar that they operated practically as independent entities. With the creation of the Dirección de Ingresos, the units were placed under one administrative head, the Director de Ingresos, appointed by the president for a two-year period. Moreover, their operations were streamlined by merging various units and separating others, so that the Ministry of Finance's new tax-collecting organization was reduced to four units: Renta de Licores, Tabaco y Fósforos; Papel Sellado y Timbres; Impuestos Directos sobre Capital, Instrucción Pública, Vialidad, Derechos Reales y Licencias de Comerciantes; and Impuestos sobre Cerveza, Destace de Ganada, Azúcar, Venta y Arrendamiento de Tierras Baldías, Explotación de Bosques Nacionales, y Patentes Mineros. Finally, in an attempt to impress on personnel the need for efficiency and probity, a Guardia Nacional major was appointed Director de Ingresos.[37]

The appointment of Guardia officers to head various government bodies became a fairly common practice. The Ferrocarril del Pacífico, nationalized in 1937, came under the direct control of Somoza with the title of *Jefe Supremo*.[38] The Ministry of Public Health was replaced by a Dirección General de Sanidad under the head of the medical corps of the Guardia.[39] The entire mail and telegraph system was militarized outright "in order to improve the service," as well as that of the Recaudación General de Aduanas after Nicaragua declared war on the Axis powers.[40] The appointment of military officers or the militarization of a government department conceivably improved efficiency to the extent that lax employees theoretically could be court-martialed, but it also allowed for greater political control of the bureaucracy since the officers appointed most likely were Somoza stalwarts. (Such was the case of the Director General de Sanidad, Colonel Luis Manuel Debayle, Somoza's brother-in-law.) It served, finally, to open up channels of administrative advancement for Guardia officers through an additional salary and opportunities for graft. At the time, however, the impression that these changes made within Nicaragua probably was that of an energetic president trying to shake up the bureaucracy and make it work better.

Another area of government that came under review was the municipal authority. Under the Constitution of 1911, the municipal governments were elected by direct popular vote for two-year periods. As occurred with the elections for president and Congress, the party in power pretty much managed the entire show. But after 1928, with the introduction of minority representation in diverse organs of government, control of the municipalities was divided among the Liberal and Conservative parties according to preelectoral arrangements. Further, under the Constitution of 1911, municipal government had exclusively economic and administrative functions. However, the dearth of material resources available to the municipalities meant that they did precious little of what the Constitution mandated.[41] Instead, the *consejos municipales* became the center of political activism of the party in power and a source of sinecures for the party faithful. Though not committed to eradicating these activities, Somoza did think that the municipalities should do more for the community and thus strengthen the role of government within society.

In order to reform the system of municipal government, Somoza decided that he needed first to control it directly. In March 1937, he issued a decree taking over the municipal government of León, claiming that the mayor had abandoned his post and that public services were neglected to the point that there was a danger of social protest (*perturbación social*). Because León was an important city, the decree read, the national government could not stand by while things deteriorated. Therefore, the president would appoint a three-man board (*junta local*) to run the city until the national Constitution was reformed or until a new municipal government was duly elected. Three days later, the municipality of Masaya was intervened under similar pretexts, although in this case the decree mentioned that riots and protests actually had taken place, in addition to the fact that the closeness of Masaya to the capital made it imperative that social peace and harmony in that city be maintained. Shortly afterward, the municipal government of Chinandega was intervened as well.[42] It should be noted that Managua, located within a Distrito Nacional since the mid-nineteenth century, already was under direct presidential control.

In August 1937 the Congress passed a law suspending all future municipal elections until the reform of the Constitution. In the meantime, the president would appoint the municipal authorities "in case of emergency or absence of the officials."[43] At this moment, municipal government throughout the country became an appendage of the national government as municipality after municipality was intervened by the president. All of the municipalities of the department of Masaya were replaced by "*juntas de vecinos* . . . under the direct supervision and control of the Central Government [in order that] they undertake public works for the progress and well-being of the inhabitants." Identical decrees applied to nine other departments; although not all municipalities were replaced at once, a clear majority did come under the control of *juntas locales* or *juntas de vecinos*. Subsequent executive decrees applied to the remaining *departamentos* and to municipalities not affected by previous decrees.[44]

Control by the central government extended beyond the appointment of *alcaldes*, *regidores*, *síndicos*, and *tesoreros*. Since the mid-1920s, the municipal councils were audited by the Tribunal de Cuentas, the national accounting office, and in 1935 the central government assumed the authority to approve the muncipal councils' annual budgets.[45] Under Somoza, a special office, the Contraloría General de Cuentas Locales, was created within the Ministry of the Interior to supervise the finances of the municipal councils. In addition to approving annual expenditures and income, the Contraloría authorized all contracts that the municipality signed with private companies and all public works that the municipality wished to undertake.[46]

Once the municipal councils were in place in keeping with the wishes and convenience of the president, regulations were issued to systematize and rationalize both human and material resources. The juntas locales were divided into three categories according to their monthly income, which also determined the number and function of their members. The regulation further stipulated that the municipality's income must be determined according to the real economic possibilities of the region and that municipal taxes should not weigh too heavily on essential goods and services. Finally, municipal spending would be distributed strictly, with 35 percent going to administration, 40 percent to improvements and public services, 10 percent to health and hygiene, and 5 percent each to debt payments, unforeseen expenses, and paper and office supplies.[47] With these measures, the central government had eliminated practically all municipal autonomy and converted the *alcaldías* into administrative arms of the government in Managua and the president of the republic.

In order to achieve administrative coordination between the central government and the municipalities, a congress of municipalities was held in Managua in December 1939. In attendance were all the presidents of juntas locales of the first two categories, who were treated to a series of speeches and talks on the old and the new municipal system, the best methods of municipal accounting, and the role of the municipalities in educational and public health programs. The minister of the interior, Gerónimo Ramírez Browne, made the point that in modern society national governments were acquiring far more responsibilities, whereas municipal governments had been declining as a result of insufficient financing, political infighting, and bureaucratic inefficiency. Under the new system, then, the municipalities focused exclusively on economic and administrative matters; the results, he said, had been very promising because municipal income had increased as had the number of public works (or, as they were called, *obras de progreso*) and because the suppression of municipal elections themselves had contributed to strengthening the peace of the towns and cities. The congress ended with the participants agreeing to raise income through new taxes, dropping others that cost more to collect than they were worth, and introducing common accounting procedures, as well as expanding municipal programs of public health, including food inspection, garbage disposal, and sewage.[48]

A second congress of municipalities was held three years later, in December 1942, by and large with the same agenda.[49] The problems that municipalities faced had not changed much in the interim. Nor had the smaller and poorer ones benefited much from all this talk; they were not even invited to attend. Although it is impossible to determine the distribution of central government funds or the amount of taxes levied at the local level, it seems likely that only the larger cities and towns benefited from the process of municipal reform. Not only were they politically more important but their economic base was sounder and larger. The smaller municipalities probably engaged only in keeping the most basic life cycle records and collecting enough taxes to pay the meager salaries of a few employees.

The Growth of the Public Sector

Given the fact that after 1937 policy initiatives in Nicaragua came principally from the central government, a proper appreciation of an increase in the state's authority must include the growth of the bureaucracy and of budget income and outlays. Although Nicaragua's economy was just as much geared to export production as any other in Central America, the central government's reliance on export duties as a source of income was balanced somewhat by its fairly substantial stake in a number of public services and by its control of the banking system. At first glance, it might seem strange that a country that was under a U.S. protectorate for so many years emerged with a fairly important public sector in the economy. But the very presence of the United States and its policy of imposing peace and order in Nicaragua had required that all sensitive financial matters come under U.S. control. That is, the public sector could draw on a number of resources that no other country in Central America had at the time. Under the Somoza regime, the size and importance of the public sector grew even more, but the basis of its fiscal and institutional strength was already in place in the early 1930s.

As noted previously, government income in Nicaragua relied almost completely on indirect taxation. The most important of these were customs duties. (See Table 3.5.) In the years prior to the Great Depression, customs contributed about half of all government income; during the depression the amount dropped to about a quarter. The extremely low figure for 1925–26 reflects the political chaos resulting from Chamorro's coup d'état; the United States did not recognize the Chamorro government nor did the U.S.-controlled Collectorship General of Customs provide Chamorro with any funds. In the latter years of the period in question, customs duties rose as a result of the increase in Nicaragua's exports to the United States during the war. Other indirect taxes, in addition to those on liquor and tobacco, included stamped paper and commercial licenses, and taxes on cattle slaughtering, sugar, and beverages.

The most important source of income after customs duties was the state's own enterprises and properties. The railroad was the biggest money earner of all. Until the 1940s, the railroad had a virtual monopoly on the transport of all exports and imports through the port of Corinto, since there was no usable highway to Corinto at the time. The port itself was also government property, as were the principal steamers on the Great Lake.[50] Thus, it is not surprising that Somoza took over the railroad and its extensive system of warehouses and machine shops in order to further his political ambitions and influence. Control of the railroad meant authority to set cargo rates or to provide special concessions to exporters and importers, which in turn gave the railroad a life-and-death power over the business community. Another important aspect of the country's infrastructure under government ownership involved the telegraph, radio, and telephone systems. In fact, there were two radio networks:

Table 3.5 Sources of Government Income, 1910–1945
(as a percentage of total income)

		Indirect				Public
Year	Customs	Liquor	Tobacco	Others	Direct	Services
1910–11	55.1	18.1	10.1	11.2	—	5.5
1915–16	45.4	21.8	13.9	18.8	—	—
1920–21	51.5	21.7	6.5	20.3	—	—
1925–26	1.8	46.3	20.0	31.9	—	—
1930–31	32.3	9.6	2.6	23.9	—	31.6
1935–36	25.5	7.7	1.5	31.2	—	34.2
1936–37	21.7	8.2	1.3	32.1	—	36.7
1938–39	15.9	11.7	2.1	34.2	—	36.2
1939–40	25.2	11.2	3.5	38.7	—	21.4
1940–41	27.6	10.6	3.7	36.3	—	21.8
1941–42	25.7	10.5	3.9	31.7	—	28.2
1942–43	25.4	13.1	4.1	23.2	—	34.2
1943–44	46.7	12.9	4.0	5.7	2.4	28.3
1944–45	39.6	14.4	4.9	6.4	3.0	31.6

Source: Ministerio de Hacienda y Crédito Público, *Memorias.* Data for 1937–38 are not available.

the Radio Nacional and the Guardia's own system, which also offered service to the public. All in all, then, the government controlled the country's basic transportation and communications infrastructure.

If the income from these government enterprises is added to that generated by the national banks, their contribution to the national budget oscillated between 20 and 35 percent of the total. Needless to say, the size of this public sector would create friction with certain elements of the private sector, which protested unfair competition and favoritism toward some over others. For Somoza, however, control over public enterprises increased the power of the state considerably and allowed him to project an image of the efficient administrator without whose presence everything would fly apart.

Budgetary expenditures during the first years of Somoza's presidency were related primarily to settling the financial problems that had accumulated during the depression years and the foreign loans of 1909 and 1917, as well as the unpaid foreign commercial debt. Up to fiscal year 1940–41, the Ministry of Finance and debt payment absorbed up to 45 percent of budgetary expenditures

Table 3.6 Budgetary Expenditures, 1930–1945 (as a percentage of total)

Year	a	b	c	d	e	f	g
1930–31	7.5	30.4	44.2	1.2	9.9	3.6	3.3
1935–36	8.0	37.0	33.8	6.6	8.7	2.4	3.4
1936–37	7.2	36.0	33.7	7.8	6.8	2.6	5.8
1938–39	4.7	30.2	27.2	6.3	9.9	2.4	19.3
1939–40	3.9	22.0	45.4	5.3	11.5	2.0	9.9
1940–41	4.0	22.7	44.4	5.5	10.5	2.6	10.5
1941–42	3.9	22.9	28.8	5.2	14.3	2.7	22.4
1942–43	3.0	19.2	20.6	5.7	44.3	3.0	4.2
1943–44	3.4	19.0	18.5	6.6	5.3	4.0	3.1
1944–45	3.2	20.4	20.3	6.7	42.5	3.7	3.2

Source: Ministerio de Hacienda y Crédito Público, *Memorias*. Data for 1937–38 are not available. Percentages are based on total budget expenditures excluding the allocations for public enterprises and the national banks, which are not available for most years.

Key: a = Legislative and judiciary; b = Armed forces and interior; c = Finance and public debt; d = Education; e = Development and public works; f = Agriculture, labor, and health; g = Others.

(See Table 3.6.) Thereafter, investment in public works became the most important budgetary item, although it should be kept in mind that a large part of the budget allocation for development and public works (*fomento y obras públicas*) reflects U.S. contributions for the completion of the Pan-American highway that Somoza negotiated with Roosevelt during his trip to Washington in 1939.

In sharp contrast to the large expenditures for infrastructure and finance, social programs followed the pattern set by previous administrations. Only rarely did spending on health, education, labor, and agriculture surpass 10 percent of the total budget, which does not say much for Somoza's avowed concern for the working class and the campesinos. Fiscal policy, in general, was geared to promoting export production through the extension of the transportation infrastructure and the maintenance of social peace, while seeking to liquidate Nicaragua's international financial obligations.

The budget's impact on Nicaraguan society can be measured partly in terms of the employment it generated. Especially during the years of economic crisis, the government became an important provider of jobs. In addition, public employment increased the size of the political clientele of the regime and, therefore, had a direct bearing on the relative strength of the country's political

Table 3.7 Public Employment, 1930–1945 (1936–37 = 100)

| | According to Budget Appropriations | | | Pan-American |
Year	Number	Index	Railroad	Highway
1930–31	5,872	(110)		
1936–37	5,321	(100)		
1937–38	6,162	(116)		
1938–39	6,898	(130)		
1939–40	6,325	(119)		
1940–41	7,678	(144)	2,203	2,250
1941–42	8,627	(162)	2,451	3,899
1942–43	8,663	(163)	2,512	
1943–44	9,030	(170)		2,624
1944–45	9,475	(178)		

Sources: Ministerio de Hacienda y Crédito Público, *Presupuesto general de ingresos y egresos de la República de Nicaragua.* Data on railroad employees are from various reports prepared for Somoza found in boxes 167, 211, and 273, AN. Data on highway construction employees for 1942–43 are from a report by John K. Flick, an engineer for the U.S. Public Roads Administration in charge of the supervision of the Pan-American highway construction in Nicaragua, box 267 AN; for 1940–42, from "Inter-American Highway, Nicaragua, Quarterly Progress Reports" for 31 December 1941 and 31 December 1942 submitted to the Export-Import Bank in Washington, Fondo Salvadora de Somoza, no. 8, AN.

forces. Public employment as reflected in budgetary appropriations increased from 5,321 in 1936–37 to a little under 9,500 nine years later. (See Table 3.7.) However, these figures do not give the entire picture. They do not include employment in government enterprises like the railroad, the ports, and various other public services, nor do they include those employed by the state banks or in public works on an occasional basis. The present employment data on these last organizations are sporadic and provide complete statistics only for 1940–44, when public employment conceivably approached 15,000 in 1941–42. Data from the 1940 census report a total of 11,941 employed by the government on a fixed basis, which is about 2,000 more than the sum of the two figures available for 1940–41 (excluding highway construction), although it probably includes those employed by the national banks, the waterworks, and the municipalities. Thus, as a proportion of the urban work force, the government may have employed up to one out of every seven or eight urban workers.[51]

Table 3.8 Public Employment by Category, 1930–1945 (1936–37 = 100)

Year	a	b	c	d	e	f
1930–31	636 (198)	2,479 (95)	1,380 (125)	380 (132)	785 (96)	212 (118)
1936–37	321 (100)	2,611 (100)	1,101 (100)	288 (100)	820 (100)	180 (100)
1937–38	307 (96)	2,673 (102)	1,297 (118)	708 (246)	976 (119)	201 (112)
1938–39	307 (96)	3,017 (116)	1,521 (138)	776 (269)	1,060 (119)	217 (121)
1939–40	287 (89)	2,322 (89)	1,446 (131)	832 (289)	1,203 (147)	235 (131)
1940–41	280 (87)	3,489 (134)	1,582 (144)	873 (303)	1,166 (142)	288 (160)
1941–42	720 (224)	3,619 (139)	1,718 (156)	1,010 (351)	1,254 (153)	306 (170)
1942–43	753 (235)	3,543 (136)	1,734 (157)	1,050 (365)	1,276 (156)	307 (171)
1943–44	761 (237)	3,610 (138)	1,834 (167)	1,191 (414)	1,305 (159)	329 (183)
1944–45	774 (241)	3,717 (142)	1,973 (179)	1,214 (422)	1,442 (176)	355 (197)

Source: Ministerio de Hacienda y Crédito Público, Presupuesto general de ingresos y egresos de la República de Nicaragua.

Key: a = Congress, executive offices, judiciary, and foreign affairs; b = Army and interior; c = Public education; d = Finance; e = Development and public works; f = Health, agriculture, and labor.

On the basis of the information available, the biggest increase in public employment between 1936 and 1945 occurred in the Ministry of Finance and Public Credit. (See Table 3.8.) This increase is consistent with the regime's attempts to increase tax collection. The second largest increase took place in the judiciary (which is included under column a in Table 3.8). The army and personnel of the Ministry of the Interior (including the Guardia Nacional in police roles) show the smallest rate of growth, no doubt as a result of the overwhelming control the Guardia Nacional exerted over the country after the death of Sandino. The increase in numbers of employees engaged in education is not insignificant but must have been due mostly to the hiring of teachers at very low salaries.

Employment in the government carried with it a political obligation, if not directly with Somoza at least with the Liberal party. To get a job in the government required a recommendation from someone in a position of authority. If that person were Somoza himself, so much the better. That is not to say that Somoza himself placed friends and supporters in this or that position. Letters to Somoza requesting a job generally were handed to his private secretary for a reply. One such example is that of José del Carmen Flores, a schoolmate of Somoza's, who wrote that he was a fellow Mason and an unconditional supporter of the regime. Therefore, he believed, he had "the right to request from you whatever you can give me" and went on to ask for a government job "that would enable me to provide bread for my children." Somoza's private secretary answered to the effect that Somoza had authorized him to place Flores in some "adequate post" but that Flores himself must report which job openings were available "so as to proceed accordingly."[52] On other occasions, the secretary instructed the job seeker to go directly to a given ministry to request a position without the president's express recommendation. But in all cases, a job in government was a political appointment that was used to maximum advantage in the days of economic hardship, especially since job openings were far fewer than job seekers.

Once in a public job, a person was expected to support the regime or, at least, not criticize it. Furthermore, there seem to have been sufficient informers who were seeking points in the eyes of their superiors. One Armando Rodríguez O., an auditor with the Contraloría Especial de Cuentas Locales, reported to his boss, the under secretary of the interior, that the mayor and other municipal employees of the town of Diriamba, in the coffee-growing region south of Managua, were all closet Conservatives who were partial to their party's membership.[53] On another occasion, a major of the Guardia Nacional, Francisco Gaitán, prepared a report for Somoza on one Hernaldo Peña, an employee of the Banco Nacional in Masaya, who was overheard speaking in a disparaging manner about the president; Peña had said that Somoza was a thief and a lout and that the Guardia Nacional officers became rich on the loans from the Banco Nacional that Somoza had authorized. Gaitán therefore recommended that Peña be fired from his job, that he be reprimanded, and that he lose all privileges that he had enjoyed until then from the government.[54]

The government bureaucracy was rewarded with occasional wage increases, although the available data do not permit a comparison with inflation rates. In February 1938 Somoza raised the salaries of all government employees between 10 percent for those with higher salaries and 60 percent for those with the lowest, but this was before the years of greatest price inflation.[55] The most attractive aspect of a government position, however, was its relative stability, particularly in times of economic decline or crisis. Thus, the bureaucracy was very loyal to the regime and could be mobilized easily to participate in demonstrations and to vote for Somoza at election time.[56] Together with the Guardia Nacional, it constituted a powerful political block that the regime controlled at all times.

Constitutional Reform

The changes advanced by the Somoza regime in the role and size of the state required a legal or ideological justification that not only incorporated policy measures already implemented but also laid the bases for future developments. Somoza and his followers frequently talked of the state's new responsibilities in a new age, and it was precisely to provide this new orientation of the state with an aura of legitimacy that Somoza was particularly interested in reforming the Constitution. Just two weeks after Sacasa left his job, the Congress began to discuss the issue of constitutional reform. Most Liberal deputies and senators were amenable to a prompt debate and approval of a new Constitution, whereas the Conservatives wished to reach some kind of prior agreement that would limit such reform. But as expected, the Liberal proposal was approved handily, with the Conservatives voting against it.[57] Congressional committees then began to work on outlines for a new charter, which were presented to both chambers in August 1938.

In the Chamber of Deputies, the committee argued for constitutional reform in terms of the need to legalize the status of the Guardia Nacional as the national army, the new situation of the municipalities since their intervention by the central government, and the changes that were required in the tax structure. The committee also considered the demands that the working class was making (which, in all justice, it thought should be addressed) as well as the constitutional provisions that would allow the minority party its proper representation in government. However, the Conservatives on the committee decided to vote against the reform outline because they believed that the real purpose behind these deliberations was Somoza's desire to extend his presidential term; instead, they insisted that constitutional reform must necessarily include explicit provisions to prevent presidential reelection. In the Senate, the Conservatives also brought up Somoza's ambitions but to no avail, as both chambers eventually approved the committee's outlines.[58] The result was a legislative decree calling for general elections for a constitutional convention that would convene on 15 December 1938.[59]

In order that the new Constitution include as far as possible the opinion of all important political factions, Somoza needed to guarantee the participation of the Conservative party in addition to that of his own Nationalist Conservatives. To that effect, he issued two presidential decrees. The first appointed a *comisión técnica* of seven members to prepare a first draft of the new Constitution. It included a majority of Liberals, but also three Conservatives, including Carlos Cuadra Pasos, the leader of the Civilista faction, who was willing to participate in the formulation of a new Constitution even though he had objected to the initiative in the congressional debates.[60]

A second decree established the procedure to assure that all participating political factions had a "proportional representation" in the constitutional convention. The preamble stated, however, that because an electoral procedure to guarantee proportional representation "according to the desirable scientific methods" was not feasible due to the electorate's lack of experience, a simpler, more empirical method should be implemented. Therefore, the decree continued, the Conservative party would regain the juridical status ("personería jurídica") that it had lost by not participating in the 1936 elections, without having to go through all of the legal paperwork. Thus, the only parties with the right to participate in the elections were the Liberals, the Conservatives, and the Nationalist Conservatives. Deputies to the convention would be assigned in a predetermined fashion according to the electoral strength of each party. For example, in Managua the party with the most votes would get five deputies, while the second and third place runners-up would each get one deputy; in a department like Chinandega there would be three for the first place and one for second, but none for third, and in León all six would be for the first-place winner. Obviously, the dice were loaded in favor of the Liberal party: forty deputies for the first-place winner, twelve for second, and four for third.[61] So much for proportional representation in Somoza's Nicaragua.

The elections held on 6 November 1938 were even more of a sham than those that named Somoza president in 1936. The Conservatives decided to abstain again, while the ballot boxes and ballots were distributed throughout the country by the quartermaster general of the Guardia Nacional. The final results were made available within twenty-four hours, a record even today in Central America. Nevertheless, the Liberals' showing was hardly encouraging: they got 10,000 votes less than in 1936.[62] The Liberals somewhat increased their vote total only in León, Jinotega, and Chontales: the first a traditionally Liberal department, the second a Guardia stronghold, and the third a Conservative bastion where the Liberals most likely made a strong effort to get out the vote and/or stuff the ballot boxes. The results for the Nationalist Conservatives were even worse; they dropped from a total of 21,582 in 1936 to 11,196 in 1938. Thus, at most Somoza could claim that his share of the votes had increased in comparison to 1936.

The Somocista-dominated Constituent Assembly produced a Constitution for Nicaragua in four months, a document with some interesting new characteristics together with the conventional provisions of constitutions past. One of the most striking aspects of the new Constitution was its definition of property. Although the document recognized that private property was inviolable, it asserted that the existence of such property was subject to the collective interest ("la propiedad en función social"), which allowed the state to tax it, restrict its sale, and expropriate it if need be. Furthermore, the Constitution explicitly stated that unused portions of latifundia would be split up to promote the development and growth of small- and middle-sized rural properties. It also acknowledged the rights of workers to a weekly day of rest, minimum salary, maximum working hours, severance pay in the event of occupational accidents, and free medical care. It even committed the state to the formation of a national social security institute.[63]

As happens frequently in Central American constitutions, the new Nicaraguan document contained contradictory provisions regarding public freedoms and political rights. The 1939 Constitution established freedom of expression, but it put outside of the law "those who make statements contrary to the public order, to the fundamental institutions of the state, to the republican and democratic form of government, to the established social order, to public morality and proper behaviour ['la moral y las buenas costumbres'], or that cause damage to third parties." Yet in the next article, it stated that freedom of the press was guaranteed and that there would be no prior censorship. It also contained provisions for preventive arrests and internal confinement under executive authority if public tranquility was threatened.

The new Constitution formalized the new approach to municipal government: every two years the president would appoint municipal councils, which would come under his direct supervision. ("They shall be subject to the economic and correctional vigilance of the Executive Branch.") Also under presidential control was the Consejo Nacional de Elecciones, as two of its three members would be named by the executive. Finally, the Constitution defined the nature and role of the country's army, to be formed by the Guardia Nacional and the police as the only armed force in Nicaragua entrusted with guaranteeing the nation's independence, its territorial sovereignty, its internal peace, and the individual rights of the citizen.

The Constitution's transitory provisions were to have the greatest immediate impact because they did exactly what the Conservatives had said they would: Somoza's term was extended all the way to 1 May 1947 and the Constituent Assembly itself became the National Congress until 15 April 1947 with no intervening elections to bother about. There would be time, therefore, to concentrate on useful activities; the regime would not be encumbered by party politics and electoral campaigns.

At his swearing-in before the Congress on 30 March 1939, Somoza stressed that the new Constitution was the product of the same national, nonpartisan efforts that had raised him to the presidency. The "traditional parties" had been haggling over constitutional reform for years but they had never reached an agreement, he said, because they had been engaged in their own petty ambitions and struggles. Now, with new institutions that guaranteed administrative efficiency and social justice, the road was open for all to participate in the achievement of the public good. He mentioned specifically those members of the Conservative party who had turned a deaf ear to their leadership's instructions to abstain from the elections and who won election on the ticket of the Nationalist Conservatives, Carlos Cuadra Pasos being the chief example of these. Somoza concluded with his well-known promise to balance the budget, stabilize the currency, make credit available to more people, build infrastructure, promote public education, and construct low-cost housing.[64]

The Liberal Party under Somoza

Somoza's appeal for unity went beyond speech making. Specific measures needed to be taken to strengthen the Somocista coalition, bring renegades back into the fold, and persuade others that there was a better future with Somoza. One of his first concerns was the Liberal party itself. After the 1936 electoral confrontation between Argüellistas and Somocistas, the party was badly split: Argüello had gone into exile and the Sacasistas were bitter following their president's overthrow. Somoza had to reinforce the Somocista wing of the party and, if possible, make it absolutely dominant. The first step he took was to reach an agreement with Argüello, who was living in exile in San Salvador. In February 1937, he sent an official delegation to talk to Argüello and tell him that he could return to Nicaragua with all guarantees whenever he wished. In August of the same year, Somoza announced that Sofonías Salvatierra, a member of the party's leftist faction and a confidant of Sandino, also could return to Nicaragua. Argüello arrived in Managua in July and immediately met with Somoza to set the basic conditions for peace between the two, including the appointment of Argüellista ministers to the cabinet.[65] With that agreement, Somoza thought that he could count on a larger volume of Liberal votes, although the 1938 elections for the Constituent Assembly did not bear out this promise. Still, he was able to neutralize a number of Liberal party leaders loyal to Argüello and strengthen party unity.

Somoza's strongest efforts to reconstitute the party took place in León. By May 1937, an Asociación Pro-Unificación Liberal had been established to promote public expressions of support for the Somoza government. The Asociación sent a letter to Somoza signed by some 450 Liberal leaders and party members in which they stated their confidence in the government and backed its policies in the face of the "difficult economic situation." Among the signers were the leading families of the department traditionally associated with the Liberal cause: the Mayorgas, the Herdocias, the Sevillas, the Sacasas, and the Debayles.[66]

Subsequent efforts were made in other departments to enlist support through a number of party activities. One fairly common procedure was the public demonstration, generally associated with a visit by Somoza to a town or a department; in June 1939, the occasion was to welcome Somoza back from his trip to the United States, where Roosevelt had received him with full honors. Somoza's trip to Washington was exploited for all it was worth, for in Nicaragua the seal of approval of the U.S. government was the strongest endorsement any politician could desire. Leaflets were circulated weeks in advance inviting the people of Granada, Masaya, and León to attend the demonstration. Free trains were made available, as well as meal tickets for a lunch in Managua.[67] On 29 June, the day of Somoza's return, about 70,000 people crowded the streets from the airport to the presidential palace, while diverse companies and individuals handed out food and drink to the welcomers.[68] The parade was headed by Somoza, and behind him came the diplomatic corps, senators and deputies, the Supreme Court, the General Staff of the Guardia, employees of the Banco Nacional and Banco Hipotecario, jefes políticos and departmental Guardia commanders, floats of diverse organizations, private automobiles and buses, sports teams, the Boy Scouts, the fire department, labor organizations, and the public at large, which suggests the order of importance of the components of the Somocista coalition.[69]

Following Nicaragua's declaration of war against the Axis powers in December 1941, Somoza visited various parts of the country to enlist the support of the people in the struggle against totalitarianism. A massive effort was made to that effect in León in July 1942. As usual, free trains provided transport for people from the surrounding towns and seven open kitchens were set up to prepare 14,000 meals. Workers and peasants received a special invitation reminding them how they had been exploited by loan sharks and how Somoza had put an end to this practice through the banking reforms and a freeze on rents. The big event, in fact, was to be the inauguration of the Casa del Obrero in León. Advance teams visited various communities to enlist the participation of men on horseback, who would provide the event with local color. On 12 July, the day of the demonstration itself, the speeches praised Somoza to the skies. Isidro Muñoz, from the Indian barrio of Subtiava, said that Somoza's government "comforts all Nicaraguans with the same paternal concern, without regard of the nefarious parties." One Tomás Montalván H. mentioned that Somoza was totally responsible for the peace and work enjoyed by all Nicaraguans and that, therefore, as of now workers and peasants should proclaim him president for another term.[70]

Another mass demonstration followed in Managua in November 1942, also organized to support the government in its struggle against fascism.[71] At all these rallies, leaflets pictured Somoza in military uniform, occasionally surrounded by the Nicaraguan and U.S. flags. By appealing to the patriotism of Nicaraguans and enveloping himself in the aura of U.S. might, Somoza projected an image of strength and stability in the face of totalitarian aggression. Even though Nicaragua never furnished troops to the Allied armies, Somoza declared that his country played an important role in the Allied effort through its contribution of raw materials, such as rubber, sesame seed oil, gold, and coconuts. Whenever possible, he tried to be seen in the company of the U.S. ambassador or attending some event at the U.S. legation.[72]

So solid did his position become that, at the beginning of 1943, Somoza thought it was time to begin his reelection campaign. The first meetings of Somocistas took place in March and April 1943, usually in the form of *cabildos abiertos* (open town meetings) under the direction of the local mayor. The apparent motive behind these cabildos was the need to reform the Constitution, which was not considered "flexible" enough for the period the country was going through, particularly regarding the requirement to provide the government with special authority to combat Nazi-fascist totalitarianism. It also was argued that the provisions of the Atlantic Charter needed to be included in the Constitution. In some cases, the cabildos claimed that the provisions of the current Constitution prohibiting presidential reelection were a barrier to the free political expression of a people in a democracy. Once the speeches and the agreements were finished with, a document was drawn up that everyone present signed before it was sent off to Somoza and/or the Congress as a form of petition. The number of signatories ranged from about 50 in the case of the smaller municipalities to over 500 in the larger ones; León reported an *asamblea popular* with 8,000 in attendance.[73]

The supposed threat to Nicaragua represented by the war against the Axis powers also served to promote the expansion of the paramilitary wing of the Liberal party called the Liga Militar Liberal Nacionalista or Liga Militar Liberal de Nicaragua. Initially, it seems to have been an association of war veterans of the Zelaya days, as well as of others who fought for the Liberal cause. In December 1937 the Liga Militar Liberal of the department of León voted to become the corps of "auxiliares de la Guardia Nacional," organized into columns and squads of 25 men each, distributed among the various towns and villages under a departmental general staff. At the time, it had about 2,600 members. Similar organizations were formed in the departments of Zelaya, Chinandega, and Managua.[74] The supreme chief of the Liga Militar Liberal was, of course, Somoza himself. Members of the organization were issued identification papers signed by him and his minister of war. As stated in this identification, the member became a part of the reserve force of the Guardia Nacional subject to its discipline and its code of honor.[75] In this manner, a certain fraction of the Liberal party came under direct military control and could be employed in a variety of political tasks.

Within the Liberal party itself, Somoza undertook to tighten control by means of an overhaul of its statutes and organization. A party convention met in León on 7–9 February 1944 and approved in quick order a number of changes in the party's platform and internal organization. The broad objectives of the party were not changed much from those approved in 1913; at most, the convention added specific references to the party's commitment to a labor code for the Nicaraguan worker, to the creation of more small- and middle-sized rural properties, and to a reform of the tax structure in order to make it more progressive.[76] More substantial changes occurred in the procedures for the election of party officials. Whereas in the past representatives to the *Gran Convención* were elected by the local assemblies of party members, the new statutes called for a national plebiscite on the basis of one delegate for every thousand Liberal votes in the most recent presidential election; though more "democratic" in the sense that delegates were voted to office directly, this change meant that the election procedure could be controlled centrally. In addition, the new statutes did away with the election of the departmental party committees; from now on, they would be appointed by the national party committee, which was elected by the Gran Convención. The departmental committees, in turn, would choose the local committees and these, the *consejos cantonales* and *clubs rurales.* That is, all direct election of intermediate and lower party bodies was eliminated.[77]

In addition to carrying out the usual political and organizational activities, the departmental and local committees apparently had the important task of channeling patronage. They were instructed to assure the implementation of "all the precepts and instructions which in matters of SOCIAL ASSISTANCE might favor all the members of the Party, under the definition of Social Assistance as the proper execution of those provisions contained in the Declaration of Principles and the Program of the Party which look to improve the lot of the proletarian class of the country." That is, they were to help party members take advantage of the government's health programs, agricultural credit, public education, and other social programs. In practice, this meant that party members would receive preference over other citizens in the distribution of government social and economic assistance. In return for patronage, party members at the local level were instructed to act as the eyes and ears of the party, or as the new statute put it, "they must report the needs of the party members and advise immediately about any activity in their vicinity considered dangerous to the Party so that the proper measures can be taken."[78]

The implementation of the new statute marked the institutionalization of a new party, no longer so much *Liberal* or *Nacionalista* as *Somocista*. The ideological rhetoric was fundamentally the same, and in some respects it was more progressive, but the machinery of the party took on a decidedly biased character as Somoza consolidated his control. The president of the republic formally became the Jefe Supremo of the party, empowered to intervene at any level and to review all important party decisions.[79] His control of party finances also gave him discretionary authority to spend the monies received from the 5 percent contribution levied on public employees' salaries, a tax that Somoza had promised to abolish in 1936.[80]

Dealing with the Loyal Opposition

The strength and the unity (albeit imposed) of the Liberals contrasted sharply with the confusion and division within the Conservative party. From the moment that the Conservatives split over whether to participate in the 1936 presidential election, they were unable to present a unified political alternative to Somoza. The reason was very simple: there were always Conservatives willing to play politics with the Somocista Liberals by backing either the

Nationalist Conservatives or the dissident wing of the *Genuino* (or *Tradicional*) Conservatives headed by Carlos Cuadra Pasos. In 1936 a group of Genuino Conservatives participated in the election on the Nationalist Conservative ticket and won some seats in the Chamber of Deputies and the Senate.

In 1938 the same faction decided to field candidates for the Constituent Assembly although the party's leadership vehemently opposed the plan. Emiliano Chamorro, by then living in exile in Mexico City, announced his rejection of any deals with the Liberals by publishing a flier in which he bitterly denounced Somoza for all the evils that had befallen Nicaragua since the 1926 Liberal uprising and declared that the Constituent Assembly's real purpose was to extend Somoza's term.[81] The Conservative party's authorities in Managua similarly instructed their representatives in the Congress to oppose the initiative for constitutional reform, but this order was not obeyed. As a result, Carlos Cuadra Pasos resigned from the Conservative executive committee under pressure from the Chamorristas. In a matter of days, however, he and his dissident Conservatives came to an understanding with the Nationalist Conservatives to unify their candidates under one slate, exactly as they had done in 1936.[82]

The dissidents explained their decision in a communiqué released on 8 October 1938. They argued that even with all the imperfections that the electoral law contained, the opportunity for the opposition to participate in the country's political debate was important and should not be discarded, especially since the Conservatives ran the risk of simply disappearing from the political map if they did not maintain a presence and make their voice heard. Furthermore, they reasoned, they would continue to defend the party's platform, which included religious freedom, respect for the family, prohibition of usury, and social justice.[83] Once installed in the Constituent Assembly, they tried to explain the difference that existed between them and the Nationalist Conservatives, which boiled down to the fact that the latter "were with the Government" but they were not. To make that point, they walked out of the Assembly when the Constitution came up for approval but returned once that issue was out of the way.[84] Meanwhile, the other Genuino Conservative party faction proceeded to expel the dissidents, claiming that they were no longer Conservatives and that, therefore, the Conservative party had nothing to do with the current state of affairs.[85]

The Nationalist Conservatives, while completely subordinate to Somoza and his political line, were not immune to internal problems either. Three of their deputies to the Constituent Assembly were members of the extreme right movement in Nicaragua, which openly voiced its opposition to democracy and whose support for Somoza was based principally on his promise to head a strong government that would eradicate violence and disorder from the country. The three deputies strongly supported constitutional reform, primarily because they *wanted* to make Somoza a lifelong president, if that were at all possible. By 1940 their outspokenness was more of a liability than an asset, given the United States's posture toward the Axis powers. In August, they were formally accused by Henri Pallais, a Liberal deputy from León, who demanded that the Senate try them for espousing "propaganda counter to the fundamental institutions of the state." Pallais said that the deputies—José Coronel Urtecho, Pablo Antonio Cuadra, and Diego Manuel Chamorro—belonged to the "Reactionary party" and that they had frequent contacts with the Spanish Falange, in addition to organizing youth groups under the name of Legiones Católicas Nacionalistas.[86]

The three men defended themselves strongly, arguing that a democratic system allowed for all political expression, as in the case of European parliaments where monarchists and communists sat side by side. Coronel Urtecho stated simply that he was in the Congress not because he believed in democracy but because he believed in Somoza, the head of the first truly national army the country had ever had and the backbone of the state. He denied that he belonged to a reactionary party, which in fact did not exist, but admitted that he was a member of a minority group within a minority party and, he asked, what danger to the country could he so represent? Cuadra relied more on legalistic arguments to defend himself, probably reflecting the influence of his father, Carlos Cuadra Pasos; he contended that all deputies enjoyed parliamentary immunity, which covered the statements that they made, and that he and his two codefendants had acted within legally recognized political parties. After the debate, the Senate voted in secret session to absolve the three deputies by a vote of 8 to 6. Once Nicaragua entered the war in December 1941, the expression of fascist ideas was prohibited, but by then the political value of the right-wing deputies for Somoza had declined and they were not heard from again.[87]

The Regime and Organized Labor

Of far greater importance for Somoza was the labor movement. Regardless of his attitude toward labor in 1936, with the passing of time he could afford less to ignore it because the war years in Nicaragua witnessed a significant increase in the number of workers employed in urban areas, a reflection of the establishment of a number of import-substituting industries and extensive public work programs, together with the development of nontraditional export production (especially in mining and rubber). In 1940, most of the 23,000 laborers engaged in manufacturing worked in artisanal shops of less than five workers each, but in 1945, 8,000 workers were employed in factories, representing fully 30 percent of the industrial labor force, while mining, construction, and transportation employed another 18,000.[88] Here was a source of potentially active political clientele, which together with other urban groups might be mobilized to further Somoza's political objectives.

Labor organizations had not grown much in the 1920s and 1930s. In part, this was due to the small proportion of industrial workers and also to the generally repressive nature of the Nicaraguan governments. But with the foundation of the Partido Trabajador Nicaragüense in 1931, the presence of organized labor gradually increased together with Somoza's interest in engaging labor's support for his political ambitions. As early as 1936, Somoza was making formal overtures to the labor movement by offering to build Casas del Obrero and low-cost housing and to initiate a program of labor legislation, including social welfare provisions in the new Constitution. One month after assuming office, Somoza attended a ceremony to lay the first stone of the Casa del Obrero in Managua.[89]

At the same time, the Congress took up the issue of a labor code at the initiative of a Liberal deputy, but Somoza withdrew his support for the measure and it died before it ever got to the floor. Somoza argued that he wanted to review the draft law and, especially, seek the counsel of the workers' organizations to improve its content.[90] The real explanation was probably that a labor code at the moment would have produced a negative reaction in the business community that would not have been offset by gains in the support of labor. Furthermore, Somoza's strategy was to prolong the political effect of a given measure as much as possible, both before and after the fact. That is, the promise of a labor code was worth as much to him as the code itself as long as the labor movement kept up its support. In the meantime, other measures could be enacted and the promise of the code occasionally dangled before the labor movement.

In September 1937 the Congress approved a law that required the Banco Hipotecario to set aside C$300,000 of its annual earnings for the construction of low-cost housing.[91] In three years, the government built all of ninety-one houses in the Colonia Somoza in Managua, a number that hardly scratched the surface of the housing problem in the country but that was exploited for its propaganda value.[92] In January 1940 the first Casa del Obrero was formally inaugurated in Managua by Somoza himself. The president delivered a flowery speech comparing the structure to a "temple" where all true workers could meet "under the august serenity of its roof" to discuss their common problems. He also insinuated that labor should return his support: "I have the right to expect that the Nicaraguan labor movement, aware of these frank and trust-worthy statements, will recognize with the same trust the renovating effort being undertaken on its behalf in a number of ways, all of which point surely in the direction of a better future for the laboring classes of Nicaragua."[93]

Somoza drew up and decreed a set of regulations for the proper administra-tion and functioning of the Casa del Obrero that pretty much restricted the workers to running a social club. The regulations prohibited political or religious discussion as well as "all communist or totalitarian activities or propaganda and all opinions in general which run counter to the public order." In addition, the Casa's board of directors would be elected by a general assembly of worker delegates from the various labor unions, but the delegates themselves would be chosen by the president on the basis of lists submitted for his consideration.[94] Significantly, a financial report for the Casa in 1942 indicates that over 91 percent of all expenditures were for liquor and parties, while only 6.4 percent were for cultural activities and social assistance.[95]

Other labor legislation included a law on industrial security that applied to mining companies and others that handled toxic materials; it authorized the government to fine those firms that did not protect their workers from indus-trial accidents, as well as establishing a minimum salary, maximum working hours, and various social benefits including free medical attention and subsi-dized food.[96] To the extent that it applied mostly to mining operations located in the isolated parts of the department of Zelaya, the effects of this law were not felt by most workers congregated along the Pacific coast. A minimum wage law that would have applied to the entire country was approved by the Chamber of Deputies but was roundly defeated in the Senate, apparently due to the opposition of landed interests.[97] The only other bit of labor legislation ap-proved prior to the labor code of 1945 was a law that entitled all workers, including rural laborers, to a weekly day off with salary.[98]

These labor laws were intended to demonstrate to workers, both organized and otherwise, that Somoza and his government were sincerely interested in the welfare of the labor class. But not all workers perceived this legislation in those terms. As a result, two principal currents of thought emerged within the labor movement. On the one hand were those who maintained that "collaboration" with Somoza was not such a terrible thing; they assumed that the workers could believe the president when he professed his desire to help laborers improve their living standards. Another tendency, generally referred to as "independent," was more cautious and understood that Somoza's statements to labor were more of a political gamble than a call to incorporate laborers into the Somocista coalition on an equal footing with other groups. Both currents came together in the Partido Trabajador Nicaragüense and within the PTN they struggled to control the leadership while Somoza, on the outside, wheeled and dealed with the two factions.

The older leadership of the labor movement was generally more inclined to talk with Somoza; these were individuals who had spent many of the previous years in prison or in exile and were willing to work within restrictive circumstances. The younger leaders, less experienced and more radical, predominated in the noncollaborationist wing of the PTN. The collaborationist leaders were quite prestigious at the time and were not mere instruments of the regime; although some leaders were "bought" by Somoza, it is not correct to assume that the labor movement had no autonomy with respect to the regime. Even the more Somocista of these were willing to act independently on occasion, as when they called for the formation of a labor party in 1941 and again in 1945 with no ties to the Liberals.[99] But for the labor movement itself, the divisions were real and worked in Somoza's favor. The most telling example of this divisiveness occurred around the time of the first national congress of the PTN, held in Managua on 31 August–1 September 1938.

Somoza previously had convened a meeting with various leaders of the PTN to offer them provisions in the new Constitution that would be favorable to the workers. At that moment, the pro-Somoza wing of the PTN was strongest and decided that a national congress of the PTN would be the best way to unite the labor movement around a program of social action with government support. Somoza, in turn, was enthusiastic about the labor congress; he issued a declaration in which he accepted the support of the PTN so that in the future the labor movement and the government might march together. But he also made it clear that this alliance would be between "nationalistic" Nicaraguans and should not be tainted by "the shadow of imported theories."[100] The PTN leadership justified its advances to Somoza as part of its search for social justice. As an editorial of the PTN newspaper, *Causa Obrera*, put it: "We want justice, and to achieve it one must be close to those that can administer it. One does not go to the desert of ineffective actions to slake one's thirst."[101]

An organizing committee for the PTN congress named in late June 1938 included three members of the collaborationist wing and two of the independent wing. They agreed to bury their differences for the time being and establish the most effective procedures for electing delegates to the congress. The congress convened in the building of the municipal council of Managua, which had been offered by Somoza, with a total of 226 delegates from the Pacific region of the country. Among other points, the congress voted to send a group to discuss with Somoza the social welfare provisions of the future Constitution, which Somoza accepted, but he reneged on his promise to include a labor representation in the Constituent Assembly. As a result, the elections for a new executive committee of the PTN favored the independent wing, and although contacts with the regime were maintained, Somoza's initial enthusiasm for labor cooled noticeably. The PTN itself collapsed in 1939 for a variety of reasons, including the rivalry between the two wings, a decline in worker interest, and an increase in government repression. In July 1939, a considerable number of PTN leaders left the country for exile in Costa Rica while others were jailed by Somoza after publishing statements critical of the regime and of living conditions in the country.[102]

After the first attempt at rapprochement between the regime and the labor movement, there followed a period of labor activism during which labor organizations limited themselves to petitioning Somoza for a redress of specific grievances—usually increases in salaries and improvements in working conditions. Such was the case of the workers of the maintenance section of the national railroad who requested an increase in salary because the fall in the value of the córdoba had been much greater than the two wage increases the government had allowed in 1938 and 1939.[103] In another instance, the Sindicato Industrial de Zapateros, whose membership totaled 458, informed Somoza of their struggle to achieve better salaries and to have them paid in cash on Saturday at four o'clock in the afternoon, to demand better treatment from the master shoemakers, and to assure that a worker would be given eight days' notice before he was fired.[104]

Demands or requests for better salaries and working conditions had to be tempered after 1941 by Somoza's declaration of war against the Axis powers and his rhetorical struggle against fascism. Labor newspapers, such as *La Verdad* and *Hoy*, emphasized Somoza's good faith in defending the rights of labor but even that did not exempt them from being closed forcibly by the regime in 1941 and 1942, respectively, when they demanded a general wage increase and a labor code. This repression was particularly evident in the case of the left-wing labor organizations, which again were trying to make their presence felt. A "Congress for Peace, Unity, and Liberation" organized by the clandestine Communist party in January 1943 in an attempt to bring together workers, employees, and students in a broad antifascist movement was broken up by the Guardia Nacional. The following month a so-called Block of Anti-Fascist Workers was organized as an umbrella group for the Communist party; on 2 May 1943, after a May Day parade demanding land for campesinos and lower food prices, its leaders were jailed.[105]

By late 1943, Somoza began to soften his attitude toward labor organizations and left-wing political groups as a counterbalance to growing opposition from university students, professionals, businessmen, and Conservative oligarchs. The Communist party, under the name of Partido Socialista de Nicaragua, emerged from clandestinity to support openly a labor code for Nicaragua, and various pro- and anti-Somoza factions of the labor movement came together in the Consejo Intergremial Obrero. That such collaboration was possible suggests that there were certain common points of view between the anticommunist Somocista labor leaders and those of the left wing, such as their opposition to the domestic right and the Conservative party, which opposed any concessions to the workers, including a labor code. Furthermore, the labor movement was still very small and weak. It had few resources to work with, both human and material, and Somoza's maneuvers weakened it even more. Its international connections were limited at the time to Mexico and Costa Rica, where labor movements were either appendages of the regime or worked closely with it.[106] But for Somoza, it was politically important to have labor, or part of it, on his side. It strengthened his image as a "national" leader both within and outside Nicaragua, and, if need be, it always could be called up with a new round of concessions in exchange for political support.

The Regime and the Private Sector

A final component of the Somocista political coalition was the private sector. At the beginning of Somoza's first term as president, most of the debate between the regime and the private sector centered on short-range solutions to pressing economic problems. Once these were resolved through currency devaluation, tax hikes, and increases in the money supply, the government's relation with business leaders was much more cooperative. With the import merchants, whose initial opposition to the maintenance of parity strongly influenced the decision to devalue, Somoza seems to have made his peace by early 1939. On 5 February in Managua, the chambers of commerce of the entire country (Managua, León, Granada, Chinandega, Masaya, and Matagalpa) hosted a black-tie banquet with one hundred guests "as a homage of friendship and recognition for the interest that the President has shown in the economic improvement of the nation." In a speech the president of the Managua Chamber, Constantino Pereira, who by then was also treasurer of the Liberal party, underlined the importance of cooperation between the government and the private sector and praised Somoza for giving the country peace, monetary stability, and a nationalized Banco Nacional. For these reasons, and because the merchants' associations were "apolitical" and independent, they had all come together from different parts of the country to give their backing to a president who was the nation's guarantor of peace, liberty, and democracy.[107]

Somoza answered with a speech of his own in which he reminded the audience that in the preceding few days he had attended celebrations to mark the completion of the first houses for workers and of the new building of the Banco Nacional; now he was with the chambers of commerce, "the strongest artery in the organic system of the republic," whose support he sought in the name of the Fatherland. He promised that his government's policies would always assure the freedom that businessmen needed to produce and exchange, that supply and demand would determine prices in the country, and that peace would be maintained by insisting on order and by keeping the government above party politics. In the speech Somoza described his government as *antipartidista* in the sense that it governed for all.

In the following years, the merchants concerned themselves with minor problems and adjustments required by the country's economy. In August 1939 they complained about the rise in import duties, and the following month about government imposition of price controls on basic goods. In December 1939 the Managua Chamber wrote to the minister of the interior describing the negative impact that the decree on maximum profits had had on commercial activity. But all chambers of commerce supported the Max plan for the reform of the banking and fiscal systems. After 1941, the publications of the Managua and León chambers contained very few comments on economic policy in general and, if so, they usually were supportive of the government. For example, the Managua Chamber's president had only one suggestion for the government in his year-end report for 1941 and that had to do with improving bureaucratic procedures in requests for dollars at the exchange commission.[108]

The government's relations with cattlemen and farmers is more difficult to trace due to a lack of information and published material. The regime's economic measures in 1937 and 1938 generally favored producers for export through currency devaluation and a rapid rise in agricultural credit. That is, Somoza's relationship with coffee producers seems to have been generally good. The only evidence found of specific grievances is a letter from the president of the Asociación Agrícola de Nicaragua to Somoza's private secretary complaining of the lack of sufficient workers to harvest coffee in the Managua area. He blamed the problem on the low price of coffee itself, which did not allow for attractive wages, but also faulted the government for not suspending work on highway construction during the coffee harvest and for not reducing the price of railway tickets for migrant workers as it had done in the past. On the contrary, highway construction had increased and labor was scarcer than ever.[109]

The government's attitude toward some of the country's cattlemen does not seem to have been as conciliatory. In the first place, cattlemen in Chontales and Boaco were mostly Conservative ranchers whose allegiance to the caudillo Chamorro made them doubtful political allies. Somoza's early measures prohibiting the export of meat for a five-year period must have produced very negative reactions among them, not to mention Somoza's own growing participation in cattle raising. Subsequently, in 1940 Somoza decreed that the subsidy that the Asociación Nacional de Ganaderos received from the government was to be suspended and that the activities of the Asociación that coincided with those of the Ministry of Agriculture henceforth would be handled exclusively by the latter. As a justification for this measure, the decree mentioned that "the defense of the agriculture of the nation requires urgently the organization of production and processing of certain export items that cannot be achieved without the intervention and the direction of the State."[110]

Somoza's policy toward Conservative landowners did not extend to all Conservative landed interests. His relations with the powerful agricultural complex of the Nicaragua Sugar Estates, Limited, in the department of Chinandega seem to have been particularly cordial, both because of the importance of its sugar production and export and because of its owners' ties with the more conciliatory factions of the Conservative party. In 1939 the president of the Nicaragua Sugar Estates and of the powerful Asociación Azucarera de Nicaragua (which included all the big and medium sugar producers) wrote Somoza requesting that the Nicaraguan embassy in Washington intervene before the U.S. Department of Commerce to seek a lower import duty and a higher quota for Nicaraguan sugar. Somoza wrote back immediately stating that he thought that the request was perfectly sound and that he had instructed the Nicaraguan ambassador in Washington to proceed accordingly.[111]

The importance of mining and banana operations to Nicaragua's exports and to Somoza's personal income established the basis for an especially warm relationship with foreign business. When Somoza visited the United States in early 1939, the Bragmans Bluff Lumber Company offered a ship of its fleet to transport Somoza and his entourage to New Orleans. H. D. Scott, the company's manager, also offered "to meet you and enjoy showing you around the city of New Orleans and return with you to—OUR Nicaragua."[112] On another occasion, when the Nicaraguan Congress began to study the law to protect workers from accidents in mining operations, the manager of the La Luz Mines, Limited, wrote to Somoza expressing his concern because the mining companies already provided their workers with medical care, subsidized foodstuffs, and potable water, while operating costs had increased as a result of the war in Europe. Furthermore, he stated, the law was discriminatory because it applied only to mining operations when there were many other firms that employed Nicaraguan laborers, too. Therefore, he requested that the president give special attention to this matter so that the law would affect not only the mining companies.[113] In the end, the law passed by the Congress applied to all firms that handled toxic materials, but its provisions regarding worker benefits did not impose any significant additional burden on the mines' operating costs. Somoza knew that if he encumbered the mining firms more than they were willing to tolerate, he risked their departure from the country and a political backlash from Nicaraguan business groups.

One sector of foreign business in Nicaragua that did not fare well under Somoza was the German coffee planter community, especially the planters who were concentrated in the northern department of Matagalpa. In less than two weeks after the attack on Pearl Harbor and Nicaragua's declaration of war on the Axis powers, all bank accounts held by nationals of countries at war with Nicaragua were frozen.[114] Simultaneously, the government took over the coffee farms and business concerns of these foreigners. In the case of the coffee growers, their entire harvest was confiscated and sold by the Banco Nacional, which then paid off the owners' outstanding debts and taxes and gave them enough money to maintain their farms and their immediate families. Anything left over remained in a frozen account with the Banco Nacional until the end of the war or until disposed of otherwise. Similar measures applied to those involved in any other production for export. The business firms of these foreigners could remain open, but they were forbidden to export or import their products.[115] A subsequent decree required that foreigners from countries at war with Nicaragua present detailed lists of all their possessions and the items they produced. It reiterated that the businesses of foreigners would continue to be operated by their owners but under the direct supervision of the Banco Nacional, which also would claim the monies received from any sale of these businesses. In February 1943, however, another decree totally prohibited such foreigners from selling or trading their properties.[116]

The final step, of course, was outright expropriation. That came in the form of a congressional resolution in September 1943 that empowered the government to take over all those businesses of enemy aliens that were considered essential to the economic health of the country and to the war effort. Once expropriated by either the Banco Nacional or the president, these properties would be auctioned off and the funds deposited in frozen accounts with the Banco Nacional.[117] Many of these properties, especially the coffee farms of the Matagalpa region, ended up in the hands of Somoza and his coterie.

In fact, Somoza from early on combined his position of national executive with that of business executive. When he signed some business contract, he frequently listed his occupation as "agricultor." A comprehensive study of the growth of his businesses is not possible at the moment, but there is sufficient evidence to determine to some extent how he prospered. Somoza's control of the credit system was fundamental, as was the information he possessed concerning government spending. That is, he was able both to speculate without much risk and to involve himself in productive investment. An example of the former involved the construction of a new airport for Managua. Somoza first bought up the land on which the airport would be built, then declared the government's decision to build the airport, then had the Banco Nacional purchase the land from him, and finally authorized the government to buy the land from the Banco Nacional. Illustrations of his investment strategy include the construction of a cement plant in 1940, in which Somoza had a 36.6 percent interest, and the operation of the first Nicaraguan insurance company, which was run by a group of his friends and relatives, all of whom occupied posts in the government.[118] But Somoza's greatest wealth came from land, which he most likely was able to acquire through the government credit system under his control. His presence as an important cattle breeder and gentleman farmer is evident as early as 1940, when his prize bulls, stallions, cows, and pigs won most first prizes in the national agricultural shows held yearly in Managua.[119]

Somoza also received income from foreign businessmen who thought it prudent to have the president of Nicaragua on their side. The foreign mining companies all seem to have given Somoza a contribution in kind on the basis of their gold production. One of these, the Compañía Minas Matagalpa, sent him U.S.$10 for each kilo of gold produced as a "voluntary and spontaneous" contribution that would continue as long as the conditions of the contracts signed between the company and the Nicaraguan government remained in effect. Under this arrangement, Somoza received U.S.$1,885 and U.S.$905 for the two semesters of 1943. William Krehm, writing in the late 1940s, figured that Somoza drew about U.S.$175,000 per year from the gold mining companies.[120]

Foreign businessmen interested in investing in Nicaragua usually had to come to terms first with Somoza. As early as 1939, he was imposing himself as a partner on one Alejandro Safié, who was interested in setting up a textile factory and flour mill. According to a draft agreement, Somoza would invest nothing of his own but would receive 40 percent of earnings in exchange for his "commercial council and cooperation so that [the firm's activities] might develop within the greatest freedom under all the rights and privileges offered by the laws of the country." After ten years, four-tenths of all the machinery and buildings would be transferred directly to Somoza's ownership; in the meantime, the company could not sell any of its properties or acquire debts over U.S.$10,000 without Somoza's express approval.[121]

From his first years in power it is evident that Somoza generally made no distinction between public service and private gain, nor did he seem to consider such behavior improper. His businesses were run directly from his office in the presidential palace and Nicaragua's diplomats and consuls abroad were as much his commercial agents as the country's official representatives.[122] Documents relating to the formation of new Somoza enterprises or to the purchase and sale of properties were duly reported in La Gaceta/Diario Oficial. Nor did Somoza's growing economic empire create much fuss within the Nicaraguan business community or the opposition Conservative party, both because it was still not large enough to step on too many toes and because in depressed economic times there was a ready market of properties for sale.

The Regime and the Disloyal Opposition

Somoza's incursions into the business world in a fairly open and normal fashion were helped by the fact that up to 1944 there was little outright opposition within Nicaragua to his government's policies or to his occupying the presidency. What political opposition there was can be defined best as a mixture of isolated incidents and the publication of diverse broadsheets and booklets, within and outside of Nicaragua. Students, at both the university and high school levels, were the most active, but they represented more of a bother than real political opposition. In February 1939, a group of students at the university campus in León objected to a portrait of Somoza that hung in the main hall; the picture was a present from Emperor Hirohito that had been embroidered in silk. The students were able to get into the hall at night and douse the portrait with acid. Those implicated were caught eventually, tortured, and jailed for some months.[123] In February 1940, the police in Managua captured a group of "communist conspirators," who turned out to be students who had printed and distributed the famous photograph of Somoza embracing Sandino shortly before Sandino was killed. Below the photograph was the phrase "The embrace of death" followed by "Yesterday he killed Sandino, today he kills the people" and along the sides were the words "hunger" and "oppression." Eight students were accused of actually printing the flier and sentenced to confinement in Little Corn Island for subversive activities and for defaming government officials; nine more were sentenced to thirty days at hard labor for distributing the fliers.[124]

Student opposition to Somoza followed an anti-imperialist and Sandinista line, but its content was still very vague. No unifying ideology emerged around which a wider political coalition could unify. For example, relations between the labor movement and university students were never good. Students did read the writings of Victor Raul Haya de la Torre and studied the Spanish Civil War, but they were bombarded with much more information and commentary from the United States, especially once World War II had begun. As one contemporary stated, it was a "lost generation" within a "dormant population."[125] This would change suddenly in 1944, when students and other social groups were drawn together in a common purpose of preventing another Somoza reelection. But prior to 1944, it was more common to see university and high school students engaged in activities supportive of Somoza and his regime.[126]

With the beginning of the war in Europe, the regime warned its opponents that any attempts to jeopardize Nicaragua's neutrality or to alter the public order would be dealt with harshly; not even members of the Congress should take advantage of their parliamentary immunity.[127] The new Constitution approved in March 1939 carried a rider called the "Ley Marcial o de Orden Público," which would take effect the moment that any of the Constitution's provisions were suspended. The Ley Marcial specifically addressed the maintenance of public order and the security of the state during "abnormal" circumstances. Under the law, the president was empowered to arrest anyone without a warrant and confine that person for an unlimited length of time. If so required, the military authorities could dissolve "at whatever cost" those groups that had caused or were taking advantage of the abnormal circumstances. Military courts would then handle all cases of treason, rebellion, mob action, and conspiracy to overthrow the government.[128] In mid-1941, the Congress approved another measure entitled "Ley de defensa de la democracia." This legislation prohibited the diffusion of all ideologies and political and social systems contrary to the country's "republican and democratic system" and against the established social order; as mentioned in the law, such systems included those espoused by the communist doctrine and the Nazi and fascist organizations. The measure also prohibited the creation of political parties in Nicaragua with international ties and the use of emblems and uniforms of foreign political groups.[129]

Needless to say, the moment that Nicaragua formally entered the war, Somoza declared a state of emergency and put the Ley Marcial into effect.[130] During the next four years, Nicaragua remained under martial law; both the right wing of the political spectrum (such as the "reactionaries" within the Nationalist Conservative party) and the communists and more radical labor activists were able to move only at their own risk and at the pleasure of the dictator. Even the "established" political groups were restricted in their activities. When the leaders of the Conservative party decided to meet in June 1943 to discuss various aspects of the political situation, they first had to request permission from the jefe político, who then consulted with the minister of the interior, after which it was determined that there were only two political parties in Nicaragua, the Liberals and the Nationalist Conservatives. Because the Genuino Conservatives had not participated in the last election, they were considered a nonparty and could not hold their meeting.[131]

These public and institutionalized measures of political control were complemented by a gamut of more insidious mechanisms typical of dictatorial regimes. Paid spies were one of the most popular forms of gathering political intelligence. In Granada, where the Conservatives and fascists were particularly active, the director of police kept a close eye on all their activities, in particular their contacts with the Jesuit order and various worker associations.[132] In Masaya, one A. P. wandered around public places presumably to overhear what Conservatives, communists, and anti-Somoza Liberals had to say about political developments.[133] In rural areas, the *jueces de mesta* not only had judicial authority but also were required to report weekly on the "situation" of their locality, including all social and political meetings. On the basis of the reports available, the jueces de mesta seem to have been individuals with very little schooling; most likely, they were campesinos who were well connected to the Liberal party or the Guardia Nacional.[134] Their importance to the regime is evidenced by the fact that they continued to function (and apparently well for the regime's needs) right up until the Sandinista triumph of 1979.

Given these constraints on political activism in Nicaragua, the only arena where opposition to the regime could be voiced more or less openly was abroad, in countries like Costa Rica, Mexico, the United States, and eventually Guatemala once the Arévalo government was installed. With the exception of the labor leaders in exile, foreign-based opposition groups were largely committed to moderate reformism and political democratization. The Comité Patriótico Abstencionista Nicaragüense with headquarters in New York City issued a manifesto in mid-1938 calling on all Nicaraguans to boycott the election for a Constituent Assembly. Otherwise, they said, Somoza's power would be completely consolidated and the only alternative course of action in the future would be armed revolt. Such a violent path, in turn, would open up the way for the penetration of "exotic doctrines" which are the natural and direct consequence of dictatorial regimes.[135]

In Mexico City, the Comité Revolucionario Nicaragüense issued a *Programa de acción* in September 1938 that described Nicaragua's political ills as a direct result of the praetorian influence left behind by the United States with the complicity of the two historic parties. That is, the problem of Nicaragua was not Somoza but the Guardia Nacional. The Liberal and Conservative parties meekly had accepted this new factor in the Nicaraguan political system and now they were suffering the consequences: Somoza and the Guardia Nacional would tame them and break them through the use of carrot-and-stick measures ("el pan y el garrote") against which they were powerless in fact, because the parties were nothing more than caudillos and traditional beliefs and practices with no real links to the people.[136]

In light of this reality, the Comité Revolucionario intended first of all to eradicate the praetorian presence and thereafter proceed to rebuild the country along new lines. That is, it sought to organize an armed opposition to the regime with popular participation and then to implement a new political and social model. Specifically, the Comité mentioned the need for land reform through the expropriation and distribution of uncultivated lands, the return of communal and *ejidal* land to their rightful owners, and the organization of new agricultural units based on cooperatives and technical and financial assistance. Second, the Comité considered that Nicaragua's agricultural base was too vulnerable to fluctuations in the world market and that, therefore, there was need for industrial development under state aegis. Industrial development, in turn, would require the implementation of varied worker legislation, including a labor code and social security. The state would also take a more direct role in promoting commercial and export activities by reforming the banking system and placing greater controls over foreign capital within the country. Third, the Comité Revolucionario called for a new foreign policy to replace that of a regime that had toyed with fascism and had not faced up to imperialism (presumably that of the United States), which had brought so much hardship to Nicaragua. In particular, the Programa stated, all those agreements that limited Nicaragua's sovereignty and controlled its finances should be reviewed and, if necessary, abolished. Finally, a new political system would be established to guarantee basic political and civil rights, municipal autonomy, and free and secular education.[137]

The position of both the Comité Patriótico Abstencionista and the Comité Revolucionario reflects a middle-class, reformist ideology that was well intentioned but had no organized links to the people. These and similar groups that developed in succeeding years were formed by disgruntled professionals and businessmen who wanted a better government for Nicaragua or, in some cases, who had experienced some direct and personal misfortune at the hands of Somoza and whose primary concern was to "get even." Although some might contemplate an overhaul of Nicaraguan society, as in the case of the Comité Revolucionario, at no time was there a call for popular organization and action to oppose the regime.

Conclusion

By 1943 the regime's position was hardly challenged within and outside the country. Local and foreign capital had been largely incorporated into the

Somocista coalition. Organized labor, while more fractious and unpredictable, also had been approached and invited to speak its mind within the limits set by the regime. Only the Chamorrista faction of the Conservative party, with its leader in exile and its activists within the country severely restricted in their movements, was publicly opposed to the regime and to Somoza. The Conservatives' weakness was compounded by their lack of clear policy alternatives and their insistence on the respect for constitutional procedures that they themselves rarely had honored in the past. Their political power base among cattlemen and ranch hands and campesinos in Granada, Boaco, Chontales, and Rivas was no match for the Somocista coalition of merchants, coffee exporters, urban laborers, government employees, and the Guardia Nacional. Other opposition groups outside of Nicaragua engaged in proposing high-sounding alternative political projects but with no real base of support within the country.

The regime, on the other hand, had strengthened the institutions of the state and placed them solidly under the control of Somoza. The economic measures undertaken in response first to the Great Depression and afterward to the world war centralized in the hands of the national executive the determination of fiscal and monetary policy, in addition to giving Somoza a large say in the credit policy of the principal banks in the country. Of particular importance in this respect was the transfer of the board of directors of the Banco Nacional to Managua and the subsequent reform of the entire banking system in 1940. By combining both an increased control over the country's finances and credit and a policy of devaluation and inflation favorable to the export producers, the regime could claim a commitment to economic reactivation without questioning the fundamental tenets of the free enterprise system. Price and exchange controls, while a limitation in principle on the operation of market forces, were not particularly effective in controlling inflation or the operation of the black market; the import merchants protested on occasion the lack of foreign exchange and the bureaucratic bottlenecks under the system of controls but in the end acquiesced to the procedures.

The municipal reforms and the growth of the national bureaucracy provided the regime with additional mechanisms of political control. The old Conservative-Liberal electoral rivalry was eliminated at the local level through the direct appointment of the municipal authorities by the president and the virtual elimination of municipal autonomy. The central government came to control virtually all public employment, a prerogative that it used to good advantage to develop support among the bureaucracy and the job seekers. And by increasing revenue and tightening collection procedures, the regime had the resources with which to finance the growth of the public sector.

To cap it all, the Constitution of 1939 provided the regime with a degree of legitimacy by defining the state along new lines of greater social and economic interventionism. The Constitution committed the state to the eventual implementation of social security legislation and to the subdivision of uncultivated latifundia to create small- and middle-sized rural properties, as well as defining property as a right with a "social function." It also confirmed previous changes in the system of municipal government and, for the first time, established the constitutional status of the Guardia Nacional as the army of Nicaragua. Finally, the Constitution gave the state extensive powers to limit expression and, together with its rider, the Ley Marcial, to arrest, incarcerate, and confine people deemed dangerous to the security of the state under procedures administered by the military courts. Of course, the Constitution did not set a timetable for the social and economic agenda it envisioned, nor did it define in clear terms when its provisions for political repression could be activated; these imponderables were left in Somoza's hands, who would exploit them to his advantage in the coming years.

The Nicaraguan state at the beginning of the 1940s thus was the result of both a process of institutional development and the rise to power of an individual who controlled the most important institution of them all, the Guardia Nacional. This mix of institutional and personal characteristics is best described in the Constitution itself when it defines the president of the republic as "personifying the nation" in addition to holding the position of chief of state.[138] But the success of the Somocista state at that time also was due to Somoza's ability to conciliate the interests of the more powerful social groups, as well as aggressively seeking the support of others who had previously been left out of the political process. The use of force as a mechanism of political domination receded in the face of political conciliation; not only was it more difficult objectively to confront the regime on military terms but also it made little sense to do so when there were channels of communication open to the chief of state (albeit only for those who accepted the rules set down by the regime). And finally, by placing himself firmly (although mostly verbally) within the alliance against fascism and totalitarianism, Somoza was able to exploit the important presence that the United States still retained among Nicaraguan political figures who had matured under the protectorate of the 1910s and 1920s. To many in Nicaragua, the sight of Somoza surrounded by the U.S. ambassador and the U.S. flag must have meant only one thing: the most powerful nation in the hemisphere did not object to Somoza's continuation in power and would not look kindly on any attempt to remove him.

At the beginning of 1944, Somoza felt as strong as ever and his plans for remaining in office even beyond 1947 were taken for granted by everyone. However, not everyone was willing to accept such a prospect lightly. As rejection of Somocismo built up, so did the levels of open confrontation, and the year 1944 brought to a head the first serious crisis of the new order, a crisis that threatened not only to disrupt the Somocista coalition but also to imperil the vital support of the United States. That Somoza survived the crisis must be attributed in good part to his ability to maneuver effectively as well as to his control over the revamped state apparatus that was largely in place by then.

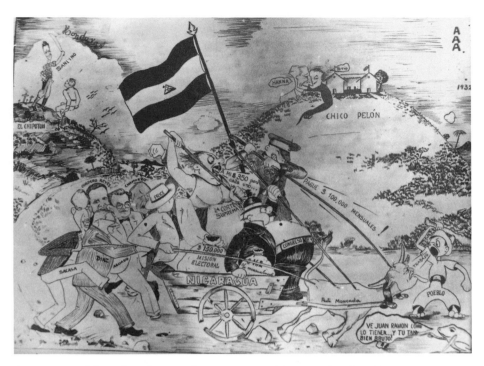

A caricature of the political scene of Nicaragua in 1932. President José María Moncada is the ox, goaded on by a cartload of politicians and the Guardia Nacional demanding money while the people demand work. On the left, Sandino brandishes a machete on his hilltop in the Segovias and, on the right, U.S. ambassador Matthew Hanna converses at his own hilltop residence. Anastasio Somoza did not yet merit a place in the caricature; the Guardia Nacional was still under American command. (Archivo Nacional de Nicaragua)

A Somocista rally in Somoto held on 5 January 1936. The placards waved by the mostly peasant crowd speak of generalities: "General Somoza will never be defeated;" "General Somoza will be the reformer;" "The enemies of the people are the enemies of the fatherland." (Archivo Nacional de Nicaragua)

A Somocista rally held in the Caribbean town of Bluefields on 1 May 1936. The placard on the left reads "The people acclaim you, the army is behind you." The photo was sent to Somoza by Captain J. Adrián Somarriba, Guardia Nacional, who obviously played a key role in the event. (Archivo Nacional de Nicaragua)

The general is received in Matagalpa by a fairly substantial crowd during the 1936 election campaign. (Archivo Nacional de Nicaragua)

Somoza campaigns in León for the presidency in 1936 carrying the American flag. The memories of U.S. occupation must have weighed heavily on the minds of many voters but Somoza, described by some as "the last marine," had no qualms about showing his true colors. (Archivo Nacional de Nicaragua)

122

Oficina Central de Propaganda
PRO GRAL. A. SOMOZA

El suscrito hace constar que el señor

Juan A. Hernández

se ha inscrito en esta oficina como partidario de la candidatura del Gral. A. SOMOZA.

Managua, 7 de Oct de 1945.

Jefe de Central de Propaganda
Pro-Gral. A. Somoza.

An example of a "magnífica," a document that proved one's allegiance to the Somocista cause. This magnífica certifies that Juan A. Hernández registered in support of Somoza's presidential candidacy for 1947. (Archivo Nacional de Nicaragua)

Somoza visited Washington in 1939, where he was received with full honors by President Roosevelt. Eleanor Roosevelt and Salvadora Somoza stand behind them. (Instituto de Historia de Nicaragua)

A street demonstration in celebration of the Allied victory places Somoza on a par with Franklin Roosevelt. This must have been one of the very few times when the hammer and sickle was waved about openly in Somocista Nicaragua. (Instituto de Historia de Nicaragua)

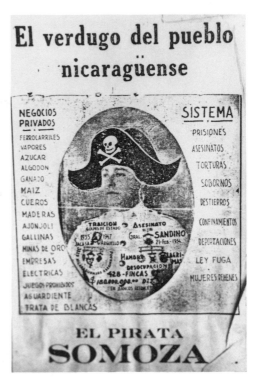

Flier attacking "the pirate Somoza" as "the executioner of the Nicaraguan people" (circa 1944). On the left are listed his private businesses, including railroads, ships, sugar, cotton, cattle, wood, gold mines, electric utilities, illegal gambling, booze, and prostitution. On the right, his political system: jails, murders, torture, bribery, exile, and summary executions. (Archivo Nacional de Nicaragua)

The entrepreneur-politician at his desk (mid-1940s). Somoza ran his businesses and the country simultaneously from the same office. (Instituto de Historia de Nicaragua)

University students in León protest the regime's gag laws during the June and July days of 1944. (Instituto de Historia de Nicaragua)

Somoza hands over the office of the presidency to Leonardo Argüello in April 1947. However, power remained largely in the hands of Somoza and the Guardia Nacional, as evidenced in Argüello's overthrow less than a month after taking office. (Instituto de Historia de Nicaragua)

Power brokers gather after the signing of the Somoza-Cuadra Pasos agreements of 1948. Carlos Cuadra Pasos, the leader of the Civilista faction of the Conservative party, third from left, stands next to President Brenes Jarquín, followed by Anastasio Somoza D., Somoza's youngest son, and Anastasio Somoza. (Instituto de Historia de Nicaragua)

Somoza and his wife, Salvadora, surrounded by rank and file of the presidential detachment of the Guardia Nacional (August 1948). Somoza sought to ingratiate himself by projecting a fatherly image among the troops. (Instituto de Historia de Nicaragua)

Somoza is awarded a diploma extended by leaders of the mechanics' and jewelers' trade unions (circa 1950). (Archivo Nacional de Nicaragua)

Nicaraguan exiles march in protest in Guatemala City inmediately after the failed overthrow attempt against Somoza in April 1954. Their placards read "Free Nicaraguans stand by Guatemala" and "War without quarter against Somoza." In a few weeks, they too will be silenced when the Guatemalan regime of Jacobo Arbenz is forced from office by a U.S.-sponsored coup. (Archivo Nacional de Nicaragua)

4 CRISIS, REFORM, & REPRESSION

. . . .

Solidly backed by the Guardia Nacional, firmly allied with the United States against the Axis powers, and supported by a widely based political coalition within Nicaragua, Somoza at the beginning of 1944 was preparing for his reelection in 1947 as if that were the most normal thing possible. As happened during the period 1935–36, groups of Liberal faithful gathered "spontaneously" to proclaim Somoza's candidacy for another term as president by drawing up a document in which they underlined that Somoza's record and the situation created by the war required that Nicaragua continue under the same government; then they all signed the paper and sent it off to Managua.[1] In June of the same year, Somoza announced in a press conference that he personally opposed presidential reelection, but that he had as much right as any other citizen to run for the presidency.[2] Already in April, the two chambers of the legislative branch had approved by the usual wide margin a constitutional amendment that would allow the sitting president to stand for a new term whenever his original term in office coincided with a declared state of international war that had lasted for at least two years.[3] Such a tailor-made amendment made it quite obvious to all that Somoza intended to stay in power for an extended period of time beyond his current term.

Somoza's desire to remain in the presidency flew in the face of the political movement in Central America at the time. After approximately fifteen years of military dictatorship, Guatemala and El Salvador were experiencing the first signs of open opposition to the governments of Ubico and Hernández Martínez. The U.S. State Department already had gauged antiregime feeling in the area and had warned its embassies in Central America to maintain the most impartial and discrete relations with both governments and opposition groups. According to the secretary of state, this was particularly important because "it is almost inevitable that this opposition will eventually come to power in some countries."[4] In the case of Nicaragua, the opposition had been quiescent for a fairly long time, with only a limited amount of internal dissenters and a number of exiled groups producing some written criticism of the regime. This changed rapidly, when during a two-week period, the regime seemed on the verge of collapsing under the pressure of violent protests.

The June and July Days of 1944

The immediate cause of open political dissent in 1944 was Somoza's desire for reelection. Within the Liberal party itself, there was a group that harbored political ambitions of its own or that concluded that Liberal principles were being compromised by Somoza's *continuismo*. While the Congress debated the reform of the constitutional provision that prohibited presidential reelection, a number of prominent Liberals publicly voiced their opposition and were forthwith thrown in jail in Managua and León. Adolfo Altamirano Browne, a Liberal deputy, subsequently requested that the Chamber of Deputies petition Somoza for their freedom, a measure that was unanimously approved by the chamber and that met with Somoza's support.[5] This was one of the first evidences of dissent within the Liberal party and Somoza at that moment was trying to avoid an open split that might lead to a serious political crisis. But Somoza's conciliatory attitude toward members of his own party was not repeated in June, when the streets of Managua witnessed the first widespread urban disturbances since the demonstrations of early 1936 that preceded Somoza's rise to power.

The initial nucleus of this urban opposition was formed by university students. In total, their number could not have exceeded 600, which was the student population of the Nicaraguan university system at the time, with about half at the Managua campus and the rest in Granada and León.[6] At a general assembly of the student body on 27 June 1944, it was agreed that a demonstration would be held that day to express support for the student movement that was struggling to remove the right-wing junta that took over the Guatemalan government after Ubico's overthrow. Throughout the afternoon, the students and others who joined them paraded up and down the streets of Managua demanding democracy and liberty in both Guatemala and Nicaragua. The crowd grew to some 2,000 people before the police and the Guardia intervened in the early evening to break it up while it was congregated in front of the military academy. About 500 demonstrators were locked up and spent the night in jail. Some of them were freed the following day while the rest spent more time behind bars. On the twenty-ninth, a group of women dressed in black marched through the streets demanding the release of those detained but it came face-to-face with a pro-Somoza demonstration that forced it to disperse.[7] In León the same day, a group of about 150 students, professionals, and farmers signed a note addressed to Somoza protesting the treatment of the demonstrators in Managua; they argued that the events in Managua at no time threatened public order nor undermined Nicaragua's rather "formal" war effort.[8] A group of labor leaders also met with Somoza to request that about 60 workers arrested during the demonstrations be set free.[9]

The nature of the demonstrations is not difficult to determine. The slogans that were heard spoke of a basically *political* opposition to the regime. Beginning with the university students, the vast majority of whom were from middle- or upper-class families, the protest caught the attention of a number of Conservative and dissident Liberal politicians; some of these individuals were arrested in the streets, while others echoed their protest by resigning from government posts. The protest march of the women dressed in black was formed by mothers and sisters of the detained demonstrators, most of them elegant ladies of the upper and middle classes who were countered by a demonstration of Somocistas described by *La Prensa* as a rabble of market vendors and women of ill repute (that is, of the lower class).[10] The manner in which the demonstrators were handled also suggests that Somoza was aware of the type of political opponents he was dealing with. At a press conference on 1 July 1944, he said that the demonstrators who were still being held would be turned over to the civil courts, even though their actions in front of military installations warranted court-martialing.[11] The following day he personally supervised the release of a number of student demonstrators; he talked with them before turning them over to their parents, chiding them for attacking him personally after all the effort he had put into building up the university.[12]

Somoza's relatively soft handling of this wave of street protests did not defuse the situation, however. On 3 July the leadership of the Liberal party met to discuss the situation, with one group demanding that the time for freedom and democracy had arrived and that Somoza should desist from his reelectionist plans or should even step down immediately.[13] The same day, Gerónimo Ramírez Brown, the minister of education and one of Somoza's earliest backers, had resigned his post to protest Somoza's closure of the university.[14] And on 4 July, both Somocistas and anti-Somocistas determined to take advantage of the U.S. Independence Day celebration to organize street demonstrations and to set forth their views. The Somocistas, no doubt, wished to call attention to their close ties with the United States, while their opponents took advantage of the date under the assumption that their demonstrations would not be repressed outright during a festivity celebrating freedom.[15]

Early in the morning of the fourth, thousands gathered around the U.S. embassy building; most of them opposed Somoza. Carlos Pasos, a businessman who had emerged as the principal opponent to Somoza within the Liberal party, gave an impassioned speech to a crowd that had grown to some 20,000. When a short while later a detachment of Guardia Nacional cadets paraded in front of the embassy, they were jeered by the crowd, as was Somoza when he attempted to make a speech from a grandstand erected for that purpose when his request to speak from an embassy balcony had been rejected by the State Department in Washington. Afterward, the crowd moved out in a street demonstration that got as far as the Mexican embassy a few blocks away before the Guardia intervened and dispersed the crowd. Nearly 500 demonstrators sought haven in the embassy itself, of which Somoza allowed nearly all to leave except for 20 leaders, who were left inside the embassy compound as refugees.[16]

On 5 July, a number of shopkeepers threatened to close their stores in protest of the arrests. When word reached the government, the Junta de Control de Precios y Comercio, then headed by the collector general of customs, Colonel Irving A. Lindberg, issued a warning that all businesses that shut their doors would be seized and liquidated by the government, while foreign shopkeepers could even be expelled from the country.[17] Cattlemen from the Conservative regions of Boaco and Chontales also had cut back on their shipments of meat to Managua, to the point that Somoza accused them of subversion and instructed the jefes políticos to threaten the cattlemen with forced requisitions of beef which the government itself would transport to Managua.[18] Thus, what had begun as a student protest now had produced a crisis within the Liberal party that threatened to tear apart the Somocista coalition; it also had opened the door for the Conservatives to express their opposition to the president.

On 7 July, Somoza decided to give a little and issued a statement declaring that he no longer sought the presidential nomination for the next term. He said that the constitutional amendment that would permit reelection under special circumstances had the support of the majority of the Liberal party, but that he was aware that insisting on the amendment might split the Liberals, a situation that would give great advantage to the opposition. Therefore, he would sacrifice his political future on behalf of party unity and would veto the amendment. He also announced that the elections to be held in 1947 would be fair and that the freedom of the press would be guaranteed. In regard to the political turmoil of the past days, he said that the government's actions in no way warranted such behavior; therefore, the only ones to blame were those who wanted to subvert the public order. In any case, he added, now that the political issue had been resolved through his veto of the constitutional amendment, there were no reasons whatsoever for more political instability and those who persisted in making problems would be treated with a heavy hand.[19]

With this measure, a good part of the crisis was resolved: Somoza conceded some things while at the same time he threatened others. Over the next few days, the last events of the crisis played themselves out. On 10 July the minister of the interior, Leonardo Argüello, resigned to protest what he considered Somoza's autocratic handling of the disturbances; he said that Somoza had never consulted his ministers or his close advisers to seek expedient and political solutions to the crisis. The mayor of León, Alberto Reyes, also resigned his post for the same reason.[20] Carlos Pasos, the dissident Liberal leader, was taken from his refuge in the Mexican embassy to speak with Somoza and arrange some kind of Liberal reconciliation, but nothing was resolved due to the distrust expressed toward Somoza by the dissidents.[21] Meanwhile, arrests continued in some parts of the country, especially in Managua and León, where most of the university students were located. In Managua, the list of imprisoned students and others involved in the street demonstrations reached a total of over ninety; included were a good number of sons of prominent Liberal and Conservative families. In León, fewer demonstrators had been arrested although the city lived under a cloud of fear and distrust.[22]

By 14 July, the first group of dissident Liberals left the country for exile in Costa Rica, including Carlos Pasos and Carlos Castro Wassmer, a Liberal caudillo from the León region. Fifteen more were confined to Corn Island, although La Prensa reported that as many as seventy were scheduled to leave for that place of internal exile. At a press conference on the fifteenth, Somoza expressed complete confidence in his control of the situation. He emphasized that during the troubled period not a single person in Nicaragua had been killed and that in a short while he would announce an amnesty so that all those exiled could return once the political passions had cooled somewhat.[23] In fact, when Somoza sent an amnesty bill to the Congress three weeks later, he issued a communiqué emphasizing that it was the government's strength that permitted it to act in a benevolent fashion and to allow political criticism so long as such criticism was expressed through legally established channels.[24]

Political Forces during the Crisis

The crisis had passed, but it hardly would be sufficient to say that the Somocista regime survived only because it was strong or because it was magnanimous and conciliatory toward its opponents. The strengths of the regime also were a direct consequence of the weakness of the opposition. Years later, Somoza admitted that he had been on the verge of resigning and leaving the country in July 1944 but the opposition's disunity allowed him to continue in office.[25] In fact, the opposition to Somoza and his regime was very heterogeneous, with little or no cohesion other than a common desire to prevent a Somoza reelection or other means of keeping Somocismo in power.

Some of the most vocal antireelectionist sentiment came from the Liberal party itself and finally took form under the name of Partido Liberal Independiente (PLI). The origins of the PLI went back to 1937, when a small group of young Liberal university graduates organized the Grupo Democrático Nicaragüense. The Grupo engaged in meetings and discussions generally critical of the budding Somoza dictatorship but never made its presence felt in the political arena.[26] By the early 1940s, as Somoza's wealth and political ambitions became more evident, discontent within the Liberal party grew until it came into the open in January 1944 during the funeral ceremonies for Manuel Cordero Reyes, a prominent Liberal who had served as Somoza's foreign minister but who had broken with the regime. Young dissident Liberals distributed leaflets during the funeral in which they denounced Somoza's regime and called on Liberal party members to join in opposing *continuismo somocista*; they signed these leaflets as *Liberales Independientes*, from whence the party later derived its name.[27]

The political ideology of the PLI was characterized consistently as anti-Somoza. Somoza stood accused of violating basic Liberal tenets of government and economics and establishing in Nicaragua a harsh form of despotism. A comprehensive indictment of the Somoza regime from the PLI viewpoint was written in January 1944 by three leaders of the Liberal dissidents: Manuel Cordero Reyes, Carlos Castro Wassmer, and Carlos Pasos. In general, they accused Somoza of violating the people's political liberties, of corrupting the Guardia Nacional and other governmental bodies, of taking advantage of the state's financial institutions for personal gain, and of destroying the independence of the judicial system. The criticism of the economic aspects of Somocismo boiled down to the unfair competitive advantage that Somoza's control over the state apparatus gave his enterprises and the political coercion he exercised through the credit system and the customs service. His direction of the national railway came in for particularly heavy criticism, both because the railway gave Somoza's cargo preferential treatment and because it had become a political tool: "The railroad is an important factor in hindering the operation of the country's businesses; it employs trivial excuses to complicate, delay or deny the delivery of goods harvested or purchased by industrialists, merchants or independent producers and uses similar methods to exercise political pressure on the citizenry."[28]

Of particular concern to the PLI was Somoza's "invasion" of the most diverse types of economic activities; his total wealth was calculated at U.S.$10 million and his annual income at about U.S.$1 million. These critics concluded that it had become practically impossible to initiate a business activity without Somoza's approval and even his participation, to which was added the following dictum: "And the worst effect of such a regime is that it destroys all initiative, weakens ongoing efforts, creates a defeatist spirit, and paralyzes the progress of the nation. . . . Such are the aspects of the Somoza dictatorship that differentiate it from others in Latin America, most of which are of an exclusively *political* type and some of them truly honest and constructive."[29] In other words, the problem was not dictatorship in itself but the type of dictatorship embodied in Somocismo.

The growth and strength of the PLI was principally in Managua, León, Masaya, and the Segovias. According to Enrique Espinoza Sotomayor, one of the founders of the PLI, the more businesses Somoza operated in a given locality, the more such activities affected the local entrepreneurs and the more easily they gravitated toward the PLI.[30] Undoubtedly, the PLI considered that it was the repository of genuine Liberal ideology as contraposed to the aberrant Somocista version, but ideology did not play an important role in its criticism of Somocismo. On some occasions, references were made to "the hungry people" and "the misery of the people," but most often it was the figure of Somoza that came under attack: "That thief? That modern gangster, that Al Capone, is your president? Will you continue to consent to such a shameful situation?"[31]

In fact, the PLI did not envision any major changes in Nicaraguan society or economy. As it stated in a communiqué issued in July 1944, it basically sought to do away with continuismo and guarantee public liberties by forcing Somoza to resign.[32] The PLI thus emerged as a party of the middle classes, akin to Arevalismo in Guatemala or to Figuerismo (later on) in Costa Rica, committed to modernizing the state by strengthening its political institutions and promoting the development of capitalism along more humane and socially responsive lines.[33]

The Conservative party's role in the crisis of 1944 was far more limited. During the demonstrations in Managua, some students of prominent Conservative families were arrested, such as Pedro Joaquín Chamorro, who later became editor of *La Prensa*, and Fernando Agüero, the future leader of the Conservative party after the death of the caudillo Chamorro in the mid-1960s. A Conservative deputy, Octavio Pasos Montiel, also was thrown in jail in spite of his parliamentary immunity.[34] But the official position of the party, as defined by a gathering of Conservative notables, was that the government and the Liberal party were responsible both for the events of the preceding days and for producing a solution to the political crisis, while they, the Conservatives, would not take advantage of the moment to further their own political goals. Instead, they called for a democratic and political solution, without spelling out exactly what shape it might take.[35] The Conservatives' abstention in part reflects the absence of exiled Emiliano Chamorro from the meeting; had he been in Managua he most likely would have advocated some sort of putsch to overthrow Somoza.[36] Instead, the Conservatives' position reflected the opinion of the more conciliatory Conservative elements, including the leader of the Civilistas, Carlos Cuadra Pasos, as well as that of the unabashedly Somocista Conservatives headed by José Coronel Urtecho. All in all, therefore, Somoza confronted primarily a rebellion within his own party.

A decisive consideration in Somoza's successful resolution of the crisis was the decision of organized labor to stay out of the problem and, in some cases, even to offer support for the regime. Somoza had taken the initiative in late 1943 to seek a better working relationship with various labor leaders. In early 1944, the Partido Socialista de Nicaragua (PSN) emerged from clandestinity and began organizing activities. In April of the same year, Somoza publicly apologized to the leaders of the PSN for having jailed them and offered to preside over a congress of workers and peasants that would bring together the two factions of the labor movement.[37]

The congress duly opened in Managua on 26 May 1944 with a speech by Somoza in which he recounted his government's policy of promoting harmonious relations between labor and capital, of generating employment, and of keeping a control on the prices of basic goods. He promised that his regime was studying a labor code that would soon go before the Congress for its approval; later on he would introduce a number of social security measures, including health insurance, pension plans, and unemployment compensation. The government also would support worker initiatives in the formation of cooperatives. He concluded with a lyrical statement of his position toward the working class: "I have wished to provide hope and faith in the future to those tough-skinned peasants who labor painfully from dawn to sunset to bring in the harvest, and to those workers in factories and shops and in the starless nights of the mines who offer generously of their sweat and blood to create the nation's wealth. Hope and faith in a future abundant in bread, laughter, and song."[38]

Somoza's speech was answered by labor leader Absalón González, an arch-Somocista who had been elected president of the congress in order to maintain a semblance of unity between the various factions. He stated that Somoza had been the first president since the days of independence who had shown any interest in the working class and who always kept his promises to the workers. He requested from the regime a labor code of "Christian inspiration" and appealed to all present to back the code as it moved toward legislative approval. But the congress declined to support Somoza's electoral ambitions, although it did give him a qualified vote of confidence that applauded his decision to enter into the antifascist coalition and to allow workers to organize and express their views openly.[39] As it turned out, the majority of the two hundred delegates to the congress belonged to the more openly Marxist factions within the labor movement, but the opposition expressed at the time by the Conservatives and business leaders to a labor code and other worker legislation made labor's support for Somoza and his regime practically inevitable.[40]

The test of fire of labor's political inclinations came precisely during the days of demonstration and repression in June and July. In Managua, a number of labor unions signed a leaflet entitled "A Serious Appeal to All Workers" in which they denounced the call for a general strike issued by the political opponents of Somoza. They argued that a strike controlled by the workers was a legitimate thing, but when it was used for other purposes it generated only hunger and misery for the working class. In this case, the call for a strike came from "those at the top, from our most reactionary and dangerous exploiters." Thus, the only legitimate strikes were those in response to the most important and immediate needs of the working class. The leaflet called for tranquility and calm so that the workers could continue to organize their unions and strengthen their organization in a climate of "democratic peace and constitutional normalcy."[41] Such a posture played directly into the regime's hands.

Simultaneously, the Comité Organizador de la Confederación de Trabajadores de Nicaragua, within which were represented the two opposing tendencies in the labor movement, issued a flier explaining its position in the face of the disturbances. It praised the university students for showing support for their peers in Guatemala who were fighting tyranny but claimed that the Nicaraguan students had been manipulated by dissident Liberals, Conservatives, and "Nazi-fascist types" whose only objective was to take over the government and milk the national budget; what began as a simple show of student solidarity had degenerated into a dangerous provocation. The committee concluded that if the students really wished to contribute to the nation's well-being, they should first reject all base political intrigues and join with the labor movement to achieve a "democratic peace," for it was only through this peace that national well-being and progress could be achieved. The alternative was "social decomposition," which was promoted by ambitious politicians who sought personal advantages "at such times when the people make the mistake of supporting them."[42] The Comité Organizador at no time spoke of backing Somoza or praised him as a national leader, but by refraining from supporting the opposition, it was giving Somoza a tacit vote of confidence.

The left wing of the political spectrum, the Partido Socialista de Nicaragua, also made known its position toward the regime. In an extensive communiqué signed by a number of labor leaders who belonged simultaneously to the Comité Organizador, the PSN criticized the Nicaraguan party system as a small clique of leaders who decided for large numbers of workers and the people in general, in the absence of a political organization of the working class itself. The PSN stated that it would fill that void as well as struggle for social justice under a program of national unity. According to the communiqué, the PSN was willing to support the Somoza regime's policies of social improvement and would subordinate its own party interests to those of the national interest. In the past, it had made the mistake of insisting on its own position: "We opposed the government of General Somoza, but we realized that we were not following a correct political line so we proceeded to rectify it. General Somoza has told us that he too is ready to listen to the voice of the people. . . . We have faith that the President of the Republic will come to an understanding with our people because HE KNOWS FULL WELL THAT NO RULER ON THE FACE OF THE EARTH CAN REMAIN IF HE FLOUTS THE POPULAR WILL." More to the point, it added: "Be assured, General Somoza, that if our people do not participate in activities against your government you may continue uneventfully in office." For its part, the PSN committed the party to oppose all actions that disrupted the public order and called on all Nicaraguans to do the same.[43]

Other labor organizations came out much more strongly for Somoza, especially groups that were organized around the Casas del Obrero. The Casa in León issued a flier urging workers to reject the call to oppose Somoza's government for the regime had provided the working class with schools, offered low-interest loans to small farmers, and promised a labor code.[44] Another group issued a flier entitled "Six Truths about General Somoza" that described the opposition to his government in particularly strong terms: "The group of professional politicians who currently oppose President Somoza are of strictly bourgeois origins, including landowners, industrialists, merchants, traitors, and in general, men who have governed the country over the course of the years organized around aristocratic castes which exploit the people." But support for Somoza in the flier was rather more qualified: "The Nicaraguan people will not accept the thesis of overthrowing one Somoza to enthrone another. As long as there are no good and experienced individuals prepared to lead the battle against the reactionary forces, the people will be at the side of General Somoza."[45]

In addition to the support for the regime expressed openly or tacitly by labor, there is evidence that the Liberal party undertook the mobilization of its followers in diverse parts of the country, through both written expressions and the physical transport of its people, to show support for Somoza. From the department of Jinotega in the north, the Liberal party loaded up seven truckloads of party faithful and sent them off to Managua to help Somoza if the need should arise. It also organized a local self-defense force in case the Guardia contingent had to be pulled out of the city of Jinotega.[46] In Managua, the local Liberal party's executive committee issued a flier calling on Liberals to close ranks around the party so that it could compete in the upcoming elections from a position of strength.[47] The Guardia Nacional, heavily Liberal in its composition, was particularly concerned about the outcome of events in July; as expressed in a letter to Somoza from Lieutenant Alfonso J. Borgen, stationed at the Ingenio San Antonio in Chinandega, "The Guardia Nacional is made up nearly exclusively of Liberals, and I believe, as do all of my colleagues, that if you abandon the Presidency we will suffer again under the boot of the Conservatives and the chains and the whip of the Chamorros."[48]

New Rules of the Game for the Media and Labor

Somoza controlled the situation in a matter of weeks, but the seriousness of the crisis forced a reconsideration of the Somocista coalition. The Liberal party had not demonstrated total allegiance to the president, and certain shop-keepers and cattle raisers made evident their distaste for the regime by attempting to close down their businesses or curtail their activities. The Guardia had stood firm, and the labor movement had made its position quite clear, although labor did not back Somoza as much as he would have liked. The bureaucracy also had pledged its loyalty to Somoza and had participated in the street demonstrations on his behalf.[49] However, there was a need to reinforce the Somocista coalition by bringing the Liberals together again, by courting labor more assiduously, and by expanding the government's bureaucratic clientele.

There was also a need to define more explicitly the role of the political opposition and of dissenting opinions within the Nicaraguan state to avoid an explosion like the one that occurred in July 1944. That is, political opposition would be permitted and it would be able to express itself but within certain limits set down by laws and the established electoral practices of years past. The ultimate objective was twofold: on the one hand, the presence of an opposition was necessary to legitimize the Somocista regime, especially in the face of attacks from critics within and outside of the country who called Somoza a dictator; on the other hand, the opportunity to express dissenting views and to participate in electoral events served to vent the pressures that built up within a restrictive political environment, in addition to keeping alive a faint hope among the opposition that someday, perhaps, the regime could be defeated on its own terms.

Of fundamental importance was that Somoza take steps to limit political expression while not imposing a total state of siege that would render Nicaraguan "democracy" a complete sham; that is, he would permit political opposition but would restrict its access to the media so that political information could not flow freely. The regime's attitude toward the media always had been ambivalent. Somoza said that he welcomed criticism of his government but that such criticism must be "constructive" and within the law. Instead, he said, newspapers had been used as mouthpieces of the political opposition to voice insulting criticism of the government to the extent that the difference between *libertad* (freedom) and *libertinaje* (libertinism) had been lost completely.[50] As soon as the July events were under control, Somoza sent the Congress a bill that would restrict the freedom of expression. He also decreed that prior censorship would be put into effect as of 5 August, with a government censor empowered to scrutinize newspaper proofs and eliminate all material considered improper under the current state of martial law enacted in

December 1941.[51] This prior censorship was lifted three days later after Somoza met with newspaper editors and extracted a promise from them that henceforth they would be accountable for the editorial line of their papers, that they would use proper language (*lenguaje de altura*), and that they would not engage in personal insults.[52]

Although prior censorship was removed, in September 1944 the Congress passed and Somoza signed into law a bill that restricted the freedom of expression. This law gave the media a number of concessions, including exemption from all taxes and free postage within the country (including that of newspapers sent by mail). However, the law specified in clear terms the instances when freedom of expression was being transgressed, including propaganda to subvert the public or social order, statements calling for civil disobedience, insulting remarks about the fundamental institutions of the state, and false news reports that sought to create panic among the business sector or the public at large. Punishments for violating the provisions of this law included fines for the lesser offenses and outright closure for the more serious ones.[53] *La Prensa*, the leading opposition newspaper, was in fact closed by the government before the law went into effect and did not reappear until the middle of 1946.

Having placed limits on the freedom of expression, Somoza then turned his attention to expanding his relations with the labor movement. The central issue during this period became the labor code, which the president had been dangling before organized labor since the late 1930s. By August 1944, a draft of the labor code was before the Congress, which approved it with a minimum of debate. At most, some Conservative senators objected to the code, claiming that it had arrived twenty-five years too early because Nicaragua had no pressing labor problems that warranted such an extensive piece of legislation. Furthermore, they said, the draft law gave little consideration to the rural worker, the campesino. As might be expected, the Liberal majority passed the law with practically no modifications.[54]

The Nicaraguan Labor Code of 1945, as the fundamental document governing the relations between labor and capital, reflected the Somocista view of the organization of economic production under the aegis of the state.[55] As such, it was more important as an instrument that allowed the state to control the relations between labor and capital than one that freed labor to reach its objectives through strikes, negotiations, and political expression. For example, the code recognized the right of all workers (and businessmen, as well) to join together in cooperatives and unions and spelled out the objectives of these sindicatos: to denounce any irregularities in the implementation of the code, to engage in collective bargaining, and to represent the membership in all labor-management conflicts and in arbitration and conciliation proceedings. Moreover, all unions first had to be legalized by the Inspección General del Trabajo, a branch of the Ministry of Labor, which could revoke a union's legal status if its membership fell below the minimum of twenty-five laborers, if it joined up with a political party or association (either national or international in nature), or if it engaged in political activities of any kind.[56]

Even the strike, a basic weapon of labor in its relations with management, was subject in the code to certain conditions and objectives that entitled the state to determine whether it was licit or not. Thus, a strike could be called legally only to achieve a "balance" between capital and labor, to seek redress of grievances due to bad treatment on the part of management, to demand the proper implementation of a collective labor agreement, or to "harmonize" all aspects of labor's rights versus capital. Furthermore, a legal strike required that at least 60 percent of the workers support it, and that it be peaceful and noncoercive. Nor could strikes be held in any organizations providing public services or in workplaces of "collective interest"; the first excluded all government employees and the second, according to the definition of "collective interest," all rural workers engaged in agriculture, cattle raising, and lumbering.[57] Thus, the workers who could decide to go on strike were a minuscule fraction of the country's labor force, and once the decision was taken to strike there was no guarantee that the authorities would allow it to proceed. The decision to strike could be made only by those workers at the work site itself; any outside labor organizers were liable to be punished, as were those workers who tried to turn the strike into a political act or who espoused violence. And finally, before a strike could be called, all attempts at mediation and conciliation had to be exhausted.[58]

Such were the number of restrictions on labor unions and their rights that it was practically impossible for a labor movement to be independent of the regime. Still, the years 1944–46 witnessed a degree of labor activism hardly seen before or after that time. From August to December 1944 there were a number of strikes in Nicaragua, the most important being that in September against the textile firm of Pasos and Arellano, partly owned by Carlos Pasos, the PLI leader. Shortly afterward a number of workers struck at the cement plant of which Somoza himself was a principal stockholder. In December, the workers employed in the construction of the Pan-American highway went on strike demanding salary increases. In all these cases, the regime was able to negotiate settlements that the workers accepted without complaint. By the beginning of 1945, however, Somoza began to crack down on unions that were dominated by socialist labor leaders and those that were making problems for industrial enterprises. In the first place, Somoza did not want the PSN to grow excessively within the labor class and challenge labor leaders who were beholden to him; in the second place, among the industrial firms there were quite a few in which Somoza was a stockholder.[59] That is, the labor movement would be allowed to grow as long as it did not threaten Somoza's political control or his own economic interests, which did not leave it much room to maneuver in.

Nevertheless, the growth of the labor movement in terms of numbers of unions and membership was impressive. In 1945 alone, 97 unions were authorized in the country, compared to 11 in all of 1944.[60] Such was the spate of union organization that the Ministry of Labor produced a model of a founding document and statutes for all labor unions to employ. By the end of 1945, the number of workers belonging to recognized unions had risen to over 14,000, of which the biggest had 167 members (the stevedors' union at Corinto) and the smallest 7 members. Most of the rest had between 30 and 50 members.[61] In any case, some of these unions probably already existed under different names and they appeared in the Ministry of Labor's records because they had complied with the new registration procedures. In 1946 the number of additional unions registered fell to 29, and in 1947 they dropped to 13. In succeeding years, few if any registered. These data indicate that Somoza's interest in union organization was largely one of temporary expediency, although one could also assume that what potential there was for union organizing within the bounds set by the labor code was pretty much exhausted by 1945.

More indicative of Somoza's attitude toward labor, however, was his policy during and after 1945. To counter the Socialist party's influence within the labor movement, Somoza gave his support to the so-called Comité Organizador de la Confederación de Trabajadores Nicaragüenses, headed by labor leaders who were willing to work with him. But the increasing strength of the Socialist party within the labor movement and its unwillingness to become a docile member of the Somocista coalition finally persuaded Somoza to crack down on its leadership; in August 1945, the government expelled from the country a first group of Socialist leaders. In spite of this, the PSN continued to maintain a strong presence within the labor movement and even dominated the founding convention of the Confederación de Trabajadores de Nicaragua (CTN) in February 1946.[62]

In the end, Somoza did not get a strong, unified labor movement to his liking, even though labor's support for his regime during the critical months of 1944 had no doubt contributed to his permanence in office. He most likely thought that his backing of a labor code and his tolerant attitude in the face of leftist political and union activism would be sufficient to keep labor unconditionally on his side. When this did not prove to be the case, the value of labor's support did not outweigh the criticism that the private sector and the Conservative party aimed at Somoza, nor did he need labor's goodwill as much once the 1944 crisis had been defused. At that moment, it became advisable to drop labor, or at least break the ties with the PSN-dominated labor unions and federations. Such was the case of the Federación de Trabajadores de Managua (FTM), which in April 1946 requested permission to hold the annual May Day parade. Somoza turned down the request under the pretext that another labor federation had already received authorization; he said that the FTM could hold a meeting at the Casa del Obrero.[63] And when a labor union dominated by the PSN struck again at the textile mill of Pasos and Arellano in December 1946, Somoza this time sided with management and had the strike declared illegal.[64]

The United States and Somoza's Reelection

The progressive break with the labor movement required that the Somocista regime reinforce its other constituent elements and seek accommodation with opposition political parties. The scheme within which this was to be accomplished was the presidential and legislative election scheduled for February 1947. Through this procedure, Somoza sought to strengthen the PLN in order to contest the election and raise popular support for the regime, while the opposition parties would be enticed to participate and to channel their political energies into the campaign. In other words, the regime needed to recoup the legitimacy it had lost during the conflictive days of June and July 1944. Because a mass political movement based on the support of labor had failed to provide that legitimacy under terms acceptable to the regime, Somoza opted for the more conventional legitimizing mechanism of an election. At most, he had to relinquish his desire for another term in office, although not even that was completely decided when he vetoed the constitutional amendment allowing for presidential reelection. In fact, his final decision not to run again for office was determined in good measure by pressure brought to bear on Somoza by the U.S. government through its ambassador in Managua.

As it happens, at the beginning of 1945 expressions of support for a Somoza candidacy were heard once more in various parts of Nicaragua. In León, which Somoza visited in January to open a religious event (and was duly photographed with the bishop), Somoza listened to a speech that encouraged him to seek another term in office following the example of the U.S. president, Franklin D. Roosevelt, who had just won a fourth term. Afterward, a campesino who expressed his support for Somoza downplayed the legal obstacles that stood in Somoza's way, stating that what the rural workers needed was land and tools to work it, rural roads, schools, and technical advice. The demands that others made on the regime, he said, were alien to the campesino: "Those freedoms which others seek do not affect us, because in the countryside we do not have the same needs as city folk."[65] That is, it was not so important that Somoza ran the country as a dictator but that he got things done.

In the following months of 1945, town meetings and conclaves of Liberal party faithful produced the usual *actas de adhesión y proclamación* signed by hundreds of Somocistas.[66] Their contents were a rehash of the 1935–36 campaign, stressing Somoza's role in keeping the peace, guaranteeing the unity of the PLN, and promoting the country's progress. The mechanisms for raising the faithful's spirits were rather conventional, too. Money and liquor seem to have been distributed abundantly, especially in July when Somoza's candidacy was proclaimed frequently. In Nandaime, near Granada, the party assembled fireworks, musicians, and 150 liters of aguardiente to put people in the mood. In the department of Jinotega the expenses for the Somocista campaign were estimated at C$10,000 and 800 liters of aguardiente were dispensed, while in the department of Estelí each town received C$200 (then U.S.$40) for expenses and about 150 liters of liquor.[67]

By the middle of 1945, there was no evidence at all that Somoza intended to abide by his 1944 promise not to seek reelection. In August, Nelson Rockefeller, then acting secretary of state, told the dictator's ambassador in Washington, Guillermo Sevilla Sacasa, that Somoza's reelection plans would create trouble for the United States and Nicaragua, and that Somoza's withdrawal from the race would be much respected and applauded.[68] When the U.S. ambassador in Managua, Fletcher Warren, spoke to Somoza some days later about this matter, Somoza told him that the proclamations of his candidacy had been carried out by his friends in violation of the law, but because they were his friends he could not very well send them off to jail. He also allowed his name to appear for reelection, he said, in order to keep certain Guardia

Nacional officers under control and prevent them from pursuing their own political ambitions, thus endangering the peace. A third reason he gave Warren for allowing his candidacy to remain was that "unfortunately" there were people in government service who wished to make as much money as possible out of their positions; were he to announce that he would not be a candidate, these people would proceed to make as much money as possible from now until the end of his administration. And finally, he argued that as long as he was a candidate, the opposition would not be able to present a viable opponent before the electorate; therefore, when the time came, he would be in a position to indicate a candidate agreeable to him and to the various elements opposing him. "At that time, we can be sure (it was clear that the president meant himself and the United States when he said 'we') that the man selected will serve patriotically and loyally the interests of Nicaragua and the United States."[69] Before Warren left, Somoza mentioned to him that he was tired and did not want to run for reelection.

With the U.S. government giving every indication that it did not look kindly on Somoza's political ambitions, Somoza then began to gamble for time. At the end of August 1945, he met again with Warren and told him that he expected the United States to provide some suggestions as to who should be the candidate for the presidency. He said that the Conservatives realized perfectly well that the next president would be a Liberal and that Cuadra Pasos, the Conservative leader, would prefer that that Liberal be Somoza himself.[70] The State Department replied that nominations for presidential candidates were a purely Nicaraguan affair, but by October Somoza was telling the U.S. ambassador that the Liberal party would probably nominate him in any event and that he had to think of some way to get out of the predicament. He said that he would go to the United States in June of the following year to attend the graduation from West Point of his son, Anastasio Somoza Debayle, and remain there until after the election in February 1947. Meanwhile, he and the State Department would determine whether or not he would continue to stand as a candidate.[71]

It is clear that Somoza needed Washington's *approval* for his candidacy, although not its direct support. In contrast to his position in 1936, when absolute noninterference was Washington's policy, Somoza now faced an explicit request from the highest levels of the State Department that he step aside as president at the end of his term. Although no action was threatened if he did not comply, Somoza realized that the United States could deny recognition to a future government headed by him, which in turn might isolate him in

Latin America. More serious, such nonrecognition would reduce his legitimacy within Nicaragua, for if the United States indicated that it did not consider Somoza's continuation in office a prerequisite for Nicaragua's stability and peace, it would do nothing to prevent his ouster. And that was the fundamental message of the United States to Somoza: it was no longer essential from Washington's perspective that he continue to run the country.

Somoza, of course, thought otherwise. As Warren pointed out in a note to the State Department, Somoza believed that he was the only guarantee for peace and order in Nicaragua. He had convinced himself that it was his duty to Nicaragua and to its people that he be reelected, and he felt "intensely" that democracy in Nicaragua called for "different expressions and different procedures" from those in the United States.[72] Somoza also insisted that he had the support of 80 percent of the Nicaraguan people.[73] By mid-November, Somoza felt that he had gained sufficient strength vis-à-vis the State Department and flatly told the U.S. ambassador that he would seek the unified support of Liberals and Conservatives for his candidacy; he said that only if he was unable to get this bipartisan backing would he step down.[74]

At this moment, in the face of Somoza's determined attitude, the State Department turned up the heat. It sent Ambassador Warren a copy of a speech by the director of the Office of American Republic Affairs, Elliot O. Briggs, delivered at the University of Pennsylvania, in which the U.S. government made its position known on the dictatorial governments in Latin America. In brief, Briggs repeated that Washington's policy was one of nonintervention but that did not prevent the administration from speaking its mind on issues of "vital importance," in this case its concern about the fact that some governments in the hemisphere had not come to power through democratic processes and others had stayed in power through unconstitutional means or without the consent of the governed. Briggs also stated that the United States would "obviously feel a warmer friendship for and a greater desire to cooperate with those governments that rest on the periodically and freely expressed endorsement of the governed. . . . The policy of non-intervention does not imply the approval of local tyranny."[75] On 29 November Warren took this speech and other documentation reflecting the State Department's displeasure with the dictator's plans to Somoza. They had a long chat.

Somoza pretended that he did not understand what all the fuss was about and asked Warren for clarification. In the fashion of diplomats and in order not to give the impression of meddling in another country's internal affairs, Warren said that he had been instructed only to hand Somoza the documentation and that he should draw his own conclusions. Because Somoza insisted on clarification, Warren said that he only could give him his "personal" opinion (which was, of course, the same as that of the State Department): Somoza was a dictator. Somoza then asked why the State Department did not tell him exactly what it wanted him to do. Warren said that for four months now he had been trying to let him know his position with regard to the U.S. government, to which Somoza replied: "As a friend, I deserve better treatment from the State Department. It should tell me exactly, and I have invited it to tell me exactly, what it wants." He then wrote out a statement in pencil in which he made "the offer to the Department of State to renounce my candidacy within not more than 30 days and to devote myself during the remainder of my administration to working toward progress and to guarantee free elections in Nicaragua during the next electoral period." He explained to Warren that he wanted thirty days "in order to arrange matters and to show he is not yielding to pressure," but Warren interpreted this as "mere temporization."[76]

The State Department then told Warren that Somoza should know that it could not accept an offer from him to renounce his candidacy, which was a purely Nicaraguan internal matter that rested exclusively on Somoza's shoulders. When Somoza learned about the State Department's position, he "seemed hurt," Warren reported, and explained that he had been misunderstood. According to Warren's telegram to the State Department, Somoza had said: "I only wanted to let the U.S. as a friendly country (the elder brother of the continent, as I say) know beforehand my decision in hope that my action would help bring tranquility to Nicaragua. I did not aim to offend or harm the U.S. in any way. . . . You tell them I did not mean to harm or offend; I only wanted to be friendly."[77]

Two weeks later, a meeting was held in Washington attended by the Nicaraguan ambassador, Sevilla Sacasa; Assistant Secretary of State Spruille Braden; and the chief of the Division of Caribbean and Central American Affairs, William P. Cochran, Jr. Sevilla Sacasa reiterated Somoza's decision to refuse the nomination for another term as president, even though "many members" of the Guardia Nacional wished him to continue in office, as well as "large sectors" of the population. Braden said that he could not comment on Somoza's decision but that "the best way to practice democracy was to practice it," even though it be a difficult process. He insinuated that Somoza would continue, as a private citizen, to exercise considerable influence in Nicaragua's development toward democracy; he made it clear, too, that being a "private citizen" meant being away from the presidency and the Guardia Nacional, and away from active politics. That is, Braden wished Somoza out of the picture completely.[78] Somoza would shortly announce his withdrawal from the race, but getting him out of the Guardia Nacional would be a different matter.

Within the Guardia Nacional there was growing concern among the younger officers that Somoza's ambitions might lead to bigger and wider problems. The U.S. military attaché, Colonel Judson, had been talking to these officers about the need for a "nonpolitical" Guardia and of the possibility that the Guardia would not receive more military assistance until the Somoza problem was cleared up. Somoza's brother-in-law, Colonel Luis Manuel Debayle, even resigned his Guardia commission to protest Somoza's reelection campaign.[79] Because he faced emphatic U.S. disapproval and the danger of Guardia dissent, Somoza's decision to renounce his candidacy should have come as no surprise; if he insisted on his original plans, he would risk alienating his most reliable bases of support without having prepared dependable alternatives. The only road open was to hold elections as promised and try to make the best of them.

The Electoral Campaign of 1947

The holding of elections in 1947 required the regime to initiate some process of "apertura." In the first place, the Conservative party of Chamorro and Cuadra Pasos did not exist legally, since it had not participated in the 1936 and 1938 elections. According to the 1923 electoral law, if it wished to participate in the next election, it needed to petition the electoral board and present lists of signatures equivalent to 5 percent of the total votes cast in the last election. In order to facilitate the return of the Conservative party to the fold, the government decreed in August 1945 that the Liberals and the Nationalist Conservatives constituted the two principal parties but that the regime recognized the "historical and legal existence" of the Conservative party and would permit it to run candidates for office without going through the process of petition and signature gathering.[80]

In the second place, the state of siege that had been in effect since December 1941 was lifted in November 1945. In part, this meant that political activities could be reinitiated without prior approval from the authorities and opened the way for demonstrations, meetings, and propaganda that had been illegal up to then.[81] And in the third place, Somoza gradually lifted restrictions on the press, as he had promised the U.S. ambassador during one of their meetings in

November 1945. *La Prensa*, which had been closed down in mid-1944, finally reappeared in June 1946 after one year and ten months of silence.[82] William Krehm, *Time* magazine's correspondent for the region, admitted to Somoza that criticism of the regime and of the president was frequent and spirited in the press, although Somoza made it clear to Krehm that when this criticism surpassed the limits of "civic and journalistic decency," the government would take action.[83]

These concessions by the regime should not be construed as evidence of a wide and truly democratic political opening. The election of 1947 and the political campaign that preceded it would develop under the peculiar characteristics of Nicaraguan "democracy" with its own "different expressions and processes" (as Somoza described it to Ambassador Warren). One of these expressions was the control of the electoral machinery itself, which Somoza proceeded to tighten in September 1945. A number of reforms of the 1923 electoral law were approved by the Congress, including one that made it more difficult for new parties to register for the election by raising the number of signatures from 5 to 10 percent of the votes cast in the last election. The Conservative party had already been granted the right to register without presenting any signatures, so this measure was aimed at the Independent Liberals (PLI), who were in the process of organizing themselves to participate in the upcoming election. Another reform gave the president the right to name two of the three members of the national electoral board, which before had been named directly by the two main parties.[84]

"Freedom of the press" was another of those "different expressions" of Nicaraguan democracy. Regardless of Somoza's promise to respect this basic freedom of liberal democracy, it applied generally only to those groups and parties that were playing the game by the regime's rules. Thus, a university student paper, *El Universitario*, was harassed by the Guardia Nacional from the moment of its founding in December 1945 until it was closed down in February 1947.[85] Nor were the Independent Liberals allowed to make use of the press unhindered; in Chinandega, the jefe político made it known to all printers that they could not produce material for the PLI without the prior approval of his office.[86] On the other hand, *La Prensa* was allowed to print rather strong editorials without much interference.[87]

What all this boiled down to was the recognition on Somoza's part of two oppositions in Nicaragua. The Conservative party was the loyal opposition whose basic quarrel had to do with power and power sharing, and hardly anything to do with Nicaraguan society and its problems. That is, Somoza could get along with the Conservatives because they did not threaten his already considerable economic empire (even though they did criticize it) or attack the original foundations of his political power: the Guardia Nacional and his link with the United States. After all, the Conservatives had governed Nicaragua for eighteen years with direct U.S. economic and military support and it was the Conservative government of Adolfo Díaz that had agreed to the formation of the Guardia. The disloyal opposition of Independent Liberals and university students who praised Sandino, on the other hand, questioned the basic premises of Somocismo by declaring its origins and its practices immoral and illegitimate, thus suggesting that political opposition to Somoza was not only a matter of preventing his reelection but also of doing away entirely with the institutions of the Somocista state and its principal actors.

Other expressions of political opposition to Somoza were impeded when they originated from those groups identified with a disloyal opposition. When the Independent Liberals and the Conservatives requested permission to hold a number of *actos cívicos* on 24 November 1946 in order to celebrate the nomination of Dr. Enoc Aguado, their joint presidential candidate, the jefe político of Managua answered that he could not authorize these events because the 1923 electoral law only referred to *actos políticos*. The jefe político even objected to the term *concentración de masas*, defining it as Marxist in its origins and therefore subversive. He asked that they repeat their request "in simple terms," but it took two more letters from the political parties to get finally a rather grudging approval from the jefe político, in which he warned them to stay away from military barracks and police stations.[88]

The non-Somocista labor movement also felt the regime's animosity toward the end of 1946. When the Federación de Trabajadores de Managua asked for permission to hold a meeting in a Managua movie house to discuss the country's problems of unemployment and the high cost of living, the jefe político denied the request, arguing that the Federación did not explain in sufficient detail the nature of its proposed meeting. He added that its leaders were identified with political movements not recognized by the state (that is, the Socialist party).[89]

Within this restrictive environment, Somoza proceeded to gear up his Liberal party for the campaign. The Liberals, of course, did not feel the limits placed on political expression and participation as did the other parties. They were also by far the wealthiest political organization in the country. At the beginning of 1946, they had accumulated a campaign chest of C$1,189,581, most of it produced by the 5 percent "contribution" on salaries that all public employees paid to the

PLN. Because little had been spent in 1944 and 1945, the contributions had piled up in the party's accounts, ready for the political campaign.[90] The party also had access to the state banks, where it could request an overdraft or a loan.[91] Finally, it had Somoza himself, with all his personal wealth. In October 1946, Somoza announced that he had contributed C$100,000 to the PLN from his own pocket and expected that other Liberals would follow his example.[92] Because large outright contributions did not seem to have materialized, the PLN mounted a campaign to raise C$1,000,000 in the form of voluntary loans that would be paid back on a monthly basis with the 5 percent from the public payroll, "if and when the PLN should win the next elections."[93]

Information on PLN spending during the electoral campaign in 1946 and 1947 is unavailable. However, data for 1944 and 1945 contained in a report by the PLN treasurer to the Gran Convención of 1946 give some idea of how the party attempted to keep its membership enthusiastic about supporting the Somocista cause. About 17 percent of expenditures went to help individual Liberal party members in need (that is, someone who was "extremely poor and a good Liberal") and to pay for funeral expenses, although these were usually very small amounts that ranged between 15 and 30 córdobas (three and six dollars at the current exchange rate).[94] Still, the number of recipients was obviously too small (at most one hundred a month) to have influenced results at the voting booths. That is, patronage distributed by the PLN to its followers in the form of public employment or special favors was far more important than the party's direct charity, although it is conceivable that expenses for propaganda and the Liberal plebiscite of October 1945, which account for more than half of all expenditures, also included outright gifts or payments for services rendered or for expressions of loyalty.

Financial solvency was one important aspect of the strength of the PLN. But it was not sufficient in itself to get out the vote. In order to persuade party members to work and vote for the PLN, the party organization had to create a sense of urgency around the 1947 electoral process. As a first step, the party held a national plebiscite among its members in October 1945 to elect representatives to the Gran Convención to be held in January 1946. According to the party's leadership, 76,000 Liberals turned out to choose 101 delegates to the convention.[95] In some parts of the country, Independent Liberals tried to persuade people to refrain from voting by distributing leaflets and halting them on roads.[96] In other parts, the PLN organization had grown weak over the years and people were skeptical about continuing to support the party or Somoza.[97] In still other areas, there was stiff competition between opposing factions to elect the representatives to the convention.[98] Nevertheless, the results were a fairly accurate gauge of Liberal support and must have indicated to the party leadership where the biggest effort had to be made for the 1947 elections.

At the Liberal convention, Somoza confirmed his decision not to run for office, but no action was taken to name a new candidate. The reason was that Somoza still wanted to bring the dissident PLI members back into the party. During the first half of 1946 meetings were held between representatives of Somoza and the PLI to seek some kind of rapprochement, although a number of the PLI leaders opposed any dealings with Somoza.[99] By June, the PLI decided to cease discussions with Somoza. Somoza made one last try in July by proposing the names of Ildefonso Palma Martínez (who as a Liberal deputy had voted in 1934 against the blanket amnesty for the killers of Sandino) and Leonardo Argüello as candidates for the presidency; according to *La Prensa*, both Somocista and Independent Liberals were inclined to support Palma Martínez, a Liberal who, unlike Argüello, was not identified with the regime. In fact, on 10 July the PLI accepted Palma Martínez's candidacy in principle, although it continued to express distrust in Somoza.[100] When another Liberal convention gathered in León in August 1946, Somoza arranged for Argüello to be the candidate; on that occasion Argüello received 98 out of 101 votes.[101]

Picking Argüello as the candidate of the PLN was an attempt by Somoza to conciliate some of the dissident Liberals. Because Argüello had resigned his post as minister of the interior in 1944 following the June and July days, he had a claim to be independent of Somoza. Furthermore, he had been an important figure in the party since the 1910s, so he might be attractive to the older party stalwarts who were not beholden to Somoza directly. Finally, Somoza produced him at the León convention as a compromise candidate when neither of the two front-runners had the absolute majority of votes needed for nomination. For Somoza, Argüello seemed the candidate most easily "manageable" if he should reach the presidency, for Argüello was rather old and Somoza assumed that having been granted his life-wish to be president, he would be willing to repay his political debt.

Whereas the PLN was able to select its candidate for the presidency with a minimum of fuss, in large part because Somoza was pretty much in control of the party, the opposition went through a year of haggling and negotiating in an attempt to present Somoza with a united front. That this would be difficult enough was evidenced by the disunity of the opposition in the crisis days of 1944. The split of the Independent Liberals from the PLN initially did not help the opposition much, either, because the PLI identified with the Liberal tradition in Nicaraguan politics and continued to attempt a negotiated solution to its differences with the Somocista Liberals.[102] Even so, the opposition was talking early on about some sort of unified effort and a single candidate to face the PLN.

The two most important forces within the opposition were the Independent Liberals and the Conservatives, although the PLI had not yet demonstrated how many votes it had taken when it left the ranks of the Somocistas. But the PLI leaders at the time must have impressed the Conservatives, because they were strong enough to insist that the presidential candidate of both parties must be a Liberal, even though it was agreed that General Chamorro would select the candidate from a list prepared for his consideration by the PLI.[103] Chamorro returned to the country in late July 1946 after ten years in exile, and the following month the PLI and the Conservatives formally signed the pact that bound them to join together to achieve victory in the 1947 elections. Under the terms of this pact, they promised, among other things, to work to save democracy in Nicaragua from the threat of continued Somocista dictatorship. Subsequently, the Independent Liberals met in a convention in León and ratified the choice of an elderly Liberal, Dr. Enoc Aguado, as the presidential candidate of the two parties.[104] Thus, the candidates of the opposing forces were both Liberals separated by their support or rejection of Anastasio Somoza's designs for the country.

For the electorate, the confusion created by all the wheeling and dealing and by two Liberal candidates running for the presidency was hardly clarified by the political platforms set forth by each candidate. Argüello described his future government as one that would continue the work initiated by Somoza in the field of social welfare by establishing a social security system, land reform, price controls, and support for labor unions. He also proposed to create a national police force within the Guardia Nacional, while the Guardia proper would be entrusted with the purely military function of defending national sovereignty. Otherwise, he promised more and better things for everyone, including large-scale "counter-illiteracy campaigns."[105] Aguado's platform was not much different; he also talked about the need to remake the Guardia into a professional force not subject to the political fluctuations of the country, as well as advocating complete respect for all political liberties and social programs that would assist the poorer groups within the society. Perhaps the only significant difference in Aguado's program was his plan to decentralize the nation's political power by strengthening the municipal councils, but even that was but a Conservative desire of years past in response to Somoza's abolition of municipal autonomy.[106]

The main issue was, of course, Somoza himself and the continuation of Somocismo. Somoza seems to have maintained a fairly low profile during the electoral campaign. He spent most of September and October in Boston, undergoing treatment for an intestinal disorder, and returned to Managua with a renewed promise that the elections would be clean and fair. However, he said that he would continue to participate in the struggle against communism, which he defined as the new challenge faced by the American republics. This concern, he noted, should not be interpreted as a desire to further his political ambitions but rather as that of a citizen interested in seeing his work continued so that Nicaraguan democracy could firmly establish itself. He concluded: "In this endeavour I am sure to have the support of important sectors of the opposition itself, either for religious reasons, economic self-interest, or a common desire to guarantee a strictly democratic organization of the state."[107] It must have been clear, therefore, that a victory for Argüello would definitely leave Somoza in the government or at least close to the president. If anything, then, the election of 1 February 1947 would be a referendum on Somocismo, the results of which might indicate the wear and tear that the Somocista coalition had suffered after ten years in power.

The Electoral Outcome

The main problem in evaluating the 1947 electoral results is that this election is generally considered to have been the most fraudulent ever held under the governments of Somoza García. Still, it is possible to reach some tentative conclusions on the basis of abstentionism and reports from election observers. To begin with, electoral registration was held on 29 July and 4 August 1946. The total number of citizens who registered to vote came to 221,590.[108] The Conservative party immediately protested the registration procedures, claiming that the party's observers were expelled from about 80 percent of the registration places and that more than 50 percent of the Conservative voters failed to register because registration officials never processed their forms.[109] In addition, *La Prensa* estimated that some 50,000 registrations were fraudulent.[110] Whatever the case, the national electoral council proceeded to organize the election on the basis of its figures, which were not much larger than those for the 1936 election, when 219,668 had registered to vote.

Table 4.1 Electoral Participation, 1936 and 1947

Department	1936 Regist. Voters	1936 Votes Cast	%	1947 Regist. Voters	1947 Votes Cast	%
Boaco	9,250	4,161	(45.0)	10,055	7,783	(77.4)
Carazo	11,189	5,875	(52.5)	11,647	8,398	(72.1)
Chinandega	14,974	8,048	(53.8)	19,499	14,657	(75.2)
Chontales	20,387	5,605	(27.5)	13,297	9,829	(73.9)
Estelí	15,994	6,237	(40.0)	9,692	7,957	(82.1)
Granada	11,041	4,836	(43.8)	11,774	8,936	(75.9)
Jinotega	8,923	4,435	(49.7)	8,856	6,276	(70.9)
León	24,215	12,248	(50.6)	24,579	19,794	(80.5)
Madriz	7,081	4,490	(63.4)	7,354	5,792	(78.7)
Managua	30,596	13,230	(43.2)	35,893	28,664	(79.9)
Masaya	14,998	6,900	(46.0)	14,176	11,504	(81.2)
Matagalpa	22,008	12,778	(58.1)	23,193	16,703	(72.0)
Nva. Segovia	4,765	3,202	(67.2)	5,472	4,348	(79.5)
Rivas	8,797	4,139	(47.1)	8,941	6,912	(77.3)
Zelaya	15,450	13,235	(85.7)	17,162	12,515	(72.9)
Total	219,668	109,419	(49.8)	221,590	169,708	(76.6)

Sources: Data for 1936 are from Consejo Nacional de Elecciones, *La verdad electoral de 1936* (Managua: Talleres Nacionales, 1937), and Recaudación General de Aduanas, *Memoria para 1932.* Data for 1947 are from *LG/DO* 51,50 (6 March 1947) to 51,58 (15 March 1947).

Election day was followed by a spate of denunciations of massive fraud. *La Prensa* claimed that voter lists were incorrectly drawn up and that many people did not vote because they could not find their polling place; at other polling places, the results were totaled incorrectly after the poll watchers were chased away.[111] At still others, the Guardia Nacional picked up the ballot boxes, which never appeared again.[112] A look at the official figures indicates that irregularities were present from the moment that voter registration began. (See Table 4.1.) In some departments, the number of voters who registered was substantially down from 1936. In Chontales, for example, voter registration dropped by nearly 35 percent, even though that department was heavily Conservative and could have been expected to register as many voters as possible. The drop for Estelí of nearly 40 percent also seems excessive. In most other departments, the increase in registered voters from 1936 to 1947 was

Table 4.2 Election Results, 1936 and 1947

| | 1936 | 1947 | | | |
Department	PLN–Natl. Cons.	PLN–Natl. Cons.	%	PLI-Cons.	%
Boaco	4,160	3,916	(50.3)	3,867	(49.7)
Carazo	5,868	4,703	(56.0)	3,695	(44.0)
Chinandega	8,046	10,674	(72.8)	3,983	(27.2)
Chontales	5,605	4,979	(50.2)	4,950	(49.8)
Estelí	6,223	5,105	(67.2)	2,492	(32.8)
Granada	4,835	5,036	(56.4)	3,900	(43.6)
Jinotega	4,435	4,658	(74.2)	1,618	(25.8)
León	12,239	14,838	(75.0)	4,956	(25.0)
Madriz	4,490	4,902	(84.6)	890	(15.4)
Managua	13,204	14,076	(49.1)	14,588	(50.9)
Masaya	6,871	6,227	(53.9)	5,331	(46.1)
Matagalpa	12,764	10,568	(63.3)	6,135	(36.7)
Nva. Segovia	3,202	2,988	(68.7)	1,360	(31.3)
Rivas	4,067	3,437	(49.7)	3,475	(50.3)
Zelaya	13,221	8,851	(70.7)	3,664	(29.3)
Total	109,230	104,958	(61.8)	64,904	(38.2)

Sources: Data for 1936 are from Consejo Nacional de Elecciones, *La verdad electoral de 1936* (Managua: Talleres Nacionales, 1937), and Recaudación General de Aduanas, *Memoria para 1932.* Data for 1947 are from *LG/DO* 51,50 (6 March 1947) to 51,58 (15 March 1947).

minimal. Among the traditionally Liberal departments, only Chinandega and Managua showed a significant increase in voter registration. On the national level, the increase in registered voters was less than 2,000 over that of 1936, as if a concerted effort had been made to restrict the registration of opposition voters as much as possible and at the same time foster the registration of Liberals loyal to the Somocista camp.

Even if massive fraud had been perpetrated, the results for Argüello (and Somoza) were not heartening; the PLN-Nationalist Conservative ticket received nearly 5,000 votes less than in 1936. (See Table 4.2.) The Liberal-Nationalist Conservative alliance got fewer votes in nine of the fifteen departments and barely held its own in four others; only in Chinandega and León, traditionally Liberal, did the PLN increase its support by a little over 2,500 voters in each case. On the other hand, the PLI-Conservative coalition won by small margins in Managua and Rivas and nearly won in Chontales and Boaco; all of these, with the exception of Managua, were Conservative strongholds.

How are we to gauge the level of fraud, if that is at all possible? The results for the PLN-Nationalist Conservative alliance need not have been inflated. The Liberals alone registered over 136,000 voters under their party label during voter registration in 1946.[113] Furthermore, that Liberal-Nationalist Conservative votes dropped from the 1936 level would indicate that not much effort was made, if at all, to manipulate the results from that angle. Most likely, it was the opposition that got shortchanged, although the opposition gave the PLN-Nationalist Conservatives only 37,532 votes to their 107,591, a result as unlikely as that offered by the regime.[114] What is clear is that the regime had suffered a decline in its political strength as far as the voting public was concerned. The schism of the Independent Liberals must have sapped the PLN of a good number of votes, and the labor movement, split as it was between Somocistas and anti-Somocistas, could not give the Argüello candidacy much support.[115]

The regime's decline in support at the polls did not necessarily mean a decline in its real strength, however. The Guardia Nacional was still loyal to its Jefe Director, although some officers were concerned about continuismo somocista and would abandon Somoza during the ephemeral Argüello presidency. The business community, which Somoza generally had favored since the banking and currency reforms of the early 1940s, had come through the war years in a climate of growing prosperity as the U.S. demand for Nicaraguan exports increased. There was some criticism of the national bank's restrictive credit policies and of the typical bureaucratic problems that business people faced when they tried to get foreign exchange to pay for imports.[116] At one point, the Banco Nacional was criticized roundly for not implementing the Max banking reforms in full, especially in regard to placing qualified people in key positions and keeping the bank's operations free of political influence.[117] This last was probably a veiled commentary on Somoza's stranglehold on credit operations, as was denounced more openly by businessmen associated with the PLI. But if the business community was critical of Somoza's government and his growing economic empire, it was careful to voice its opinions in private; in public business associations at most suggested improvements in the operations of the economic system.[118]

All in all, the reaction to the electoral results and Argüello's victory was rather limited. In León, a group of PLI and Conservative leaders issued a flier in which they denounced Somoza for "taking the polls by force," thus invalidating Argüello's election; they claimed that Aguado had received 95 percent of the votes cast. Argüello was nothing more than a representative of the dictatorship, they said, so that the struggle for democracy was just beginning and it would continue until freedom was obtained.[119] And in Masatepe, a small town to the southeast of Managua in the coffee-growing district, about two hundred opponents of the Liberal camp threatened to disrupt a victory party being held by some Argüellistas. They clashed with a contingent of Guardias who intervened, with the result that one Guardia was relieved of his rifle and others were hit with stones. Later in the day, the group insulted the Guardia patrols with the very offensive epithet of "hijos de la gran puta" while they cheered General Chamorro.[120]

These limited expressions of disgust with the Somoza regime were nothing compared to the problems that Argüello himself would create. Between his electoral victory on 1 February and his accession to office on 1 May 1947, the president-elect met with diverse political, labor, and business groups, as well as with officers of the Guardia Nacional, to hear their comments and suggestions on the new government's policies. His speech before the Congress on the day he assumed the presidency reflected a decision to head a government of a different character and policies than those of the past. He said he would seek to eliminate the abuses committed by previous governments, especially in the bureaucracy, where private interests had displaced public service. He did recognize that the Somoza government had made significant improvements in the country's infrastructure and social services, but that more had to be done, especially in the field of education and literacy.[121] In general, Argüello espoused a conventional liberal program and cautiously indicted Somoza's regime for presumably deviating from true liberal principles.

Once in office, Argüello proceeded to effect changes in personnel, moves that sought to undermine Somoza's hold on the bureaucracy and the Guardia Nacional. He issued orders for the immediate closing of all illegal games, such as lotteries and gambling; this decision affected a number of public employees and Guardia officers who were on the take. The general manager of the Ferrocarril del Pacífico, an old Somoza crony who allowed the railway's supplies and machine shops to be used by Somoza enterprises, was replaced by a North American with experience in the business.[122] Argüello also wanted to demilitarize those public services that Somoza had put under Guardia control during the war years, such as the public health service, the customs, the communications network, and the railroad itself; Somoza wished to retain this measure because it extended his authority beyond that of Jefe Director of the Guardia alone.[123] The bottom line, of course, was the Guardia Nacional itself. Argüello was well aware that Somoza's power would be little diminished if he retained his position as Jefe Director. In April, he apparently had come to an agreement with Somoza to the effect that as president he would not alter the officer corps of the Guardia at all.[124] Somoza meanwhile drummed up support for his own position within the Guardia; recruits and officers honored Somoza with banquets and speeches in which they promised to follow him to the end.[125]

The breaking point between the two men came when the Congress, firmly under Somoza's control, proceeded to appoint the three *designados a la presidencia*, who would be directly in line to replace the president should he leave office. Needless to say, the three so named were Somocistas. Argüello, in turn, replaced on his own initiative the director of communications, the Managua chief of police, the inspector general of the army, the head of the general staff, and the commanding officer of the presidential guard with men loyal to him, thus violating the agreement he had reached with Somoza in April.[126] On May 25, Argüello informed Somoza that he was to leave the country and that his resignation as Jefe Director would be announced immediately afterward. Somoza apparently agreed to go but asked for a few days to arrange his affairs. That was more than enough time for him to organize the overthrow of Argüello, which came in the early morning hours of the following day when the Guardia Nacional took control of the National Palace and the military headquarters at the Campo de Marte and cut off the communications of the presidential residence. Argüello refused to resign as president but finally agreed to go to the Mexican embassy as an exile. He took with him the seals and sash of office, claiming to the bitter end that he was still president of the republic.[127]

A week after the coup, the Congress convened and resolved to fire Argüello on the grounds that he had demonstrated his incapacity to run the government, he had refused to endorse the Congress's choice of the designados, and he had sown divisions within the Guardia Nacional thereby threatening its unity and discipline.[128] To replace him, the Congress named Benjamín Lacayo Sacasa, a Somoza puppet. Although the reasons and the circumstances were different, 1947 was similar to 1936, when Sacasa was eased out of the presidency. By keeping control of the coercive apparatus of the state, Somoza set down his own rules of the game and continued to play with advantage.

Conclusion

The basic problem faced by the Somoza regime in 1944 had to do with the breakdown of the political consensus that had been developed since the overthrow of Sacasa in 1936. For the first time, open opposition to the regime was expressed in the streets of Nicaragua and the legitimacy of the state itself was called into question. However, the character of the demonstrations both against and in support of Somoza had more to do with the regime than with the fundamental organization of the state. The criticism voiced by the dissident Liberals and some Conservatives thus did not include the elimination of the more important state institutions, such as the Guardia Nacional, the national banking and railroad system, or even the two-party system itself. And those who supported the regime did so out of party allegiance or because they sought specific concessions from Somoza (as in the case of the labor movement). The crisis of 1944 was not as serious as might have been the case if opposition to the regime had been combined with a rejection of the basic organization of the state.

Furthermore, the breakdown of the political consensus was quite limited; in addition to its spontaneous origins and limited organization, it generally involved urban groups and was led by middle-class politicians and activists whose contact with the masses was slight and not too friendly. Other than overthrowing Somoza, the movement never offered anything concrete other than "democracy" and "freedom," terms that Somoza himself had used in the past to identify his government with the struggle against fascism and totalitarianism. For the people who witnessed the struggle, the choice between Somoza and his opponents was not at all clear. And in the minds of the labor leaders who sought an improvement in the lot of the workers, Somoza even was perceived as progressive or, conversely, Somoza's opponents were classified as reactionary and oligarchic.

In the face of this opposition, the regime did two very simple things. In the first place, it engaged in repressive measures to set the limits to the opposition it could tolerate, both by sending out its soldiers and shock troops to control the street demonstrations and by placing administrative limits on the freedom of expression. In this manner it proved its willingness to act drastically while at the same time keeping the repressive measures within bounds, that is, at a level proportional to the threat the regime itself faced. Somoza could boast that no one had been killed in the troubles and that those detained were released quickly except for some who were sent into exile within or outside of the country.

The second thing the regime did involved a longer-term policy of stretching out hands to both supporters and opponents in order to re-create the consensus of the previous decade. The political opponents within the Conservative party were offered a chance to measure their strength with the Somocista Liberals in an election they perceived would be honest enough to warrant participation. Even the dissident Liberals in the PLI accepted the challenge and were forceful enough to get one of their own, Enoc Aguado, chosen as a common candidate for a combined opposition effort. The labor movement, a strange hybrid of Somocista and Marxist tendencies, accepted the promise of a labor code as a symbol of good faith and potential opportunities for the future. The PLN, with better funding and a newly strengthened organization, could be counted on to deliver the votes of the faithful; in addition, by selecting a member of the old guard of the party as their presidential candidate, the Liberals might expect to recover some of the ground they had lost with the split of the PLI. Finally, Somoza had to reconcile his own position within the Nicaraguan political system with his most influential erstwhile backer, the United States. Somoza's fawning and wheedling in the presence of the U.S. ambassador need not be interpreted as evidence of fear or weakness; he simply was acknowledging the huge power that stood behind the ambassador, a power that could not be challenged but from which some concessions might be extracted. And because Somoza knew that the United States was more concerned about the prospects of political breakdown and violence than with his own continuation in office, he was able to play for time.

In the end, therefore, none of the groups opposing Somoza went so far as demanding his resignation as president before the end of his term as a precondition for reaching a settlement. Once the electoral alternative had been accepted by the Conservatives and the Independent Liberals, once the opposition's media (*La Prensa*) had been reinstated, once the labor movement had been awarded the labor code, and once the United States had become convinced that Nicaraguan stability would not be threatened by Somoza's insistence on remaining in office until 1947, Somoza could give up his reelectionist ambitions without weakening his political position.

Others might have perceived that Somoza had been put on the defensive by the events of June and July of 1944 and that his eventual decision not to seek another term in office was a reflection of a significant decline in his regime's strength. But the opposition of Conservatives and Independent Liberals could do nothing to reverse the fraudulent electoral outcome in 1947. Nor could President Argüello subvert Somoza's control over the Liberal party and the Guardia Nacional without inviting his own ouster from office. Somoza was president no longer, but he never ceased directing the Guardia Nacional and the Liberal party and, through them, the apparatus of the state.

5 COURTING CONSERVATIVES & CAPITALISTS

· · · · · · · · · · · · · · · ·

Argüello's overthrow was a completely unexpected event. The speed with which Argüello and Somoza had attempted to eliminate the other left most of the country's political actors on the sidelines. It was not until Argüello sought asylum in the Mexican embassy one day after the coup against him that the repercussions of and reactions to his ouster became evident. Within the country, diverse groups reacted in a variety of ways, ranging from cautious support for a political solution to outright rejection of any deals with Somoza. Abroad, the most important response was that of the United States, but the reaction to events in Nicaragua spread to practically all the Latin American republics. Therefore, Somoza had to maneuver on two levels to recover what legitimacy was left the regime after the electoral fraud and the Argüello fiasco. That he was able to impose a new government and conserve his position as Jefe Director of the Guardia Nacional suggests a developed skill not only in weighing political options but also in acting quickly and decisively to remain ahead of his opponents.

The Creation of a New Government

The first order of business that Somoza faced was the replacement of Argüello with a president who would finish out Argüello's term. Benjamín Lacayo Sacasa took over the job as *Primer Designado* but that apparently did not suffice in terms of political legitimacy. On 6 June, Lacayo Sacasa announced that elections would be called to form a Constituent Assembly that would reconcile the two historic parties and reestablish political concord in the country. A few days later, a government decree set elections for 3 August 1947 in which only the Nationalist Liberals and the traditional Conservatives would be allowed to participate.[1] The regime was attempting to engage the Conservatives in a political solution to Argüello's overthrow by starting out with a clean slate in the form of a national agreement between the two principal parties that would not in itself justify the coup but would bury it in the past.

The Conservatives initially showed interest in playing the game. The executive committee of the party met and agreed to talk with Provisional President Lacayo, while at the same time it announced that it did not support the demand of the Independent Liberals that Argüello be returned to office as the precondition for any political settlement. The only thing that the Conservatives wanted was a guarantee that the elections would be clean and the results respected. When the Conservative party leadership met with Lacayo on 18 June, they requested a postponement of the date for elections so as to give them more time to organize. They also demanded a complete overhaul of the electoral rolls to eliminate all irregularities, which in the opinion of the Conservatives were so numerous as to invalidate any election. After the meeting, General Chamorro announced that Lacayo had not accepted the Conservatives' demands and that, therefore, the Conservatives would abstain from participating in the elections.[2] An attempt some days later by the Conservative leader, Carlos Cuadra Pasos, to arrange a meeting between Somoza and Chamorro to seek a political agreement failed to materialize.[3]

While Somoza handled the Conservatives through political means, he dealt with the labor and political left movements through repression. A decree of 5 July 1947, signed by Provisional President Lacayo, sent the main leaders of the Socialist party off to internal exile on the island of Ometepe in Lake Nicaragua. They were not accused of doing anything illegal except belonging to a political group that espoused a foreign ideology prohibited by the Constitution. The danger was perceived in terms of what they might do, such as disturb the public order, interrupt the "peaceful" reorganization of the state's institutions then in progress, and introduce communist ideas that could "subvert the established social and political system."[4] By mid-1947, then, Somoza had broken entirely with the left and now looked to an alliance with the Conservatives as the most efficient way of reaching a new national consensus that would guarantee the survival of the regime.

Not even the Guardia emerged unscathed from the Argüello episode. When the deposed president went into exile at the Mexican embassy, eleven officers of the Guardia went with him.[5] Somoza presumably purged some 150 additional officers who opposed his continued direction of the Guardia or who had expressed support for Argüello's policies.[6] But he retained his position as Jefe Director, which was never again challenged in any serious manner. As Jefe

Director, and as minister of war in Lacayo's and succeeding cabinets, he remained in direct control of the Guardia and pretty much in control of the government as well.

With the threat of possible trouble from the left defused and the Guardia under control, the elections for the Constituent Assembly were held as scheduled on 3 August. However, the results appear to have been so meager that the official tallies were not even published in La Gaceta/Diario Oficial. In Managua, according to La Prensa, no more than 5 percent of the electorate bothered to vote, most of these public employees who were concerned about keeping their posts.[7] One measure of the degree of voter apathy was the number of voters who registered in the department of Chinandega on 7 and 14 July 1947. According to the president of the departmental executive committee of the PLN, 6,058 Liberals and 1,813 Conservatives registered, giving a grand total of 7,871.[8] Compared to the 19,499 who registered to vote in the 1947 presidential election, only 40 percent did so for the Constituent Assembly election in a heavily Liberal department.

Undoubtedly, the speed with which the regime called the election prevented a more thorough campaign to get out the vote, although the Liberals' main concern was to hold the election as soon as possible and not worry too much about how many showed up at the polls. Nor was the election itself that important to the electorate, since there was no choice but to vote for the PLN or the Nationalist Conservatives, who were reactivated by Somoza in view of the Conservatives' abstention. In any case, Somoza got the Constituent Assembly he needed to give the change in government a facade of legitimacy. Lacayo Sacasa stressed this point on the day he opened the Assembly's discussions. He said that both the Conservatives and the Liberals were of the opinion that a Constituent Assembly was the solution and that even though the Conservatives decided not to participate in the election, that part of the population that desired to express its opinion was free to do so. In addition, his government respected the citizens' liberties, even though a couple of newspapers had to be closed down for expressing "subversive" opinions and a group of individuals (the Socialist leaders) were confined to the island of Ometepe for engaging in "communist propaganda" and planning "terrorist" activities in Managua and other cities in the country. All in all, Lacayo said, the country was at peace and the government was in control of the situation.[9]

The installation of the Constituent Assembly came none too soon. In the wake of Argüello's overthrow, no country in Latin America or the United States was willing to recognize Lacayo Sacasa's government. More serious was the

United States's decision to stop all military assistance and training to the Guardia Nacional and to remove the American director of the Nicaraguan Military Academy.[10] Furthermore, it was not clear if the Nicaraguan delegation to the Rio conference just then about to begin would be seated as the official representation of a legally constituted government.

Somoza's concern with the United States's position had emerged in early August, when he held talks with the U.S. ambassador and offered to produce a new Constitution in line with North American worries about regional security and military strength. He specifically promised to include provisions to outlaw all "Communist propaganda and activities" and to empower the Nicaraguan executive to allow military bases on national soil in moments of continental emergency.[11] By the time the Rio conference opened on 21 August, the Constituent Assembly had elected a new president of Nicaragua to complete Argüello's term; he was Victor Román y Reyes, an elderly gentleman and an uncle of Somoza, whose inaugural speech to the Constituent Assembly on 20 August was notable only for a call for national unity, in particular to wayward Liberals and recalcitrant Conservatives.[12] The United States still did not recognize the new government, but Somoza's control of the situation was more than evident. The Department of State so informed the U.S. embassy in Managua: "whether we like it or not," said the department's cable, the government of Román y Reyes had all "the attributes and qualities of stable de facto government." In addition to maintaining public order in Nicaragua, the government was meeting all its international obligations. Therefore, the United States had to ask whether it would continue to be stable, even though it was a puppet of Somoza. The cable concluded that there was little chance of strictly constitutional or more representative government in the future.[13] Nonetheless, the United States withheld diplomatic recognition for another nine months, until after the Pan American conference in Bogotá in April 1948.[14]

The pressure exerted from abroad by diplomatic nonrecognition was the opportunity that a number of Conservatives had been waiting for to attempt a coup de force. As coup attempts go in Nicaraguan history, it was one of the sorriest: on 7 September, small bands of armed men attacked the mining operation of La India to the north of Chinandega and the port of Muelle de los Bueyes on the Rama River in Zelaya department. The Guardia Nacional lost a number of soldiers to the attackers but quickly chased them away and proceeded to hunt them down. A week later, the Guardia General Staff informed the country that the leaders of the attacks had been captured and that they had confessed to links with the Conservative party, especially with General Chamorro, who supposedly had promised them abundant rewards once the coup succeeded.[15] Chamorro, in fact, went into hiding and remained there until he requested and received a safe conduct from the government to leave Nicaragua on 27 September.[16] Others were not so lucky: reports from Chinandega, Granada, Masaya, and various other parts of the country mentioned numerous arrests of Conservatives and Independent Liberals. However, the government seems to have been satisfied that members of the PLI were not involved in the coup attempt and these individuals, including Carlos Pasos, were freed at the beginning of October.[17] The Conservatives who remained behind bars were released in November after a delegation from the party met with Somoza.[18] And on 29 November, the government finally let former president Argüello leave for exile in Mexico, where he died two weeks later.[19]

In a matter of six months, then, the entire Argüello episode and its sequel of a Conservative boycott of elections, an attempted coup, and diplomatic isolation had been managed successfully and the regime emerged relatively intact from it all. Now it was only a matter of tying the loose ends together and organizing a new coalition to guarantee the country and the regime a period of political calm. In this sense the initiative had already been taken by Carlos Cuadra Pasos when he wrote to Somoza and Chamorro on 30 June 1947.

Softening Up the Conservatives

Cuadra Pasos, as the leader of the so-called Civilista faction of the Conservative party, was concerned primarily with the problems of national unity and the danger of popular restlessness that he detected at moments when the government was perceived as weak or indecisive or, worse still, illegitimate. In his mind, national unity could only come about through a consensus of the country's two main parties and their respective leaders, Somoza and Chamorro. However, he also considered the existence of a third force, the Guardia Nacional, which was beholden to one of the two national leaders and his party. In his words:

> . . . the current situation is confused by the following: absence of legitimate supreme authority; a de facto government within the international order; a strong-willed opposition, which becomes more daring with each passing day; an Army, the central element, moderated in its actions to date by its discipline and which keeps the peace through the fear pro-

duced by its military efficiency. This situation is aggravated by the disturbances resulting from the growing unconformity of the masses, expressed
in methods unknown in our previous civic strife (which even in their
barbarity reflected a sense of chivalry); the increasing probabilities of civil
war; the decline in our economy and the threat of hunger. Up to the
present, a number of freedoms have served as safety valves for the venting
of political passions: freedom of the press, relative freedom of association,
and freedom of expression. But the guarantor of this apparent peace is the
Army, controlled in its deadly procedures by its good discipline.[20]

For Cuadra Pasos, the threat of anarchy was real enough, particularly in
view of the illegitimate character of Argüello's election, his subsequent overthrow, and the new Lacayo government. Only a new government elected
through free balloting could revitalize the national consensus and provide it
with the respect and the legitimacy it so urgently needed. But in order to
guarantee a free election, it would be necessary to take the Guardia Nacional
out of politics, which Cuadra Pasos proposed to accomplish by a promise from
both parties that its institutional structure and permanence would not be
altered.[21] To reach this objective, and to prevent any outbreak of violence
("perturbación," as Cuadra Pasos put it), it was imperative that Somoza and
Chamorro get together as soon as possible.

Somoza's response was positive, at least in terms of meeting with Chamorro
under the sponsorship of both principal parties. But General Chamorro, who
probably had more quarrels with Cuadra Pasos than with Somoza, replied in
very cautious terms. His interpretation of the political moment in Nicaragua
was that the Liberals had been greatly weakened by the departure of the
Independent Liberals and that Somoza, therefore, was the leader of only "a very
small number of eastern Liberals" (of the eastern part of the country, where the
Liberal party was weak to begin with). Furthermore, Chamorro insisted that
Argüello also must be a party to any arrangement, as Argüello still retained
extensive international sympathies. In sum, Chamorro believed that he should
get together with Somoza *and* Argüello to organize a free election and proceed
with the transformation of the Guardia Nacional into an apolitical body as
stipulated by the agreement signed twenty years earlier by the U.S. chargé
d'affaires, Dana Munro, and then foreign minister, Carlos Cuadra Pasos.[22]

Chamorro's rejection of the Cuadra Pasos proposal by insisting on conditions that Somoza would never agree to was in line with his belief that the time
was ripe for a coup de force. He must have believed that U.S. disapproval of the

overthrow of Argüello had weakened Somoza's control of the Guardia and threatened his leadership of a divided PLN.[23] Thus, he probably reasoned that a few armed attacks against Guardia posts would persuade the populace to support a rebellion, as well as induce Guardia officers to break with Somoza and overthrow him. Instead, the utter failure of this attempt resulted in Chamorro's loss of control of the Conservative party, or at least opened the way for the Civilistas to take the political initiative after the commotion following the uprising had subsided. Once again, it was Cuadra Pasos who offered to reach an agreement with Somoza and seek a political accommodation that would bring long-term peace to Nicaragua.

On 23 December 1947, Cuadra Pasos wrote to Somoza and offered his analysis of the national situation. He expressed his deep concern about the absence of diplomatic recognition for the Román y Reyes government, as well as at the increasing number of Nicaraguan exiles who were moving about in Central America and Mexico looking for arms with which to overthrow the Nicaraguan government. In his opinion, the main reason for this situation was the illegitimate nature of the Román y Reyes government, but with the recent death of former president Argüello, neither of the opposing political factions had a greater claim to legitimacy than the other. It was therefore necessary and possible to work for a new national consensus and pave the way for a legitimate regime on the basis of impartial and honest elections (in his words, "that electoral freedom or a fiction close enough to that freedom which has calmed public passions in the past"). He conceded that the Román y Reyes government could remain in office for another two years while the national election was organized, but that it would be necessary to allow the Conservative party a share of government posts in order for it to supervise and guarantee that everything be done correctly. Thus, the Conservatives should be given positions on the national electoral board, as well as in the legislative and judicial branches of government. These measures, together with a national amnesty for political offenses committed up to that time, would calm the country's political passions and lead to diplomatic recognition.[24]

Somoza's reply was generally receptive, although he stated that Cuadra Pasos's worries about the possibility of violence and anarchy within Nicaragua were exaggerated because the Guardia Nacional remained disciplined and in total control: "I am able to assure you that the opposition does not possess the necessary force to unleash a civil war that would lead the people to a massacre and jeopardize the stability of the legitimate government." Somoza said that he was more concerned that the possibility of civil unrest might lead to the penetration of communist ideology and practices, which could jeopardize continental security. Otherwise, he rejected Cuadra Pasos's belief that the Román y Reyes government was illegitimate and mentioned the diplomatic recognition just then extended to his government by Costa Rica and the Dominican Republic as proof of that legitimacy. Nevertheless, he said he welcomed the opportunity to reach a political agreement with the more "moderate" elements of the Conservative party that would lead to national elections in which each of the "historic" parties would gauge the real measure of its popular base of support. He concluded by inviting Cuadra Pasos to draw up a draft of a pact to lay the framework for those elections.[25]

By the beginning of 1948, then, the basis for a comprehensive political agreement was taking shape. The Constituent Assembly was about to finish writing the new Constitution and the Conservatives, denied the leadership of Chamorro and his more confrontational policies, could only look to the moderate and conciliatory Cuadra Pasos and his faction for guidance. The labor movement and leftist groups had been disbanded, jailed, and exiled. No other political options had a chance of success and military insurrection had just proved futile. Without a doubt, Somoza was operating from a position of considerable strength, as could be evidenced in the provisions of the new Constitution and the Somoza–Cuadra Pasos pact of January and February 1948.

The new Constitution was in most respects a rehash of the previous document of 1939; it did, however, include some significant changes as well as a number of symbolic concessions to the Conservatives. In the first place, the Constitution's preamble invoked the name of God, one of the Conservatives' constant preoccupations ever since the Liberals struck the divinity from the country's chief political document. In the second place, it did not include the provision found in the 1939 document that empowered the state to divide unused portions of latifundia and foster the growth of small- and middle-sized landholdings; the Conservative cattle barons considered this provision a constant threat to their properties. Of interest to the United States was the outright prohibition of all communist and fascist parties, as well as those with international connections. Another special provision made it easy for the Nicaraguan Congress to allow the passage of foreign troops across the country and the installation of foreign military bases on national territory in case of a continental emergency. And of special interest to Somoza was Article 283, which granted the Jefe Director of the Guardia Nacional exclusive control over all transfers and appointments within the Guardia, about which he needed to inform only the president of the republic.[26] Doubtless, the Argüello episode had taught Somoza that the only person he could trust in Guardia Nacional matters was himself.

The new Constitution "legitimized" the Román y Reyes government by extending its term of office to May 1952 and by turning the Constituent Assembly into the regular legislative branch of government up to April of the same year. However, the legitimacy accorded to the government by the Constitution was less important than that provided by the Somoza–Cuadra Pasos agreement of 26 February 1948. By appearing to bring together the two main political groups in the country, the agreement opened the way for the renewal of diplomatic recognition by the American republics and for the participation of the Conservatives in governmental functions, which gave the appearance of national, bipartisan unity. In fact, Cuadra Pasos signed the agreement on behalf of "a considerable group of conservatives who have remained in opposition," and not as an official representative of the Conservative party as such. Still, the agreement established as a primary objective the holding of free elections within three years, by which time it was hoped that the Conservatives, under the persuasion of Cuadra Pasos, would become an official party to the agreement.[27]

As suggested by Cuadra Pasos's letter of 23 December 1947 to Somoza, the agreement stated that every effort would be made to guarantee fair elections in 1952. To begin with, the Conservatives would be consulted on the formation of a new national electoral council and the corresponding departmental councils. Furthermore, the Guardia Nacional would maintain a strict neutrality during the electoral process under the supervision of a bipartisan commission that would recommend appropriate measures to this end. A general amnesty also would be decreed to free all those in prison for political offenses and to permit the political exiles to return to Nicaragua. In this manner, the Conservatives could aspire to win a significant share of political power in the country, if not the presidency of the republic itself. But the agreement went even further: it gave the Conservatives an immediate share of governmental posts through a number of executive decisions and legislative legerdemain.

First, under the terms of the agreement, seven deputies and four senators of the Conservative party "in opposition" would be "elected" in a special election to be held shortly. Provision for this election had been included in the recent Constitution, but the agreement expressly stated that the Liberals would refrain from participating "in order to allow for the election of the Conservative representatives from the opposition" (to distinguish them from the Nationalist Conservatives, who were not in opposition). Second, the Liberals would see to it that one vacancy appeared in the Supreme Court and in each appellate court, such positions to be filled by Conservative lawyers. Third, the Conservative party would be entitled to a "just participation" on the boards of directors of the state's banks and public service institutions, as well as in all special diplomatic missions and delegations to international conferences. Fourth, a majority of the municipal councils in those departments where the Conservatives got the most votes in the 1932 presidential election and where they presumably retained a majority of the votes would be turned over to the Conservatives. Finally, the implementation of the above provisions was contingent on diplomatic recognition of the Román y Reyes government by the rest of the governments of the continent; if this recognition did not materialize, the agreement would not take effect.

The agreement, thus, gave something to everyone. It confirmed the legitimacy of the Román y Reyes government in the eyes of at least part of the opposition and projected this recognition and legitimacy to the international sphere. It contained written guarantees that the next election would be *really* free and honest and gave the Conservatives a limited representation in local government according to the results of what could be construed as the last free and honest election in the country's history. It also guaranteed the Conservatives a minority representation in the legislative and judicial branches of government and the possibility of putting some of their people (or at least those of Cuadra Pasos) into publicly owned enterprises; in this manner, the Cuadra Pasos Conservatives could aspire to control part of the patronage the regime dispensed and thereby strengthen their own following within the Conservative party. That all this was done with the highest patriotic zeal of guaranteeing the country's peace and prosperity did not alter the basic fact that it was a political deal that provided mutual advantages to both signatories.

So it was perceived by General Chamorro, who blasted the agreement in a communiqué he issued in Guatemala City on 2 March 1948. He said the agreement lacked any popular support because it was signed by a representative of a "group" of Conservatives and by the leader of a Liberal party that was only a shell of its former self since the departure of the Independent Liberals. In Chamorro's view, the only political alliance with real popular support was the one that won the 1947 elections: the Conservative-PLI coalition. He therefore could only reject the Somoza–Cuadra Pasos agreement out of hand and call for continued opposition to Somocismo.[28] In fact, he had no other options.

The remaining groups opposing Somoza were in a similar bind. Their impotence was best reflected in a little booklet they had published in Bogotá in the month preceding the Ninth Pan American Conference that was to be held in that city in April 1948. Under the collective name of Frente Nacional pro Libertad de Nicaragua, the Chamorrista Conservatives and Independent Liberals and two organizations unheard of until then, the Asociación Nacional Femenina and the Unión Democrática de Obreros y Campesinos, described and denounced the Somocista regime in terms of its predatory business practices and its disrespect for basic democratic freedoms. They linked Argüello's overthrow directly to his attempt to cut the umbilical cords that nurtured Somoza's businesses at the expense of the public's interest: "His first measures in office attempted to stop the dictator Anastasio Somoza from continuing to use the resources of the public enterprises of the Nation, and of the Guardia Nacional, for private benefit on his uncountable urban and rural properties, thus striving to rehabilitate the country's economy with the Nicaraguan people's own funds that Somoza has squandered during many years for his exclusive personal gain." The Frente Nacional then proceeded to list Somoza's control of the Guardia Nacional, of the major banks and public services, and of the state's bureaucracy, which together created a veritable political monster: "We find ourselves . . . facing a formidable machine of centralized control over each and every one of the country's activities: a totalitarian power, exercised by a single and unpredictable hand, that shapes the classical Caesarean pyramid of authority."[29]

Faced with this awesome power, the Frente Nacional could only suggest to the Pan American Union that it mediate between the opposing political forces to bring about a transition to democracy by supervising free elections, reorganizing and depoliticizing the Guardia, and replacing Somoza with an interim junta.[30] The problem was that Somoza had already mediated his own transition to "democracy" with Cuadra Pasos, including an ample political amnesty for everyone implicated in crimes against the state and the special election of Conservative representatives to the Congress; he was not going to allow any international meddling in Nicaragua's internal affairs.[31] Somoza's maneuvering paid off when the Pan American conference resolved that all countries in the hemisphere reestablish diplomatic relations, which opened the way especially for renewed U.S. recognition of the Managua government.

The Grand Coalition

The intransigent opposition to the regime was at a dead end, having lost its call for international censure of Somoza and remaining outside of the deal that

Cuadra Pasos had negotiated in February 1948. Thus, it was faced with one of two alternatives: remain in opposition to Somoza by refusing any contact or deal with the regime, or oppose Somoza under the guise of a loyal opposition subject to conditions and limits set by the regime itself. The first alternative in a sense suggested that there would be moments in the future when outright opposition might triumph as long as it cultivated an image and a practice unsullied by any deal with Somocismo. Such a position foresaw that a time would come when popular opposition to the regime would be so strong that it could be swept away entirely; to lead such an opposition it was necessary to have certain political qualifications, among which the most important would be a history of unwavering struggle against the dictatorship. This was the position adopted by the PLI and certain youth and student organizations, as shall be seen later on.

The second alternative envisioned a policy of negotiations and political pressure brought to bear on the regime from within in order to achieve evolutionary changes, specifically a move toward an effective two-party system ("las paralelas históricas," as it was termed) with an apolitical Guardia Nacional standing watch over the functioning of the electoral mechanism and the routine succession of governments. This was the position adopted by the Civilistas within the Conservative party, a strategy they hoped would gradually win over the more recalcitrant elements, especially the followers of General Chamorro.

The period from 1948 to 1950 was precisely a time of struggle within the Conservative party to define its political options. Initially, the Chamorristas were on the side of the radical opposition. Chamorro himself was seeking to organize an armed revolt against Somoza and was a party to the founding document of the Legión del Caribe together with José Figueres of Costa Rica and Juan Rodríguez García of the Dominican Republic.[32] Inside Nicaragua, the Civilistas struggled to retain influence within the party structure, although they were a minority and were occasionally supplanted by Chamorristas.[33] Even Somoza became concerned about the delay in the ratification of the Somoza–Cuadra Pasos agreement by the plenum of the Conservative party.[34] Finally, Chamorro agreed to discuss a political solution to the impasse and returned to Managua in January 1950.

A series of talks between Chamorro's emissaries and Somoza resulted in a number of meetings between the two leaders in March 1950. Chamorro was primarily concerned that the next elections be honest and initially demanded that the recently created Organization of American States (OAS) supervise the balloting. But Cuadra Pasos made it known that he would participate in the election with his Civilistas with or without OAS supervision. On 31 March 1950, Chamorro and Somoza reached an agreement on a new political pact that fixed 21 May 1950 as the election day for both a Constituent Assembly and a new president. The pact also guaranteed that the Conservatives would get twenty seats in the Constituent Assembly and that the new Constitution would provide for the direct election of municipal authorities. In addition, Conservative politicians would be placed in the posts of minister of finance and of education.[35]

This Chamorro-Somoza pact was ratified by the national executive committee of the Conservative party on 2 April 1950. *La Prensa* reported that it was approved by a vote of 10 to 3 but that many of those present at the deliberations as observers were dissatisfied with the pact. Chamorro was forced to make a public statement explaining why he had decided on such an about-face after years of intransigent opposition: he said that he had struggled consistently to end the Somoza dictatorship and had sought allies and weapons to *revolucionar*, but that these efforts always had ended in failure. Therefore, upon returning from his last period of exile, he had decided to change his tactics and proceeded along the lines of political accommodation. He asked all Conservatives to think carefully about the pact in order to understand its logic and its importance.[36] Three days later, Somoza and Chamorro sat down and signed the Pacto de los Generales, thus laying the basis for a new political coalition and a new start, so to speak, for both historic parties.[37]

Once the agreement was signed, the Congress formally proceeded to set the date and the procedure of the upcoming election, which would be held "based on electoral freedom and minority representation" but under "the communist threat."[38] Sixty deputies to a Constituent Assembly would be elected, with forty seats going to the majority party and seventeen to the minority party, plus three that would include the defeated presidential candidate and the two living, popularly elected ex-presidents (Somoza and Chamorro). Only the Liberals and the Conservatives could participate because the constitutional procedure for registering new parties would be held in abeyance. In order to guarantee the "fairness" of the elections, the departmental electoral boards would be reorganized, with the Conservatives having a majority in those departments where they won in the 1932 elections, that is, Chontales, Granada, Rivas, Matagalpa, and Boaco, their traditional strongholds; on all other departmental boards, the Liberals would have a majority. Once the Constituent Assembly was seated, it would proceed to choose new members of the judicial branch, with the Supreme Court getting three Liberals and two Conservatives, and the appellate courts in Granada, León, and Masaya obtaining a minority of Conservative judges.

The Congress also set down a list of principles that would have to be incorporated into the new Constitution. Among the most important was that of a minority representation of one in all plural administrative and political bodies, including the boards of directors of the state banks and the public services, the municipal councils, and all international missions. In the reorganization of the municipal councils, the representation of the majority and minority parties would be as reflected in the results of the 1932 elections. Also contained in the new Constitution would be the principles of a nonpartisan national army, absolute electoral freedom, freedom of expression, and eventual suffrage for women, as well as a prohibition against presidential reelection. In a very obvious way, then, through negotiations between Liberals and Conservatives and the congressional decree that gave form to the entire procedure, the electoral event had been resolved before it was even held. What remained was choosing the presidential candidates, working out party platforms, and proceeding with the electoral campaign.

The Conservatives took the whole thing very seriously in that the leadership, at least, thought that for once the cards were not stacked against its candidates. A *junta de notables*, under the direction of Chamorro, chose Emilio Chamorro Benard, a prominent businessman from Granada, as its presidential candidate and drew up a program of government that generally coincided with the Liberals' stated commitment to social security and a minimum salary for workers, civic and political equality for women, extension of the public school system, expansion of the highway network, and the construction of hydroelectric dams and irrigation systems. The Conservatives explicitly "differed" from the Liberals in that they took a stand on the need to teach Christian dogma in schools to combat communism, to respect the church and its sacraments, and to cut back on alcohol consumption and decrease its importance as a source of public revenue. However, the Liberals under Somoza had never bothered the church nor had they been soft on communism, while an expressed desire to reduce alcohol intake was an issue with which anyone could agree. Perhaps the only substantial issue that distinguished the Conservatives was their support for "unrestricted freedom of commerce," which was generally understood to mean the right of the export producer to receive his earnings in dollars and to be able to negotiate them freely on the open market.[39] But not even this was much of an issue once the córdoba had stabilized in the postwar period.

The really important issue for the Conservatives was Somoza's promise to guarantee an open campaign and to respect the electoral results. A broadside issued by the Conservative leadership in León stated that for the first time in many years the party was participating in elections that would be truly free and honest based on serious agreements signed by both established parties and the personal guarantee of Somoza himself. Their choice of Chamorro Benard as their presidential candidate, a man with no political experience or following, was itself indicative of the Conservatives' desire to present a fresh image.[40] Not even Somoza's nomination as the Liberal presidential candidate at the party's convention in León on 22 April or his accession to the presidency through senatorial appointment upon the death of Román y Reyes on 7 May seems to have dampened the Conservative leaders' enthusiasm. General Chamorro issued a manifesto stating that Somoza's appointment as provisional president did not add to his already considerable power nor was it a sufficient excuse to drop out of the race. The Conservatives also took it upon themselves to widely circulate a memorandum that Somoza sent to all Guardia Nacional officers and civil authorities on 9 May ordering them to behave impartially and allow the campaign and the elections to proceed in the greatest liberty.[41] Seen in the light of these actions, the Conservatives' main adversary does not seem to have been Somoza but voter apathy, especially as a result of the negative impression caused by Chamorro's perceived surrender to Somoza in the Pact of the Generals. Thus, the Conservative leadership had to convince the party faithful that 1950 would not be a replay of 1947 and that they were not acting from a position of weakness.

During the campaign the Conservatives seem to have been allowed a fairly free run of things. On 2 May they held a large demonstration in Managua with 75,000 people in attendance; the marchers carried banners critical of *continuismo somocista* and claimed to have achieved the turnout without the usual Somocista lure of booze, money, and food. Other large demonstrations were reported in Granada and Masaya.[42] That is not to say that there was none of the usual harassment by the local authorities or the threat of armed thugs of the Reserva Civil.[43] But the Conservative leadership at no time threatened to withdraw from the race and the election was held as scheduled on 21 May.

The results of the election proved a disaster for the Conservatives, who received less than one-quarter of all the votes and won a bare outright majority only in Granada. (See Table 5.1.) Their other traditionally supportive departments (Boaco, Chontales, and Rivas) came through with a little more than 45

Table 5.1 Election Results, 1950

Department	Liberals	%	Conservatives	%	Total
Boaco	4,476	(52.2)	4,106	(47.8)	8,582
Carazo	6,706	(71.5)	2,666	(28.5)	9,372
Chinandega	14,395	(85.2)	2,498	(14.8)	16,893
Chontales	5,406	(52.4)	4,906	(47.6)	10,312
Estelí	6,796	(82.5)	1,439	(17.5)	8,235
Granada	4,340	(46.9)	4,911	(53.1)	9,251
Jinotega	6,231	(86.7)	957	(13.3)	7,188
León	22,468	(92.0)	1,951	(8.0)	24,419
Madriz	5,286	(89.9)	595	(10.1)	5,881
Managua	26,319	(75.0)	8,754	(25.0)	35,073
Masaya	8,561	(67.0)	4,209	(33.0)	12,770
Matagalpa	14,848	(74.6)	5,047	(25.4)	19,895
Nva. Segovia	4,437	(86.9)	667	(13.1)	5,104
Rivas	4,320	(54.5)	3,609	(45.5)	7,929
Rio San Juan	3,307	(83.2)	669	(16.8)	3,976
Zelaya	15,401	(86.4)	2,417	(13.6)	17,818
Total	153,297	(75.6)	49,401	(24.4)	202,698

Source: Consejo Nacional de Elecciones, El juicio electoral de 1950 (Managua: Talleres Nacionales, 1956), pp. 354–55.

percent of the votes. In all the rest, the Liberals won by substantial or overwhelming majorities. As usual, reports of electoral chicanery were widespread; the Conservative representative on the electoral council affixed his signature to the final results only after listing a number of irregularities including incorrect vote counts, intimidation at the polls, and the absence of Conservative poll watchers at some booths. Yet the Conservatives presented only one specific demand for annullment of the results: this was in a small canton in Boaco and involved all of ninety-six votes.[44] Even La Prensa recognized that Somoza had won and that the Guardia Nacional had behaved correctly; it suggested that the Conservatives' poor showing was the result of widespread abstention. After the vote totals were published, the Conservative party issued a manifesto stating its nonconformity with the electoral results but promising that it would continue to participate in the political process as a "sentinel" of the nation's interests. That is, it would abide by the terms of the Pact of the Generals but would not curry any favor of the government party.[45]

Economic Expansion and Institutional Reform

The Somocista electoral victory of 1950 was only the most visible manifesta-
tion of the regime's power at the beginning of the 1950s. It had resisted and
overcome a number of challenges both from within and from abroad and
seemingly had emerged strengthened by it all. Its political enemies had been
co-opted or silenced by the sheer weight of its presence. By conciliating and
confronting diverse social and political groups, Somoza had consistently retained the upper hand. But it was not only a matter of political ability in
dealing with the regime's opponents that contributed to its permanence. The
"formidable machine of centralized control" described by the Frente Nacional
pro Libertad de Nicaragua in 1948 was synonymous with the political and
administrative institutions that had grown since the 1930s and that constituted the foundation of the regime's strength. In fact, the survival of the
regime was possible precisely because the Nicaraguan state, as structured and
directed by fifteen years of Somocista domination, had acquired the resilience
and the cohesion to withstand successive attacks and crises.

In the decade of 1935–45, the development of the state under the Somocista regime had occurred under generally very trying economic circumstances. The weight of the Great Depression had reduced considerably the
material resources available for state building; thus, the regime was forced to
attempt a more efficient organization of the bureaucracy and to extract as
much income as possible through a variety of new and extended taxes in order
to enhance the state's power and presence. After 1945 the situation was
reversed, as material resources became more abundant to the point where the
state had difficulty in absorbing and administering its share of the national
income. This new situation was the direct result of the economic boom that
began in a limited manner during the postwar years and then exploded to
record levels after 1950.

Underlying this economic expansion was a rapid increase in the value of
Nicaragua's exports, which practically quadrupled between 1946 and 1956,
while imports increased to an even greater extent. The export boom was fueled
by a significant increase in demand and in prices on the world market for
coffee, Nicaragua's traditional export product; the average price of a pound of
exported Nicaraguan coffee climbed from U.S.$0.168 in 1946 to U.S.$0.527
in 1951 and to U.S.$0.629 in 1956. However, the most dramatic increase in
the country's export production was in cotton, which up to 1949 had been
grown and exported in negligible amounts. By 1955 cotton had superseded

Table 5.2 Government Income and Expenditures, 1945–1956

Year	Income in C$	Income in U.S.$*	Expenditures in C$	Surplus/ Deficit
1945–46	52,908,606	10,581,721	57,683,888	4,775,282
1946–47	77,128,808	15,425,761	66,285,236	10,843,572
1947–48	59,082,290	11,816,458	64,627,342	(–) 5,545,052
1948–49	78,365,921	15,673,184	76,658,161	1,707,760
1949–50	69,159,084	13,831,816	66,199,235	2,959,849
1950–51	90,316,688	18,063,337	81,409,515	8,907,173
1951–52	117,509,624	23,501,924	112,034,294	5,475,330
1952–53	154,497,174	30,899,434	145,693,549	8,803,625
1953–54	183,309,700	36,661,940	174,400,774	8,908,926
1954–55	209,836,171	41,967,234	232,651,800	(–) 22,815,629
1955–56	282,573,405	40,367,628	253,345,131	29,228,274

Source: Ministerio de Hacienda y Crédito Público, *Memorias*, especially those for fiscal years 1954–55 and 1955–56, which contain comprehensive statistics for the period 1945–56.

*The exchange rate was 5:1 until July 1955, when it was officially dropped to 7:1.

coffee as the country's principal export, while the entire coastal plain from Managua to Chinandega had been despoiled of its remaining forest cover and converted into vast cotton fields. Sesame seed and wood exports also experienced significant increases, but at a much lower volume than cotton. Gold production held steady during the entire period, although its importance to the country's economy remained limited given the enclave-type nature of its production and export.[46]

The economic boom was translated immediately into a marked increase in the level of revenue collected by the government. In dollar terms, government income quadrupled between 1946 and 1956, while expenditures more than quadrupled. (See Table 5.2.) Obviously, this expansion was a function of the increase in foreign trade and, particularly, of imports, which still were the basis of the government's revenues: customs duties increased as a proportion of total government income to over 60 percent for a few years in the 1950s, comparable to their importance during the predepression years of the 1920s. (See Table 5.3.) As a consequence, other sources of income declined proportionately, although indirect taxes as a whole still accounted for two-thirds to four-fifths of total revenue.

Table 5.3 Sources of Government Income, 1945–1956
(as a percentage of total income)

Year	Indirect a	b	c	d	Direct*	Public Services	Public Borrowing
1945–46	37.2	16.2	6.1	6.4	2.9	27.2	4.0
1946–47	35.2	9.1	4.3	5.1	1.9	24.2	20.2
1947–48	49.4	14.7	7.6	7.2	2.4	18.7	—
1948–49	41.9	12.1	6.6	6.4	1.7	18.3	13.0
1949–50	47.8	14.1	8.5	8.6	2.6	13.0	5.4
1950–51	57.7	12.0	7.0	7.8	2.5	13.0	—
1951–52	57.3	11.1	6.7	7.6	2.2	10.5	4.6
1952–53	61.3	8.7	6.5	7.4	2.1	11.0	3.0
1953–54	58.0	8.7	6.4	7.4	5.4	10.4	3.7
1954–55	56.2	8.7	6.4	7.4	9.8	8.5	3.0
1955–56	64.5	6.4	5.0	6.1	8.3	8.1	1.6

Source: Ministerio de Hacienda y Crédito Público, *Memorias.*
Key: a = Customs; b = liquor; c = tobacco; d = others.
*Includes capital and, after 1953, income taxes.

The increase in public revenue allowed for considerable growth of the public sector in the country's economic and social development, although the distribution of budget expenditures did not vary to any great extent during the postwar years. (See Table 5.4.) What is striking is the change in the distribution of expenditures when compared to the first ten years of the Somocista regime. (See Table 3.6.) The proportion of funds allocated to the public debt and national finance and to public works declined considerably, although their absolute amounts increased during the entire period given the rapid increase in overall budget expenditures. On the other hand, the proportion of budget expenditures for the armed forces and the interior ministry increased significantly after the low point of 1943–44; this increase was particularly large after 1950, when the threat of armed resistance, as perceived by the regime, grew to dangerous levels. Similarly, the percentage expenditure for education practically doubled during the period 1945–56 when compared to the previous ten-year period. There was also a perceptible increase in the budget allocations for health and agriculture.

The increase in government expenditures was not matched by a proportional increase in public employment, nor was the proportional increase in

Table 5.4 Budgetary Expenditures as a Percentage of Total, 1945–1956

Year	Legislative/ Judicial	Armed forces/ Interior	Finance/ Public Debt	Education	Public Works/ Develp.	Agri. Labor Health	Others
1945–46	5.0	26.4	19.7	10.0	30.7	4.5	3.7
1946–47	4.5	26.1	22.7	10.5	28.8	3.7	3.7
1947–48	4.5	26.9	27.3	11.1	20.9	5.4	3.9
1948–49	4.4	25.0	27.2	10.5	23.1	5.1	4.7
1949–50	5.0	34.0	28.0	10.0	11.3	4.3	7.4
1950–51	4.4	33.6	22.4	9.8	16.8	6.3	6.7
1951–52	4.3	31.3	21.0	11.1	20.4	5.9	6.0
1952–53	3.3	30.7	18.5	12.4	17.0	6.9	11.2
1953–54	3.3	27.8	18.0	11.2	21.8	9.4	8.5
1954–55	2.9	37.8	17.5	9.3	18.7	7.3	6.5
1955–56	2.8	31.7	19.7	10.0	19.2	8.7	7.9

Source: Ministerio de Hacienda y Crédito Público, *Memoria 1955–56.*

public employment as great as that experienced between 1936 and 1945. During this first period, public employment rose by 78 percent with a budget that nearly doubled in size (see Tables 3.2 and 3.7), while during the years 1945–56 public employment rose by only 60 percent with a budget that quadrupled in size. (See Table 5.5.) There are two reasons for this difference. On the one hand, the proportion of public funds earmarked for investment purposes increased from 15.9 percent of total budget expenditures in 1945 to 34.7 percent in 1956, while on the other, that for goods and services (including salaries) dropped from 84.1 percent to 65.3 percent in the same period.[47] In sum, the average salary increased while the proportion of public funds allotted to salaries declined, thus explaining in part the smaller proportional increase in public employment when compared to total budget outlays.

The increase in public employment in some sectors would suggest a growing interest of the regime in social programs. The number of employees in the field of education, most of them teachers, grew from over 2,100 in 1945 to around 4,000 in 1956. (See Table 5.6.) Those employed in health, agriculture, and labor showed the greatest increase of all, and within this group the number of health personnel grew the most (from 375 in 1949–50 to 907 in 1955–56). However, as can be observed in Table 5.7, the percentage distribution of public employment during the ten years in question remained remark-

Table 5.5 Public Employment, 1945–1956 (1936–37 = 100)

Year	According to Budget Appropriations		Railroad	Others
	Number	Index		
1945–46	9,837	185		
1946–47	10,305	194		
1947–48	10,546	198		
1948–49	11,470	216		
1949–50	11,392	214		
1950–51	11,326	213	1,870	
1951–52	11,917	224	2,036	423
1952–53	12,599	237	1,964	472
1953–54	14,742	277	1,991	618
1954–55	14,943	281	2,256	706
1955–56	15,772	296	2,152	

Sources: Ministerio de Hacienda y Crédito Público, *Presupuesto general de ingresos y egresos de la República de Nicaragua.* Data on railroad employees for 1951–52 is from Fondo S. de Somoza, no. 6, AN; for 1950–51 and 1952–53 to 1955–56, from United Nations, CEPAL, *El desarrollo económico de Nicaragua* (Mexico: United Nations, 1967), p. 171.

ably consistent. With the exception of health, agriculture, and labor, a group that encompassed the smallest proportion of public employees, the remaining categories oscillated up and down by only a few percentage points, a fact suggesting that increases in public employees were made across the board and not in response to any specific policy objective. Furthermore, the vast majority of public employees were still engaged in purely administrative, fiscal, and police functions.[48]

The regime's concern about economic development was not reflected as much in the distribution of its bureaucracy as in its attempts to improve its efficiency and to establish new governmental institutions designed to increase public support for the private sector. Not since the banking and fiscal reforms of the late 1930s and early 1940s did the regime engage in such a flurry of decision making involving the creation of new taxes and public institutions aimed at preparing the way for a qualitatively different role for the state in national development. From now on, economic and fiscal matters and the overall issue of economic development presumably would be resolved in the light of technical studies, commission reports, recommendations of international advisory groups, and the creation of new government bodies. These

Table 5.6 Public Employment by Category, 1945–1956 (1936–37 = 100)

Year	a	b	c	d	e	f
1945–46	786 (245)	3,711 (142)	2,165 (197)	1,192 (414)	1,589 (193)	394 (219)
1946–47	828 (258)	3,862 (148)	2,331 (212)	1,210 (420)	1,566 (191)	508 (282)
1947–48	852 (265)	3,895 (149)	2,388 (217)	1,202 (417)	1,626 (198)	585 (325)
1948–49	812 (253)	4,256 (163)	2,769 (251)	1,193 (414)	1,726 (210)	714 (397)
1949–50	812 (253)	4,338 (166)	2,718 (247)	1,432 (497)	1,491 (182)	601 (334)
1950–51	820 (255)	4,385 (168)	2,577 (234)	1,304 (453)	1,494 (182)	746 (414)
1951–52	845 (263)	4,402 (169)	2,722 (247)	1,478 (513)	1,589 (194)	881 (489)
1952–53	828 (258)	4,463 (171)	3,191 (290)	1,385 (480)	1,615 (197)	1,117 (621)
1953–54	864 (269)	5,125 (200)	4,061 (369)	1,797 (624)	1,610 (196)	1,285 (714)
1954–55	908 (283)	5,240 (201)	3,992 (363)	1,694 (588)	1,774 (216)	1,335 (742)
1955–56	929 (289)	5,505 (211)	4,000 (363)	1,846 (641)	2,099 (256)	1,393 (774)

Source: Ministerio de Hacienda y Crédito Público, *Presupuesto general de ingresos y egresos de la República de Nicaragua.* The figure for those employed in public education in 1955–56 is an estimate.

Key: a = Congress, executive offices, judiciary, and foreign affairs; b = Army and interior; c = Public education; d = Finance (and economics after 1949–50); e = Development and public works; f = Health, agriculture, and labor.

changes were prompted by the increased presence of bilateral and multilateral institutions, such as the Economic Commission for Latin America (ECLA), the International Bank for Reconstruction and Development (IBRD), and the Point Four foreign aid program of the Truman administration, institutions that provided technical and financial assistance for development programs but that required guarantees that such assistance could be handled adequately by the recipient country. From the point of view of the Nicaraguan government, the growth of budgetary income demanded an evaluation of the capabilities of governmental institutions to disburse these monies in a manner most consonant with the requirements of capitalist economic growth.

The first attempt at rationalizing the government's institutional structure since the early 1940s came in November 1948, when the Congress passed a law that assigned to each ministry the specific administrative and political functions it was responsible for carrying out.[49] It authorized a cabinet made up of nine ministries, a Jefe Director of the Guardia Nacional, a minister for the Distrito Nacional (the city of Managua), a president of the Tribunal de Cuentas (national accounting office), and a Fiscal General de Hacienda, who would

Table 5.7 Public Employment as a Percentage of Total, 1945–1956

Year	a	b	c	d	e	f
1945–46	8.0	37.7	22.0	12.1	16.2	4.0
1946–47	8.0	37.5	22.6	11.7	15.3	4.9
1947–48	8.1	36.9	22.6	16.4	15.5	5.5
1948–49	7.1	37.1	24.1	10.4	15.1	6.2
1949–50	7.1	38.1	23.8	12.6	13.1	5.3
1950–51	7.2	38.7	22.8	11.5	13.2	6.6
1951–52	7.1	36.9	22.8	12.4	13.4	7.4
1952–53	6.6	35.4	25.3	11.0	12.8	8.9
1953–54	5.9	34.8	27.5	12.2	10.9	8.7
1954–55	6.1	35.1	26.7	11.3	11.9	8.9
1955–56	5.9	34.9	25.4	11.7	13.3	8.8

Source: Ministerio de Hacienda y Crédito Público, Presupuesto general de ingresos y egresos de la República de Nicaragua.

Key: a = Congress, executive offices, judiciary, and foreign affairs; b = Army and interior; c = Public education; d = Finance (and economics after 1949–50); e = Development and public works; f = Health, agriculture, and labor.

represent the government in all legal proceedings involving fiscal matters. Although most functions of the diverse ministries and the other offices remained unchanged, one important innovation was the creation of a Ministry of Economics, charged with developing economic development policies, setting monetary and banking guidelines, carrying out research into new areas for productive investment, and overseeing price fluctuations and controls. All ministry personnel would be appointed or removed by the president, but in the case of the Ministry of Economics there would be an additional qualification: its personnel would be chosen on the basis of "recognized technical expertise" given the special tasks entrusted to it. In other words, an attempt would be made to depoliticize the formulation of economic policies in order to enhance the state's legitimacy in setting national development objectives.

A second step taken by the regime was the creation of the Consejo Nacional de Economía in June 1949.[50] Under the president's authority, the Consejo would be responsible for the "general economic policy of the nation"; specifically, it would seek to increase the efficiency of the public sector in implementing the country's economic programs, to promote research into economic matters that would help the Ministry of Economics formulate policies, and to make the public aware of the need for orderly and harmonious economic development. The Consejo itself would be made up of the ministers of economics, finance, development, and agriculture, and the president of the Banco Nacional. Under the Consejo, a Junta Técnica de Economía staffed by professionally trained individuals would carry out the studies and produce the recommendations needed to formulate policy. Finally, a third body called the Junta Consultiva would advise the minister of economics on the requirements and the problems of those institutions and groups involved in the country's economic activities. On this Junta Consultiva would sit representatives of the Managua Chamber of Commerce, of the Sociedad Anónima de Cafeteros, of the Cooperativa Nacional de Agricultores, and of the Asociación Agrícola de Nicaragua, as well as any similar organizations created in the future. In this manner, the private sector achieved a direct and formal line of access to the highest level of the government.

A presidential decree of February 1953 gave the Consejo Nacional de Economía even more wide-ranging authority, including that to develop national economic plans, coordinate the economic projects of diverse government bodies, advise on fiscal matters, and contract technical assistance.[51] It also required that all offices of the executive branch and autonomous government bodies submit proposed economic legislation for review by the Consejo, which would then give its opinion directly to the president. The Consejo was empowered to call before it any government employee to explain and justify the merits of his or her agency's policies. In sum, the Consejo became a kind of superministry of economic development that sought to bring coherence and efficiency to public and private investment under the aegis of the state.

The state's role was not limited only to planning and offering recommendations for action. Under a presidential decree of March 1953, the Instituto de Fomento Nacional (INFONAC) came into existence as a public corporation with its own capital endowment and the authority to contract further financial obligations. In order to achieve its objectives of a more diversified and enlarged national production capability, the Instituto could provide technical and financial assistance to those private firms engaged in production for both export and the internal market. In particular, INFONAC would seek to provide assistance in those areas of production that private capital was loath to invest in; it could even purchase stock in a company or proceed directly to found a business enterprise that would be sold off to the private sector once it turned a profit. The institute also was authorized to purchase for resale all sorts of agricultural machinery, animal stock, and fertilizers and pesticides, as well as to operate grain silos. The government would put up C$50 million over the years 1952–62 to start operations, but INFONAC could otherwise receive private deposits, sell stock, and negotiate loans from local and foreign credit sources.[52] In a number of respects, therefore, it took over functions that previously had been handled by the Banco Nacional and its subsidiary, the Compañía Mercantil de Ultramar, such as loans for industrial development and imports of capital goods and raw materials.

Although INFONAC was a public institution, its board of directors included a representative of the agricultural sector, another of the industrial sector, and a third of the minority party, all chosen by the president on the basis of lists submitted to him by the diverse trade associations and the Conservative party. The rest of the board consisted of the ministers of economics, finance, development, and agriculture, as well as the general manager of the Banco Nacional—all presidential appointees. INFONAC's formal status as an "autonomous" institution, therefore, was questionable, given that five of its eight board members were named directly by the president; it was as much under the control of the executive branch of government as the Banco Nacional. Nevertheless, it represented an attempt to remove the state's contribution to economic development from the control of older and presumably more inefficient and politicized institutions, such as the Banco Nacional and the Banco Hipotecario, and place it in the hands of a more technically competent organization.

Fiscal Policy and Economic Development

The creation of new institutions attuned to the needs of national development was no easy solution to the more complex fiscal and administrative problems that the Somocista state had inherited from years past and that appeared all the more glaring in times of economic boom, especially when the regime attempted to involve itself more directly in establishing economic policy. The fiscal system, in particular, had changed little since the reforms introduced by Somoza in the late 1930s and still retained important characteristics that went even further back in time. In 1952 George Garvy, an adviser on public finance contracted by the IBRD at the invitation of the Nicaraguan government, prepared an exhaustive report on the country's fiscal system in which he suggested that the Nicaraguan system was entirely inadequate to meet the needs of a rapidly growing national economy.[53] To begin with, the tax structure retained features that severely limited the state's taxing ability, such as an almost exclusive reliance on indirect taxes, the absence of an income tax, a very limited property tax, and practically no progressive features in the system as a whole. Export taxes, which could be construed as a direct tax on the income of export producers, yielded only 8.8 percent of total revenues and that because a sliding tax on coffee and cotton exports was established in 1951.[54] Otherwise, professionals, rentiers, merchants, and landowners only paid a nominal property tax, frequently figured on the basis of grossly undervalued properties, when they paid any tax at all; Garvy calculated that in 1951, fewer than 13,500 individuals and business firms paid property taxes.

In addition to its regressive characteristics, the tax system was terribly complicated. New taxes had been placed upon old ones so that a given object might be taxed several times before it finally reached the consumer. Garvy noted, for example, that gasoline was subject to eight different taxes in addition to import duties, consular fees, and two municipal taxes levied in Managua. Evasion of tax payments also meant that the cost of collecting some taxes absorbed a large part of the yield or even exceeded it, the stamp tax being a case in point. Finally, given its extreme reliance on import and excise taxes, the tax structure was highly inelastic; that is, the volume of tax collection depended on the amount of goods imported or consumed and thereby provided the state with a very weak foundation for financing a program of long-range economic development.

In light of the above, Garvy concluded that "the present tax system is at the point where it has become an obstacle to the economic development of the country." Its regressive nature only depressed the standard of living of the people, mostly poor farm workers and subsistence farmers, while the absence of direct income taxes had not induced the higher-income groups to channel more of their savings into productive investment. Any attempt to increase tax revenue by imposing more of the same old taxes was doomed to failure; only new taxes falling on those groups until then immune to taxation could increase income, among which the most important would be a general and progressive income tax, "the foundation of all modern tax systems."[55]

Increasing government income was only one side of the coin. As Garvy observed, the capabilities of the government to spend were severely restricted by an administrative structure that had changed little since the days of fiscal austerity in the 1930s and 1940s. The Ministry of Finance was charged, in theory, with performing the functions of revenue administration, general accounting, government purchasing, and budget preparation. In practice, it was little more than a "combined collection and disbursing office performing routine functions" headed by a minister who centralized all decisions but who spent between 60 and 80 percent of his time signing checks and talking with visitors. For example, the preparation of the budget, which was the minister's exclusive responsibility, involved the formulation of rather unsound estimates of income that were then reconciled with spending requests from the different government offices. The budget was then presented to the Congress, which made only nominal changes. The result was that estimates of government revenue usually fell short of actual income while expenditures boiled down to a list of salaries grouped by departments and bureaus without any attempt to detail nonsalary expenditures.[56]

That is not to say that there were no priorities either explicit or implicit in the government's spending. As observed in Table 5.7, the percentage distribution of government employees according to various administrative categories remained quite stable during the period 1945–56, from which one might conclude that the regime assigned equal importance to all its branches. However, in moments of fiscal crunch the regime was forced to make choices on government outlays that clearly reflected its scale of preferences. Such an occasion arose in 1949, a year when the coffee harvest dropped by more than half and the outlook for fiscal year 1949–50 appeared critical. The government requested the assistance of the International Monetary Fund (IMF), which sent a technical mission to Nicaragua. That mission produced the typical IMF recommendation for such a situation: reduce government expenditures as much as possible.[57] In line with this position, the minister of finance, León Debayle, worked out a plan to reduce government spending for the coming fiscal year in order to bring it into line with an expected drop of 30 percent in customs revenues. Otherwise, Debayle figured that the fiscal deficit would run over C$15 million and would bring on a new round of pronounced inflation.

Debayle's plan contemplated budget cuts figured on the basis of the 1948–49 projected expenditures. There would be an across-the-board cut of approximately 33 percent for all departments except the executive offices and defense (primarily the Guardia Nacional), which would remain unchanged. Thus, the required saving of C$15 million would be achieved without affecting "those basic services of the state that must remain unaltered," namely the armed forces.[58] Although the plan conceivably would produce the results expected, it was more the product of an exercise in applied arithmetic than a thought-out fiscal strategy; Debayle simply lopped off C$15 million from the previous budget, set aside an unchanged amount for defense, and finally adjusted downward the remaining appropriations by 33 percent regardless of the social or economic impact. As it turned out, real spending for fiscal 1949–50 was greater than Debayle's projection, but all government branches did end up spending less than in the previous fiscal year, with the exception of defense.

The first measure to overcome this kind of budget improvisation took the form of a five-year development plan put together in 1952 under the supervision of the Consejo Nacional de Economía on the basis of an IBRD technical mission report. The plan envisioned the investment of at least U.S.$59.3 million of government funds plus an additional U.S.$16.7 million in foreign loans to complete the principal highway network and build numerous feeder roads, modernize the railway, improve water and sanitation facilities in the main cities and towns, increase electric production and build a national grid, expand coffee and livestock production, create new industries, reduce illiteracy, and promote vocational and technical training.[59] The plan aimed to increase per capita income by 15 percent over the next five years, which the IBRD thought entirely possible given the export boom at the time and the availability of foreign credit sources.

The second step taken to strengthen the country's finances was the introduction of an income tax in December 1952. As approved by the Congress, the law exempted from income tax payment all nonprofit organizations, as well as personal income received from national lottery prizes, inheritances, donations, interest-bearing accounts, and insurance payments. Otherwise, all those with incomes in excess of C$20,000 yearly (about U.S.$4,000) were required to file an income statement and pay a minimum tax of 4 percent, which increased progressively to 18 percent for those with annual incomes in excess of C$1 million.[60]

Finally, the government contracted numerous loans with the IBRD and the Export-Import Bank through the Banco Nacional for the development of infrastructure. Between 1951 and 1956, the IBRD lent Nicaragua a total of U.S.$16.3 million for highway construction, electrical generation, and port improvements, among others. The Export-Import Bank came through with U.S.$600,000 for the Managua electric system, giving a grand total of U.S.$16.9 million, an amount only slightly larger than the U.S.$16.7 million envisioned in the five-year development plan.[61]

A thorough evaluation of the impact of these administrative and fiscal measures on the development of Nicaraguan society and its economy lies outside the scope of this study. However, a number of inferences can be drawn with regard to the role of the state in determining or influencing economic policy during the period 1945–56. In the first place, the regime's efforts to improve its bureaucratic efficiency do not seem to have been entirely successful. The observations Garvy made in 1952 regarding excessive ministerial centralization and the lack of coordination to avoid unnecessary duplication of bureaucratic functions were echoed again in 1956 by Modesto Armijo, a close adviser to Somoza on fiscal matters. Armijo believed that the country's explosive economic growth after 1950 had forced the state to increase its public responsibilities far beyond its real capabilities; the result was widespread improvisation and excessive centralization of decision making. He proposed several changes in the number and functions of the government's ministries in order to better define bureaucratic jurisdictions, eliminate unnecessary posts to achieve greater efficiency, and generally rationalize the state apparatus.[62]

Years later Armijo's findings were repeated in far greater detail by the Consejo Nacional de Economía, which emphasized the continued duplication of administrative functions and the excessive centralization of authority in the government ministries. It also criticized the lack of proper mechanisms for the selection of government personnel, which it attributed to the old custom of favoring friends and relatives above personal merit (although it did not mention party affiliation as a criterion for government employment). Bureaucratic disorganization meant that any attempt at serious economic and social planning by the government would fall short of its objectives, as José M. Castillo, secretary of the Consejo, duly reported to Somoza in April 1956. Castillo said that serious planning, and not just stopgap measures, required the preparation of adequate economic and social statistics and the formulation of alternative development plans so that the government could act on a firm footing. Up to that moment, Castillo said, the government's planning had been more reactive than premeditated, that is, there had not been any real planning to speak of.[63]

The problem that none of these technocrats touched on was the fundamentally political nature of public employment, in which the state's bureaucracy constituted a political clientele that needed to be expanded and given preference by the regime for partisan reasons. The lack of proper selection criteria for government employees, the disorganized growth of the bureaucracy, and the duplication of administrative functions obviously reduced efficiency—but efficiency was not the main or only objective.

A second inference is that fiscal reform as recommended by the IBRD mission did alter somewhat the proportion of direct tax revenue. After 1953–54, with the introduction of the income tax, the amount of direct taxes as a proportion of total income rose from under 3 percent before 1952 to a little over 8 percent in 1955–56. (See Table 5.3.) However, the importance of indirect taxes did not drop in any appreciable way but instead stayed around 80 percent of total revenue. On the one hand, there were clear limits to how much direct taxes could be raised, determined in large part by the skewed distribution of income in Nicaragua at the time. The IBRD figured in 1952 that 25 percent of gross national product accrued to about 1 percent of the population and that the boom in export earnings only aggravated this situation; for example, it estimated that between 70 and 75 percent of the coffee and cotton crops were produced by some 950 growers.[64] Thus, by fiscal year 1959–60, only 2,208 individuals and 572 business enterprises paid any income tax at all.[65] On the other hand, the continued heavy reliance on indirect taxation, especially customs duties, resulted in part from the weight of the economic boom of the 1950s and the relative ease with which these duties could be collected without having to undertake profound changes in the administrative system.

Third, the state's role in promoting economic growth did increase noticeably as of 1950. Government spending was routed in increasing amounts and proportions for investment purposes whereas the proportion spent on current expenses declined. (See Table 5.8.) This was particularly true with the creation of INFONAC and the negotiation of loans with multilateral credit institutions after 1953. Furthermore, government investment proved much more dynamic than that of the private sector. (See Table 5.9.) Between 1950 and 1956, private agricultural investment showed no clear upward trend and nonagricultural private investment grew by only two and a half times, whereas public investment nearly quadrupled.[66]

Fourth, public investment was heavily concentrated in the development of economic infrastructure, especially road and bridge building and electric power generation and distribution, which absorbed between 65 and 80 percent of all government investment between 1950 and 1956. On the other hand, social and communal services were favored with from one-fifth to one-fourth of public investment, of which about half was investment in urban infrastructural improvements.[67] Some comparative statistics on the socioeconomic development of Nicaragua tend to back up the conclusions that can be reached on the basis of the above fiscal data. (See Table 5.10.) That is, the regime committed itself to heavy investment in economically important ventures while it barely held its own, if at all, in social programs.

In general, then, the state's development policies signaled a clear opening

Table 5.8 Government Investment and Current Expenses,
1945–1956 (in million 1958 C$)

Year	Investment	%	Current expenditures	%	Total expenditures
1945	24.4	(15.9)	128.8	(84.1)	153.2
1946	38.4	(23.6)	124.0	(76.4)	162.4
1947	41.0	(27.5)	107.9	(72.5)	148.9
1948	33.4	(18.0)	152.3	(82.0)	185.7
1949	20.5	(11.4)	159.7	(88.6)	180.2
1950	27.2	(16.6)	136.2	(83.4)	163.4
1951	32.3	(19.6)	132.7	(80.4)	165.0
1952	53.1	(26.3)	148.9	(73.7)	202.0
1953	68.1	(29.3)	164.7	(70.7)	232.8
1954	74.9	(28.7)	186.4	(71.3)	261.3
1955	88.4	(32.1)	187.3	(67.9)	275.7
1956	102.7	(34.7)	193.3	(65.3)	296.0

Source: Nicaragua, Consejo Nacional de Economía, Análisis del desarrollo económico y social de Nicaragua, 1950–1962, (Managua: N.p., 1964), p. 68.

Table 5.9 Gross Public and Private Investment,
1945–1956 (in million 1958 C$; 1950 = 100)

Year	Public		Private Agricultural		Nonagricult.		Total	
1945	24.4	(90)	29.1	(39)	73.7	(84)	127.2	(67)
1946	38.4	(141)	33.9	(45)	66.8	(76)	139.1	(73)
1947	41.0	(151)	39.8	(53)	99.1	(113)	179.9	(95)
1948	33.4	(123)	41.4	(55)	106.1	(121)	180.9	(95)
1949	20.5	(75)	41.9	(56)	132.3	(150)	194.7	(102)
1950	27.2	(100)	75.1	(100)	88.0	(100)	190.3	(100)
1951	32.3	(119)	70.1	(93)	113.3	(129)	215.7	(113)
1952	53.1	(195)	98.4	(131)	178.3	(203)	329.8	(173)
1953	68.1	(250)	63.4	(84)	218.4	(248)	349.9	(184)
1954	74.9	(275)	96.0	(128)	271.3	(308)	442.2	(232)
1955	88.4	(325)	109.2	(145)	244.6	(278)	442.2	(232)
1956	102.8	(378)	86.0	(115)	218.9	(249)	407.7	(214)

Source: United Nations, CEPAL, El desarrollo económico de Nicaragua, (Mexico: United Nations, 1967), p. 44.

Table 5.10 Assorted Statistics on Nicaraguan Social
and Economic Development: 1950–1956

Year	Highways and Roads (kms)	Power Generators (mw)	Tractor Imports	Hospital Beds	Primary School Enrollment	Population Ages 6–13
1950	1,880	20.6	125	2,114	126,367	229,700
1951	2,440	26.3	345	2,114	121,496	238,792
1952	2,715	26.4	283	2,055	124,785	249,221
1953	3,100	33.2	306	2,072	125,171	259,432
1954	3,310	37.8	713	2,072	131,637	269,696
1955	3,687	40.2	604	2,129	135,977	280,188
1956	4,087	42.4	83	2,242	139,896	291,416

Sources: Data on highways are from United Nations, CEPAL, *El desarrollo económico de Nicaragua* (Mexico: United Nations, 1967), p. 172, and Dirección General de Estadística, *Boletín de estadística*, no. 8 (September 1960): 77; on power generation, IBRD, *The Economic Development of Nicaragua* (Baltimore: Johns Hopkins University Press, 1953), p. 174; on tractor imports, from Pedro Belli, "Prolegómeno para una historia económica de Nicaragua de 1905 a 1966," *Revista del Pensamiento Centroamericano* 30, no. 146 (January–March 1965): 18; on hospital beds, from Nicaragua, Dirección General de Estadística y Censos, *Resumen estadístico 1950–1960*, 2d ed. (Managua: N.p., June 1961), p. 39; on school-aged population and enrollment, from Nicaragua, Consejo Nacional de Economía, *Análisis del desarrollo económico y social de Nicaragua, 1950–1962* (Managua: N.p., 1964), p. 186.

toward the propertied classes through a number of fiscal and financial decisions coupled with the political pact signed by Somoza and Chamorro that presumably buried the old Conservative-Liberal rift for good. After 1950, a new set of social and economic priorities replaced the more populistic and partisan rhetoric that had characterized the Somocista regime of the previous fifteen years. Furthermore, a new set of rules of the game enabled hitherto excluded social groups to participate in the economic and political decisions handed down by the government.

The Regime and the Private Sector

One of the most evident changes registered in this new period of the Somocista regime involved the country's financial system. Up until 1950, the government

Table 5.11 Public and Private Bank Credit
Operations, 1945–1948 (in thousand C$)

	1945	%	1946	%	1947	%	1948	%
Private Banks								
JRE Tefel	453	(0.7)	658	(1.0)	725	(0.9)	691	(0.8)
Caley Dagnell	943	(1.5)	2,012	(3.1)	2,514	(3.2)	2,574	(3.0)
Banco de Londres	5,653	(9.2)	5,759	(9.0)	4,504	(5.8)	5,499	(6.5)
Total	7,049	(11.4)	8,429	(13.1)	7,743	(9.9)	8,764	(10.3)
State Banks								
Caja Cred. Pop.	1,162	(1.9)	1,363	(2.1)	1,210	(1.6)	1,226	(1.5)
Banco Hipotecario	7,873	(12.7)	7,672	(12.0)	26,462	(34.0)	27,815	(32.8)
Banco Nacional	45,861	(74.0)	46,695	(72.8)	42,413	(54.5)	46,998	(55.4)
Total	54,896	(88.6)	55,730	(86.9)	70,085	(90.1)	76,039	(89.7)
Total, All Banks	61,945		64,159		77,828		84,803	

Source: Juan María Castro Silva, Nicaragua económica (Managua: Talleres Nacionales, 1949), pp. 103–10. The significant increase in loans offered by the Banco Hipotecario as of 1947 was made possible by a large bond issue of C$22.5 million that year.

banks handled the vast majority of the country's institutional credit operations. (See Table 5.11.) Between 1941 and 1948, at no time did the state's banks handle less than 86 percent of all bank credit. In addition, there was no important private Nicaraguan bank; the banking firms of JRE Tefel and Caley Dagnall usually handled between 2 and 4 percent of total credit operations during a given year, with the foreign-owned Banco de Londres handling from approximately 6 to 10 percent. Thus, the stranglehold that the state banks had on Nicaraguan users of bank credit was nearly complete. The control that Somoza exercised over the banks, in turn, was a potent political tool in the system of political domination.

After 1950, the state's monopoly on bank credit operations was altered with the creation of the first important Nicaraguan private banks in the country's history. One of these, the Banco de América, can be identified as part of the political opening of the Somoza-Chamorro pact of 1950: among its founders were some of the old leading Conservative families of the Granada region, such as the Chamorros, the Pellas, and the Benards. These families were very active in cattle raising and commerce, and in the case of the powerful Nicaragua Sugar Estates, Limited, group, they controlled much of the country's sugarcane growing and refining within the San Antonio sugar mill complex in the northwestern part of the country. The other private bank, the Banco Nicaragüense, was founded in 1953, one year after the Banco de América. The Banco Nicaragüense grew out of the association of the main cotton growers of the León and Chinandega region and its operations initially were limited to the support of cotton growing in these departments. Later on, during the decade of the 1960s, both the Banco de América and the Banco Nicaragüense extended their operations to the entire country and became the nuclei of extensive financial and business conglomerates.[68]

The initial financial importance of these new banks to the country's credit system cannot be gauged on the basis of the available evidence. It does seem probable that during the 1950s their role remained secondary to that of the state's Banco Nacional and Banco Hipotecario and that their eventually extensive holdings within the Nicaraguan economy came about during the 1960s as a result of the period of economic growth linked to the Central American Common Market. Nevertheless, their appearance in the early 1950s can be interpreted as part of the economic and political *apertura* the regime provided the country's principal non-Somocista economic groups.

Another aspect of the government's economic policies that indicates an opening, albeit indirectly, to Conservative economic interests was the increased support for cattle raising. The government, which authorized all beef exports, permitted increased exports of cattle on the hoof after years of severe restrictions. Until 1956, yearly cattle exports were up to four times greater than in 1946.[69] In addition, INFONAC's credit policy showed a clear pattern in favor of the development of the national cattle industry; of the C$20,930,348 in foreign loans that INFONAC negotiated between 1954 and 1960, over one-half went to purchase thoroughbred cattle and milk plant and meat packing equipment. Its most important single industrial investment was the construction of the IFAGAN slaughterhouse and meat-packing facility, which absorbed one-fifth of all its industrial investment during the period 1954–60. In addition, INFONAC opened branch offices in the departments of Chontales, Boaco, and Rivas, the main centers of the Conservative cattle-raising activities.[70] All of these commercial and financial decisions would seem to be a logical follow-up to the Pact of the Generals and the creation of the Compañía Nacional de Productores de Leche, which brought together Somocista and Conservative ranching interests.

Perhaps the most important element in the regime's policies toward the Conservatives, however, was the tolerance or benign neglect with which the principal leaders of the opposition were treated in terms of their property or businesses. Somoza never touched their property even after they were thrown in jail or tossed out of the country. Emiliano Chamorro, for example, returned from his years of exile to resume the personal direction of his farms.

Nor did Somoza ever attempt to break into the businesses of the Granada oligarchy. On the contrary, he seems to have been very respectful of the more important Conservative capitalists and their business ventures, an attitude that was particularly evident in the case of the sugar-growing and processing conglomerate of the Ingenio San Antonio. Just after the Pact of the Generals was signed, the government authorized an increase in the retail price of sugar from C$0.10 to C$0.15 per pound.[71] A few months later, F. Alfredo Pellas, general manager of Nicaragua Sugar Estates, Limited, proposed to Somoza that the government grant the company special rail and dock rates, as well as fiscal concessions, in order to proceed with the construction of facilities to export the refinery's surplus molasses, which up to then was being thrown away at the rate of one and one-half million gallons a year.[72] In November 1954, Pellas again wrote to Somoza requesting government authorization for an increase in Ingenio San Antonio's sugar export quota for the agricultural year 1954–55 to 300,000 quintals;* he figured that Ingenio San Antonio and its associated sugar mills would produce 800,000 quintals, while the others (including Somoza's installations at Montelimar) would reach 100,000 quintals, all of which would leave 400,000 quintals for export after subtracting the sugar required for internal consumption.[73] It is not clear how the regime responded to these requests, but it seems highly unlikely that the government would turn them down given the enormous weight that Ingenio San Antonio had in the national economy.[74]

The regime's relations with the private sector were not entirely devoid of friction. By the early 1950s the Somozas were a business empire on the same level as some of the much older families of Granada and León and had expanded into some very profitable ventures in addition to those acquired during the war years, which were mainly in agriculture and urban real estate. By 1950, Somoza was the principal shareholder of the internal airline, LANICA, and had set up his own liquor plant, Fábrica de Licores Bell. In 1953, he founded the sole national merchant marine company, MAMENIC Line, and also moved into the textile industry.[75] But the rest of the private sector does not seem to have been so concerned with the Somoza business holdings, as was the

*One quintal equals a little over one hundred pounds.

case in the early 1940s, due in part to the flourishing economy of the 1950s, which provided ample opportunities for many of the country's capitalists. In addition, the economic control exerted by the state's enterprises declined with the creation of the new private banks and the construction of the highway network as an alternative to the state railway. The typical complaints now voiced by Nicaraguan business associations had to do with government controls on imports and foreign exchange and with increased taxation.

These were old complaints that went back to the depression years of foreign exchange scarcity and had continued through the war with the government's import controls and rationing policies. When the war ended, the need for these controls declined as the supply of imported goods, mostly from the United States, increased and Nicaragua's accumulated dollar reserves were made available to importers. Nevertheless, the regime kept a handle on foreign exchange and import operations. In October 1945, a presidential decree allowed unrestricted imports of essential consumer goods but kept a lid on luxury items, which required special permits from the Comisión Reguladora de Comercio. In addition, all exports continued to be subject to authorizations extended by the Banco Nacional, together with the conventional stipulation that foreign exchange earnings would be deposited with the Banco Nacional in córdobas at the official exchange rate of 5:1. Nor was the private holding or purchase of foreign currency allowed.[76] But even with these measures, the country by 1947 practically had exhausted its dollar reserves in a shopping binge abroad. In early 1948 another executive decree placed greater restrictions on imports of luxuries and increased the proportion of the cash deposit required to purchase dollars.[77] In April 1949, the decline in export earnings required a further restriction on imports; a Comisión de Cambios replaced the Comisión Reguladora de Comercio and proceeded to enlarge the list of nonessentials and luxury goods. By the end of 1949, the Comisión de Cambios became simply a Contralor de Cambios, but the functions of all these government offices were basically the same: to control the distribution of scarce foreign exchange without having to take the politically costly step of devaluation.[78]

Devaluation finally came, albeit in stages. The executive decree of December 1949 setting up the Contralor de Cambios included a provision that allowed export producers to sell up to 20 percent of their dollar earnings on the open market, adding that dollars to pay for nonessentials and luxury imports only could be acquired in that fashion. Subsequently, in November 1950, a law approved by the Congress established a new exchange rate of 7:1 for all imports, although the official exchange rate remained at 5:1 (that is, the government's foreign loan obligations and imports would be figured on the lower rate). In turn, imports would be classified according to three categories: essentials, semiessentials, and nonessentials. The last two would be subject to additional deposits of one and three córdobas per dollar while the foreign exchange request was being processed.[79] In July 1955, the official rate for the córdoba finally was dropped to 7:1.[80] In sum, even in times of economic boom the regime retained its control of foreign exchange operations. All of these measures laid the basis for a stream of complaints from the private sector associations.

The Banco Nacional was the main target of criticism, given both its administrative control of foreign exchange operations and its preponderance in the nation's credit transactions. In late 1947, the Managua Chamber of Commerce stated that the Banco Nacional's operations were deficient in all respects and that a better alternative would be a purely autonomous central bank not under the direct control of the executive branch of government; such a "Banco Central Sociedad Anónima" would look after the country's finances in a more impartial manner and not automatically lend the government the monies it requested to tide over a budget deficit. According to the Managua Chamber, such frequent loans to the government not only increased inflationary pressures but also restricted the bank's ability to make loans to the private sector.[81] The Cooperativa Nacional de Agricultores, S.A., echoed a similar complaint in 1951 when it requested that the Banco Nacional's credit limits be raised in accordance with the inflation rate and that the bank's board of directors meet more often to speed up the processing of loan requests.[82]

But it was the exchange controls that received the most criticism. The León Chamber of Commerce stated flatly in July 1950 that eighteen years of state direction of the economy ("economía dirigida") had not yielded good results and that the exchange control mechanisms were largely to blame, in addition to the fact that foreign exchange always had been distributed to favor some and hurt others. Now was the time, the León Chamber said, to correct this policy, "to free commerce from the heavy weight of the controls in order to enter into a new era of economic readjustments and individual liberties, which is the basic condition to achieve success in the development of the country's finances."[83] At the same time, the chambers of commerce of the entire country met with the board of directors of the Cooperativa Anónima de Cafetaleros and worked out a plan to reform the exchange control regulations that would leave 80 percent of all foreign exchange in the hands of the exporters for free convertibility.[84]

This would invert outright the current proportion of foreign exchange distribution set by the government.

In February 1951, the Managua Chamber of Commerce complained that procedures to request foreign exchange were excessively complicated and that the Banco Nacional bureaucrats dragged their feet in processing the forms.[85] And when the first bilateral free trade agreement was reached with El Salvador the following month, the Managua Chamber again insisted that if free trade in goods was to be allowed, then it also was natural that free currency convertibility should go along with it.[86] In May 1953, the Managua Chamber repeated its complaints, adding that the system "has created a situation that is untenable for nearly all branches of private enterprise."[87] In early 1956, according to the chamber, the situation created by exchange controls and high duties had made imported goods both expensive and scarce in Nicaragua to the point that "thousands" of Nicaraguans were traveling to Costa Rica and Honduras to purchase what they needed.[88]

During this entire period the government stood by its policy of exchange controls. As a matter of fact, ever since September 1939, when it was first established, the Congress had reenacted religiously every year the "estado de emergencia económica," which placed restrictions on the constitutional right of freedom of commerce and under which the government justified the system of exchange controls.[89] That this situation of "economic emergency" remained in effect right up to 1956 and beyond was patently absurd from a strictly economic point of view; Nicaragua's economic situation in the 1950s hardly was similar to that of the late 1930s. Furthermore, in all likelihood it would have been sufficient to decree the state of economic emergency during specific periods when there was a decline in exchange earnings (such as occurred in 1949–50) or an excessive demand for dollars (as happened in 1947).

Instead, a chronic state of economic emergency must be explained in terms that are not altogether economic. In the first place, a totally free market for foreign exchange most likely would have resulted in fairly substantial swings in the exchange rate with the consequent fluctuations in the price of imports; such a situation would have meant political costs for the regime that it was not willing or able to absorb. Second, the politically charged environment that characterized the Nicaraguan economy was conducive to capital flight, so that an uncontrolled foreign exchange market could drain the country of its foreign currency reserves in a short period of time. And third, there can be no doubt that government control of foreign exchange was a potent political tool, just as control of bank credit had been during all the years of Somocista rule.

Although the black market offered an escape valve to the purchaser of foreign exchange in the same sense that private credit was an alternative to the Banco Nacional, the costs also were higher (in addition to the fact that it was illegal). Thus, an importer, a planter, or an industrialist preferred to work through the exchange control mechanism if at all possible while avoiding any open political opinions.

In addition to objecting to government controls on banking and foreign exchange, the private sector voiced its opposition to new taxes and social services that required additional contributions from the business community. The Managua Chamber of Commerce and the Cooperativa Nacional de Agricultores publicly objected to the income tax proposal put forth by the government in late 1952, arguing that its objective of redistributing the tax burden could not be reached as long as the myriad of indirect taxes on consumption were not rescinded.[90] The Managua Chamber also criticized the creation of the social security system in mid-1956 because of the large contributions that the private sector and the workers would have to make, although the measure in itself, the chamber said, could be construed as an important advance in the struggle for social rights (even though it might have been "politically motivated"). The Social Security Institute answered back that Nicaraguan industries had good profit margins that would allow them to cover their contributions, and that it was not right to deny workers their rights just to keep production costs low.[91]

One of the most revealing examples of the regime's attitude toward the private sector was a meeting that Somoza held with representatives of the Cooperativa Nacional de Agricultores on 29 November 1955. The representatives had requested the interview to discuss problems in the production of cotton, in particular the low yields and the low prices paid by the mills for raw cotton. They argued that the campesinos were receiving good salaries and that they were much better off than before, to which Somoza replied that he had never heard that the campesinos had ever been badly off during his administration. He then proceeded to lecture them on the nature of Nicaraguan capitalism: "Us farmers are rolling dice all the time. . . . On a given year we have a good harvest and then we swim in money; the next year both harvest and prices collapse and the situation changes entirely." He added: "When we earn a lot of money, for example, it never crosses our mind to offer the government a small part of our earnings for public works to benefit the country. You know that there are many such projects under construction and that loans have been contracted that have to be paid. All of us should sacrifice something at this

moment." Furthermore, the difficult economic times would separate the efficient farmers from those who had rented land at high prices to grow cotton but
who paid little or no attention to their farms. In any case, he said that *he* would
continue to plant cotton as usual.[92]

To the specific requests for help made by the planters, Somoza offered to put
together a commission composed of representatives of the Compañía Mercantil de Ultramar, the Banco Nacional, and the Cooperativa to look into the
planters' profits and losses and come up with some aid package that would
help those who really needed and deserved help. But he definitely rejected the
suggestion that part of the country's foreign exchange reserves be channeled
into agricultural credits, that railroad freight rates be reduced, or that growers
be paid for their cotton at a preferential exchange rate. He said that he would
consider a reduction in taxes on fertilizers and fuel, an extension on loan
repayments for machinery, a reduction of the prices charged by the cotton
gins, and lower handling rates at the ports. That is, the regime was willing to
provide limited help to the private sector in a moment of economic downturn
but otherwise expected businessmen to survive under the unwritten laws of
the capitalist system. Furthermore, the state's ability to help was limited by the
general economic situation of the country at the time. Somoza's reference to
outstanding loans and ongoing government investments suggested that the
government, too, had to look out for its own solvency. Thus, hard times had to
be shared by regime and private sector, a situation that Somoza, the politician-
businessman, most likely understood better than most.

Conclusion

Friction and debate between the Somocista regime and the traditional political
opposition and private entrepreneurs involved mostly matters of form and not
of substance. The process of negotiations leading up to the Pact of the Generals
between Somoza and Emiliano Chamorro did not require that Somoza give up
any significant portion of political power. Nor did it involve fundamental
changes in the Nicaraguan state. By promoting the appearance of power
sharing through predetermined electoral results and minority party representation in certain government bodies, the regime was able to enhance its
legitimacy without jeopardizing its control of the coercive apparatus (the
Guardia Nacional) or the principal institutions of the state (the national banks,
the economic development agencies, and the government ministries). For its

part, the Conservative opposition came to accept the need for a rapprochement with the regime after it realized that its overthrow through the traditional means of the *golpe de estado* was impossible and, perhaps most important, that there was no fundamental difference between Liberals and Conservatives after all. Carlos Cuadra Pasos, the most eloquent spokesman for the conciliatory wing of the Conservative party, expressed more concern about possible social explosions and political instability than about achieving a more representative government or improving the lot of the people. The Pact of the Generals in the end vindicated Cuadra Pasos's position and allowed the Conservatives to accept defeat gracefully.

Relations between the regime and the private sector followed similar lines of tension and conciliation but never of outright rupture. Undoubtedly, those entrepreneurs not tied into the Somoza group of companies ("the loaded-dice group," as Jaime Wheelock has described it) resented the advantages of preferential access to credit and foreign exchange. The IBRD, in its study of Nicaraguan economic development, attributed the low levels of capital formation in Nicaragua to a cautious attitude on the part of private investors, which they, in turn, attributed to a lack of confidence in the government and its policies. This was understandable, said the IBRD, because "political factors have often played a role in determining credit allocations, in approving new industries, and in various indirect, psychological ways." On the other hand, the IBRD observed that private enterprise also had been unduly cautious, seeking safe investments or quick returns: "It has engaged in land or real estate speculation or has sought profits from importing and exporting or from usury rather than from increased production."[93]

The IBRD's comments are not completely fair to the Nicaraguan business community. Although political factors were an important influence in the private sector's decisions to invest and produce, its performance during the postwar years was typical of a capitalist export economy that responded principally to stimuli from abroad. In other words, that this response was "speculative" had more to do with conditions in the world market for Nicaragua's export products than with internal conditions. Nicaraguan entrepreneurs simply did what they knew best how to do. And even though some of them might have complained about the regime's economic and development policies, their main concern was that the country remain at peace, that social stability be guaranteed at all costs, and that investments produce the best return possible. The Somocista regime responded adequately to these demands, particularly after it reached an agreement with the Conservatives in

1950. The Pact of the Generals, therefore, must be understood not only as Chamorro's capitulation to Somocista hegemony in the political and military spheres but also as a natural consequence of the demand of landowners and merchants that a new national consensus replace the old system of power struggles so plagued with uncertainty and fraught with violence. Chamorro, that symbol of eternal opposition and the last of the old-style caudillos of Nicaragua, who had fought Zelaya and Moncada and Somoza, had become a total anachronism within the new Nicaraguan state.

6 DEFENDING & OPPOSING THE REGIME

· · · · · · · · · · · · · · ·

By 1950 the regime of Anastasio Somoza had acquired the basic form and components that would characterize it until the death of the dictator in 1956. It formally had made its peace with the Conservative party through a number of pacts and limited political and bureaucratic participation that not only allowed for Conservative politicians to hold public posts but also had extended the helping hand of the state to diverse Conservative business groups. Moreover, the regime undertook to implement a policy of economic development that generally favored all businessmen and landowners within the geographic spheres of both Liberal and Conservative influence. Finally, it had carried out, with varying degrees of success, a number of fiscal and administrative measures that sought to update the state apparatus in keeping with the changing economic and political environment of the 1950s. All of these measures were taken within a period of marked economic expansion, which both required that the state adapt its practices to the new economic realities and made possible the regime's uninterrupted continuation in power.

But the regime's political alliances and the favorable economic conjuncture did not eliminate all of Somocismo's weaknesses. The continued presence of Somoza at the head of the government was not to the liking of everyone, much less of all Conservatives. Chamorro himself and his faction within the Conservative party remained critical of Somoza and his government. In addition, significant numbers of Nicaraguans remained in political groups that openly espoused the need to eliminate Somocismo, in particular the Independent Liberals, not to mention the Nicaraguan exiles who practically made a living by hatching plots and trying to implement them. In other words, the regime could not let down its guard and give the opposition of all stripes the benefit of the doubt for its good behavior. The coercive apparatus of the state and the political arm of Somocismo had to be buttressed constantly in preparation for any eventuality as well as to demonstrate to everyone that the Guardia itself and the Liberal party were under, and in, complete control. Somoza's reelection plans also required that the party machinery remain strong even though electoral manipulation and fragmentation of the opposition made a defeat at the polls for the Partido Liberal Nacionalista (PLN) highly unlikely.

The Liberal Party

As the political arm of the Somocistas, the PLN performed the vital function of rallying popular support for the regime and of getting out the vote on election day. The PLN was, above all, a very efficient electoral machine that was geared up in the period immediately preceding en electoral event. As had occurred in 1936 and in 1945, PLN activitists again engaged in the organization of "spontaneous" meetings of Somocista Liberals to proclaim the presidential candidacy of General Somoza beginning in the latter part of 1949 as well as in mid-1954 (for the 1956 elections).[1] These proclamations of the Somoza candidacy were sometimes held in an open plaza as a public meeting although most often they took place in the municipal building or in the house of the local Liberal caudillo. After drawing up a declaration in which Somoza's attributes were listed in glowing terms, those present signed and committed themselves to work for the campaign. Subsequently, the proclamation was sent off to Managua, where the Somoza newspaper *Novedades* made it a point to publish the event as part of a supposedly widespread grassroots movement demanding that Somoza remain in office.

A variant on the public proclamation of Somoza's candidacy was the individual confession of political faith to the Somocista camp. A "Libro Rojo" was kept in each municipality in which all Liberals were registered. New converts to the fold had their names included and simultaneously signed statements in the presence of witnesses explaining why they had become Somocista Liberals after years of belonging to the Conservative party or to none at all. Usually, Somoza's commitment to peace and progress was emphasized in comparison to the lack thereof on the part of the Conservatives and Emiliano Chamorro; such was the case of Anibal Hernández and Ricardo Irigoyen of Ometepe Island, who claimed in their statements that the Conservatives "are opposed to the nation's culture and progress and only want disorder and violence through which they always have bloodied the Nicaraguan soil."[2] In Jinotepe, department of Carazo, seven inhabitants of the village of La Conquista signed up during August 1956 after years of belonging to the Conservative party, explaining that they appreciated the peace and progress that Somoza had given Nicaragua in stark contrast to "the horrors, the mistakes, and the intranquility under which the Conservative leaders kept the Republic in years past."[3] Such conversions need not have been totally sincere or unsolicited; one Tomás Adolfo Martínez, president of the local Liberal committee in Ometepe Island, sent Somoza the conversions of Hernández and Irigoyen mentioned above with a note stating that these were "two new supporters who, together with the others that I have sent you, will contribute as good *Somocistas* to the triumph of your candidacy."[4] Obviously, Martínez was seeking to win points with Somoza through the recruitment of party members.

These proclamations and individual commitments were followed during the presidential campaign itself by larger meetings in which party leaders or Somoza himself gave speeches and the crowd was regaled with food, liquor, and fireworks. When Somoza arrived in Rivas in February 1950 for a rally in support of his candidacy, 1,500 people showed up; they were provided with 400 liters of aguardiente and issued small cards, popularly called *magníficas*, with a photograph of Somoza and the printed message: "The bearer of this card attended the proclamation of General Somoza's candidacy for the Presidency of the Republic. Rivas, 26 February 1950."[5] In both cases, affixing a signature to a list and carrying a magnífica granted the individual a public recognition of his Somocista militancy which would come in handy when dealing with the authorities or requesting some favor from the powers that be.

The PLN's campaigns ended with massive rallies in León and elsewhere for which all the state's resources were pooled to bring the people out. The railroad and the government's trucks provided free transportation, while food and drink kept the people in place as Somoza and his retinue made the rounds and gave their speeches.[6] In general, the PLN left nothing to chance: people took electoral campaigns seriously even though they might have attended the rallies and *proclamaciones* for any number of reasons, including personal convenience or peer pressure. Whatever the motivation for actively supporting Somocismo, popular mobilization was a key element of the regime's strategy to maintain its presence and control the population. In addition to keeping the party apparatus in working order, it also brought the people together to support a figure and an organization with which each individual could identify and from which some tangible benefit might be forthcoming.

In fact, the PLN did promise things that were of some interest to the average citizen, the campesino and the urban worker; it had an ideology and a platform that were publicly broadcast through fliers and pamphlets. For the 1950 election, the PLN drew up a platform that offered to open up virgin lands for colonization by small farmers and promised to extend title to those campesinos who currently were working on state-owned lands. For the urban worker, the PLN offered a social security system and increased state investments in public health, electrification, and housing. In Somoza's own words, "I want the Nicaraguan people to be a wholesome people, living in decent and happy homes and imbued with simple virtues."[7]

In 1956 the PLN offered to continue pursuing the "profound transformations" that the country had experienced over the previous six years, in particular those that directly benefited the workers such as the social security system and the public school network.[8] This is not to say that the regime's actual accomplishments in any way approached what it had promised. A case in point is the repeated pledge in the 1956 platform to push through a *ley agraria* to permit campesinos to assume ownership of state lands they might be farming, an offer that had been made previously in 1950. Still, the inclusion of political promises appealing to the workers and campesinos suggests that Somocismo at least recognized their importance in generating electoral support.

The PLN also continued to stress that its ideology and its practical accomplishments set it apart from the other political currents in Nicaragua at the time. Of particular relevance to the Somocistas were the 1945 labor code, the low-cost housing projects, the income tax, and the social security legislation of 1956, all of which contrasted with the Conservative party's stance of generally opposing all legislation that involved the state in regulating the relations between capital and labor or in directly assisting low-income groups. As a consequence of these measures, Somocista publications described Nicaragua as emerging from a semifeudal order of backwardness and social injustice; the new order, in contrast, sought to raise the living standards of the people through a policy of economic development and "social equilibrium," while fighting all "extremist" ideologies of the left and the right (although the communist "menace" was mentioned much more often as the main enemy).[9]

Ideology and party programs may have been important for the party's leadership and certain urban social groups, but in a country with high levels of illiteracy and a large rural population, these probably were not priorities in the minds of most people. The PLN's presence was much more significant in a physical sense, in the form of party members, local caudillos, block and district organizations, and the influence that could be exerted through them. Keeping that party organization in working order and sufficiently financed was an ongoing concern of the leadership, although the intense activity occurred at election time or at some moment of serious political tension within the country, as happened in 1947, in 1954 during an armed uprising, and again with Somoza's assassination in 1956.

The party's formal structure remained unchanged after the reforms that Somoza introduced in 1944, through which the power of its national authorities increased noticeably. At the top of the structure was Somoza himself, the *jefe máximo*. Under him, the Junta Directiva Nacional y Legal administered the party through a full-time paid staff in Managua, with the departmental committees under the control of the local caudillos, individuals who generally held some post in the Congress or in the government bureaucracy. In the towns and the rural areas, the party committees seem to have been under the control of lesser caudillos and the jueces de mesta.

During an electoral period, however, the party's activities became much more widespread and its structure expanded. In addition to the "regular" party structure there sprouted up all sorts of committees of diverse Liberal groups dedicated to the cause of Somocismo. The most common were the so-called *comités de propaganda pro-General Somoza*, whose sole function was to push Somoza's candidacy (which was a foregone conclusion, anyway) and thereafter to contribute to the electoral activities themselves. In the department of Madriz, for example, the Comité Departamental de Propaganda set up seven local committees with a total of 114 party faithful committed to furthering Somoza's candidacy in 1950; these local committees in turn organized 91 *comisiones de propaganda* to undertake specific campaign activities.[10] For the 1956 election, in addition to the PLN structure itself, there appeared a considerable number of electoral organizations that seem to have resulted from local initiatives seeking to impress Somoza with their loyalty and drive. Thus, in Nueva Segovia we find the Frente Liberal Nacionalista, in Chontales a Sub-Comité Liberal de Obreros and a Sub-Comité de Obreros y Campesinos Liberales Nacionalistas pro Anastasio Somoza García, in Managua a Comité Central Ferrocarrilero Pro-Somoza, in Masaya a Frente Obrero Somocista, in Chinandega a Comité de Compactación Liberal, and so on.[11] There even was an attempt to create a national federation of so-called Frentes Populares Liberales Somocistas headed by Nicolasa Sevilla, a Somocista stalwart famous as a rabble-rouser in Managua.[12]

The most important electoral committee was, of course, the one at the top: the Comité Nacional de Propaganda Pro-Candidatura del General Anastasio Somoza. For the 1956 election, it included the bigwigs of the PLN, who made up the national committee composed of twenty-two individuals. Thirty-eight additional party members made up an advisory council, and fifty-eight ran specific committees (finance, publicity, press, radio, social assistance, membership, and legal advice).[13] But the weight and importance of this national committee most likely were based on the funds it disbursed during the campaign. As in previous years, most of the party's funds came from the 5 percent contribution of public employees' salaries, a sum that increased markedly during the 1950s as a result of the growth of the government payroll: from July 1947 to December 1949, the PLN received slightly over C$2 million from the 5 percent contribution, which amounted to something like C$69,000 per month, but from April 1950 to December 1955 it received C$8.9 million, or C$128,000 per month.[14]

During a campaign period the party's expenses were concentrated heavily in the media. Those outlays and "other" campaign expenses together accounted for over 80 percent of total party expenditures during the period 1950–52.[15] "Other" campaign expenses cannot be broken down on the basis of the available information, but additional party documents give some clues as to the nature of Somocista electoral persuasion. Liquor remained an important element and its contribution to the cause was quantified in precise terms: party planners projected the distribution of aguardiente by department during the 1950 campaign on the basis of the 1947 Liberal vote and a consumption per capita of 0.4 liters, for a total of 43,369 liters (rounded off to 46,800 to account for "derrame" or spillage). They also figured how much each vote would cost in each department based on the level of Conservative strength, the distances to be traveled, and the overall "political resistance of the opposition." Thus, Carazo, a small department heavily penetrated by Somocismo, was assigned C$3.00 per projected voter, as was León, where the Liberals would have no trouble winning. But Chontales, Matagalpa, Rivas, Boaco, and Granada were assigned C$5.00 per voter due to the strength of the Conservative party and the larger distances between settlements, while Managua and Masaya each got C$4.00 per voter because the strength of the two parties was generally balanced. Zelaya, huge and sparsely settled, was assigned C$10.00 per prospective voter.[16] Each projected vote for the PLN therefore cost on the average C$4.75 including a small sum for "unforeseen expenses." Presumably, these monies paid for food, transportation, banners, fireworks, music, podiums, and other expenses.

The 1950 campaign cost the PLN approximately C$1.4 million, according to party treasurer Castellón (see n. 15), but for the 1956 campaign the party accumulated a total of nearly C$5 million for expenses. Of course, the revenue that the PLN received through the 5 percent contribution was not its only source of funding, although it was surely the most important. In a crunch, the PLN could get a loan from the Banco Nacional, which would be paid back later with monies from the 5 percent fund. In addition, the PLN sold bonds to individual party members and others, promising to repay the value of the bond during the following presidential period. For the 1956 campaign, for example, the PLN printed and put on the market bonds for a total value of C$1 million in denominations of 10, 25, 50, 100, 500, and 1,000 córdobas; it promised to repay them "through lotteries as of 1 March 1957."[17] On other occasions, special party events were financed with funds provided by both the national PLN headquarters and private donations at the local level. Such was the case of Somoza's campaign trip to León in February 1956, which cost nearly C$77,000; of this amount, the PLN provided C$40,000 and the rest consisted of private donations in cash and kind (mostly cattle) and the proceeds from the sale of about 5,500 liters of aguardiente provided by the local government excise office.[18]

The Guardia Nacional

By these various methods, the Liberal party delivered the votes that legitimized the Somocista victories at the polls. However, such votes did not suffice to legitimize the regime's continuation in power in the sense of persuading the diverse opposition groups that Somoza was legally and constitutionally the president of the republic. The regime's existence and continuation in office were doubtless predicated on the control of the state's elements of coercion, principally the Guardia Nacional and various paramilitary groups in the country. In fact, the political machinery employed by the regime was an organically integrated fusion of the Liberal party and the Guardia Nacional, with Somoza the undisputed chief of both. The members of the Guardia were all Liberals, but even more so Somocistas, while the Liberal party members worked closely with the Guardia to impress upon the populace that the coercive power of the state was their own party's coercive power, too.

The interrelationship between the Guardia and the Liberal party was particularly in evidence in the late 1940s, when the regime's legitimacy within and outside Nicaragua was at a low level following the Argüello fiasco and Somoza's reelection plans. The attempted Conservative coup of September 1947 also

must have provided grounds for concern: in the months immediately following the attack on the Guardia posts of Muelle de los Bueyes and La India, the
Guardia and the Liberal party proceeded with all haste to reorganize the party's
paramilitary groups in defense of the regime since the old Liga Militar Liberal
apparently had fallen into disrepair. The new groups that were formed usually
were called "Reserva Civil de la Guardia Nacional" and were made up of
"Nationalist Liberal friends."[19] Such groups of "Reserva Civil" sought to cooperate with the Guardia in the maintenance of peace and order by following
instructions handed down by Guardia officers and reporting any "suspicious
activity"; furthermore, they could carry weapons, which they were expected to
use "responsibly."[20]

How many individuals were involved on a national scale in these groups of
Reserva Civil is impossible to gauge. The *actas de fundación* mention numbers
that range from 23 for a small company in Valle de la Gracia near Chinandega all
the way to a battalion organized in Masaya that had 322 members distributed in
nine companies.[21] In the department of Estelí, a battalion of 1,152 was organized and divided into four companies. But the largest contingent appears to
have been set up in Chontales, where the Conservative threat was perceived to
be most serious; in that department, a total of 2,492 "auxiliares de la Guardia
Nacional" had been inducted into the paramilitary structure by December
1947.[22] Considering that Chontales only had 85 regular Guardias stationed
within its boundaries in 1947, the incorporation of nearly 2,500 reserves at least
gave the impression of a massive increase in Guardia strength.[23] Not that the
Guardia's real firepower increased in the same proportion, of course; most of the
members of the Reserva Civil probably were not trained in the use of military
weapons, even though a number of them were authorized to own pistols and
hunting rifles. Whatever the case, the real objective behind this militarization of
Liberal party members was to provide a show of force in the face of a threatened
Conservative uprising and to place the Liberal political machine on an emergency footing that would allow for rapid mobilization should the need arise.

With or without Reservas Civiles or the Liberal party itself, the final arbiter in
moments of crisis was the Guardia Nacional. After the purge of dissident officers following Argüello's ouster, the Guardia remained totally loyal to the regime and was rewarded with substantial increases in its budget, even though
total troop strength generally declined until 1953. (See Table 6.1.) The decline
in the number of enlisted men was undoubtedly a reflection of the regime's confidence in its ability to control any situation as well as a greatly improved quality
of armament. The United States played a key role in this respect through

Table 6.1 Guardia Nacional Strength, 1946–1956 (1946 = 100)

Year	Officers	Enlisted Men	Total
1946	345 (100)	3,290 (100)	3,635 (100)
1947	n.a.	n.a.	3,546 (97)
1948	373 (108)	3,162 (96)	3,535 (97)
1949	394 (114)	3,544 (108)	3,938 (108)
1950	386 (112)	3,201 (97)	3,587 (99)
1951	402 (117)	2,962 (90)	3,364 (93)
1952	418 (121)	2,803 (85)	3,221 (89)
1953	458 (133)	2,814 (86)	3,272 (90)
1954	470 (136)	2,981 (91)	3,451 (95)
1955	n.a.	n.a.	4,155 (114)
1956	526 (153)	3,865 (118)	4,391 (121)

Source: Ministerio de Guerra, Marina y Aviación, *Memorias.* Data for 1947 and 1955 are from Nicaragua, Cuartel General de la Guardia Nacional, *Informe consolidado de fuerza de la Guardia Nacional*, box 351, and Fondo S. de Somoza, no. 11, AN. Troop strength is reported on or about 15 April of each year.

large increases in military assistance and training as part of its strategy to counter the nationalist government of Guatemala under Arbenz. In 1952 a U.S. Air Force mission arrived in Nicaragua, with the U.S. Army following suit the next year. In 1954 a Military Assistance Program was initiated.[24] As a result of these agreements, added to purchases of equipment that Somoza engaged in on his own, Nicaragua came to have the largest air force in Central America by 1955.[25]

In addition to the purchases of equipment and training that contributed to greater identification with the institution and its chief, Guardia personnel also were rewarded with attractive salaries and opportunities for enrichment through informal channels. During the period 1945–56, the average monthly salary of an officer rose by nearly two and half times, and that of an enlisted man by nearly three times.[26] Officers generally spent a lifetime in the service of the Guardia, with occasional leaves of absence from active duty to work in a Somoza enterprise or to occupy some diplomatic post abroad. While Guardia officers were on active duty, the abundant opportunities for graft and corruption must have increased their total income considerably.

Enlisted men also could participate in the take, but their opportunities were more limited. Nonetheless, for an enlisted man a Guardia career does not seem to have been unattractive; he was assured of medical care and could appeal to

Somoza himself for assistance in moments of financial difficulty. Somoza cultivated this personal contact with his men in the force by granting them special audiences and identifying himself with the smallest of their grievances. In a speech he gave at a dinner honoring his sixtieth birthday, Somoza underlined his commitment to the Guardia and its men; he said that they should consider him "as the benefactor of the poor and the humble of the Guardia Nacional . . . as a brother and a father." He announced then that all members of the Guardia, his "friends and brothers," would receive a lighter with his signature engraved on it so that every time they took a smoke they would remember their "Jefe, Compañero, Padre, y Hermano." As a result of these generally favorable conditions for the Guardia's common soldier, the number of yearly reenlistments ran more than double that of new enlistments from 1947 to 1956.[27]

The Guardia's role in Nicaraguan society was a varied one. It included police functions and the defense of the national territory; the first was obviously the most important, since Nicaragua never was threatened by outside invasion.[28] But most important by far was its defense of the regime, which, in practice, meant assuring that no Chamorrista plot or other uprising could succeed and that no insurgence within the Guardia could spread throughout the force. To that end, a majority of the Guardia's troops and personnel were stationed in the Managua area, where they could be watched more carefully by the Jefe Director and, should the need arise, dispatched to any part of the country on short notice. In addition, troop concentration in Managua was the last line of defense for the regime in case of armed insurrection. As can be seen in Table 6.2, the increase in Guardia strength as of 1954 was due largely to the concentration of more troops in Managua; not even strongly Conservative departments were assigned many more soldiers. By December 1955, over 60 percent of the force was stationed in Managua and outlying areas.

The limited increase in Guardia strength in the departments of the interior no doubt also reflects the degree of political control that the central government exercised over them through nonmilitary measures. In addition to the Liberal party structure and the paramilitary organizations, the Guardia Nacional ran political intelligence operations on a widespread basis, relying on paid spies as well as members of the Liberal party and the Reserva Civil who made it a point to eavesdrop at opposition events and talk to opposition leaders.[29] Finally, the total control that the Guardia exercised on the right to bear arms and its monopoly on military weaponry gave it an overwhelming superiority of firepower over any group or combination of groups that might attempt a

Table 6.2 Guardia Nacional Troop Distribution

	May 1947	%	July 1951	%	June 1954	%	Dec. 1955	%
Managua*	1,704	(48.1)	1,834	(55.2)	2,092	(56.9)	2,703	(61.6)
3d. Bat. (Granada, Masaya, Rivas)	302	(8.5)	257	(7.7)	253	(6.9)	293	(6.7)
4th. Bat. (Chontales, Boaco)	157	(4.4)	141	(4.2)	157	(4.3)	176	(4.0)
5th. Bat. (León, Chinandega)	281	(7.9)	237	(7.1)	227	(6.2)	255	(5.8)
6th. Bat. (Nueva Segovia, Estelí, Madriz)	341	(9.6)	264	(8.0)	333	(9.0)	345	(7.8)
7th. Bat. (Matagalpa, Jinotega)	243	(6.9)	176	(5.3)	156	(4.2)	194	(4.4)
8th. Bat. (Zelaya)	359	(10.1)	299	(9.0)	352	(9.6)	312	(7.1)
Others	159	(4.5)	115	(3.5)	108	(2.9)	113	(2.6)
Total	3,546		3,323		3,678		4,391	

Source: Nicaragua, Cuartel General de la Guardia Nacional, *Informe consolidado de fuerza de la Guardia Nacional*, box 351, and Fondo S. de Somoza, nos. 1, 11, AN. The choice of data on troop distribution for specific dates is solely a reflection of its availability.

*Includes Presidential Guard, troops of Second Batallion stationed in Managua and Carazo departments, Managua police force, General Staff, Military Academy, Air Force, and others stationed permanently or transient in Managua.

violent action against the regime. Chamorro's decision to come to terms with Somoza undoubtedly was a reflection of his realization that the regime was virtually invulnerable to armed pressure and that the most that he could achieve was a modus vivendi that allowed for some degree of political activism and a share of government posts.

The Civic Opposition

Not everyone shared Chamorro's appreciation of the political situation of Nicaragua nor was Chamorro himself ever totally committed to a subservient role for the Conservative party or for himself, as demonstrated by the events of April 1954. However, the more straightforward groups that opposed Somoza, those that called for an end to Somocismo and for changes of one sort or another in the socioeconomic structure, represented a departure from the traditional Conservative party or even the PLI. It was a new opposition, frequently critical of both the PLI and the Conservatives, either because of their demonstrated inability to rid the country of the Somozas or, worse still, because they had come to terms with the regime. Thus, as it consolidated its position, the Somocista regime gave rise to an opposition whose rhetoric, tactics, and organization were substantially different from those of years past.

Three types of opposition to the regime can be identified in the years following the Argüello fiasco: a "civic" opposition, an exiled opposition, and an armed opposition. These categories were not mutually exclusive; at any time a member of the civic opposition might join up with a group involved in an attempt to violently overthrow the regime, while exiled opponents were involved with equal ease in supporting political or military strategies against Somoza. However, the absence of a unified front among the different opposition groups substantially diluted their efforts to rid the country of Somoza; instead, the facility with which the regime handled these diverse groups enhanced its image as a powerful and stable government that could set its own terms in the political debate.

The civic opposition evolved out of the old party structures of both Conservatives and Liberals. The Liberal offspring, the Partido Liberal Independiente, was undoubtedly the most pervasive presence within the civic opposition. Ever since its appearance in 1944, the PLI had remained fully opposed to Somoza, rejecting any kind of pact or agreement to bury its differences or to join in a governing coalition. It had no trouble in forming a coalition with the Conservatives for the 1947 election, but it broke with the party in 1950 when Chamorro came to terms with Somoza and agreed to run a candidate in the elections that year. The problem with the PLI was that its claim to opposition was basically only that: it was against Somoza, against presidential reelection, against any pact. But it never made clear what it stood for.

To begin with, the PLI retained the official platform and statutes of its ancestor, the PLN, until 1961, when a national assembly of the party decreed a new set of its own. In this sense, the PLI was hardly a real alternative to the Somocista PLN.[30] With the middle class (doctors, lawyers, pharmacists, teachers, and university students) as its principal political clientele, it was never able to make inroads into the industrial labor sector and, much less, among the rural workers and small landowners. Nor did it receive much support, either moral or financial, from the business community, with the result that the PLI always was strapped for cash.[31] To compound its difficulties, the PLI was never a legally recognized party, so that its only means of participating in an election was in coalition with the Conservatives, which it did but once—in 1947, when Dr. Enoc Aguado, the PLI leader, was the coalition's candidate for president.

Because it had no legal existence of its own, the PLI could function only with difficulty between the periods of electoral campaigning. It thus had few opportunities to recruit new party members and never found it easy even to hold meetings of its leadership at the regional or national level; furthermore, the Guardia Nacional often watched its activities, which required a certain amount of clandestine behavior by the party members.[32] And finally, the PLI retained an anti-U.S. streak that it expressed in terms of its supposedly Sandinista origins and its rejection of U.S. backing for Somoza. In contrast to the PLN and the Conservatives, the PLI apparently never engaged in formal communications with the U.S. embassy in Managua, which in Nicaraguan politics was considered a prerequisite for a minimum level of political activity.[33]

In sum, the predicament of the PLI was that as its prestige grew over the years as a staunchly anti-Somocista group, its real force as a political movement waned following the initial euphoria of the events of 1944. The problem was that some of its leaders were in exile, such as Carlos Pasos, who had been living in Costa Rica since 1947, while the others had fossilized the party structure by not opening up positions for newer and younger members. The national convention of the PLI that met in León in February 1956 was headed by the same governing board ("junta directiva") that had led the party since 1944. On a more fundamental level, the party stood accused by some of its more prominent leaders of neglecting its ties to the popular masses and of limiting its activities to political confabulations ("intrigas de alcoba") and meetings of small numbers of individuals.[34] It could be argued, of course, that within the constraints imposed upon political activities by the regime there was not much more that it could do. Nonetheless, as time went by the level of dissatisfaction among the more activist and impatient party members was bound to grow and new channels and methods of political expression and dissent appeared.

Within the Conservative party there were also voices critical of the party's actions and its ideology (or lack thereof). As early as 1947, Carlos José Solórzano, a Conservative leader, published a booklet outlining a future plan of action for the Conservatives. In his La ideología que debe sustentar el Partido Conservador de Nicaragua, Solórzano stated that the Conservative party had never developed a coherent and complete ideology but had limited its pronouncements to electoral platforms that reflected immediate concerns at the expense of a long-term blueprint for Nicaraguan society. On the other hand, he said, the Liberals of the Somocista or Independent version were no longer a viable ideological alternative. Instead, the future political struggle in Solórzano's mind would be between conservatism and socialism; the latter was a real political alternative, "a more modern ideology, more demagogical and more gratifying to the passions and the desires of the masses." To counter this threat, the Conservatives could not turn to the left, because that would run contrary to their respect for traditional values of family, religion, and individual freedom, nor would such a shift fit into "our geographical situation, which at the moment ties us to the influence of the United States." Nor could the Conservatives turn to the right, because that would identify them with clericalism and the defense of capitalism and social privileges. Instead, the proper position would be in the center and *above* the right and the left, a true reflection of Nicaragua's social reality and the needs and aspirations of the people as a whole.

Solórzano argued that Nicaragua was Christian country, and therefore the party should base its ideology on the Christian ethic. Second, Nicaraguan society was experiencing at increasing levels the conflict between capital and labor, a solution for which required a turn toward socialism, albeit a type of "spiritual socialism" espoused at the time by President Arévalo of Guatemala. Third, even though this socialism would favor the workers and the peasants, it did not mean the expropriation of the capitalists but a recognition of the right of the working class to benefit more fully from the fruits of its labor. Finally, the society the Conservatives should work for would recognize the "natural inequalities" present among men but would seek to lessen those inequalities at least at the economic level without going the way of materialist, egalitarian socialism of the Soviet type. In sum, Solórzano said, "we must accept the Christian and humanitarian side of socialism. If our party, as is the duty of any group of true Christians, does not stand next to the worker instead of the capitalist, our ideology will be at the service only of a small class, whose exploitative tendencies it is necessary to correct."[35]

Three years later, in 1950, Rafael Paniagua Rivas wrote another short piece on the Conservatives' future political line. In addition to the Conservative maxims of respect for traditions, religion, and a transcendent conception of man and society, Paniagua Rivas argued that change within the party was necessary if its "historic mission" were to be carried out, especially in view of the party's excessive "opportunism" and its lack of solidly founded guiding principles. He stressed the need for an equilibrium between authority and liberty, and a rejection of extreme liberal individualism as well as of the dictatorship of the proletariat of the Marxists. To that end, the new order the Conservatives should strive for would be "Social Christian," in which the needs of the individual would balance out with the requirements of the society, private property would satisfy both individual and social functions, capital and labor would work harmoniously, and material goods would be equitably distributed to further the common good. In turn, ample participation in government was the political correlate of this new social and economic order.[36]

These ideas of ideological reform within the party were picked up by the younger party members who organized a group called Juventud Conservadora, which was led by the sons of older Conservatives from the Granada region. They not only demanded a new orientation for the party but a change in its leadership as well. They were particularly critical of Emiliano Chamorro and those Conservatives who occupied posts in the various branches of government by virtue of the Pact of the Generals of 1950 but who did nothing to improve the lot of the people.[37] They also criticized the old leadership for not allowing new blood into the higher party echelons and for employing the same tactics that Somoza used to railroad the election of party authorities within the PLN.[38] In their stand, the Juventud Conservadora was supported editorially by La Prensa, which had just come under the direction of Pedro Joaquín Chamorro Cardenal upon the retirement of his father, Pedro Joaquín Chamorro Zelaya. Carlos Cuadra Pasos, the éminence grise of the party, also endorsed the Juventud and its leader, José Joaquín Cuadra, his son.[39]

Under pressure from the main opposition newspaper, from the party youth, and from party stalwarts disgruntled with the leadership of General Chamorro and the old guard, the Conservative Gran Convención held in Managua in February 1954 agreed on a number of important changes in the party's political stance and program. It formally declared that it opposed any form of "continuismo" of the Somozas, either through a constitutional amendment or the election of another Somoza to the presidency, both of which it considered a violation of the 1950 pact. The party promised to use "all the resources at its disposal" to thwart such an event, including alliances with all other opposition political forces and electoral abstention as a measure of last resort. These were hardly new tactics in the party's recent history, but they did signal that the spirit of the 1950 agreement was very much in doubt and that collaboration with the Somoza regime would not be continued, which was one of the

Juventud Conservadora's demands. The party convention also approved a resolution in support of free and unhindered labor union organization and the implementation of a land reform program on public or privately unutilized lands. Both of these resolutions represented important departures from the party's line of the previous decades, when the Conservatives had opposed the 1945 labor code and any talk of land redistribution. Finally, the party repeated its support for a nonpolitical Guardia Nacional and for improving the remuneration and equipment of its troops, obviously an attempt to undercut Somoza's own control and prestige within the Guardia.[40]

Although the 1954 convention represented a shift in the Conservatives' political posture, the old guard still maintained a stranglehold on the party's leadership. Chamorro was able to impose his candidates for the major party posts, including the president of the party's *junta directiva*, Emilio Chamorro Benard, who was elected by a vote of 99 to 1, with Carlos Cuadra Pasos occupying the vice-presidency by the same vote margin.[41] It was not until the decade of the 1960s that a new generation of Conservatives came to the fore under the leadership of Fernando Agüero; this was due not only to the ambitions of the younger Conservatives but also to the deaths of Chamorro and Cuadra Pasos themselves. Thus, during the 1950s the Conservatives remained what they had always been: a party with a closed leadership structure, a program of government with little substance, and only one important political asset, Chamorro himself.

In addition to the traditional opposition to the regime represented by the Conservatives and the Independent Liberals, a number of other political groupings emerged in the years following the 1947 political crisis. None of them ever became consolidated as a permanent fixture in the country's political system nor did they ever win much popular support. Such was the case of the Unión Nacional de Acción Popular (UNAP), founded by students at the university at Managua in 1948 under a Social-Christian inspiration.[42] In the early 1950s, UNAP entered the political arena seeking alliances with the established political parties. It defined its objectives at that time as a struggle against Somocismo, communism, and social injustice.[43] It faulted the Somoza regime in particular for the evils that had befallen Nicaragua, including the corruption of the theory and the practice of democracy under an unpopular Guardia Nacional and the excessive centralization of political and economic power. As a result, UNAP said, the Nicaraguan population was disillusioned and frustrated, indifferent to the corruption in the government, and thus prone to the appeals of the communists.[44]

As Somoza's reelection plans became more obvious, UNAP took it upon itself to organize the opposition in an electoral block; in July 1955 it held a rally of the opposition where the speakers included representatives of the PLI, the Conservatives, some small opposition groups, and labor leaders from the left. At this meeting, the formation of the Frente Defensor de la República (FDR) was formally announced.[45] By early 1956, the FDR had become the opposition's chief weapon in the struggle against Somoza. It organized meetings, sold bonds, published fliers, set up departmental committees, and denounced government repression of its activists, all of this under the slogan "Democracia representativa—no reelección."[46] But the FDR rejected openly any support from the Marxist left, arguing that it opposed the communists both on ideological grounds and because they had once before allied themselves with Somoza.[47]

The Labor Opposition

The FDR's rejection of the left meant fundamentally a rejection of certain labor unions, because the left had no political organization that was able to operate openly or clandestinely in Nicaragua. Leftist activities, therefore, were limited to union organizing and the publication of a newspaper and occasional leaflets. Nor was the FDR's rejection of the left translated into significant loss of political support in the campaign against Somoza. The labor movement was terribly fractured, infiltrated, and generally weakened since the repression of opposition labor leaders during and after 1947. Part of the movement identified openly with the regime, another part was an occasional collaborator, and a third group was formally illegal although the regime allowed it to exist. According to an internal report prepared in February 1953 by the Comité de Unidad y Reconstrucción Sindical (CURS), a front for a Marxist labor group, the Confederación General del Trabajo (CGT) represented the "Peronist" tendency within the labor movement. It occasionally made tepid anti-imperialist statements and demanded social security legislation and reforms of the labor code, but it engaged in discussions with Somoza and some of its leaders received money from the government. At most, the CGT demonstrated a minimum of autonomy in its calls for labor unity, including a willingness to hold talks with the Marxist left. A second group, the Federación Sindical Nacionalista (FSN), was openly Somocista and its work consisted primarily of making propaganda for the government. Its leaders, according to the CURS, were all *orejas* (paid government spies) whose main function was to keep an eye on the activities of CURS. A third group, the Asociación de Sindicatos Libres, had just come into existence with the support of the building trade workers and the U.S. embassy; it called for labor unity but explicitly insisted on the exclusion of the communists.

Despite the existence of a number of labor federations and movements, the CURS report underlined the fact that the majority of Nicaraguan industrial workers remained unorganized in the mines, the lumber companies, the sugar and cotton mills, and a variety of urban factories, due in large part to the repressive practices of a regime that prohibited workers to come together and discuss common problems. Members of the CURS were particularly targeted for repression; they claimed that some of their cohorts were expelled from the CGT simply for requesting a pronouncement in favor of world peace. The lack of CURS's legal standing was particularly troublesome, according to the report, and among the recommendations was a call for increased efforts to achieve unity with the other labor organizations and the need to emerge from a clandestine status into open activism. In particular, the report proposed to deemphasize political or ideological stands and replace them with a more bread-and-butter approach that would appeal to workers.[48] All in all, the report reflects a basic impotence on the part of the more radical elements in the labor movement to do much more than press for accommodation with the regime and the other labor organizations, while at the same time recognizing that the regime did allow for some labor activism and that its main interest was in the control or co-optation of the leadership.

In fact, the regime never relied on any massive repression of the labor movement, preferring instead to apply selective pressures to maintain high levels of disunity within the movement. The CGT was a case in point. As the largest federation, it included factions openly identified with and opposed to the regime, with a third group trying to maintain some level of autonomy (the so-called Peronist group). When the leadership of the CGT met in Managua in April 1953 to plan for a congress that would work for the unity of the labor movement, the more leftist members objected to inviting the Federación Sindical Nacionalista because of its obvious ties to the regime, while the pro-Somoza groups objected to inviting the Unión General de Trabajadores (UGT) because it was led by the socialists Juan Lorío and Armando Amador.[49] The struggles within the CGT still continued in 1955, when Somoza's reelection campaign was in full swing and he was seeking support from the labor movement; one group, under the name of Unión Popular Nacional de Obreros y Campesinos (UPNOC), was forced to quit the CGT for attempting to "politicize" the labor movement in favor of the Somoza candidacy.[50]

In the end, the CGT issued a statement critical of the situation of the Nicaraguan worker, which it attributed to the fact that the economic boom was benefiting only a small minority of the wealthier inhabitants of the country. The CGT, therefore, requested that the government decree an increase in salaries and extend more credit to the small and medium producers of basic foodstuffs. On the other hand, the organization recognized that the regime had favored the working class through the creation of the social security institute and praised Somoza for his offer to promulgate an agrarian law. The CGT thus decided to "[support and defend] decisively the government of Somoza in its policy of social improvements."[51] This was precisely what the regime looked for: a recognition by the labor movement that Somoza took the working class into consideration in his government's program and that his government was willing to listen to grievances and do something about them to some extent at least.

In truth, the labor movement could not do much more. Laws already on the books governing the existence and the functioning of labor unions and organizations gave the government an enormous amount of leeway and discretion to place limits on what unions could and could not do. Subsequent legislation expanded this authority even more. A *Reglamento de asociaciones sindicales* issued as a presidential decree in May 1951 defined in no uncertain terms what labor unions were for: to raise the "moral standing" of their members; to set up and manage cooperatives; to improve the intellectual, social, and physical conditions of the workers; and to obtain the unity of labor and capital. The Reglamento also stated clearly what they could not do: espouse communist or other "harmful" ideas, engage in political activities or join up with political parties for the same purpose, promote or support "illegal" strikes, and employ violence or pressure to achieve their ends. In addition, labor unions were required to provide the Ministry of Labor with complete lists of their members every six months; the ministry also could attend all union meetings to ensure that the provisions of the Reglamento were being observed. In fact, the ministry could dissolve a labor union if it did not comply with the stipulations contained in the Reglamento. Finally, the formation of labor federations was restricted in important respects. Federations could be organized only on a departmental basis; that is, labor unions from various departments could not organize a national federation. Nor was the federation of urban with rural unions allowed, so as to keep campesinos separate from factory workers. Only legally constituted departmental federations could proceed to form a national confederation and once constituted, federations and confederations were allowed to provide exclusively moral and economic support to their affiliated unions engaged in some labor conflict.[52]

The Casas del Obrero, already under government supervision since their creation in the 1940s, came under even stricter control. An executive decree of January 1951 declared that most Casas del Obrero in the country had not kept their account books in order and that their boards of directors had not been registered formally with the Ministry of Labor. Therefore, the ministry henceforth would name the boards of directors directly from lists presented by the various labor associations affiliated with the respective Casa. (Previously, under the old Reglamento issued in 1940, the boards were chosen by a general assembly.) Finally, the Casa's funds would have to be deposited with the Banco Nacional and monthly financial reports sent to the Inspección General del Trabajo of the Ministry of Labor. The ministry also could remove the board of directors totally or partially and name new directors if the board did not carry out the ministry's functions correctly.[53]

Despite this restrictive legislation, Somoza's public posture before the labor movement was one of open support for the working class. His message to the workers on May Day 1950, full of praise for his accomplishments and future plans, emphasized that his activities as a businessman and property holder "have not dried up in the least the fountains of justice that flow from my heart nor my passionate calling as a worker."[54] Labor leaders of all stripes wrote him requesting support for better wages and labor legislation, as well as seeking an appointment to speak to him in person.[55] He personally attended the signing of a new labor contract of the dock workers at Corinto that he had helped negotiate after weeks of agitation and work stoppages during the month of December 1955.[56] A leaflet put out by a Sub-Comité de Obreros y Campesinos in Chontales department went to the extreme of describing Somoza as "the first worker of the country," a man who left his executive office and went to work in the fields like any other peon.[57]

But the "first worker" also decided how far laborers could go in pressing their demands or expressing their views. His May Day message of 1950 warned against the most serious threat facing the Nicaraguan working class, that of international communism. He believed that the Nicaraguan workers would keep their distance from this menace "because if at some ill moment the siren of Soviet propaganda made its way among you, skulking and poisonous, everything would be lost. Communism eliminates all vestiges of liberty and establishes a barbaric despotism under which men become slavish robots of the state." In this vein, Somoza ordered in June 1953 the suspension of the weekly newspaper *Orientación*, a publication of the leftist UGT. *Orientación* had become openly critical of the capitalist system and of U.S. investments in Nicaragua, opinions that went one step too far within the limits set by the regime. But no reprisals were taken against the editors and contributors; as Minister of the Interior Modesto Salmerón explained, the objective was to close the paper and that had been achieved.[58] The following year, seven individuals were dragged before a court and accused of printing and distributing a leaflet critical of U.S. imperialism and intervention in Nicaragua.[59]

Censorship, Repression, and the Exiled Opposition

The limits set on the expression of labor unions and leftist ideologues applied to all groups within the civic opposition. All faced censorship, a policy that the regime had built up and refined over the years. Control over the written and spoken word was fundamental both to prevent the growth of an opposition whose activities eventually might become impossible to stop and to set down the rules of the game within which the opposition, in fact, could operate. The law on freedom of expression passed in September 1944 had remained on the books throughout this period; it prohibited the publication of material considered subversive to the public and social order or that incited people to disobey the country's authorities. But this law expressly forbade prior censorship of the media. In the wake of the Conservative uprising of September 1947, however, President Román y Reyes issued an executive order that contemplated prior censorship for those newspapers that infringed the limits of the freedom of expression contained in the 1944 law; in such cases, the president could prohibit the circulation of the offending issue of a newspaper.[60]

In July 1948 the Congress passed a law that repeated most of the provisions of the 1944 measure and set up a national tribunal composed of newspaper owners, Supreme Court justices, mayors, and jefes políticos that would judge those cases of infringement of the law.[61] Still another law passed in September 1953 abolished this special tribunal but made violation of the freedom of the press a criminal offense to be handled by the regular court system; in addition, this new law made any "offensive" criticism of the established authorities or of "friendly" foreign governments a punishable crime, and it prohibited anyone who belonged to a political party with international connections from owning a printing shop or a newspaper.[62] Finally, an executive decree of February 1955 specifically prohibited the circulation of any book, magazine, or other type of printed material that contained "communist propaganda."[63]

These administrative controls were complemented by outright corruption of the news media through payments to reporters and publishers. In one case, the Ferrocarril del Pacífico paid out about U.S.$3,500 to thirty individuals who worked for newspapers and radio stations during the period January–October 1952.[64] These "dádivas" or gifts were a form of bribery that guaranteed that the reporter or the publisher would present the news in the most favorable terms to the government or would refrain from publishing unduly critical material. This was an important consideration in a country where, according to the government's own admission, most of the newspapers formally did not follow the ruling party's line: in 1955, of the nine papers in Nicaragua, four were *gobiernista* or Nationalist Liberal and the remainder were Conservative, Independent Liberal, or simply independent.[65]

The combination of governmental corruption and legal restraints on the news media made it very difficult for the opposition to mount a concerted campaign against the regime; any criticism or call for action considered excessive by the government resulted in the immediate implementation of any of a number of measures at the government's disposal. Such was the case with *La Prensa* in March 1956, when Pedro Joaquín Chamorro published an editorial that in a very discrete fashion called upon the opposition to step up its political activities in light of Somoza's reelection plans. Chamorro wrote that the opposition only could effect real changes in Nicaragua when "all the members of these organizations [of the opposition] are willing to become heroes of the fatherland; when the day comes to pass that the men on the street, who do not seek a government post but who do love their fatherland and want to see it rid of oppression, come together and decide to suffer the attacks of the shock troops of the regime; only until that day can the democratic organizations demonstrate their civic strength."[66] The government immediately interpreted these words as a call to violent action against the authorities and took *La Prensa* to court. But the judge who heard the case eventually threw out the government's suit, stating that "the shock troops of the regime" were not the same as "the government's forces" and that resistance to those forces might be passive in any case.[67]

Such was the nature of freedom of expression in Somoza's Nicaragua. Restrictions and punishments were accompanied by apparently conciliatory measures, but the overall effect, as Chamorro wrote in an editorial in *La Prensa* on 13 March 1956, was to place such limits on the activities of opposition organizations so as to effectively prevent any real change from occurring in the country. In such an environment, some groups opted for removing themselves from the political system entirely and left the country to carry on their opposition from the relative safe haven of exile. Others were either forced to leave by threats or forcibly ejected from Nicaragua by the authorities. Once abroad, they still were not entirely free from the grasp of the Nicaraguan regime, as Somoza's diplomats and agents continued to exercise surveillance over their movements and pressured foreign governments to restrict their activities.[68] Nevertheless, they still were able to publish and organize with much greater freedom than their colleagues who remained in Nicaragua.

The exiled opposition was particularly active in Costa Rica and Mexico, where the opportunities for publishing and organizing were relatively good. From these countries, there issued a stream of communiqués and broadsides denouncing the regime and the collaborationist elements within the Nicaraguan political system and calling for a new social and political order. From San José, Costa Rica, the Partido Revolucionario Nicaragüense (PRN) published a newspaper, *Revolución*, during the years 1953–55. But few of these publications ever circulated in Nicaragua; their circulation abroad probably was limited, too. Still, their presence was worrisome to Somoza since their activities partially annulled the image that he wished to project abroad of a country internally at peace and of a population generally satisfied with his government.[69]

The danger that the exiled groups represented for the regime within Nicaragua, however, was minimal. On the one hand, their political expression was fundamentally a criticism of the Nicaraguan political system under Somoza and a call to the Nicaraguan population to rise up and overthrow the dictator. For example, the Pact of the Generals of 1950 generated much criticism among the exiled opposition because it was seen as a treasonous step on the part of Emiliano Chamorro. The Partido Revolucionario en el Exilio put out a leaflet in Mexico City demanding that Somoza and Chamorro hang from the same lamppost because Chamorro was nothing but the representative of the San Antonio sugar interests, whose main concern was to keep their properties safe from Somoza's greed. The Partido Revolucionario therefore called on all Nicaraguans to abstain from voting as a way of protesting the political system.[70]

On the other hand, the exiled opposition espoused a set of social objectives that, with few exceptions, hardly differed from the Somocista regime's stated policies. Such was the case of the PRN, which published its program in August 1953. Its list of objectives was a "more and better" version of what Somoza had been talking about for years: more highways, support for the working class, improvements in public health, extension of the educational system, political rights for women, and distribution of small plots of land for poor farmers.[71] The Unión Revolucionaria Democrática (URD), which included among its leaders some members of the PRN, repeated similar objectives upon its founding in Mexico City in 1954. At most, the URD recognized the need to incorporate the masses in the struggle against Somoza and to replace the traditional political dynamic of interelite competition ("de cúspide a cúspide") with a more generalized confrontation of the regime. It suggested that up to that moment both the opposition and the regime had utilized the masses for their own elitist ends: "the popular supporters of the opposition, as well as those of the Somocistas, lack all political education, do not know what their own parties believe to be the national problems, and ignore the solutions that their parties put forth." Both Somoza and the traditional opposition needed an unthinking and uncritical following that could go out into the streets and shout and vote accordingly. Or as the the URD put it: "In sum, with a real party, an ideology, and a program, Somoza would be in danger; without them, the opposition is doomed."[72]

The characteristic that determined the activities and the objectives of the exiled opposition was, in the final analysis, the class origin of its leadership, which was little different from that of the PLN, the PLI, or even the Conservative party. The Comité Central of the PRN was made up of three lawyers, one civil engineer, one journalist, five medical doctors, one general, one colonel, and one worker.[73] The founding group of the URD did not differ much, either. Thus, while the PRN criticized U.S. policy for supporting Somoza (although it claimed not to be "anti-yanqui") and spoke highly of Sandino, it rejected any alliance with the left, which "always has feigned ignorance of Latin American realities in order to follow obediently the orders of its Russian masters." Facing the other side of the political spectrum, the PRN sought to destroy "the bureaucratic and landholding oligarchies that hinder the progress of Nicaragua."[74] Not surprisingly, the PRN received expressions of support from the exiled Venezuelan leaders of Acción Democrática, Rómulo Gallegos and Rómulo Betancourt.[75] The URD also rejected the inclusion in its ranks of any communist or "friend of these," while underlining its support for the private sector and free enterprise.[76]

In general, the Nicaraguan opposition in exile projected an image and a program of a social democratic nature, much in line with similar movements and parties in Costa Rica, Guatemala, and Venezuela at the time. Their vision of the future was that of a Nicaragua without Somoza, of a state more attuned to the needs of the masses, of policies of social and economic development implemented by a regime that included greater participation in its decision making and that sought to institutionalize democratic practices and methods in the selection of the country's leadership. In their view, the objective was "the creation of an honest and efficient government to direct the building of our future."[77]

The exiled opposition was aware that its public denunciations were necessary to discredit and, if possible, weaken the regime, although in themselves these were not sufficient to bring down Somoza. They continued to make as much trouble for Somoza as possible, using all means public and legal, as well as clandestine and illegal: "we will repeat once and again, until it becomes a national obsession, the idea that Somoza is the essential obstacle that impedes the progress of Nicaragua, that he is, we insist, the number one public enemy of Nicaragua and of all Nicaraguans."[78] Eventually, they believed, public opinion would become so inflamed that Somoza would fall in the face of widespread demonstrations, general strikes, and public mayhem. Nor did they exclude armed insurrection, "but that is an aspect which we politicians are not familiar with. It is for others to plan and execute it. However, it is clear that its chances of success will be greater if it takes place within a climate of opposition and active resistance to Somoza, and not in that environment of passive conformity which confronted the men of April."[79]

The Armed Opposition

The reference to "the men of April" was to the failed armed revolt of 1954 in which a number of ex-Guardia Nacional officers and civilian members of the Partido Revolucionario Nicaragüense and the Unión Revolucionaria Democrática played a leading role. This was the first serious military undertaking against Somoza, clear evidence that some Nicaraguans were willing to take up arms to unseat the dictator. In 1947 Emiliano Chamorro and Rosendo Argüello, of the Conservative party and the PLI, respectively, had become parties to the so-called Legión del Caribe. But the Legión never got around to tackling Somoza; at most, it helped Figueres in his successful coup in Costa Rica in 1948. Chamorro's pact with Somoza in 1950 was, in part, a tacit recognition of the enormous military superiority of the Somocista regime and of the need to come to terms with it. Nevertheless, among the exiles in Costa Rica and Guatemala the idea of a military strike remained strong, especially among those members of the Guardia Nacional who had been cashiered by Somoza after the events of 1947.[80]

The main problem faced by these exiles was how to organize an attack and defeat Somoza and the Guardia Nacional militarily. Chamorro's attempt in 1947 was a clear lesson in how *not* to do it; that is, there was no sense in attempting sporadic or spontaneous attacks on isolated Guardia posts when the mass of the force was located in Managua and when Somoza's aviation could cover the entire country at will. Nor was it sensible to expect popular uprisings in support of a military action given the political control exerted by the PLN and paramilitary organizations throughout the country. The only viable alternative was a strike at the very heart of the regime's military machine, the Managua general headquarters of the Guardia Nacional and Somoza's own executive offices. By knocking out the central command and Somoza himself (either through assassination or capture) it could be expected that the rest of the Guardia's structure would collapse for lack of leadership and direction. There was even a historical antecedent for such a strategy: Chamorro's coup of 1926, the so-called *Lomazo*, which enabled the caudillo to take over the government with a minimum of fuss and little bloodshed, and Somoza's own attack on the fortress of Acosasco in León in 1936.

The organization of the strike involved getting money, buying weapons and transporting them to Nicaragua, and recruiting sufficient men within the country to use the guns against the regime. Money was raised from a variety of sources, including the Mexican comic Mario Moreno ("Cantinflas"), who gave U.S.$10,000, and the President of Cuba, Carlos Prío Socarrás. The plotters themselves, some of them men of means, put up money of their own.[81] Arms were then purchased in Mexico, including 100 automatic rifles, 325 carbines, 10 boxes of grenades, and assorted small arms, but apparently few munitions in view of the fact that only a series of short confrontations were expected. The weapons were transported to Costa Rica by air, where the plotters had Figueres's support. In San José, the plotters met with emissaries of Emiliano Chamorro, who agreed to furnish them with 6 safe houses and 300 men in Managua, which together with the 25 conspirators in San José who would infiltrate into Nicaragua added up to a total of 325 men. Eventually, at the end of March 1954, the weapons were transported across the southern Nicaraguan border and placed on boats for the trip up the Great Lake to a hacienda belonging to a Conservative sympathizer near Granada. From the hacienda, the weapons were trucked to another hacienda on the outskirts of Managua itself, where they were unpacked, cleaned, and made ready for use. This hacienda became the headquarters for the operation and here Emiliano Chamorro showed up with the men he promised, but instead of 300 there were only 80. Nor were other safe houses made available. Things had gotten off to a bad start.

Four groups were organized: two would attempt to intercept Somoza on his way to his farm at Montelimar on the Pacific coast (although no one was quite sure where Somoza really was), another would storm the Managua police headquarters of El Hormiguero, and a fourth would attack and take La Loma, the hill in Managua where the presidential palace was located. In the last two cases, the plotters would be seriously outnumbered because only 15 men were assigned to take El Hormiguero and 30 to attack La Loma, where a detachment of 100 Guardias was on duty permanently. The officer in charge of the attack on La Loma refused to go in with so few men, even though the element of surprise might have given them the edge. At this moment, the plan began to unravel; it unraveled further when on 5 April 1954 one of the plotters arrived to inform the rest that the government knew of the plot and that it was time to pack up and leave in a hurry. The two trucks were loaded up again and together with some of the men headed south on the Pan American highway; some 25 kilometers from Managua, they were intercepted and disbanded by a contingent of Guardias. Some men were killed outright in the hills covered with coffee bushes while others escaped only to be captured later on. The rest of the plotters sought asylum in the embassies of Guatemala and Costa Rica.

The government immediately decreed a state of siege and martial law in order to avert, in its terms, a situation of civil war. It also offered rewards of 10,000 córdobas each for information leading to the capture of seven ex-Guardias and eight civilians involved in the plot.[82] Somoza himself announced that the principal objective of the plot was to murder him but that at no moment did the uprising receive any support from the people, who recognized the importance of maintaining the peace that the regime so strenuously had worked to attain. He also underlined that the Guardia Nacional had remained totally faithful to its Jefe Director.[83] A month later, Somoza called a meeting of the diplomatic corps and the press at the presidential palace, where he displayed a cache of weapons, including some of Eastern European origin, discovered on the Pacific coast, so he said, in support of the conspirators; he ventured that they probably had been left there by a Soviet submarine that most likely meant to return later on with reinforcements.[84] Thus, Somoza could claim that Nicaragua had been saved in the space of a few weeks from the horrors of a civil war and a Bolshevik seaborne invasion thanks to the efficiency and speed with which the government and the Guardia Nacional had responded to these threats.

The suppression of the uprising was followed by a widespread repression of all anti-Somocista groups in the country. Many Conservative and Independent Liberal party members ended up in jail, from where they were taken to court and accused of sedition and attempted murder. The most prominent of these, such as Pedro Joaquín Chamorro and Arturo Cruz, received jail sentences that were commuted to house arrest after about one year; they were amnestied by Somoza in May 1956.[85] In the case of General Chamorro, then a senator, the Supreme Court found him and two other members of Congress guilty of attempted rebellion and sentenced them to house arrest; they also were amnestied after a year.[86] Finally, the state of siege imposed in April 1954 was lifted except for Managua and Carazo in July 1954 and for the entire country in April 1955.[87] "Normalcy" returned to the country after one year, while the surviving conspirators and their suspected sympathizers in Nicaragua were released from jail after two years. In this manner, the regime demonstrated its leniency with those who supposedly had learned their lesson and proved to everyone else that it did not fear to let its enemies back into the political system.

The Last Campaign

By early 1956 Somoza was on the road to a third nomination for president. On a campaign visit to León in February, he accepted his position as a candidate for the Liberal party's nomination, stating that the Rubicon had been crossed and there was no turning back.[88] In the following months, the diverse opposition groups all declared their intention to abstain from the electoral process if Somoza insisted on being a candidate. The Frente Defensor de la República (representing the Conservatives), the UNAP, the PLI, and the small Partido Renovación Nacional issued a manifesto stating that twenty years of Somoza rule in Nicaragua were hardly a strong guarantee that there could be fair elections; furthermore, if Somoza or some relative of his insisted on running for president, they would not participate.[89] The opposition did not name a candidate to oppose Somoza, but it did organize political acts to rally support for its anti-reelectionist stance in order to achieve the highest possible levels of abstention.

The regime allowed the opposition some leeway in its activities. Large rallies were held in Granada, where the FDR claimed an attendance of 10,000 people, and in Boaco, with a Conservative crowd estimated by *La Prensa* at 20,000. In both cases, however, the opposition said that the government impeded people from freely traveling to the cities and of arresting others after the rallies were over.[90] And in León, where the FDR opened its antireelectionist campaign in July, only 700 people showed up under the threat of armed goons and the competition of a simultaneous baseball game in Managua to which the railroad offered free transportation.[91] In August General Chamorro denounced other incidents of selective threats and imprisonments in various parts of the country, including that of a number of Conservatives who were tossed in jail in Chinandega "for speaking badly of Somoza"; the judge fined each one C$40 before setting them loose under the threat of another term in jail if they repeated the offense.[92]

Somoza's reelection plans and the opposition's antireelectionist activities came to a halt on 21 September 1956. On that day, Somoza was in León to accept the Liberal party's nomination for president, which by then was nothing but a formality. After the nomination and Somoza's acceptance speech, a celebration for the party faithful was held at the Casa del Obrero. An uninvited guest also made his way into the Casa, avoiding the lax security measures taken at the entrance. He moved toward the dais where Somoza sat with his wife and party dignitaries, pulled a revolver from his pocket, and fired a number of bullets point-blank at the dictator. Somoza's bodyguards shot him dead immediately, but Somoza was mortally wounded; he died one week later at the Gorgas Hospital in the Panama Canal Zone, where he had been flown on the instruction of President Dwight D. Eisenhower.

Somoza's executioner, Rigoberto López Pérez, was a Nicaraguan student and poet who had decided to sacrifice his life in exchange for that of Somoza's. He had lived for some time in El Salvador, where he came into contact with Nicaraguan exiles. There he decided to rid his country of Somoza and taught himself to use a handgun. That this plot never reached Somoza's spies was probably a consequence of the fact that so few people were involved, perhaps no more than ten. Nor did the opposition bigwigs like Chamorro or Aguado ever hear about the preparations. In fact, Somoza's assassination was organized and executed outside of the traditional opposition party structure of the PLI or the Conservatives.[93] On the other hand, to the extent that the event caught everyone unprepared, from the dictator's own security apparatus to the leaders of the Conservatives and the PLI, no one was able to build upon what López Pérez had done already. Instead, it was the regime that reacted—and with a savagery unheard of until then. Thousands of members of all stripes of the opposition landed in jail or were confined to their homes in a form of house arrest. A more select group was hauled before a military court and accused of participating in the assassination; some of the prisoners were convicted and sentenced but then released early in 1957 just before the next general election.[94]

The regime's repression seems to have been more in line with a preventive policy and the wrath of the two Somoza sons at the attempt on their father's life. At no moment was the regime ever in danger of toppling as a result of Somoza's death. Luis Somoza, the older son, had occupied a seat in the National Congress as a deputy since August 1950; he was elected president of the Chamber of Deputies in April 1951 and president of the Congress when both houses held joint sessions. When Somoza was shot, Luis immediately occupied the presidency pro tem and subsequently the Congress, with the tacit support of the Conservative congressmen, voted to have him finish his father's term.[95] The other son, Anastasio, Jr., had a similarly spectacular career in the Guardia Nacional after graduating from West Point in 1946. After the overthrow of Argüello he was named head of the presidential military staff and in 1950 director of the Military Academy, from whence he rose to become chief of the General Staff of the Guardia Nacional and acting Jefe Director when his father began his last election campaign.[96] While their father languished in Panama, both sons remained in Managua, thereby providing direction within the government and the army. When Somoza died finally on 29 September, the only thing left to be done was to bury him; a state funeral was held on 2 October 1956, during which maybe over 100,000 Nicaraguans accompanied Somoza to the Managua cemetery.[97] His remains lay there for a little less than twenty-three years, under the huge statue of a *guardia*, until they were hastily disinterred and transported to Miami by Anastasio, Jr., in the final moments before the Sandinista triumph of 19 July 1979.

CONCLUSION

. . . .

With the death of Anastasio Somoza García, the presidency of Nicaragua was occupied by his son Luis and the direction of the Guardia Nacional fell to his other son, Anastasio Somoza Debayle. What before had been under one head was now divided between two Somozas. However, it would be a mistake to see in this transfer of political and military power a dynastic phenomenon in the sense that the Somoza name of and by itself legitimized political authority. Since 1936, there had been presidents who were not Somozas and there would be others later on. In any political system, someone (either an individual or a group) must wield supreme power, someone must make decisions, someone must represent the authority of the state. The problem, therefore, is not one of determining who wields power but in deciding in whose interest power is wielded. This question must be answered, of course, in terms of concrete, specific measures that the state takes and that benefit some groups in society more than others.

   The state will claim to exist for the benefit of all the inhabitants within a given territory who are willing to abide by the rules set down by the state itself. But to the extent that social differences exist within society, access to political power and the rewards of political power will favor some more than others. In capitalist societies, the wealthier social classes will have the greatest advantages of influence and will demand that their interests be looked after before those of any other. The government that is able to satisfy the requirements of these economically powerful groups and that is able to put together a political coalition that meets with the approval of the owners of capital and wealth, in general, will provide a capitalist society with stable political direction and management.

Somocismo and Political Alliances

The entire twenty years of Anastasio Somoza's political control in Nicaragua were an uninterrupted effort at social and political alliance formation. Though it is true that Somoza came to the presidency by force, his 1936 coup was followed by a succession of measures and policy statements that sought to provide his regime with the political legitimacy it lacked due to its unconstitutional origins. So obvious were Somoza's attempts at alliance formation that his years at the head of the government and of the Guardia Nacional can be broken down into periods each characterized by a specific set of social and political actors within the ruling coalition.

From 1933 to 1943, the Somocista coalition was of a multiclass nature, so determined in order to face the harsh times of the depression by appealing to a variety of social groups and rewarding those whose participation was most vital to pull the country out of the economic slump. Thus, although the regime had warm words for the labor movement and it took measures aimed apparently at benefiting the wage earner, both middle class and working class, its principal and most lasting measures sought to help the coffee growers and the import merchants: devaluation, inflation, fiscal and banking reform, and the development of economic infrastructure all were intended to make Nicaragua's exports more competitive in the world markets by lowering labor costs and assuring sufficient capital for the requirements of economic expansion. That Somoza, his family and his cronies, benefited from these measures of economic stimulation does not mean that they were the only ones to do so or that they benefited the most.

Above and beyond the immediate advantages that they provided Somoza and his group, these measures set the bases for the modern, albeit underdeveloped and dependent, capitalist state in Nicaragua around which the different economic interests in the country could operate and prosper. And for those who were rewarded "negatively," who were forced to carry the brunt of the economic and fiscal measures, there was always the promise of a better future spelled out in some detail (such as social security legislation, a labor code, and land reform) and a number of small concessions, such as price controls, industrial safety legislation, and Sunday rest, which did not increase production and distribution costs significantly for export producers or import merchants.

From 1944 to 1947, and in response to a challenge to its authority from within the ranks of the PLN itself, the regime tilted toward the left by actively seeking the support of the urban laboring class. The seriousness of the threat to the regime, coupled with opportune U.S. pressure, forced Somoza to rethink his plans for continuation in office and consider a political alternative, which in the person of Leonardo Argüello can be construed as an attempt to seek a political accommodation with disenchanted Liberals. However, the size of the demonstrations during the July days of 1944 already had convinced the regime that it was necessary to organize its own base of popular support and neutralize potential labor opposition by creating a whole network of labor unions and finally implementing the labor code. But no measures were taken to harm the interests of the entrepreneurs, except to expropriate the land of German coffee growers and harass a small number of businessmen who joined the PLI.

From this perspective, the Argüello fiasco must be seen as a fluke, that is, an unexpected event that put great strains on the regime and the Guardia Nacional for a short time and that some political actors, such as General Chamorro, sought to exploit for their own ends. But not even armed uprisings, international censure, and U.S. pressure were enough to remove Somoza from his position of power in the Guardia Nacional or keep him out of the government. Instead, the events of 1947 must have convinced Somoza that his only reliable political allies were precisely the traditional enemies of his Liberal party, the Conservative oligarchs from Granada, whose conciliatory wing headed by Carlos Cuadra Pasos was willing to go out of its way to form a grand alliance with the Liberals.

From 1947 until 1956 (and thereafter), the modern Nicaraguan state came of age as the two principal political groups in the country reached fundamental agreements on the rules of the political game. Beginning with the understanding between Somoza and Cuadra Pasos and culminating in the Pact of the Generals, both parties set aside their minimal ideological differences and their already antiquated regional outlook and proceeded to share legislative and judicial functions within new economic times of boom and developmentalist policies. The state designed its activities and its institutional organization to back up this new economic and political orientation within which coffee and cotton growers, ranchers and dairymen, industrialists and merchants all could prosper in a secure environment. A strongly anticommunist ideological component in the regime's rhetoric, together with a controlled political environment and overwhelming coercive superiority, were fundamental conditions for creating entrepreneurial confidence and maintaining social order. The regime retained its links with the labor movement and proceeded to implement its promises in the field of social security and limited redistribution of the country's wealth through the income tax, but at no time did it give the private sector reasons for concern that it might be abandoning its commitment to capitalist development. Much more important, in this respect, was the regime's attitude toward foreign lending and assistance, which was channeled mostly into basic infrastructure and investments in agricultural and industrial production.

Throughout these three periods, the United States, undoubtedly part of the Nicaraguan political system and an important variable in the political outcomes within the country, expressed outwardly very different policies toward the Somoza regime. During the first period in question, the United States insisted on strict nonintervention in Nicaraguan internal politics. Such nonintervention, part of the Good Neighbor policy of the Roosevelt administration, obviously favored the stronger elements within the Nicaraguan polity, particularly Somoza and the Guardia Nacional, at the expense of the weaker groups. The insistence of the United States that Nicaraguans resolve their own problems without Washington's tutelage provided Somoza with an open ticket to proceed with his ambitions without the threat of U.S. retaliation. With Somoza in the presidency, strict nonintervention turned into diplomatic recognition and open support for the regime's employment and development projects (particularly highway construction) that Somoza had negotiated with Roosevelt during his visit to Washington in 1939. The world war was just around the corner and the United States needed reliable allies in Central America; in addition, Nicaragua could provide some important raw materials for the war effort.

With the war drawing to a close, and in response to increased antidictatorial sentiments in Central America, the United States began to distance itself from Somoza when he insinuated his desire for another term in office. The 1944 disturbances in Managua, orchestrated around the U.S. Independence Day, provided Washington with visible evidence of Somoza's unpopularity among certain important sectors of the Nicaraguan population: the urban middle class and the Conservative opposition, in addition to dissident Liberal entrepreneurs and intellectuals. That Somoza was able to defuse the crisis with a mixture of political and repressive measures indicated to Washington that he could not be pushed out that easily. The United States thus proceeded to pressure Somoza to give up his reelection ambitions but did not try to evict him from office before his term was up. Nor did Washington insist that Somoza give up his post of Jefe Director of the Guardia Nacional when Argüello assumed office in 1947. And so when Somoza overthrew Argüello, the U.S. response of temporary nonrecognition of Somoza's puppet was a slap on the wrist compared to what it might have done if it had really wanted Somoza out of the picture.

After 1948, with the Cold War already taking shape and security interests of prime concern to Washington's policy planners, the United States came to see Somoza as more of an asset than a liability. This seems to have been the case particularly after the turn to the left of the Guatemalan government under Arbenz in 1950. From then on, Nicaragua, under one Somoza or another, was the perennial and loyal ally of the United States in Central America, always ready to lend a hand in the anticommunist crusade.

In summary, the Somoza regime's continuation in office was threatened only at very specific moments and for relatively short periods of time. The Somocista alliance generally held firm, even in trying times, and Somoza always was able to count on the Civilista Conservatives. Thus, in 1944, 1947, and 1954, the years of gravest danger to the regime, Somoza had to face only certain social groups whose combined strength never got anywhere near the levels required to overthrow him and his government.

Somocismo and Institutional Development

The strength of the Somocista political alliance was combined with the regime's commitment to institutional development. Regardless of the personalistic appearance of the regime, within which Somoza took most of the credit and little of the blame, there was always a preference to provide institutional solutions to political and administrative problems. In the purely political sphere, the regime worked to involve organizations in the search for accommodation and consensus, even creating opposition groups when no others were willing to compete with the PLN in electoral events. A sort of two-party system was imposed on Nicaragua within which elections, power-sharing formulas, and political pacts were all part of the attempt to force institutional solutions within the political process. In this manner, the local caudillos gradually declined in importance as determining factors in political outcomes. They continued to exist, as landowners and businessmen, in the towns and cities, but they no longer were able to mount political initiatives on their own. They were disarmed largely back in 1927 under the terms of the Tipitapa agreement and were weakened further by the emergence of the Guardia Nacional as the only armed body in the country. Within the Liberal party, the Somoza reforms of 1943 practically eliminated all local autonomy in the selection of lower- and middle-echelon organizational units. And within the Conservative party, the decline of the caudillos was best exemplified by the decline of General Chamorro himself, whose years of exile and disastrous attempts at overthrowing the Somoza regime in 1947 culminated in the Pact of the Generals.

In bureaucratic and administrative terms, the development of the state's apparatus also was helped by institutional innovations. On the one hand, these were implemented to promote the state's own policy objectives, such as social security, financial stability, and economic growth and development. On the other hand, by promoting the growth of public institutions, the presence of the state became more widespread in terms of the bureaucracy itself and the fiscal weight exercised by the state's taxing power. That is not to say that government revenues increased under the Somoza regime in a proportion larger than the value of exports nor did the state reduce its dependence on customs duties as a source of income. The regime sought to maintain the essential public services required for the reproduction of the economic and social system; it did not wish to tax out of existence private enterprise, either local or foreign, Liberal or Conservative.

The principal and strongest institution within the apparatus of the state was, of course, the Guardia Nacional. The problem in the case of the Guardia is to determine how institutionalized it really was. From the perspective developed by Richard Millett in his *Guardians of the Dynasty*, the Guardia Nacional comes across as a praetorian force beholden to one man and to his family. Undoubtedly, the Guardia was closely identified with Somoza García and, later on, with Somoza Debayle, both of them father figures and benefactors to the rank and file and colleagues and partners in business to the officer corp. Its internal organization was subject to the political manipulations necessary for Somoza to maintain his control over the Guardia; promotions and demotions were in response as much, if not more, to political motives as to merit and professional considerations. In this light, it can be argued that the most important state institution was the least institutionalized in its internal operation. However, its role in the Nicaraguan state was similar to that of other Central American armies: a last resort to internal political opposition and unrest and the most visible and stable institutional support for the regime. And within the Somocista political coalition of Liberals and Conservatives, the need for a strong Guardia Nacional was never questioned nor was its elimination ever called for. At most, attempts were made to remove Somoza from his post as Jefe Director via administrative procedures, as in the case of Argüello's failed move in 1947, or the use of force, as in the April 1954 putsch.

As it was, the Nicaraguan polity had to accept the Guardia Nacional with a Somoza at its head. This was the price paid by the dominant political and economic groups for guarantees of the peace and security necessary for their continued activities.[1] In this respect, the Guardia Nacional arguably was as much an institution as any other in the Nicaraguan state; if it failed to achieve the levels of efficiency and rationality typical of an institution in a developed, capitalist society, the same can be said of most other public and private institutions in Nicaragua. Finally, the fact that the Guardia survived intact the assassination of its Jefe Director in 1956 is perhaps the best evidence of its institutional cohesion, albeit around the person of another Somoza. Nor is there any reason to doubt that it would have survived as such under a Jefe Director with a different surname.

Somocismo and Political Opposition

The political consensus surrounding the existence of the Guardia Nacional was all the more important given the continued presence in Nicaragua of a variety of opposition groups that threatened the social and political peace that both the Liberal and Conservative leadership defended. But the presence of a political opposition had become an integral part of the political system. To begin with, it was a fact of Nicaraguan political life, which had a long history dating back to the nineteenth century. Over time, the traditional opposition, either Liberal or Conservative, lost its meaning as a political alternative. By the 1920s Liberals and Conservatives were openly seeking formulas for bipartisan governments, and after 1936 they openly collaborated. Somoza's challenge was to complete this national political reconciliation and to bring in the final remnants of traditional, intransigent opposition elements, such as General Chamorro.

Somoza could have achieved his goal of national political reconciliation along two different paths: he could have used force to repress opposition to his regime, or he could attempt to persuade the opposition that it had no future as an alternative to his government while persuading others that the opposition was no real alternative in terms of a program of government, either. In fact, he used both approaches. The opposition was repressed during those moments when it was perceived by the regime as having overstepped the limits explicitly or implicitly defined by the state. Such was the case in 1944, 1947, and 1954, when the regime felt itself directly threatened either by civic opposition or armed rebellion and considered that a harsh response was warranted to return the opposition's activities to more acceptable or controllable levels. The opposition was treated with greater tolerance at other moments, particularly when the regime needed to burnish its image at home and abroad. The most patent expressions of political conciliation were the various pacts signed by Somoza with the leadership of the Conservative party that enabled it to participate in electoral events and guaranteed it a minimum number of legislative and judicial posts.

It should be stressed that the opposition the regime felt comfortable with was the loyal opposition, the opposition that believed in the "two-party system" and recognized the paramount importance of political accommodation. The Independent Liberals were allowed to exist and act, albeit under restrictive circumstances, but they were never offered a seat in the Congress or a position within the judicial system. As opposed to the Conservatives, the PLI was intrinsically anti-Somoza, against all his businesses and his continued political presence. By contrast, the Conservative oligarchy already had made its fortune and only needed guarantees to continue to prosper. That is, it was willing to negotiate with Somoza because Somoza's conditions were acceptable and what he had to offer was attractive.

By bringing together Conservative and Liberal parties and by co-opting their leadership, the Somoza regime could control effectively the Nicaraguan people. In the cities, the PLN machinery was able to oversee the bureaucracy and infiltrate and influence the labor movement. In the rural areas, the landowners of both parties continued to hold sway over the campesinos and colonos. To control the masses, therefore, it was only a matter of controlling the top levels of society. In some areas of the country, the PLN attempted to recruit members by taking them away from the Conservatives, but it does not seem that this was an important consideration in the two parties' competition for votes. Within a system of elite politics, the party dynamic was resolved through agreements at the top and political participation was more a function of directives from the leadership. Thus, when the Conservatives decided to contest an election, as in 1928, 1932, 1947, and 1950, the proportion of votes cast increased significantly. (See Table C.1.)

The existence of a "loyal" opposition, however, did leave open certain political spaces within which a more intransigent opposition might survive and make itself felt to some extent. That these spaces existed does not mean that the regime thought it convenient to retain them. More likely, their existence was part and parcel of the loyal opposition as a whole, the cost the regime had to pay for the continued presence of a political sparring partner that legitimized in part Somoza's claim that Nicaragua was a democracy. These

Table C.1 Participation in National Elections

Year	Total Population	Total Votes	% Votes/Population
1928	698,612	133,663	19.1
1932	733,942	130,114	17.7
1936	771,320	109,419	14.2
1938	790,817	88,775	11.2
1947	977,944	169,708	17.4
1950	1,049,611	202,698	19.3

Sources: For election results, see Tables 2.2, 4.1, and 5.1, as well as n. 62 in chapter 3. Total population has been calculated on the basis of census results for 1920, 1940, 1950, and 1962. See also CELADE's estimates for five-year intervals in Nicaragua, Oficina Ejecutiva de Encuestas y Censos, *Boletín demográfico*, no. 5 (December 1978): 5.

spaces were filled by the opposition media (especially *La Prensa*), the smaller opposition parties and groups (the PLI, UNAP, Juventud Conservadora, Frente Defensor de la República), the university, and the labor movement. Within these groups it was possible for more forthright opponents of the Somocista regime to act openly without incurring the immediate repression of the Guardia. For example, the PLI served for a time as an umbrella for various individuals who later formed part of the founding group of the Frente Sandinista de Liberación Nacional (FSLN). What obviously was not tolerated was armed opposition of any sort. Armed opponents to the regime, either Conservative or Liberal or whatever, were repressed without hesitation. The regime was absolutely clear on the need to maintain a complete monopoly on the use of force. This was so in the case of both the caudillo network, especially the Chamorristas, and the exiled opposition.

Otherwise, the openly repressive aspects of the regime seem to have been fairly muted, as if Somoza was not prepared to make enemies unnecessarily. Conservative troublemakers were exiled or they were jailed or confined to internal exile and then released, but their properties were not expropriated or confiscated. The PLI, for all its anti-Somocismo, was allowed to exist, although its more radical leaders were exiled. This limited repression was also a reflection, no doubt, of the relative weakness of the opposition. Why repress more than necessary?

The weakness of the opposition needs to be explained. In the first place, it was hopelessly fractured. Oligarchs of the Conservative party had much more in common with Somoza than they did with anti-Somoza labor leaders or even

Independent Liberal entrepreneurs, which made it impossible to bring them all together as a viable political alternative to the Somocista regime; in other words, some sectors of the opposition preferred Somoza to any other alternative apart from themselves. In the second place, the opposition was basically anti-Somoza, which suggests that its message probably did not mean much to the people whose everyday concerns were quite different from those expressed in the rhetoric of the opposition leaders and groups. Finally, the opposition did not offer anything radically different from those things that the regime promised and claimed to deliver, or it phrased its political platform in terms that were so vague and high-sounding that they meant little or nothing at all to the general population.

The opposition could gain ground against Somoza and Somocismo only by evolving from a stance that was basically antiregime to one that was antisystem or antistate, by rejecting Somocista "democracy" and all those who played by its rules, and by building a military and political coalition that could defeat the PLN and the Guardia Nacional. Neither the Conservatives, the PLI, nor the UNAP were able or willing to meet this requirement. It was left to the FSLN, organized in 1961, to initiate a new opposition to Somocismo and its allies that sought not only to do away with the regime but also to overhaul the state itself.

The Nicaraguan State under Somoza García

The weakness and divisiveness of the opposition to the Somoza regime should not detract from the strength of the Nicaraguan state under Somoza García. The Somoza regime provided those things that the country's business and agricultural interests demanded: peace, social order, adequate government support and stimulus for economic expansion, and all of this at the lowest cost possible. It minimally satisfied labor through its ideological discourse and by offering some concessions, including the labor code and social security provisions. It tolerated opposition activities, particularly during electoral periods, and allowed fairly extensive criticism of its policies and performance. In this sense, the regime contained features found in governments of conventional liberal democracies, with the important exception, of course, that in Somoza's Nicaragua a single person permanently situated in or near the highest office of the state required that most matters crossed his desk. The question that must be asked is, What difference would a democracy have made? What would an elected government headed, for example, by General Chamorro have done differently? What policies would have been implemented by a government of the PLI had it come to power, and how much opposition would it have tolerated from the left or from labor?

The answers to these questions hinge on a proper understanding of the Nicaraguan state. Things probably would not have developed much differently if Somoza had not come to power or if he had not remained as head of the Guardia Nacional for so long. This is so because the Nicaraguan state during the Somoza regime represented an overall consensus among the politically dominant groups on the desirability of export-oriented, capitalist economic growth and the need to guarantee the institutional and coercive powers of the state to foster and assure such growth. The conflicts that erupted now and then between different political actors were limited to differences that remained confined to the upper echelons of the society, notwithstanding the level of violence and animosity that they might have generated.

The only significant aspect of Nicaraguan political development and of the Nicaraguan state that would have been different in the absence of a Somoza in power was the Somoza business empire. Without a doubt, Somoza's businesses and properties grew under the shadow of the state's financial and fiscal institutions. If Somoza had not been around to take advantage of the opportunities that political power offered to enlarge his businesses, others would have taken his place, although economic power might not have been so centralized and concentrated as it was under Somoza. In this respect, the Somoza businesses are more important as a causal explanation of eventual revolution in Nicaragua than of the formation of the state. The Nicaraguan state as it evolved under Somocista control undoubtedly favored Somoza's business interests and those of his cronies, but it must be emphasized that the state's institutions and policies were not designed primarily or exclusively to favor such business interests. They were designed to promote the development of a capitalist, export economy and to retain control over a population whose labor kept that economy producing. But the constant growth of the Somoza businesses eventually stepped on too many toes and split the Liberal-Conservative, Somoza and non-Somoza business consensus and contributed to a crisis within the state itself during the 1970s.

Pedro Joaquín Chamorro already foresaw this development in 1956 when, just a few days before Somoza was shot, he wrote an editorial in La Prensa about what the future had to offer capitalists and laborers in a Nicaragua under continued Somocista control. He said that those capitalists who sought to remain on good terms with the regime were unaware of the great danger that it posed to their interests, not because of any progressive social program that Somoza had in mind but because Somoza's own "supercapital" would one day devour them entirely. Nor should laborers think that by cozying up to Somoza they might assure their long-term interests; what would happen, Chamorro wrote, was that Somoza's supercapital also would render the labor movement impotent in the face of the enormous economic power then concentrated in the hands of the dictator. For both laborers and capitalists, then, Somoza's wealth would turn into outright monopolistic control from which there would be no return.[2]

What Chamorro had perceived was one of the root causes of revolution in Nicaragua. The Nicaraguan state, organized under Somoza García's regime as an instrument of political and economic conciliation, gradually proved incapable of defusing the increasingly tense relations between the Somoza business empire and the rest of the Nicaraguan bourgeoisie. When the state finally was perceived as being hopelessly partial to one sector of the dominant class, it lost its character of a "state for all" and became a state perceived as only or mostly for the Somozas.[3] Undoubtedly, some Nicaraguans had diagnosed this condition in the early 1940s, most visibly in the case of the entrepreneurs and professionals who formed the PLI in hopes of ejecting Somoza from his posts in government and the Guardia Nacional; their justification for abandoning Somoza was precisely his greed combined with his monolithic control of the state's apparatus, that is, his refusal to share political power and economic advantages. A similar statement was made in 1948 when Somoza's opponents tried to discredit his regime at the Pan-American conference in Bogotá. However, the level of discontent with the regime was not sufficient at that moment to create a situation of unresolvable conflict. The growth of the Nicaraguan economy after 1945, and particularly after 1950, created enough economic opportunities for most everyone to benefit and postponed the crisis until years later.

In a sense, it could be argued that Somoza García set down the rules of the game and that his sons, Luis and Anastasio, Jr., set about breaking them. But such an interpretation is overly simplistic. The process of economic concentration in the hands of the Somozas, accelerated by their control of the state apparatus, need not be seen as an abnormal characteristic of capitalist economic development, particularly in a dependent and poor society such as Nicaragua, where the amount of wealth to spread about is particularly limited. Furthermore, economic concentration benefited not only the Somozas but other sectors of the Nicaraguan entrepreneurial class as well. Finally, economic concentration did not hinder the state's continuing ability to extract resources from the population in order to finance basic governmental services necessary for the maintenance of peace, social order, and economic growth.

Economic concentration did increase the competition for survival and advancement among economic groups but of itself does not explain the emergence of revolutionary pressures in Nicaragua. Economic growth provided the state with the material resources to consolidate its institutional and coercive hold over the population but did not contribute to strengthening its legitimacy. It is quite possible that Somoza García's first years in power were favorably looked upon by a majority of Nicaraguans who took an interest in the political life of the country. However, the permanence of a Somoza in high public office, the increasingly visible corruption of the bureaucracy and the Guardia Nacional, and the openly subordinate role of the Somoza regime to the interests of the United States in the region all contributed to a decline in the legitimacy of the regime and of the state. Already in the 1950s there were groups and individuals who were willing to use force to rid the country of the Somoza regime. In the years following Somoza García's death, there were attempts to organize revolutionary movements in the countryside, inspired doubtlessly by the success of the Cuban guerrillas under Fidel Castro. But these movements never took hold nor did their leadership remain committed to a long struggle against the regime; these were more exercises in heroics than in revolution. It was the creation of the FSLN in 1961 that took the issue of the regime's legitimacy to its ultimate limits. By reviving the figure of Sandino and all he stood for, and by adding a design for a new Nicaraguan state, the FSLN was able to constitute the basis for a protracted struggle against the Somocista regime. The struggle of the Sandinistas, which for a long time seemed to be getting nowhere, did begin to undermine the legitimacy of the established order by calling into question its origins and its reason for being.

The final crisis of the Somocista state occurred precisely when its strength began to decline in the face of the crumbling unity of the governing coalition of Liberals and Conservatives in the 1970s, combined with the growing legitimacy accumulated by the insurgent forces under the FSLN after years of difficult struggle and innumerable reverses. It was then that the Somocista state, apparently so strong, durable, and legitimate, collapsed under a cloud of fire and smoke as the people took to the streets to build barricades and rid the country, once and for all, of a government that seemed destined to last forever. As the saying goes, "No hay mal que dure cien años ni cuerpo que lo resista" (No illness lasts for a hundred years nor can anyone resist it for so long).

NOTES

. . . .

Abbreviations

AN   Archivo Nacional de Nicaragua
ASG   Anastasio Somoza García
FRUS   U.S. Department of State, *Foreign Relations of the United States*
IHCA   Instituto Histórico Centroamericano
LG/DO *La Gaceta/Diario Oficial*

Introduction

1. The most important elaboration of this approach is Chapman's "The Age of the Caudillo." In the case of Somoza, two examples of this approach are Millett, "Anastasio Somoza García," and Krehm, *Democracias y tiranías en el Caribe*, chapter 7. Along similar lines, see also Grieb, *Guatemalan Caudillo*. These writers emphasize the personal characteristics of the dictators in explaining their rise to power and their permanence in office, which is not to deny the validity of their arguments but only to point out that dictators and dictatorial regimes exist within a given environment that influences their policies and limits their political options much like occurs in any other political system. See, for example, the persuasive arguments of Paul Lewis in his *Paraguay under Stroessner* and, particularly, Charles Anderson's "Nicaragua: The Somoza Dynasty," from which I got abundant insights into the functioning of dictatorial regimes.

2. Perry Anderson, *Lineages of the Absolutist State*; Wallerstein, *The Modern World System I*; North and Thomas, *The Rise of the Western World*. Although Anderson and Wallerstein employ a generally Marxist approach as opposed to North and Thomas's neoclassical orientation, all would agree that the role of the state was decisive in promoting capitalist development.

3. Laski, *The State in Theory and Practice*, and the various contributions in Tilly, *The Formation of National States in Western Europe*.

4. Laski, *The State in Theory and Practice*, pp. 88–99. For a lucid analysis, see also Stepan, *The State and Society*, pp. 3–45.

5. O'Donnell, "Apuntes para una teoría del estado," pp. 196–99. Additional insights on the state's role and the issue of the state's independence from given social classes

("state autonomy") can be found in Held, "Central Perspectives on the Modern State," pp. 23–43; Skocpol, "Bringing the State Back In," pp. 9–14, and *States and Social Revolutions*, pp. 24–29; and Hamilton, *The Limits of State Autonomy*.

6. Kaplan, *Formación del estado nacional en América Latina*, pp. 43–46.

7. Oszlak, "The Historical Formation of the State in Latin America," pp. 16–24. Oszlak relies on the writings of J. P. Nettle and Philippe C. Schmitter to develop these points.

8. Ibid., pp. 11–14.

9. Ibid., pp. 16–22. Oszlak develops his ideas within a concrete historical case in *La formación del estado argentino*.

10. Torres Rivas, "Poder nacional y sociedad dependiente," pp. 178–83. See also his "La formación el estado y del sector público."

Chapter 1

1. This and the following discussion of Nicaraguan colonial history draws on Radell, "An Historical Geography of Western Nicaragua," pp. 59–64, 97–98, 112–22, 137–39, 148–57; Woodward, *Central America*, pp. 29–30, 35–39; and MacLeod, *Spanish Central America*, pp. 51–55, 277–79.

2. Wortman, *Government and Society in Central America*, chapter 6.

3. Ibid., p. 205. A very good collection of documents on the Central American independence movements is Meléndez, *Textos fundamentales de la independencia centroamericana*.

4. For a detailed analysis of the issues involved in this conflict, see Woodward, *Central America*, pp. 88–111. See also Gallardo, *Las constituciones de la República Federal de Centro-América*, for an analysis of the federal experiences in Central America and a complete anthology of the federal constitutions. Karnes's *The Failure of Union* provides a comprehensive historical overview of the forces favoring and rejecting political union in the isthmus.

5. Wortman, *Government and Society in Central America*, pp. 235–36.

6. Ibid., p. 271.

7. Velázquez, "La incidencia de la formación de la economía agroexportadora," pp. 12–13. See also Lanuza, "La formación del estado nacional en Nicaragua," pp. 99–109.

8. Humberto Belli, "Un ensayo de interpretación sobre las luchas políticas nicaragüenses," pp. 13–14.

9. Velázquez, "La incidencia de la formación de la economía agroexportadora," pp. 13–14, 19.

10. Barahona Portocarrero, "Estudio sobre la historia contemporanea de Nicaragua," p. 32.

11. Stansifer, "Una nueva interpretación de José Santos Zelaya." A detailed analysis of Zelaya's regime and policies can be found in Teplitz, "The Political and Economic Foundations of Modernization in Nicaragua."

12. Barahona Portocarrero, "Estudio sobre la historia contemporanea de Nicaragua," p. 33.

13. Nicaragua Sugar Estates, Ltd., *Ingenio San Antonio*, pp. 4–5.

14. Zelaya's overthrow has been amply documented. For a number of interpretations, see Cox, *Nicaragua and the United States*, pp. 707–10; Findling, "The United States and Zelaya," chapter 8; and U.S. Department of State, *The United States and Nicaragua*, pp. 6–7. See also my unpublished paper, "The Stages of United States Intervention in Nicaragua, 1910–1912." More general analyses of U.S. policy objectives in Central America and Nicaragua, in particular, can be found in Callcott, *The Caribbean Policy of the United States*, chapter 5, and Langley, *The United States and the Caribbean*, chapter 2.

15. For the texts of these agreements, see Decimal Files, 27 October 1910, 817.00/1469 1/2, General Records of the U.S. Department of State, Record Group 59, National Archives, Washington, D.C.

16. Pedro Belli, "Prolegómeno para una historia económica," pp. 5–6. A comprehensive account of U.S. financial policy in Nicaragua can be found in Hill, *Fiscal Intervention in Nicaragua*; for a wider perspective on U.S. strategic interests and their relation to financial issues, see Tulchin, *The Aftermath of War*, chapter 5.

17. Pedro Belli, "Prolegómeno para una historia económica," pp. 7, 19–20. For a general description of Nicaragua's economy in the 1920s, see Cumberland, *Nicaragua*.

18. Valle Martínez, "Desarrollo económico y político," pp. 19–20.

19. Ibid., pp. 22–25.

20. See Frazier, "The Dawn of Nationalism and Its Consequences in Nicaragua," pp. 132–83, for a detailed analysis of the U.S. role in the selection of Nicaraguan presidents and the implementation of electoral events.

21. Nicaragua, Ley electoral, *LG/DO* 27,71–74 (3–6 March 1923).

22. See, for example, Stimson, *American Policy in Nicaragua*, pp. 8–12.

23. A cogent explanation and apology of U.S. policy toward Nicaragua is provided by Stimson, *American Policy in Nicaragua*, pp. 90–129. See also Kamman, *A Search for Stability*, and Munro, *The United States and the Caribbean Republics*, chapters 5–6.

24. Valle Martínez, "Desarrollo económico y político," pp. 26–27.

25. Stimson, *American Policy in Nicaragua*, pp. 56–57, 63–64.

26. Ibid., pp. 71–72, 78–79.

27. Millett, *Guardians of the Dynasty*, pp. 70–71.

28. Cuadra Pasos, *Posibilidades de existencia del comunismo en Nicaragua*, pp. 4–5, 6–7.

29. Cuadra Pasos, *Obras*, pp. 572–73.

30. Cuadra Pasos, *Posibilidades de existencia del comunismo en Nicaragua*, pp. 12–13.

31. José Coronel Urtecho, interview with author, Managua, 28 November 1984. See also Tirado, *Conversando con José Coronel Urtecho*, pp. 112–18.

32. Partido Liberal Nacionalista, *Estatuto constitutivo*, articles 4, 14.

33. Gutiérrez Mayorga, "Dos etapas en la historia del movimiento obrero de Nicaragua," pp. 161–64.

34. Ibid., pp. 166–68, 185–92.

35. Partido Liberal Nacionalista, *Estatuto constitutivo*, pp. 21–32.

36. Computed on the basis of the 1920 census. Cantarero, using the same census, estimates that 84 percent of all Nicaraguans were engaged in agriculture but only 8.4 percent in manufacturing. See Cantarero, "The Economic Development of Nicaragua," p. 61.

37. Dodd, "United States in Nicaraguan Politics," p. 212.

Chapter 2

1. Salvatierra, *Conciliación democrática de los partidos políticos de Nicaragua*, pp. 27, 29–31, 41–43.

2. For a detailed discussion of these points, including Somoza's selection as Jefe Director, see Millett, *Guardians of the Dynasty*, pp. 125–36, 149–50.

3. A comprehensive account of the military aspects of the struggle is found in Macaulay, *The Sandino Affair*.

4. These points are made by Gregorio Selser in his seminal work, *Sandino: General de hombres libres*, especially pp. 153–56, 174–76, 215–16.

5. Black, *Triumph of the People*, p. 25. See also Macaulay, *The Sandino Affair*, pp. 158–60.

6. Macaulay, *The Sandino Affair*, p. 247; Selser, *Sandino*, pp. 276–83.

7. Macaulay, *The Sandino Affair*, pp. 245–46.

8. *Mercurio*, no. 29 (November 1931) and no. 42 (December 1932).

9. See *LG/DO*, 1933: 37,39 (17 February); 37,52 (4 March); 37,88 (22 April).

10. Macaulay, *The Sandino Affair*, p. 237. These are the official U.S. Marine figures; Macaulay thinks that only figures on marine casualties are "undoubtedly correct."

11. Millett, *Guardians of the Dynasty*, p. 152. See also Guardia Nacional, Departamento de Inteligencia y Operaciones, "Informes" for 1 July, 1 October, and 1 November 1933, box 143, AN.

12. See Millett, *Guardians of the Dynasty* (pp. 152–61), for a well-documented description of events surrounding the death of Sandino and the roles of Somoza and U.S. Minister Arthur Lane in the affair.

13. Ibid., pp. 169–74.

14. *LG/DO*, 1934: 38,163 (23 July); 38,180 (14 August).

15. *LG/DO* 38,259 (19 November 1934).

16. *LG/DO* 38,248 (6 November 1934).

17. *LG/DO* 35,243 (13 November 1931).

18. *LG/DO* 36,195 (12 September 1932).

19. *LG/DO* 34,221 (1 October 1930); 38,259 (19 November 1934). The government simultaneously authorized the municipalities countrywide to create rural credit institutions with monies raised through special taxes determined by the central government. The same law established the first of these credit institutions in the municipality of Chinandega to assist small- and medium-sized farmers with loans of up to C$300 at 9 percent interest for six years. *LG/DO* 38,213 (24 September 1934). The

problem with both the Banco Hipotecario and these Institutos de Crédito Rural was that the amounts with which they had to work were simply insufficient.

20. *LG/DO* 39,203 (12 September 1935).

21. *LG/DO* 37,121 (2 June 1933).

22. The León Chamber of Commerce defended this point of view with particular insistence. *Mercurio*, no. 47 (May 1933). It criticized the government for signing a loan agreement with New York banks for only U.S.$1.5 million when the country needed four times that amount. *Mercurio*, no. 51 (September 1933). On occasion, a wounded patriotism influenced these arguments; *Mercurio* claimed that Nicaragua must demand from the United States a better financial arrangement after being sucked dry by U.S. bankers. The paltry three million dollars received by Nicaragua as part of the Bryan-Chamorro Treaty also should be renegotiated. *Mercurio*, no. 52 (October 1933).

23. On 16 August 1934 the Managua Chamber of Commerce wrote President Sacasa requesting a devaluation of the córdoba in order to increase the supply of dollars and to improve credit operations in the country. Devaluation also would stimulate export producers and, in combination with protective tariffs, encourage production for local consumption. *Boletín*, no. 1 (August 1935).

24. *Boletín*, no. 3 (October 1935).

25. *Boletín*, no. 5 (December 1935).

26. Irving Lindberg, Collector General of Customs, to Provisional President Carlos Brenes Jarquín, Managua, 22 June 1936, box 73, folder "aduanas," AN.

27. In his inaugural address, Sacasa requested that all Nicaraguans seek a "simple and frugal" existence. Nicaragua, Presidencia de la República, *Mensaje inaugural del señor Presidente de la República Dr. Juan Bautista Sacasa leido ante el Congreso Nacional el 1 de enero de 1933*, p. 6. In December 1935, Sacasa reported that the fiscal deficit had been reduced to about C$30,000 a month but that additional economies were unlikely and an increase in taxes was impossible "within the circumstances." Nicaragua, Presidencia de la República, *Mensaje del Presidente de la República Dr. Juan Bautista Sacasa al Honorable Congreso Nacional del 15 diciembre de 1935*, p. 11.

28. See *LG/DO*, 1933: 37,17 (23 January); 37,29 (6 February); 37,35 (13 February); 37,36 (14 February); 37,40 (18 February); 37,116 (27 May).

29. *LG/DO*, 1933: 37,15 (20 January); 37,104 (12 May); and 1934: 38,45 (22 February); 38,206 (13 September).

30. *LG/DO* 38,160 (19 July 1934). This procedure of bureaucratic musical chairs was a standard solution to discrepancies between the two parties over appointments to public office. It allowed the minority party a certain measure of power while leaving the majority party with the final say.

31. Partido Liberal Nacionalista, *Política liberal concerniente a los convenios de conciliación*, pp. 4–11, 42–44.

32. Information on these committees is provided by Sánchez, *La vieja guardia*, a collection of articles, photographs, and documents on the origins of the Somocista cause and, in particular, of those individuals who from the beginning were true Somocistas. Minister Lane's opinions can be found in Minister in Nicaragua to Secretary of State, March 15, 1935, *FRUS, 1935*, 4:842–46.

33. ASG to Leonardo Somarriba, Managua, 10 December 1934, box 75, folder "documentos," AN.

34. Baltasar López to ASG, Chichigalpa, 11 December 1934, box 65, folder 34.11, AN.

35. Letters sent from La Concordia, 15 January 1935, with approximately 95 signatures; from Estelí with 70; from Corinto with 90; from Bluefields with 40; and from Jinotega, 11 March 1935, with 80. A group of Somoza sympathizers in León took the form letter and turned it into a broadside. Box 289, AN.

36. A rally that Somoza organized in November 1935 in Managua to further his candidacy drew only 2,000 people, even with the promise of free liquor and money. Millett, *Guardians of the Dynasty*, p. 171.

37. "Algunos amigos me piden cartas de recomendación; a muchos tendré que dárselas. Espero sabrás disimular estas molestias." Agustín Sánchez Vijil to ASG, Jinotepe, 3 July 1935, box 65, folder 34.5, AN.

38. Contribution by Agustín Sánchez Vijil in Sánchez, *La vieja guardia*, no page.

39. ASG to Ambrosio Parodi, Managua, 5 December 1934, box 75, folder "documentos," AN.

40. Box 72, folder "Guardia Nacional," AN.

41. Sargeant Gámez to ASG, Boaco, 16 March 1936, box 69, folder "elecciones," AN.

42. Captain Hermógenes Prado to ASG, Estelí, 6 February 1936, box 72, folder "elecciones," AN.

43. J. R. Sevilla to Juan B. Sacasa, León, 13 January 1936; Horacio Fonseca to Juan B. Sacasa, Juigalpa, 8 March 1936; and J. M. Icaza to Juan B. Sacasa, León, 21 April 1936—all in box 68, folder "elecciones," AN.

44. Letters to Juan B. Sacasa from jefes políticos in Juigalpa, 25 January 1936; Matagalpa, 24 and 27 January 1936; and Estelí, 25 January 1936—all in box 68, folder "informes," AN.

45. Rodolfo Espinoza to Juan B. Sacasa, Managua, 24 February 1936, box 73, folder "elecciones," AN.

46. Julio César Saenz, "Como liberal hablo . . . ," in Sánchez, *La vieja guardia*, no page.

47. Espinoza, *El liberalismo debe renovar su ideología y su actuación*.

48. Box 65, folder 34.11, AN.

49. Box 211, AN. The use of the term *aristocracy* in this flier no doubt refers to the Granada oligarchy, considered by the Liberals as the successors to the colonial Criollo class.

50. Speech in Chinandega, 25 December 1934, in Sánchez, *La vieja guardia*, no page.

51. Meeting held on 9 November 1934, in Sánchez, *La vieja guardia*, no page.

52. Medardo Lanzas to ASG, León, 26 March 1936, and Roberto Chacón to ASG, Corinto, 9 January 1936, box 69, folder "elecciones," AN.

53. Box 270, AN.

54. Julio César Saenz, "Como liberal hablo . . . ," in Sánchez, *La vieja guardia*, no page.

55. Millett, *Guardians of the Dynasty*, pp. 174–75.

56. Horacio Argüello B., et al., *Interpretación de las propuestas.*

57. *La Prensa*, 14 May 1936.

58. Ibid.

59. *La Prensa*, 23 May 1936.

60. *La Prensa*, 31 May 1936.

61. For a detailed description of the events that transpired during the first semester of 1936, see Millett, *Guardians of the Dynasty*, pp. 174–78. Somoza's authority and influence were not limited to the larger events only. He used his position to extend favors of all sorts to people who sought his assistance. María Peralta wrote President Sacasa requesting that he authorize a gambling operation similar to the one Somoza had granted to a couple of other women. On the margin, Sacasa wrote that he could not authorize something that was forbidden by law and ordered that Somoza's action be investigated. María Peralta to Sacasa, Bluefields, 1 August 1935, box 65, folder 34.7, AN. Along similar lines, Rosalío González complained to Somoza that Eduardo Dávila's bar in León had been raided by the police who were looking for "a certain business which he runs there" (most likely a gambling operation), but that Dávila was a staunch Somocista and would Somoza please do something about this. Furthermore, says González, such actions gave the impression that the Somocista movement was declining in strength, "especially among the floating masses which are so important." Rosalío González to ASG, León, 26 March 1936, box 69, folder "elecciones," AN.

62. The meetings in Washington with Federico Sacasa are summarized in Memorandum by the Assistant Chief of the Division of Latin American Affairs (Beaulac), 1 October 1935, and Memorandum by the Chief of the Division of Latin American Affairs (Wilson), *FRUS, 1935,* 4:877–79, 883–86. For the U.S. position on "violence," see Minister in Managua to Secretary of State, 18 June, 26 September 1935, ibid., pp. 862–64, 872–73.

63. Millett, *Guardians of the Dynasty*, pp. 178–80. President Sacasa put down his own version of the events in Sacasa, *Cómo y por qué caí del poder.*

64. *LG/DO* 40,135 (20 June 1936).

65. *FRUS, 1936,* 5:841.

66. *La Prensa*, 18 June 1936.

67. *La Prensa*, 19 June 1936. See also ASG to Agencia de Noticias Trens in Mexico City, Managua, 16 September 1936, box 66, folder "informes," AN.

68. Emiliano Chamorro, *Autobiografía*, pp. 101–2.

69. Alejandro Salvatierra to Carlos Brenes Jarquín, Managua, 30 June 1936, in *Boletín*, no. 10–11 (May–June 1936).

70. Asociación Agrícola de Nicaragua to Carlos Brenes Jarquín, Managua, 2 July 1936, in Nicaragua, Secretaría de Agricultura y Trabajo, *Memoria* for 1938, pp. 29–31. The Asociación Agrícola was founded in 1934 to defend the interests of agricultural producers; its income came mostly from a special tax of C$0.05 on each sack of coffee exported and C$0.02 on each sack of sugar produced.

71. H. D. Scott to ASG, Puerto Cabezas, 27 September 1936, box 72, folder "inglés," AN. Some months later he wrote to a Liberal politician expressing his faith in Somoza: "there is no one, I am sure, who would give Americans better service than he." Scott to Mariano Argüello, Puerto Cabezas, 12 November 1936, box 72, folder "inglés," AN.

72. Nicaragua, Decreto ejecutivo liberalizando el cambio de divisas, *LG/DO* 40,227 (16 October 1936).

73. Cámara Nacional de Comercio e Industrias to Ministro de Hacienda, Managua, 20 October 1936, box 66, folder "informes," AN. See also *Boletín,* no. 14–15 (September–October 1936).

74. Irving Lindberg, Collector General of Customs, to Carlos Brenes Jarquín, Managua, 22 June 1936, box 73, folder "aduanas," AN.

75. Pérez Bermúdez and Guevara López, *El movimiento obrero en Nicaragua,* pp. 18–27, 39–42, 51–54.

76. Gould, "The Nicaraguan Labor Movement and the Somoza Regime."

77. Juventud Obrera to ASG, Managua, 20 February 1936, box 73, folder "actas y acuerdos," AN.

78. Nicaragua, Impuesto adicional al alcohol, *LG/DO* 40,177 (14 August 1936).

79. Teniente José N. Castillo to ASG, Siquía, 15 July 1936, box 66, folder "informes," AN.

80. In Chontales, for example, the caudillos were mostly Conservative ranchers, although some gave their support to Somoza through the Nationalist Conservative party. A report to Somoza listed three of these caudillos and the votes they could deliver: Cornelio Bravo Duarte with 600, Ufredo Argüello with 400–500, and Manuel Lacayo with 50. E. J. Moncada to ASG, Juigalpa, 20 August 1936, box 66, folder "elecciones," AN.

81. Guillermo E. Cuadra to Pedro A. Rodríguez, Managua, 24 April 1936, Fondo Felipe Rodríguez Serrano, AN.

82. ASG to Pedro Alejandro Rodríguez, Managua, 27 January 1936; Jacinto Suárez Cruz to Pedro A. Rodríguez, Managua, 12 April 1936; and Eligio Alvarez to Pedro A. Rodríguez, Managua, 25 February 1936—all in Fondo Felipe Rodríguez Serrano, AN.

83. Rafael Córdova Rivas, interview with author, Managua, 22 June 1984.

84. *La Prensa,* 2, 3, 12 September 1936.

85. J. Solórzano Díaz to ASG, Managua, 26 September 1936, box 66, folder "elecciones," AN; J. Solórzano Díaz to ASG, Managua, 28 September 1936, box 66, folder "varios," AN; J. Solórzano Díaz to ASG, Managua, 7 October 1936, box 66, folder "informes," AN. The Nationalist Conservatives figured that it would cost them C$16,000 to register 40,000 voters on 1 November 1936 for the December elections, an amount that was duly requested. See J. Solórzano Díaz to ASG, Managua, 20 October 1936, box 73, folder "elecciones," AN.

86. Minister of Finance to General Manager of the Banco Nacional, Managua, 5, 19, 27 November 1936, box 73, folder "ministerios," AN. These letters are instructions from the minister to the bank to transfer funds from a special account to Dr. Humberto Guevara, treasurer of the Partido Conservador Nacionalista.

87. In Boaco, the Liberals and the Nationalist Conservatives each fought to register voters under their party's name to the extent that they were annulling each other's efforts and thus damaging Somoza's campaign. Captain E. Matamoros to ASG, Boaco, 6 November 1936, box 69, folder "informes," AN.

88. Millett, *Guardians of the Dynasty,* p. 181.

89. Carlos D. García to ASG, Managua, 7 October 1936, box 66, folder "informes," AN. García had just returned from a trip to the northern departments where he was engaged in campaign activities.

90. J. Solórzano Díaz to ASG, Managua, 14 November 1936, box 73, folder "elecciones," AN. Solórzano, president of the Nationalist Conservatives, said that his party had about 3,000 men in the Ocotal region who would vote for Somoza but that he needed C$1,400 to buy them food and drink to assure their presence on election day.

91. Minister of Finance to ASG, Managua, 2 October 1936, box 73, folder "informes," AN.

92. Partido Liberal Nacionalista, *Informe de las actividades desplegadas por el Comité Departamental de Propaganda*. The bonds to finance the campaign were sold at the national level under the title *certificados de crédito liberal*. They would be repaid after 30 April 1937 with the proceeds of the contribution of 5 percent on salaries of all public employees. For an example of this type of bond, see box 292, AN.

93. Figures for 1928 and 1932 were calculated on the basis of electoral data in Recaudación General de Aduanas, *Memoria* for 1932, pp. 53–55. The figure for 1936 is from Consejo Nacional de Elecciones, *La verdad electoral de 1936*, pp. 169–80. I am assuming that these electoral results are correct on the whole. The 1928 and 1932 elections presumably were supervised impartially by the U.S. mission; in the following years, when Conservatives and Liberals discussed power-sharing arrangements, they referred to the 1932 election as an accurate barometer of voter preference. The 1936 election was supervised, if at all, by the Guardia Nacional. The Consejo Nacional de Elecciones was not an impartial body, either. Still, I believe the results are valid because they do not reflect a Somoza landslide (which might have provided grounds for suspicion) and the levels of abstention are consistent with the electoral strength of each party as reflected in the 1928 and 1932 elections.

94. J. Solórzano Díaz to ASG, Managua, 20 October 1936, box 73, folder "elecciones," AN.

95. Millett, *Guardians of the Dynasty*, p. 181.

96. Douglas and Morgan, *Nicaragua and the United States*.

97. See Sandino's letter to his general, Francisco Estrada, of 24 May 1933, and another to President Sacasa of 19 February 1934, in which he characterizes the Guardia Nacional as an unconstitutional body because of both its creation under U.S. auspices and its independence from presidential authority. Ramírez, *Augusto C. Sandino*, pp. 336, 379–80.

Chapter 3

1. The quotations and summary of Somoza's speech here and in the next two paragraphs are from Presidencia de la República, *Mensaje inaugural del excmo. señor Presidente de la República, General Anastasio Somoza, al Honorable Congreso Nacional, el 1 de enero de 1937*, pp. 8–9, 11–12, 14–18.

2. Nicaragua, Recaudación General de Aduanas, *Memoria* for 1940, p. 32. An internal memorandum prepared by the Departamento de Emisión of the Banco Nacional describes the mining operations in detail. The four largest mines (La Luz Mines Ltd., Neptune Gold Mining Co., Compañía Minera La India, and Compañía Minas Matagalpa), all foreign-owned, produced U.S.$3,014,147 of gold in the period January–June 1943, which represented 76 percent of the total production of U.S. $3,950,431. On the value of that production, they paid a *contribución voluntaria* to the Nicaraguan government of U.S.$45;212, that is, one and one-half percent of total production. The remaining mines, much smaller in size, simply sold to the government between 12 and 50 percent of their output, according to contract. Memorandum of Departamento de Emisión del Banco Nacional, Managua, 8 October 1943, box 229, AN.

3. *La Prensa*, 17, 21 February 1937.

4. Alejandro Salvatierra, Secretary of Managua Chamber of Commerce, to Minister of Finance, Managua, 4 February 1937, in *Boletín*, no. 18–19 (January–February 1937): 8–12. The León Chamber of Commerce backed this position, too. *Mercurio*, no. 93–95 (March 1937): 8–9, 24–25.

5. Miguel Silva S., Secretary of Managua Chamber of Commerce, to ASG, Managua, 1 June 1937, box 86, folder "junio de 1937," AN.

6. Nicaragua, Decreto de reorganización de la Comisión de Control de Operaciones de Cambio, *LG/DO* 41,164 (2 August 1937).

7. Managua Chamber of Commerce to ASG, Managua, 7 December 1937, *Boletín*, no. 29 (December 1937): 19–20.

8. Asociación Agrícola de Nicaragua to ASG, Managua, 30 November 1937, *Boletín*, no. 29 (December 1937): 21–25.

9. *La Prensa*, 11 December 1937; Nicaragua, Decreto liberalizando la negociación de divisas internacionales, *LG/DO* 41,281 (23 December 1937).

10. Eduardo Mendoza to Board of Directors of Managua Chamber of Commerce, in *Boletín*, no. 31 (February 1938): 4–11. Mendoza believed that the board had been unjustly criticized by some merchants who thought that it had not defended strongly enough the interests of the merchants.

11. *Boletín*, no. 32 (March 1938): 9–12 and no. 33 (April 1938): 13–14.

12. Nicaragua, Reglamento del decreto liberalizando la negociación de divisas del 23 diciembre de 1937, *LG/DO* 42,14 (19 January 1938).

13. Nicaragua, Decreto prohibiendo el libre comercio de divisas dentro del país, *LG/DO* 42,121 (9 June 1938).

14. Nicaragua, Decreto de control de precios, *LG/DO* 41,159 (16 March 1937).

15. Nicaragua, Ley de ganancias máximas para mercaderías de primera necesidad, *LG/DO* 42,17 (22 January 1938).

16. *LG/DO* 42,86 (27 April 1938).

17. Memorandum from Chambers of Commerce of Chinandega, León, Granada, Masaya, Matagalpa, and Managua to ASG, Managua, 8 February 1938, in *Boletín*, no. 31 (February 1938): 25–28.

18. Constantino Pereira to Members of Managua Chamber of Commerce, Managua, 11 February 1938, in *Boletín*, no. 31 (February 1938).

19. Asociación Nacional de Ganaderos de Nicaragua to ASG, Managua, 9 June 1937, box 86, folder "junio 1937," AN; Managua Chamber of Commerce to Minister of Agriculture and Labor, Managua, 22 June 1937, box 84, folder "mayo 1937," AN. This ban seems to have been in effect only during 1937, when 15 head of cattle were exported. In the following years, cattle exports increased, reaching over 13,000 head in 1939 and then oscillating from around 1,500 to 7,000 during the war years.

20. Krehm, *Democracias y tiranías en el Caribe*. Krehm was *Time* magazine's reporter for Central America in the 1940s. His very readable impressions about the region's heads of state, some of whom he knew personally, were published in English thirty years after the Spanish edition.

21. *La Prensa*, 19 February, 4 June 1938.

22. *Boletín*, no. 25 (August 1937): 9–13.

23. Ministerio de Hacienda y Crédito Público, *Memoria* for 1936–37, pp. IV–VI. Taxes were raised on gasoline in June 1937 and July 1938. *LG/DO* 41,133 (24 June 1937); 42,145 (9 July 1938). They were raised on alcohol in August 1937, January 1938, and September 1939. *LG/DO* 41,168 (6 August 1937); 42,15 (20 January 1938); 43,209 (27 September 1939). Tobacco taxes were raised in August 1937 and October 1939. *LG/DO* 41,173 (13 August 1937); 43,219 (9 October 1939). In February 1938 the taxes on alcohol, tobacco, and sugar all were raised 100 percent to coincide with the fall of the córdoba. *LG/DO* 42,25 (1 February 1938). For sale and inheritance taxes, see *LG/DO* 43,278 (20 December 1939) and 44,18 (22 January 1940).

24. *La Prensa*, 25 December 1937, 19 May 1938.

25. Nicaragua, Decreto rebajando el impuesto al café exportado, *LG/DO* 43,277 (19 December 1939).

26. Nicaragua, Ministerio de Hacienda y Crédito Público, *Memoria* for 1939–40, p. XXXIV.

27. *LG/DO* 44,242 (29 October 1940).

28. Nicaragua, Ley del Banco Nacional de Nicaragua, *LG/DO* 44,242–244 (29–31 October 1940).

29. Nicaragua, Ley general de instituciones bancarias, *LG/DO* 44,244–245 (31 October–2 November 1940).

30. Nicaragua, Ley de intereses; and Ley que reorganiza el control de cambios, *LG/DO* 44,246 (4 November 1940).

31. Nicaragua, Ley de reorganización del Banco Hipotecario de Nicaragua, *LG/DO* 44,246–247 (4–5 November 1940).

32. Nicaragua, Ley orgánica de la Caja Nacional de Crédito Popular, *LG/DO* 44,247–248 (5, 8 November 1940).

33. Nicaragua, Ley de reorganización de la Compañía Mercantil de Ultramar, *LG/DO* 44,245–246 (2, 4 November 1940).

34. For lists of credit operations, see boxes 137, 144, 216, 238, 274, 275, 283, 303, 316, 322, 334, and 339, AN. A sampling of letters of recommendation can be found in box 293, folder "correspondencia firmada por el señor Presidente," AN. A systematic analysis of the Banco Nacional and Banco Hipotecario loans would throw much more

light on the importance of credit as a political tool. For example, as can be observed in box 293, AN, some of the largest loan requests that Somoza recommended were from Guardia Nacional officers.

35. Nicaragua, Decreto de control de importaciones, *LG/DO* 43,206 (23 September 1939); Decreto de control de precios y ganancias, *LG/DO* 43,199 (13 September 1939); Ley de inquilinato, *LG/DO* 43,211 (29 September 1939); Ley sobre medicamentos estancados, *LG/DO* 43,248 (13 November 1939); Decreto de creación de la Junta de Control de Precios y Comercio, *LG/DO* 45,274 (17 December 1941); Decreto ampliando las funciones de la Junta de Control de Precios y Comercio, *LG/DO* 48,39 (23 February 1944).

36. Irving A. Lindberg, Collector General of Customs, to ASG, Managua, 23 June 1943, box 216, AN.

37. Nicaragua, Ministerio de Hacienda y Crédito Público, *Memoria* for 1939–40, pp. LVII–LVIII; Decreto de creación de la Dirección de Ingresos, *LG/DO* 43,250 (15 November 1939).

38. Nicaragua, Decreto de disolución de la corporación "Ferrocarril del Pacífico de Nicaragua" incorporado bajo las leyes del estado de Maine, Estados Unidos de América, *LG/DO* 41,69 (6 April 1937).

39. Nicaragua, Decreto de supresión del Ministerio de Higiene Pública y creación de la Dirección General de Sanidad, *LG/DO* 41,94 (12 May 1937).

40. *La Prensa*, 5 March 1938; Recaudación General de Aduanas, *Memoria* for 1941, p. 20.

41. Nicaragua, Constitución Política de 1911, *LG/DO* 16,13 (17 January 1912), articles 145–47. While autonomous in theory, the municipalities were subordinate to the central government for the approval of their tax schedules and for auditing procedures. Nicaragua, Decreto legislativo relativo a la fiscalización y control de cuentas municipales y otras, *LG/DO* 39,171 (5 August 1935).

42. Nicaragua, Decreto presidencial interviniendo la municipalidad de León, *LG/DO* 41,59 (16 March 1937); Decreto presidencial interviniendo la municipalidad de Masaya, *LG/DO* 41,62 (19 March 1937). In the case of Chinandega, see *LG/DO* 41,75 (13 April 1937).

43. Nicaragua, Decreto legislativo suspendiendo elecciones municipales, *LG/DO* 41,187 (30 August 1937).

44. Nicaragua, Decreto ejecutivo creando juntas locales en varios departamentos del país, *LG/DO* 41,188 (31 August 1937) (quotation); 41,189–190 (1–2 September 1937); 42,154 (22 July 1938); and 44,26 (31 January 1940).

45. Nicaragua, Decreto legislativo de fiscalización y control de cuentas municipales y otras, *LG/DO* 39,171 (5 August 1935).

46. Nicaragua, Ley de fiscalización de las cuentas municipales y de otras juntas locales, *LG/DO* 41,189 (1 September 1937).

47. Nicaragua, Reglamento para el funcionamiento de juntas locales y de la Contraloría General de Cuentas Locales, *LG/DO* 42,132 (23 June 1938).

48. Nicaragua, Ministerio de Gobernación y Anexos, *Anales del primer Congreso de Municipalidades de Nicaragua*, pp. 9–10, 26–34, 117–29.

49. Nicaragua, Ministerio de Gobernación y Anexos, *Programa del segundo Congreso de Municipalidades de Nicaragua*. See also box 199, folder "Ministerio de Gobernación," AN.

50. The railroad was nationalized in April 1937; by then, the Nicaraguan government owned all the shares and its board of directors functioned in Managua. Nicaragua, Decreto de disolución de la corporación "Ferrocarril de Pacífico de Nicaragua" incorporado bajo las leyes del estado de Maine, Estados Unidos de América, *LG/DO* 41,69 (6 April 1937). Another law altered its internal structure, abolishing its board of directors and placing it under a general manager directly responsible to the president, who became its Jefe Supremo. Nicaragua, Ley constitutiva de la empresa del Ferrocarril del Pacífico de Nicaragua, *LG/DO* 44,238 (24 October 1940).

51. Data from 1940 census are cited by Valle Martínez, "Desarrollo económico y político," p. 58. The 1940 census is rather a mystery. It is cited frequently in demographic and economic analyses but a copy of the census itself was not found. The economically active population of Nicaragua according to the 1940 census was 331,161, of which 257,963 was engaged in agriculture, which leaves a total of 73,198 employed in the urban areas. This last figure is divided by 11,941, the total employed by government according to Valle Martínez (p. 58). Figures on the economically active population are from the 1940 census as cited by U.S. Department of Commerce, *Country Economic Reviews*, "Nicaragua," vol. 3 (August 1946): 9.

52. José del Carmen Flores to ASG, Managua, 23 March 1940, box 143, AN.

53. Armando Rodríguez O. to Under Secretary of the Interior, Managua, 19 August 1942, box 199, folder "Ministerio de Gobernación," AN.

54. Major Francisco Gaitán to ASG, Masaya, 25 May 1946, box 312, AN.

55. Nicaragua, Decreto ejecutivo elevando sueldos de empleados públicos, *LG/DO* 42,33 (11 February 1938).

56. During the 1930s, particularly, people looked to the regime for solutions (*remiendos*) to their economic problems, thus strengthening the bureaucratic clientele of the governing party. Enrique Espinoza Sotomayor, interview with author, Managua, 11 March 1985.

57. *LG/DO* 40,182; 40,197; and 40,219 (21 August, 8 September, 6 October 1936).

58. *LG/DO* 42,244 (10 November 1938); 43,9 (12 January 1939).

59. Nicaragua, Decreto convocando a elección para Asamblea Constituyente, *LG/DO* 42,176 (18 August 1938).

60. Nicaragua, Decreto presidencial creando Comisión Técnica que elaborará un anteproyecto de Constitución, *LG/DO* 42,195 (9 September 1938).

61. Nicaragua, Decreto estableciendo la modalidad para elección de Asamblea Constituyente, *LG/DO* 42,195 (9 September 1938).

62. *La Prensa*, 15 October 1938.

63. The discussion here and in the next two paragraphs is drawn from Nicaragua, Constitución Política de 1939, *LG/DO* 43,68 (23 March 1939), articles 63–70, 100–104, 128–30, 220, 303–6, 326, 335. Somoza already had anticipated social welfare provisions for the new Constitution in his speech before the Constituent Assembly on 15 December 1938. He said that the Constitution would include "those matters

regarding our forms of production and distribution of wealth, which in our country have not yet resulted in problems of a serious nature but which I consider necessary to prevent by extending an adequate protection to labor and capital on the basis of principles of social justice which would underscore the need for the closest cooperation and solidarity as the cornerstone of the relations between Capital and Labor." Nicaragua, Presidencia de la República, *Mensaje del excmo. señor Presidente de la República, General Anastasio Somoza, en el acto de inauguración de las sesiones de la Honorable Asamblea Nacional Constituyente el 15 de diciembre de 1938*, p. 9.

64. Nicaragua, Presidencia de la República, *Discursos cruzados entre el Presidente de la Asamblea Nacional Constituyente, Dr. Roberto González, y el excmo. señor Presidente de la República, general de división A. Somoza, en el solemne momento de recibir de nuevo la alta investidura de Presidente de la República para el período constitucional comprendido entre el 30 de abril de 1939 y el 1 de mayo de 1947*.

65. *La Prensa*, 16 February, 21 July, 8 August 1937.

66. Box 81, folder "mayo de 1937," AN.

67. Box 115, folder "jefatura política de Masaya," AN.

68. *La Prensa*, 30 June 1939.

69. Box 116, AN.

70. The speeches cited are found in boxes 204 and 212, folder "manifestaciones públicas," AN. See various broadsides issued for the occasion in box 183, AN.

71. Box 227, AN.

72. On 7 November 1940 a demonstration was held in front of the U.S. legation commending Roosevelt's support for Great Britain. Somoza, who was inside with the ambassador, stepped out on a balcony and delivered a speech to the crowd. He mentioned the strong friendship between Nicaragua and the United States and congratulated Roosevelt on his recent reelection, a theme that would be used more frequently as Somoza's own reelection plans developed. *La Prensa*, 8 November 1940.

73. Copies of these *actas* can be found in AN: box 235; box 216; box 228; box 237, folders "jefatura política de Chontales" and "jefatura política de Boaco"; and box 223. Box 216 contains a list of places and dates where "popular assemblies" had been held up to 23 May 1943; they add up to fifty-three.

74. Box 78, folders "agosto" and "diciembre de 1937," AN. In particular, see a letter from Felipe T. Flores, "General de Brigada y Comandante Departamental de la Liga Militar Liberal de León," to ASG, León, 3 December 1937. Box 78, folder "diciembre de 1937," AN. See also box 133, folder "Partido Liberal," and box 200, folder "Liga Militar Liberal de Nicaragua," AN.

75. See box 265, AN, for an example of identification papers issued to one Santiago Morazán in Managua on 19 October 1937.

76. Partido Liberal Nacionalista, *Declaración de principios*, pp. 27–30.

77. Ibid., pp. 40–45. According to the Electoral Law of 1923, these bodies were called Junta Directiva Nacional y Legal (JDNL), Junta Directiva Departamental y Legal (JDDL), and Consejos Locales. The terminology applied to every political party in the country.

78. Ibid., pp. 45–47, 49.

79. Ibid., pp. 52–54. According to the statutes, "all matters of great importance to society or that refer to government bodies will be submitted to his high counsel."

80. Although records on party finances are rather spotty prior to 1944, documents available indicate that the funds received from government employees were used mainly to pay for the party's Managua headquarters, while smaller amounts were handed out to individuals and groups who backed the PLN (newspapermen, students, the Nationalist Conservatives). See letters from the minister of finance to the Banco Nacional authorizing payments against the "Fondo Especial—5% Empleados Públicos," box 112, AN.

81. Chamorro's flier dated 25 June 1938 reflects the caudillo's lack of political and ideological consistency. He attacked Somoza for assassinating Sandino "with malice aforethought, thus perpetrating the most horrible of crimes on the bravest and most heroic guerrilla of our time," when the Conservatives in 1934 were clearly in favor of an amnesty for those involved. He ended his statement by appealing to all the "pueblos de Indoamérica" (using Sandino's terminology) to sanction the Nicaraguan tyrant; in particular, he appealed to Cárdenas, who had just proclaimed Mexico's economic independence (when Chamorro never was much concerned with Nicaragua's sovereignty). Box 100, AN.

82. *La Prensa*, 14, 24 September 1938. According to the agreement between the two parties, of the eighteen deputies assigned to the opposition, the Nationalist Conservatives got eleven and the Genuino Conservatives seven. *La Prensa*, 5 October 1938.

83. *La Prensa*, 9 October 1938.

84. *La Prensa*, 12 January, 23 March 1939.

85. *La Prensa*, 1 April 1939.

86. Coronel Urtecho, *Carta política del señor José Coronel Urtecho al general Emiliano Chamorro*; LG/DO 44,227 (10 October 1940) (quotation). Coronel Urtecho argued that it was time for Nicaragua to enter a long period of peace and reconstruction under a *jefatura nacional*. He believed that elections, parliaments, and political parties were unnecessary for Nicaragua's future.

87. LG/DO 44,227–231 (10–16 October); 44,268–282 (3–19 December); 44,284 (21 December 1940). Both José Coronel Urtecho and Pablo Antonio Cuadra are currently visible faces in the Nicaraguan political scene. Cuadra codirects the newspaper *La Prensa*, while Coronel Urtecho is a respected poet openly supportive of the Sandinista Front.

88. Gould, "The Nicaraguan Labor Movement," pp. 4–5.

89. Box 67, folder "varios," AN.

90. LG/DO 41,56 (12 March 1937).

91. Nicaragua, Ley sobre construcción y adquisición de la vivienda obrera y sobre préstamos para edificaciones, LG/DO 41,205 (22 September 1937).

92. Nicaragua, Ministerio de Hacienda y Crédito Público, *Memoria* for 1940–41, pp. XX–XXI.

93. Box 113, AN.

94. Nicaragua, Estatutos para la administración de la "Casa del Obrero de Managua," LG/DO 44,13 (16 January 1940).

95. Box 235, AN.

96. Nicaragua, Ley sobre seguridad industrial, *LG/DO* 44,139 (24 June 1940).

97. *LG/DO* 44,163 and 44,191 (25 July and 28 August 1940).

98. Nicaragua, Decreto de descanso semanal obligatorio, *LG/DO* 44,202 (10 September 1940), and Reglamento del descanso semanal obligatorio, *LG/DO* 44,267 (3 December 1940).

99. Gould, "The Nicaraguan Labor Movement," pp. 9–10.

100. Box 95, AN. The document has no date but was issued somewhere between June and August 1938. Somoza's meeting with PTN leaders was held on 10 June 1938. *La Prensa*, 11 June 1938.

101. Cited in Pérez Bermúdez and Guevara López, *El movimiento obrero en Nicaragua*, p. 127.

102. Ibid., pp. 142–43, 146–51, and 162–66.

103. Employees of the Talleres del Ferrocarril del Pacífico to Manuel Parajón, general manager of the railroad, Managua, 5 September 1939, box 102, AN. A total of 135 workers signed this petition.

104. Antenor Serrano, secretary general of the Sindicato Industrial de Zapateros, to ASG, Managua, 8 August 1939, box 116, AN.

105. Pérez Bermúdez and Guevara López, *El movimiento obrero en Nicaragua, fascículo 5*, pp. 17–33, and *fascículo 6*, pp. 5–13, 16–18.

106. Gould, "The Nicaraguan Labor Movement," pp. 10–11. At the time Mexican labor was categorically in favor of collaboration between the PTN and Somoza, especially in the area of constitutional reform and in the formation of a broad-based popular movement. María López Pérez de F. to Carlos Pérez Bermúdez, Mexico City, 15 October 1938, box 104, AN.

107. The quotations here and in the next paragraph are from *Boletín*, no. 43 (February 1939): 1, 3–7.

108. *Mercurio*, no. 121–124 (May–August 1939), and no. 132–135 (April–June 1940); *Boletín*, no. 50 (September 1939), no. 53 (December 1939), no. 67 (February 1941), and no. 79 (February 1942). The total number of businesses organized under the various chambers of commerce was not very large. In 1937 the Managua chamber had a total of 66 members; by 1941 it had risen to 102 and in 1943 to 169. Of the members in 1941, 69 were involved in import-export, 5 in banking, and 3 in coffee exporting; the rest covered a gamut of other service and manufacturing activities. However, the weight of the Managua Chamber resided in the membership of the country's most important firms, both foreign and national: Pan American Airways, West India Oil Company (a subsidiary of Standard Oil of New Jersey), Bragmann's Bluff Lumber Company (a subsidiary of Standard Fruit Co.), Grace and Company, Nicaragua Sugar Estates, Limited, Pellas y Compañía, and Ferrocarril del Pacífico. The León Chamber of Commerce had 114 members in 1943 but the number had dropped to 92 in 1945, nor were its members as influential as the important firms associated with the Managua Chamber. See *Boletín*, no. 23 (June 1937), no. 71 (June 1941), and no. 114 (February 1945). See also *Mercurio* no. 141 (December 1943), and no. 142 (January 1946).

109. José Frixione to J. Ramón Sevilla, Managua, 10 January 1940, box 143, AN.

110. Nicaragua, Decreto trasladando funciones de la Asociación Nacional de Ganaderos al Ministerio de Agricultura y Trabajo, *LG/DO* 44,98 (4 May 1940).

111. Silvio Pellas to ASG, Granada, 26 January 1939, and ASG to Pellas, Managua, 31 January 1939, box 113, AN.

112. H. D. Scott to ASG, Puerto Cabezas, 4 February 1939, box 114, AN.

113. Frank Cameron to ASG, Siuna, 20 September 1939, box 111, AN.

114. Nicaragua, Decreto ejecutivo de bloqueo de propiedades y valores de nacionales de Alemania, Italia, y Japón, *LG/DO* 45,275 (18 December 1941).

115. Nicaragua, Decreto interviniendo fincas de café y comercios de extranjeros en cuanto a comercialización se refiere, *LG/DO* 45,275 (18 December 1941).

116. Nicaragua, Reglamento de firmas o personas afectadas por el decreto de propiedades de extranjeros bloqueados, *LG/DO* 46,38 (20 February 1942); and Decreto prohibiendo a extranjeros de países en guerra disponer de sus propiedades, *LG/DO* 47,32 (16 February 1943).

117. Nicaragua, Ley sobre bienes pertenecientes a nacionales de países en guerra con Nicaragua que deben custodiarse, *LG/DO* 47,190 (8 September 1943).

118. Nicaragua, Contrato de construcción del aeropuerto Las Mercedes, *LG/DO* 46,19 (28 January 1942); and Autorización para que el gobierno compre al Banco Nacional los terrenos del aeropuerto Las Mercedes, *LG/DO* 46,214 (6 October 1942). Data on the cement plant can be found in "Contrato para construir fábrica de cemento," *LG/DO* 44,204 (12 September 1940), and in various letters in Fondo Salvadora de Somoza, no. 12, AN. Data on the insurance company are found in a letter, dated 6 February 1943, sent by the firm to one of its clients. Box 216, AN. The president of the insurance company was José Benito Ramírez, Somoza's private secretary; the secretary was Guillermo Sevilla Sacasa, Somoza's son-in-law and ambassador in Washington; the treasurer was Rafael A. Huezo, general manager of the Banco Nacional; and a board member was Luis Manuel Debayle, the Director General de Sanidad, head of the Guardia Nacional's medical corps, and Somoza's brother-in-law.

119. Nicaragua, Secretaría de Agricultura y Trabajo, *Memorias* for 1940–44. The only field he did not compete in was chicken raising.

120. C. Carleton Semple, general manager of Compañía Minas Matagalpa, to ASG, Matagalpa, 25 August 1943, 20 January 1944, Fondo Salvadora de Somoza, no. 8, AN. See also Krehm, *Democracias y tiranías en el Caribe*, p. 175; Krehm's figure is based on contributions to Somoza of U.S.$17 per kilo of gold produced plus an additional amount equivalent to 2.25 percent of total production.

121. Box 114, AN. This draft agreement with Safié has no date but was found in a box corresponding to 1939 documents.

122. Box 183, "folder órdenes y pedidos para haciendas del señor Presidente," AN. In box 167, folder "misceláneas," AN, the administrators of Somoza's coffee farms request gasoline and other supplies that will be picked up in trucks driven by sergeants and corporals of the Guardia Nacional. For the business role of Nicaragua's diplomats, see for example, N. A. Portocarrero, consul general in New York, to ASG, New York, 6 March 1941, box 166, AN. Portocarrero informed Somoza of contacts he had made to sell diverse Nicaraguan goods, especially leather products.

123. Rafael Córdova Rivas, Eduardo Pérez Valle, and Octavio Caldera, interview with author, Managua, 26 June 1984.

124. *La Prensa*, 25 February 1940; Fondo Salvadora de Somoza no. 6, AN; Nicaragua, Decreto de confinamiento, *LG/DO* 44,57 (8 March 1940).

125. Córdova Rivas, Pérez Valle, and Caldera, interview with author, Managua, 26 June 1984.

126. A high school student association, the Unión Nacional de Estudiantes, with links to the Liberal party, was formed in October 1936. Lacayo, *590 días de acción estudiantil*, pp. 6–9. At the university level there was the Frente Universitario de Acción Liberal, which provided legal and medical assistance to indigent people. José M. Zelaya to ASG, Managua, 20 July 1943, box 228, AN.

127. *La Prensa*, 15 June 1940.

128. Nicaragua, Ley Marcial o de orden público, *LG/DO* 43,75 (12 April 1939).

129. Nicaragua, Ley de defensa de la democracia, *LG/DO* 45,138 (30 June 1941).

130. Nicaragua, Decreto de aplicación de la Ley Marcial, *LG/DO* 45,267 (9 December 1941).

131. Gustavo Manzanares to Captain Ambrosio Parodi, Managua, 23 June 1943; Parodi to Leonardo Argüello, Managua, 24 June 1943; and Parodi to Manzanares, Managua, 25 June 1943—all in box 218, AN.

132. Lieutenant Domingo Ibarra to ASG, Granada, 6, 23 January, 8 March 1940, box 127, folder "jefatura política de Granada," AN. Ibarra was fired eventually, apparently for his excessive zeal in persecuting Conservatives.

133. A. P. to Guardia Nacional, Managua, 20 May 1939, box 116, AN.

134. Box 116, AN. The reports required that the jueces de mesta inform the Ministry of the Interior about petty crime, homicides, bootlegging, and school attendance, as well as "social and political meetings." The reports in this box are mostly from the year 1939.

135. Box 104, AN.

136. Comité Revolucionario Nicaragüense, *Programa de acción*, pp. 4–6.

137. Ibid., pp. 7–24.

138. Nicaragua, *Constitución Política de 1939*, article 201.

Chapter 4

1. For example, about 790 Liberals got together in Jinotega on 2 February 1944 (under the direction of the mayor) to celebrate Somoza's birthday and proclaim him a candidate for a new presidential period. Box 75, AN. In San Rafael del Sur, nearly 600 inhabitants did the same on 26 March 1944. Box 247, folder "jefaturas políticas y alcaldías," AN. A considerable number of the "signatures" on some of these proclamations seem to have been written by the same hand, which suggests that the illiterates had their names inserted by someone else or that names were being invented.

2. *La Prensa*, 24 June 1944.

3. *La Prensa*, 20, 26 April 1944.

4. Secretary of State to Certain Diplomatic Representatives in the American Republics, 2 February 1944, *FRUS, 1944*, 7:1391–92.

5. *La Prensa*, 4 May 1944.

6. U.S. Department of Commerce, *Country Economic Reviews*, "Nicaragua," vol. 3, no. 33 (August 1946): 2.

7. *La Prensa*, 29 June 1944.

8. Fondo Salvadora de Somoza, no. 3, AN.

9. *La Prensa*, 30 June 1944.

10. *La Prensa*, 29 June 1944.

11. *La Prensa*, 1 July 1944.

12. *La Prensa*, 2 July 1944.

13. *La Prensa*, 4 July 1944.

14. Gerónimo Ramírez Browne to ASG, Managua, 3 July 1944, Fondo Salvadora de Somoza, no. 3, AN.

15. An internal memorandum sent to ASG by an unidentified adviser on 3 July 1944 expressed the need to get Somoza's followers into the streets to demonstrate to the United States that the majority of Nicaraguans continued to back the regime; this was "absolutely indispensable" to retain Roosevelt's "support" for ASG. Fondo Salvadora de Somoza, no. 8, AN.

16. *La Prensa*, 5 July 1944.

17. Fondo Salvadora de Somoza, no. 8, AN.

18. ASG to jefes políticos of Boaco and Chontales, Managua, 12 July 1944, box 258, AN.

19. *La Prensa*, 6 July 1944; for a copy of the statement, see Fondo Salvadora de Somoza, no. 8, AN.

20. *La Prensa*, 6, 11 July 1944. Argüello had been minister of the interior since November 1940. He had opposed Somoza's political ambitions in 1936; in 1944 he continued to uphold liberal principles of constitutional democracy that were incongruent with Somoza's ambitions and his own participation in a Somoza government. See his letter of resignation in Fondo Salvadora de Somoza, no. 6, AN.

21. *La Prensa*, 11 July 1944.

22. *La Prensa*, 7 July 1944; Open letter from university students to ASG, León, 11 July 1944, Fondo Salvadora de Somoza, no. 3, AN.

23. *La Prensa*, 15 July 1944.

24. *La Prensa*, 4 August 1944.

25. Edgardo Buitrago, interview with author, León, 23 March 1984. Buitrago was a Conservative deputy in the 1950s who met Somoza on a number of occasions for political reasons.

26. *Paso a paso*, no. 5, 23–30 November 1984. This is currently the official paper of the PLI. In this issue, Alejandro Zúñiga Castillo, one of the founders of the PLI, writes a brief history of the party. An internal document of the party entitled "Breve historia del Partido Liberal Independiente" (mimeograph, undated) traces the origins of the PLI to Sandino, whom it describes as "the staunchest and most solid foundation of the Independent Liberal program."

27. Enrique Espinoza Sotomayor, interview with author, Managua, 11 March 1985. Espinoza was one of the original members of the Grupo Democrático Nicaragüense and a founding member of the PLI.

28. Cordero Reyes, Castro Wassmer, and Pasos, *Nicaragua bajo el régimen de Somoza*, pp. 4–11 (quotation, p. 8).

29. Ibid., pp. 13–14.

30. Espinoza Sotomayor, interview with author, Managua, 11 March 1985.

31. See a number of fliers distributed by the PLI during the June–July days of 1944, Fondo Salvadora de Somoza, no. 8, AN.

32. *La Prensa*, 18 July 1944.

33. Of the fourteen founders of the PLI, twelve were lawyers or doctors. *Paso a paso*, no. 5, 23–30 November 1984. Some of the founders of the PLI envisioned a stronger role for the state, as described in a manifesto (never published) of 1937 written by Espinoza Sotomayor, Salvador Buitrago Ajá, Alejandro Zúñiga Castillo, and five others. They stressed the need for a massive educational effort under state direction, a reform of the tax system in order to make it more progressive, an agrarian reform of state-owned lands, labor legislation, and national industrialization. They also espoused eugenics according to the "latest methods." Espinoza Sotomayor, *Partidos políticos*, pp. 112–16; this is Espinoza's thesis for his law degree.

34. *La Prensa*, 29 June 1944.

35. *La Prensa*, 5 July 1944.

36. Chamorro makes no mention of the 1944 events in his autobiography.

37. Gould, "The Nicaraguan Labor Movement," pp. 10–11. An undated memorandum by one Manuel Mendoza to ASG provided an outline of a policy to win over labor's support by seeking to place Somocista labor leaders in top union positions. In that manner, Mendoza said, "the labor movement will act with reasonableness and moderation in its advanced and indispensable socialist demands." Fondo Salvadora de Somoza, no. 8, AN.

38. Fondo Salvadora de Somoza, no. 6, AN.

39. *La Prensa*, 28 May 1944.

40. Gould maintains that labor's favorable response to Somoza's promises "can only be understood in the context of a young, potentially expansive labor movement, weakened by internal divisions, constantly harassed by management and seriously threatened by the possibility of a right-wing takeover." Gould, "The Nicaraguan Labor Movement," pp. 12–13.

41. Fondo Salvadora de Somoza, no. 8, AN. This particular flier is signed by the labor unions of shoemakers, printers, electricians, masons, carpenters, teamsters, and chauffeurs.

42. A copy of this flier was given to me by Jeff Gould, who came across it in the National Archives in Washington.

43. "Manifiesto a la Nación del Partido Socialista de Nicaragua," Colección Centroamérica, legajo 4, no. 638, IHCA.

44. "No estamos con los agitadores del orden público," Colección Centroamérica, legajo 4, no. 583, IHCA.

45. "Seis verdades sobre el Presidente Somoza," Fondo Salvadora de Somoza, no. 6, AN.

46. J. David Zamora to ASG, Jinotega, 6 July 1944, box 267, folder "listas del Partido Liberal," AN.

47. Fondo Salvadora de Somoza, no. 3, AN.

48. Lt. Alfonso J. Borgen to ASG, Chichigalpa, 5 July 1944, box 262, AN.

49. See various statements of support addressed to Somoza by the railroad and telegraph workers in box 248, AN.

50. Press conference as reported in *La Prensa*, 10 June 1944.

51. *La Prensa*, 5 August 1944. On 28 July 1944, the minister of the interior already had written all directors of newspapers insisting that their news reports correspond to "reality." He stressed that criticism of the Guardia Nacional, in particular, no longer would be tolerated, because it was "above political interests" as guarantor of the nation's institutions and the democratic system. *La Prensa*, 29 July 1944.

52. *La Prensa*, 8 August 1944.

53. Nicaragua, Ley sobre la libertad de emisión y difusión del pensamiento, *LG/DO* 48,188 (7 September 1944).

54. *LG/DO*, 49,19 (27 January 1945); 49,42 (23 February 1945).

55. As of January 1992, the code was still in effect.

56. Nicaragua, Código de trabajo, *LG/DO*, 49,23 (1 February 1945), articles 193, 198–99, 203–4.

57. Ibid., articles 222–29.

58. Ibid., articles 251–64, 302–13.

59. Gould, "The Nicaraguan Labor Movement," pp. 22–27.

60. Nicaragua, Secretaría de Agricultura y Trabajo, *Memoria* for 1944, p. 133, and for 1945, p. 9. The *Memoria* for 1945 claims that "over 100 unions" had been registered during that year, but a review of *LG/DO* indicates that the total was around 97.

61. According to Jeff Gould, the total of organized workers by mid-1945 was over 17,000 in 100 unions; these represented more than 50 percent of all mine, transport, and factory workers and roughly 25 percent of all the nonagricultural economically active population. Gould's figure is four times larger than the official figure. If his data and his sources are correct, and I have no reason to doubt this, they probably included all unions and their membership—whether legally registered or not in the Ministry of Agriculture and Labor. See Gould, "The Nicaraguan Labor Movement," p. 17.

62. For a comprehensive analysis of the Somoza regime's relations with the labor movement during 1944–45, see Gould, "The Nicaraguan Labor Movement," pp. 28–39.

63. ASG to the Federación de Trabajadores de Managua, Managua, 26 April 1946, box 320, folder "organizaciones obreras 1946," AN.

64. Gould, "The Nicaraguan Labor Movement," pp. 40–41. For additional documentation on this labor conflict, see box 320, folder "organizaciones obreras 1946," AN.

65. *Elite*, no. 53 (January 1945); box 295, folder "discursos pronunciados por amigos del señor Presidente," AN.

66. These "actas de adhesión y proclamación" can be located in the following boxes of the Archivo Nacional: 281, 282, 285, 286, 294, and 296.

67. Manuel Urbina B., jefe político of Granada, to Lt. Francisco Aguirre Baca (Granada, 27 July 1945); Major L. Delgadillo, comandante departamental of Jinotega, to Lt. Francisco Aguirre Baca (Jinotega, 27 July 1945); L. Alfaro to various PLN groups in Estelí (July 1945), box 295, folder "telegramas varios," AN.

68. Rockefeller summarized this conversation in a letter to the U.S. ambassador in Managua. Acting Secretary of State (Rockefeller) to Ambassador in Nicaragua (Warren), 7 August 1945, *FRUS, 1945*, 9:1215.

69. Memorandum of conversation by the ambassador in Nicaragua (Warren), 10 August 1945, *FRUS, 1945*, 9:1215.

70. Ambassador in Nicaragua (Warren) to Secretary of State, 29 August 1945, *FRUS, 1945*, 9:1217.

71. Ambassador in Nicaragua (Warren) to Secretary of State, 22 October 1945, *FRUS, 1945*, 9:1219.

72. Ibid.

73. Ambassador in Nicaragua (Warren) to Secretary of State, 9 November 1945, *FRUS, 1945*, 9:1221.

74. Ambassador in Nicaragua (Warren) to Secretary of State, 15 November 1945, *FRUS, 1945*, 9:1222.

75. Secretary of State to Ambassador in Nicaragua (Warren), 23 November 1945, *FRUS, 1945*, 9:1222–23.

76. Ambassador in Nicaragua (Warren) to Secretary of State, 29 November 1945, *FRUS, 1945*, 9:1225–28.

77. Ambassador in Nicaragua (Warren) to Secretary of State, 1 December 1945, *FRUS, 1945*, 9:1228–29.

78. Memorandum of conversation, by Chief of Division of Caribbean and Central American Affairs (Cochran), 17 December 1945, *FRUS 1945*, 9:1229–30.

79. Millett, *Guardians of the Dynasty*, pp. 206–7.

80. Nicaragua, Decreto reconociendo a los dos partidos políticos principales, *LG/DO* 49,175 (22 August 1945).

81. Nicaragua, Decreto levantando suspensión de garantías constitucionales decretada en 1941, *LG/DO* 49,255 (30 November 1945).

82. Ambassador in Nicaragua (Warren) to Secretary of State, 30 November 1945, *FRUS, 1945*, p. 1227; *La Prensa*, 11 June 1946.

83. ASG to William Krehm, 27 September 1945, box 294, AN.

84. Nicaragua, Reforma a la ley electoral de 1923, *LG/DO* 49,216 (11 October 1945).

85. See a series of articles published in *El Nuevo Diario*, 19–22 December 1982, by Eduardo Pérez Valle. Pérez Valle was a university student in the mid-1940s and edited *El Universitario*, a weekly that lambasted Somoza and praised Sandino as often as it could. *El Universitario* finally closed down when the government forbade printers to accept its copy. Pérez Valle, interview with author, Managua, 13 June 1984. The government tried to close down El Universitario in March 1946 under the juridical

prohibition of printing "subversive propaganda," in this case the "doctrine of Sandinismo," which was identified by the government with communism. Carlos A. Morales, minister of the interior, to Supreme Court, Managua, 9 March 1946, Fondo Salvador de Somoza, no. 6, AN. The Supreme Court, however, issued an injunction and *El Universitario* appeared for another year.

86. Ernesto Pereira to ASG, Chinandega, 6 September 1945, box 287, folder "jefatura política de Chinandega," AN.

87. *La Prensa* criticized Somoza for attempting to impose his successor by fiat, and of using the government of Nicaragua for his own profit, to the extent that he would make alliances with communists to keep himself in power. "La opulencia epulónica del gobernante es un constante insulto a la miseria del pueblo nicaragüense." *La Prensa*, 13 June, 18 December 1946.

88. Carlos Pasos and Salvador Buitrago Díaz to Major Ambrosio Parodi and Alfredo Castillo, Managua, 7, 14, 20 November 1946, and Alfredo Castillo to Carlos Pasos and Salvador Buitrago Díaz, Managua, 12, 19, 20 November 1946, box 317, AN.

89. Manuel Pérez Estrada and Edmundo Leets C. to Major Ambrosio Parodi, Managua, 7 November 1946, and Alfredo Castillo to Manuel Pérez Estrada, Managua, 12 November 1946, box 317, AN.

90. Partido Liberal Nacionalista, "Informe que rinde la Junta Directiva Nacional y Legal del PLN a la Gran Convención," León, 20 January 1946, pp. 11–13, box 336, folder "juntas directivas del PLN," AN.

91. On 31 October 1945, ASG, as president of the Junta Directiva Nacional y Legal of the PLN, wrote to the Banco Nacional requesting an overdraft for C$180,000 to be paid back in six months with the proceeds of the 5 percent public employees' contribution. He even offered to allow the bank to discount the sum directly from each salary check. Box 321, folder "Banco Nacional de Nicaragua, 1946," AN.

92. *La Prensa*, 26 October 1946. Somoza's contribution could be seen easily as a worthwhile investment.

93. José M. Zelaya, secretary of the Junta Directiva Nacional y Legal of the PLN, to ASG, Managua, 19 December 1946, box 336, folder "juntas directivas del PLN," AN.

94. Report by PLN treasurer, Camilo López Irias, to ASG, national president of the PLN (Managua, 18 January 1946), box 336, folder "juntas directivas del PLN," AN. See also monthly financial reports in AN: Fondo Salvadora de Somoza, no. 8; box 267, folder "listas del Partido Liberal"; and box 310.

95. Partido Liberal Nacionalista, "Informe que rinde la Junta Directiva," pp. 8–10.

96. Carmen Noguera, jefe político of Jinotega department, to ASG, Jinotega, 22 October 1945, box 282, AN.

97. Edmundo Rostrán B. to ASG, Managua, 1 August 1945, box 310, AN. Rostrán had been in the Bluefields area, where he noted much corruption and bad treatment toward the population among officers of the Guardia Nacional. In the important Siuna mining district, only 170 people had come out to proclaim Somoza's candidacy on 29 July 1945, when the adult population of the district was over 4,000.

98. Marco Tulio Martínez, secretary of the Comisión Departamental Electoral de Chontales, to ASG, Juigalpa, 30 October 1945, box 286, AN. In the Acoyapa district of

Chontales, the results obtained by the two factions clearly reflect the importance of caudillo politics in the area; in the polling places there the losing faction got no votes and the winning faction all of them.

99. Carlos Castro Wassmer, the PLI caudillo from León, distributed a leaflet in which he announced his return from exile and declared his complete distrust of Somoza. All of Somoza's offers were simply measures to gain time, he said; the real solution must begin with Somoza's resignation and the formation of a new government that could guarantee free elections. Leaflet attached to letter sent to ASG by Felix Medina, Telica, 30 April 1946, box 339, AN.

100. La Prensa, 18 June, 7, 10 July 1946.

101. La Prensa, 13, 14 August 1946.

102. As a matter of fact, the PLI retained the same statutes and ideological principles as the PLN right up to 1954, when it drew up its own platform. Orlando Blandino, interview with author, León, 26 March 1984.

103. Memorandum sent to General Emiliano Chamorro by a joint committee of the PLI and the Conservative party, Managua, undated but most likely late 1945, box 310, folder "archivo especial de documentos políticos," AN.

104. La Prensa, 18 August, 3 September 1946.

105. Argüello, Plataforma política para el período presidencial 1947–1953.

106. The PLI-Conservative platform can be found in La Prensa, 18 August 1946 and succeeding issues.

107. Guardia Nacional, no. 167 (October 1946): 7.

108. Typewritten table with registration and electoral results, dated 8 March 1947, box 344, AN.

109. La Prensa, 30 July 1946.

110. La Prensa took registration results of 1928 and 1932 and projected them to 1946 according to assumed population growth, claiming that they could not be in excess of 180,000. La Prensa, 7 September 1946.

111. La Prensa, 4 February 1947.

112. Alvaro Ramírez G., interview with author, Managua, 16 January 1984. Alvaro was a poll watcher at the time.

113. Internal memorandum of the PLN (undated), Fondo Salvadora de Somoza, no. 13, AN.

114. La Prensa, 25 February 1947. The opposition claimed that the Somocistas only got more votes than the opposition in the department of Madriz, a claim that is obviously exaggerated.

115. Only the labor movement called Obrerismo Organizado de Nicaragua, founded in 1923 by Liberal politicians, came out openly for Argüello in exchange for concessions such as a labor representation in the National Congress, social security, and distribution of land to peasants. See its manifesto of 15 September 1946, box 314, AN.

116. The "Primer Congreso de Cámaras de Comercio y Producción de Nicaragua," held in December 1944, requested more credit on easier terms from the Banco Nacional, the creation of a rural police force, the reduction of railway rates, and reforms of the labor code as dictated by experience. Boletín, no. 112 (December 1944).

117. Editorial in the *Boletín*, no. 133 (September 1946).

118. As a case in point, the annual report for 1945–46 presented by the president of the board of directors of the Managua Chamber of Commerce limits its commentaries to bureaucratic bottlenecks in the public administration; it makes no reference to the wider economic and social problems faced by the country. *Boletín*, no. 131 (July 1946). The León Chamber of Commerce limited its observations to the excessively high prior deposit that the Banco Nacional required for the purchase of foreign exchange and to the need for the construction of the León-Sébaco highway that would open up the Pacific coast directly to the northern highlands. See *Mercurio*, no. 142 (January 1946), and no. 147 (January–February 1947).

119. Fondo Salvadora de Somoza, no. 13, AN.

120. Report on a riot ("amotinamiento") of political opponents in Masatepe prepared by Lts. Domingo Torres R. and Gonzalo Matus L., Managua, 19 February 1947, Fondo Salvadora de Somoza, no. 6, AN.

121. Nicaragua, Presidencia de la República, *Discurso pronunciado por el doctor Leonardo Argüello el 1 de mayo de 1947 ante el Congreso Nacional al tomar posesión de la Presidencia de la República*.

122. *La Prensa*, 11 May 1947.

123. *La Prensa*, 16 April 1947.

124. *La Prensa*, 13 April 1947.

125. *La Prensa*, 13 April, 13 May 1947.

126. *La Prensa*, 17, 23 May 1947.

127. For a detailed account of the events leading up to the coup and the coup itself, see Millett, *Guardians of the Dynasty*, pp. 208–11, and *La Prensa*, 28 May 1947.

128. *LG/DO* 51,114 (2 June 1947).

Chapter 5

1. *La Prensa*, 6, 10, 11 June 1947.

2. *La Prensa*, 17, 18 June 1947.

3. *La Prensa*, 2 July 1947.

4. Nicaragua, Decreto de confinamiento, *LG/DO* 51,142 (5 July 1947). See also Armando Amador, *Origen, auge y crisis de una dictadura*, for a detailed description of the government's repression of the labor movement during 1946–48. An important leader of the PSN, Amador was exiled by Somoza in 1947.

5. Millett, *Guardians of the Dynasty*, p. 211.

6. Rafael Córdova Rivas, interview with author, Managua, 22 June 1984. Enrique Espinoza Sotomayor also claims that Somoza had to fire one-third of the officer corps after the coup. Espinoza Sotomayor, interview with author, Managua, 11 March 1985. According to official data, the Guardia had 373 officers at the end of 1947, compared to 345 in April 1946. If Córdova Rivas's figure is correct, the officer corps either grew rapidly between April 1946 and May 1947 (which does not seem likely) and thus was

able to absorb the purge with no decrease in numbers, or Somoza rapidly replaced the purged officers after May 1947. See Nicaragua, Secretaría de Guerra, Marina y Aviación, *Memorias* for 1946 and 1947.

7. *La Prensa*, 5 August 1947. *Novedades*, the Somoza newspaper, reported a total of 108,487 votes deposited, with the PLN getting 91,261 and the Nationalist Conservatives 17,226. *Novedades*, 11 August 1947. On the basis of these figures, the Liberal turnout dropped by 13 percent compared to their showing in February.

8. Salvador Guerrero, president of the Junta Directiva Departamental y Legal of the PLN in Chinandega, to ASG, Chinandega, 17 July 1947, box 24, AN(A).

9. Nicaragua, "Mensaje presidencial del Dr. Benjamín Lacayo Sacasa a la Asamblea Constituyente al iniciar sus sesiones el 19 de agosto de 1947," *LG/DO* 51,177 (20 August 1947).

10. Millett, *Guardians of the Dynasty*, p. 211.

11. Chargé in Nicaragua (Bernbaum) to Secretary of State, Managua, 7 August 1947, *FRUS, 1947*, 8: 864–65.

12. Nicaragua, "Mensaje inaugural del Dr. Victor Román y Reyes ante la Asamblea Constituyente al asumir las funciones de Presidente de la República," *LG/DO* 51,178 (21 August 1947).

13. Acting Secretary of State to Embassy in Nicaragua, *FRUS, 1947*, 8:865–66.

14. Secretary of State to U.S. Diplomatic Representatives in the American Republics except Nicaragua, 30 May 1948, *FRUS, 1948*, 9:108.

15. *La Prensa*, 17 September 1947.

16. Chamorro was taken to the Managua airport in a U.S. embassy car accompanied by the first secretary of the embassy, the Salvadoran minister, and Anastasio Somoza, Jr. *La Prensa*, 28 September 1947.

17. *La Prensa*, 16, 28 September, 4 October 1947.

18. *La Prensa*, 1 November 1947.

19. *La Prensa*, 30 November, 16 December 1947.

20. Carta del Dr. Carlos Cuadra Pasos a los Generales Somoza y Chamorro, Granada, 30 June 1947, in Nicaragua, Ministerio de Relaciones Exteriores, *Realidad política de Nicaragua*, p. 64.

21. Ibid., pp. 65, 67.

22. Carta del General E. Chamorro al Dr. Carlos Cuadra Pasos, Managua, 2 July 1947, ibid., pp. 72–73.

23. Chamorro makes no mention of the failed coup of 7 September in his autobiography. He says only that his life was threatened and that he had to leave Nicaragua again for exile in Guatemala. Chamorro, *Autobiografía*, p. 105.

24. Carta del Dr. Carlos Cuadra Pasos al General Anastasio Somoza, Managua, 23 December 1947, in Ministerio de Relaciones Exteriores, *Realidad política de Nicaragua*, pp. 103–11.

25. Carta del General Anastasio Somoza al Dr. Carlos Cuadra Pasos, Managua, 30 December 1947, ibid., pp. 112–18.

26. Nicaragua, Constitución política de 1948, *LG/DO* 52,16 (22 January 1948).

27. Carlos Cuadra Pasos, *Mensaje a los Conservadores de Nicaragua*, p. 11. For the text of the Somoza–Cuadra Pasos agreement, see ibid., pp. 11–14.

28. Emiliano Chamorro, "Declaración al Partido Conservador de Nicaragua y al pueblo nicaragüense en general," Guatemala, 2 March 1948, Tomo 24 (B-31), Archivo no. 5, gaveta 2, no. 4, IHCA.

29. Frente Nacional pro Libertad de Nicaragua, *La verdadera realidad política de Nicaragua*, pp. 28–29, 45.

30. Ibid., pp. 47–51.

31. Nicaragua, Decreto de amnistía, *LG/DO* 52,56 (11 March 1948). The amnesty decree specifically called on recalcitrant opponents (i.e., Chamorro) to return and participate in an orderly and evolutionary process "that would avoid violent means of action and achieve a complete national harmony." Nicaragua, Decreto presidencial convocando a elección especial para senadores y diputados conforme acuerdo entre el PLN y políticos Conservadores, *LG/DO* 52,76 (10 April 1948). This decree allowed all "historic" parties to participate, that is, the PLN and the Conservatives; under the Somoza-Cuadra Pasos agreement, the PLN refrained from presenting candidates and thereby allowed all four senators and seven deputies run by the Conservatives to win unopposed. As a consequence, the Nationalist Conservatives were tossed aside, having outlived their usefulness to the regime for the time being.

32. The *Pacto de Alianza* signed on 16 December 1947 by Chamorro and Rosendo Argüello, on behalf of the PLI, committed the participants to pool their economic and military resources to overthrow the governments of Costa Rica, Nicaragua, and the Dominican Republic and replace them with democratic regimes. As each country was "liberated," it would help in the struggle against the remaining dictatorships until all were freed. President Arévalo of Guatemala was called upon to act as mediator in the case of irreconcilable differences among the participants.

33. See the manifesto published by the supporters of Cuadra Pasos denouncing the replacement of Civilista party officials in Boaco, Granada, and Rivas. "Manifiesto: El grupo conservador civilista denuncia los procedimientos ilegales de ciertas entidades del Partido," Managua, 29 September 1949, Editorial La Prensa, T-24 (B-31), Archivo no. 5, gaveta no. 2, no. 6, IHCA.

34. ASG to Carlos Cuadra Pasos, Managua, 7 December 1949, Fondo Salvadora de Somoza, no. 8, AN.

35. *La Prensa*, 17, 21 January, 22 February, 30, 31 March 1950.

36. *La Prensa*, 2 April 1950.

37. The Pact of the Generals was preceded by a business deal between the two men. The Compañía Nacional de Productores de Leche, S.A. was organized in February 1950 with Chamorro as president of the board and Somoza as vice-president. It became the largest dairy plant in the country. *LG/DO* 54,39 (23 February 1950). For examples of the stock issued, see Fondo Salvadora de Somoza, no. 7, AN.

38. Nicaragua, Decreto convocando a elecciones para Asamblea Constituyente y Presidente de la República, *LG/DO* 54,75 (15 April 1950).

39. *La Prensa*, 16, 20 April, 18 May 1950.

40. Partido Conservador de Nicaragua, "Manifiesto de la Junta Directiva Departamental y Legal del Partido Conservador de Nicaragua al pueblo de occidente," León, 21 April 1950, Fondo Salvadora de Somoza, no. 9, AN. Chamorro Benard was described as a man of impeccable credentials "because he is a complete stranger to our political scene."

41. Partido Conservador de Nicaragua, "Manifiesto de la Junta Directiva Nacional y Legal del Partido Conservador de Nicaragua a los Conservadores y todos los que con nosotros quieren luchar por acabar con el continuismo," Managua, 10 May 1950, Colección Centroamérica, legajo 4, no. 588, IHCA; "Comité de Propaganda Chamorro-Benard reproduce la circular del señor Comandante General de la República," Managua, 10 May 1950, Colección Centroamérica, legajo 4, no. 607, IHCA.

42. La Prensa, 23 April, 2 May 1950.

43. See, for example, a couple of letters from Emiliano Chamorro and Gustavo Manzanares to the president of the Consejo Nacional de Elecciones, Managua, 24 April 1950, complaining that the Guardia forbade a radio broadcast of a Conservative manifesto in Managua and that traffic policemen did not allow trucks carrying Conservative demonstrators to proceed from Managua to Granada in Fondo Salvadora de Somoza, no. 13, AN. See also reports of harassment against Conservatives in León, Jinotega, and Matagalpa in La Prensa, 14, 18 May 1950.

44. Nicaragua, Consejo Nacional de Elecciones, El juicio electoral de 1950, pp. 352–54, 359–60.

45. La Prensa, 23 May 1950. La Prensa's editorial for that date said in part: "And now we only have to say to General Somoza: This time you have the right conditions to become a perfect ruler. Nobody will accuse you in your face that you have usurped the government." The Conservative party's position is in La Prensa, 3 June 1950.

46. Nicaragua, Recaudación General de Aduanas, Memorias for 1949 and 1956. See also U.S. Department of Commerce, Country Economic Reviews, "Economic Review of Nicaragua in 1947."

47. Ibid., p. 68. Public investment grew at an annual rate of 26.6 percent during the period 1950–55, a much higher figure than the annual rate of overall economic growth of 8.3 percent for the same period. Nicaragua, Consejo Nacional de Economía, Oficina de Planificación, Análisis del desarrollo económico y social de Nicaragua, pp. 1–16.

48. Even at the Ministry of Development and Public Works, the overwhelming majority of permament employees were engaged in running the national mail and telegraph services.

49. Nicaragua, Ley creadora de los ministerios de estado y otras dependencias del Poder Ejecutivo, LG/DO 52,249 (13 November 1948).

50. Nicaragua, Decreto de creación del Consejo Nacional de Economía, LG/DO 53,132 (20 June 1949).

51. Nicaragua, Ley que reforma el decreto de creación del Consejo Nacional de Economía de 1949, LG/DO 57,36 (13 February 1953).

52. Nicaragua, Ley creadora del Instituto de Fomento Nacional (INFONAC), LG/DO 57,60 (13 March 1953).

53. IBRD, Mission to Nicaragua, *The Fiscal System of Nicaragua*.

54. Nicaragua, Impuesto sobre ingresos netos a productores de café y algodón, *LG/DO* 55,263 (7 December 1951).

55. IBRD, *The Fiscal System of Nicaragua*, pp. 5–8.

56. Ibid., pp. 61–66.

57. President Victor Román y Reyes to Cabinet Ministers, Managua, 6 June 1949, Fondo Salvadora de Somoza, no. 3, AN.

58. León Debayle to ASG, Managua, 6 June 1949, Fondo Salvadora de Somoza, no. 3, AN.

59. IBRD, *The Economic Development of Nicaragua*, pp. 5–12.

60. Nicaragua, Ley de impuesto sobre la renta, *LG/DO* 56,300 (31 December 1952).

61. For details of the loan agreements, see *LG/DO* 55,167 (11 August 1951); 55,171 (17 August 1951); 55,274 (20 December 1951); 57,227 (2 October 1953); 59,125 (22 September 1955); 59,260 (16 November 1955); and 60,212 (19 August 1956).

62. Armijo Mejía, *Ideas sobre la organización del ejecutivo*, pp. 2–10. Armijo eventually became minister of public works in the government of Luis Somoza D.

63. Consejo Nacional de Economía, *Análisis del desarrollo económico y social de Nicaragua*, pp. 293–99; José M. Castillo to ASG, Managua, 13 April 1956, box 45, AN(A).

64. IBRD, *The Economic Development of Nicaragua*, p. 75.

65. Consejo Nacional de Economía, *Análisis del desarrollo económico y social de Nicaragua*, p. 246.

66. Between 1950 and 1956, from 20 to 40 percent of all private investment went into nonproductive ventures such as the construction of homes and buildings. CEPAL, *El desarrollo económico de Nicaragua*, p. 56.

67. Ibid., pp. 57, 59.

68. For an extensive analysis of these two banking firms and their subsequent development, see Wheelock Román, *Imperialismo y dictadura*, pp. 144–58.

69. Recaudación General de Aduanas, *Memoria* for 1940, p. 100; *Memoria* for 1949, p. 89; and *Memoria* for 1956, p. 78.

70. Nicaragua, Instituto de Fomento Nacional, *Realizaciones*.

71. Interviews with author: Dr. Mario Flores Ortiz, Managua, 15 May 1984; Enrique Alvarado, Managua, 13 May 1985.

72. F. Alfredo Pellas to ASG, Granada, 11 September 1950, box 58, AN(A).

73. F. Alfredo Pellas to ASG, Managua, November 1954, Fondo Salvadora de Somoza, no. 12, AN.

74. In 1953 the Ingenio San Antonio produced about 75 percent of the country's sugar while employment in all the country's sugar mills accounted for 47 percent of the total industrial labor force. Nicaragua, Ministerios de Economía y del Trabajo, *Antecedentes del Seguro Social en Nicaragua*, pp. 61–64.

75. For summary data on these enterprises, see *LG/DO* 49,154 (26 July 1945); 50,137 (28 June 1946); 57,185 (12 August 1953); and 57,291 (18 December 1953).

76. Nicaragua, Ley reguladora del comercio, *LG/DO* 49,218 (15 October 1945).

77. U.S. Department of Commerce, *Country Economic Reviews*, "Economic Review of Nicaragua in 1947," p. 1; Nicaragua, Reformas a la ley reguladora del comercio, *LG/DO* 52,76 (10 April 1948).

78. Nicaragua, Decreto-ley de nivelación de cambios, *LG/DO* 53,79 (7 April 1949); and Reformas al decreto-ley de nivelación de cambios, *LG/DO* 53,276 (17 December 1949).

79. Nicaragua, Ley reguladora·de cambios internacionales, *LG/DO* 54,238 (9 November 1950). This law transferred the purchase and sale procedures of foreign exchange directly to the Department of Issue of the Banco Nacional and abolished the post of Contralor de Cambios.

80. Nicaragua, Ley reguladora de cambios internacionales, *LG/DO* 59,145 (30 June 1955).

81. Managua Chamber of Commerce, *Boletín*, no. 146–147 (October–November 1947), pp. 3–5.

82. Board of directors of the Cooperativa Nacional de Agricultores to its members, Managua, 26 May 1951, Fondo Salvadora de Somoza, no. 3, AN.

83. Cámara de Comercio de León, *Mercurio*, no. 155 (July 1950): 13, 15.

84. Managua Chamber of Commerce to Consejo Directivo del Departamento de Emisión del Banco Nacional, 12 February 1951, *Boletín*, no. 170 (March 1951).

85. *Mercurio*, no. 155 (July 1950): 13, 15.

86. *Boletín*, no. 171 (April 1951): 38–39.

87. *Boletín*, no. 189 (May 1953): 1–2.

88. *Boletín*, no. 213 (February–March 1956): 3–4.

89. Nicaragua, Decreto del estado de emergencia económica, *LG/DO* 43,208 (26 September 1939). Subsequent renewals of the decree usually occurred in October of each year; the last one during Anastasio Somoza's presidency was published in *LG/DO* 59,230 (10 October 1955).

90. *Boletín*, no. 185 (October–November 1952).

91. *Boletín*, no. 215 (June 1950): 3, 8. Social security required that the business contribute a sum equivalent to 8 percent of the worker's monthly salary; the worker would put up 4 percent.

92. *La Prensa*, 30 November 1955. It is possible that Somoza's rather negative attitude toward the cotton growers was partly in response to the excessive expansion of cotton production that had resulted in a substantial decline in the supply of basic foodstuffs. As he put it, "everyone is into cotton growing." As a matter of fact, in June 1955 the government had to prohibit the export of corn, beans, sorghum, potatoes, rice, and fresh vegetables. Nicaragua, Ley de defensa al consumidor de artículos nacionales de primera necesidad en tiempos de escasez, *LG/DO* 59,134 (17 June 1955) and 59,136 (20 June 1955).

93. IBRD, *The Economic Development of Nicaragua*, p. 100. Within this perspective, a case could be made that Somoza was one of the very few farsighted entrepreneurs in the country at the time, in addition, of course, to the fact that he had many advantages over other businessmen.

Chapter 6

1. For data on these activities, see Lt. Gonzalo Matus, Guardia Nacional, to ASG (Ciudad Darío, 27 October 1949) and Justo Jarquín to ASG (La Paz Centro, 23 October 1949), box 10, AN(A). A comprehensive collection of "proclamaciones" for the 1956 election can be found in box 96, folders "proclamaciones de julio a septiembre de 1954" and "proclamaciones y correspondencia PLN 1955," AN(A).

2. Signed declaration by Aníbal Alemán Hernández and Ricardo Irigoyen González (Alta Gracia, Ometepe Island, 27 May 1956), box 47, folder "Partido Liberal 1956," AN(A).

3. Box 107, AN(A). Similar declarations of late 1954 for the department of Boaco can be found in box 96, "folder Boaco," AN(A).

4. Tomás Adolfo Martínez to ASG (Alta Gracia, Ometepe Island, 27 May 1956), box 47, folder "Partido Liberal 1956," AN.

5. *La Prensa*, 28 February 1950. For the 1956 election, the PLN put out a special magnífica for female supporters of Somoza in view of the possible congressional approval of female suffrage. *La Prensa*, 1 April 1954.

6. Somoza's nomination in León for the 1950 election brought together over 20,000 supporters. *La Prensa* reported that government bureaucrats were brought in from Managua while the jueces de mesta organized the campesino contingents from the outlying areas. *La Prensa*, 23 April 1950. A similar rally in February 1956 drew over 30,000 people. *La Prensa*, 15 February 1956.

7. The electoral platform of the PLN is included in Nicaragua, Presidencia de la República, *Mensaje del excelentísimo General de División Anastasio Somoza leído ante el Honorable Congreso Nacional al tomar posesión de la Presidencia de la República para el período constitucional que se inicia el 1 de mayo de 1951*, pp. 12–16, 25–27.

8. Partido Liberal Nacionalista, *Plataforma de gobierno que el General Anastasio Somoza presenta a la Gran Convención del Partido Liberal Nacionalista, al ser proclamado su candidato presidencial para el período 1957–1963*. See also Nicaragua, Presidencia de la República, *Mensaje que el Presidente de la República, General de División Anastasio Somoza dirige al Honorable Congreso Nacional al inaugurar las sesiones ordinarias correspondientes a su VI período constitucional el 15 de abril de 1956*, pp. 106–8.

9. See Valle Rios, *Por qué los obreros y los campesinos estan con Somoza*, pp. 1–6, and Juventud Liberal Nicaragüense, *Recopilación de la Asamblea General de Juventud Liberal Nicaragüense del 2 de febrero de 1952*, pp. 29–38.

10. José Santos García, secretary of the Comité Departamental de Propaganda pro-General Somoza, to ASG (Somoto, 17 October 1949), box 10, AN(A).

11. For an extensive collection of these documents, see box 107, AN(A).

12. Luis Enrique López Castro, secretary of the Comité Nacional de los Frentes Populares Liberales Somocistas, to Junta Directiva del Comité Nacional pro-Candidatura General Somoza (Managua, 2 September 1956), box 107, AN(A).

13. See a collection of letters and documents of the Comité Nacional organized for the 1956 election in box 107, AN(A).

14. See reports prepared by the PLN's treasurer, José María Castellón, on 5 January 1950 and 6 January 1956, Fondo Salvadora de Somoza, nos. 9, 12, AN.

15. See report prepared by PLN treasurer, J. M. Castellón, Managua, 21 January 1953, Fondo Salvadora de Somoza, no. 6, AN.

16. See various typewritten documents of the Comité Nacional de Propaganda Liberal of the PLN (Managua, n.d.), Fondo Salvadora de Somoza, no. 8, AN.

17. Report by Castellón of 6 January 1956 cited previously. See also Fondo Salvadora de Somoza, no. 9, AN. Included in this set is an example of a C$10 bond issued by the Comisión de Hacienda del Comité Nacional pro-Candidatura Presidencial General Anastasio Somoza.

18. "Informe de la Tesorería del Comité Central Pro-Festejos a Anastasio Somoza García," León, February 1956, Fondo Salvadora de Somoza, no. 11, AN. The sale of aguardiente as a fund-raising mechanism involved the purchase of the liquor free of taxes from the government excise office and its resale at a lower-than-normal price, with the PLN pocketing the difference. See René Schick, secretary to ASG, to Rafael A. Huezo, Minister of Finance (Managua, 9 August 1956), box 107, AN(A).

19. Such was the case in Chinandega, department of Chinandega, where about sixty individuals got together for that purpose. Jesús Solano Cerda to ASG (Chichigalpa, 29 October 1947), box 353, AN. Another group organized in the municipality of Chinandega called itself "compañía de civiles liberales." Tomás Céspedes Cepeda, jefe político of Chinandega, to ASG (Chinandega, 30 October 1947), box 342, AN.

20. See founding document of the Reserva Civil at the San Antonio sugar mill (Chichigalpa, 3 November 1947), box 107, AN(A).

21. "Acta de fundación" of the "Julio César" departmental battalion (Masaya, 7 December 1947), box 107, AN(A).

22. "Acta de creación" of the Reservas Civiles of the department of Estelí (Estelí, 7 December 1947), and List of members of the auxiliares of the Guardia Nacional in Chontales department (Juigalpa, December 1947), box 107, AN(A).

23. Cuartel General de la Guardia Nacional (Managua, Loma de Tiscapa), Informe consolidado de fuerza de la Guardia Nacional a 17 de mayo de 1947, box 351, AN.

24. Millett, Guardians of the Dynasty, p. 213. For texts of these agreements, see LG/DO as follows: 56,294 (23 December 1952); 57,276 (1 December 1953); and 58,138 (22 June 1954). LaFeber, Inevitable Revolutions, especially pp. 106–11, places U.S. military policy in Central America at this time within the wider scope of U.S. concerns in Latin America as a whole.

25. Millett, Guardians of the Dynasty, p. 214.

26. See Nicaragua, Ministerio de Guerra, Marina y Aviación, Memorias for years 1945–56, which provide total amounts spent on salaries for officers and enlisted men.

27. La Prensa, 3 February 1956. Between 1947 and 1956 there were 3,201 enlistments and 7,493 reenlistments, which gives a proportion of 1:2.34. See Nicaragua, Secretaría de Guerra, Marina y Aviación, Memorias for years in question.

28. Somoza did engage in saber rattling with Honduras in the late 1930s over disputed territory in the Cabo Gracias a Dios region. He also was involved in a number of plots against his sworn enemy, José Figueres of Costa Rica.

29. See, for example, intelligence reports of one Inocente León who reported directly to General Francisco Gaitán, the minister of war, during the period 1950–54 on the activities and opinions of leaders of the PLI and the Conservative party. Fondo Salvadora de Somoza, nos. 2, 8, and 14, AN.

30. Orlando Blandino, interview with author, León, 26 March 1984. See also Selva, *Cero política*, pp. 25–26.

31. Dr. Alonso Castellón, interview with author, León, 10 April 1984.

32. Author interviews with Blandino and Castellón cited above. Fear of government repression apparently kept people from openly joining the party and having their names registered in the party's books, even though privately they expressed support for the PLI and its activities. Alejandro Zúñiga Castillo, interview with author, Managua, 16 March 1985.

33. Juan Sandoval, interview with author, León, 26 March 1984.

34. Reinaldo Antonio Tefel, interview with author, Managua, 11 June 1984. See also a manifesto signed by the PLI leadership in León, including at the time Tomás Borge, *La Prensa*, 9 October 1955; a speech by Adán Selva before the Gran Convención of the PLI at León, *La Prensa*, 28 August 1956; and Selva, *Cero política*, p. 26.

35. Solórzano, *La ideología que debe sustentar el Partido Conservador de Nicaragua*, pp. 5–12.

36. Paniagua Rivas, *Los principios fundamentales del conservatismo*, pp. 3–11.

37. See, for example, the speech by José Joaquín Cuadra on the occasion of the formation of a group of Juventud Conservadora in the town of Diriomo near Granada. *La Prensa*, 28 April 1953. A few months later, at a Conservative party meeting honoring General Chamorro in Granada, a member of Juventud Conservadora openly attacked the General for his demagoguery and inconsistency. *La Prensa*, 28 May 1953.

38. *La Prensa*, 17 November 1953, 7 February 1954.

39. *La Prensa*, 18 February 1954.

40. *La Prensa*, 16 February 1954. For a complete text of the resolutions, see Partido Conservador de Nicaragua, Junta Directiva Nacional y Legal, *Documentos y resoluciones del Partido Conservador de Nicaragua*, pp. 37–48.

41. *La Prensa*, 17 February 1954.

42. Reinaldo Antonio Tefel, interview with author, Managua, 11 June 1984. A detailed analysis of UNAP's origins and development, as well as of the entire Christian Democratic movement, is found in Walker, *The Christian Democratic Movement in Nicaragua*, especially pp. 24–42.

43. *La Prensa*, 12 December 1953.

44. *La Prensa*, 15 September 1955. UNAP's analysis is contained in a communiqué published in its entirety by *La Prensa*. The list of signatories is a revealing example of the polarizing effects of the Sandinista revolution on contemporary Nicaraguan politics; it includes Emilio Alvarez M., a leader of one of the current factions of the Conservative party, Ernesto Cardenal, who was minister of culture in the revolutionary government, and Arturo Cruz, who was active in the exiled opposition to the Sandinista government. Pedro Joaquín Chamorro, editor of *La Prensa*, joined UNAP's leadership the following year.

45. *La Prensa*, 26 July 1955.

46. See issues of *La Prensa* for 11 February, 3 March, 30 May, 5, 17 July, and 4 September 1956.

47. *La Prensa*, 19 January 1956. *La Prensa* even editorialized that Somoza's government was still full of Marxist labor leaders and teachers. *La Prensa*, 20 January 1956.

48. Comité de Unidad y Reconstrucción Sindical, Untitled report on the situation of the Nicaraguan labor movement, February 1953. The report was prepared in San José, Costa Rica, where representatives of the CURS engaged in talks with the Comisión Obrera Sindical, the Costa Rican leftist labor movement. Somoza was able to get a carbon copy of the report. Fondo Salvadora de Somoza, no. 6, AN.

49. *La Prensa*, 9, 11 April 1953.

50. *La Prensa*, 28 August, 22 September 1955.

51. *La Prensa*, 4 January 1956.

52. Nicaragua, Reglamento de asociaciones sindicales, *LG/DO* 55,93 (10 May 1951).

53. Nicaragua, Reglas generales para el manejo y administración de la Casa del Obrero, *LG/DO* 55,10 (18 January 1951).

54. Anastasio Somoza, "Mensaje a los trabajadores," Managua, 1 May 1950, Fondo Salvadora de Somoza, no. 13, AN.

55. See, for example, the following: Workers of the San Antonio sugar mill to ASG (San Antonio, 4 November 1947, box 353, AN) thanking him for supporting their demands; CGT to ASG (*La Prensa*, 25 June 1950) requesting that the government provide more credits to large farmers to generate employment, that landless peasants receive small plots, and that speculators and hoarders of basic foodstuffs be prosecuted; Bernardo Otero U., member of the junta directiva of the CGT, to ASG (Managua, 22 June 1951, box 77, AN[A]) requesting an appointment to discuss various matters; Domingo A. Sánchez, general secretary of the Nueva Federación de Trabajadores de Managua, to ASG (Managua, 21 September 1951, box 77, AN[A]) requesting that rent controls be retained.

56. *La Prensa*, 12, 13 December 1955.

57. Leaflet entitled "Alerta, obreros y campesinos de Nicaragua," issued by the Sub-Comité de Obreros y Campesinos" of San Pedro Lóvago, Chontales department (1 February 1956), box 47, folder "proclamaciones comités liberales candidatura ASG," AN(A).

58. *La Prensa*, 11, 12, 16, 18 June 1953; Anastasio Somoza, "Mensaje a los trabajadores," Managua, 1 May 1950, Fondo Salvadora de Somoza, no. 13, AN (quotation).

59. *La Prensa*, 26, 27, 31 April 1954. Included among the seven were Manolo Cuadra, a well-known poet, and Manuel Pérez Estrada, a labor leader who also had worked for *Orientación*. The rest included a couple of doctors, a labor leader, a writer, and the owner of the printing shop.

60. Nicaragua, Decreto normando la censura previa de acuerdo a la ley de libertad de emisión del pensamiento, *LG/DO* 51,206 (24 September 1947).

61. Nicaragua, Ley de libertad de emisión y difusión del pensamiento, *LG/DO* 52,166 (31 July 1948).

62. Nicaragua, Ley de libertad de emisión y difusión del pensamiento, *LG/DO* 57,202 (1 September 1953).

63. Nicaragua, Decreto prohibiendo la circulación de propaganda comunista, *LG/DO* 59,31 (8 February 1955).

64. Fondo Salvadora de Somoza, no. 1, AN.

65. Modesto Salmerón, minister of the interior, to René Schick, secretary to the presidency, Managua, 17 November 1955, , box 96, folder "Ministerio de Gobernación (2do. semestre 1955)," AN(A). Of a total daily circulation of 59,800 newspapers, Salmerón figured that only 26,000 belonged to newspapers identified outright with the regime and of these, the Somoza newspaper *Novedades* accounted for 20,000.

66. *La Prensa*, 13 March 1956.

67. *La Prensa*, 17 March, 7 April 1956.

68. See, for example, a list of 53 Nicaraguan exiles, including 22 ex-Guardia Nacional officers, who lived in Costa Rica and Guatemala (Managua, 9 January 1949). Fondo Salvadora de Somoza, no. 3, AN. See also Benjamín Odio, minister of foreign affairs of Costa Rica, to the Costa Rican minister of public security (San José, 17 May 1949) transcribing a list of 109 Nicaraguans who, according to the Nicaraguan minister in Costa Rica, were engaged in "activities against the regime of that country." Fondo Salvadora de Somoza, no. 6, AN. Guillermo Sevilla Sacasa, Nicaraguan ambassador in Washington, informed Somoza (Washington, 4 January 1950) of a conversation he had had with Pedro Estrada, head of the Venezuelan secret police, on the activities of Nicaraguan and other exiles in Costa Rica and Guatemala. Fondo Salvadora de Somoza, no. 3, AN.

69. At one point, Somoza even engaged the services of a company in New York City to place articles in the U.S. press favorable to his regime and stressing the peace and progress that Nicaragua enjoyed under his rule. M. Mark Sulkes to ASG, New York City, 11 February 1949, Fondo Salvadora de Somoza, no. 6, AN.

70. The leaflet was sent to ASG by Alejandro Argüello Montiel, Nicaraguan minister in San José, Costa Rica, where it circulated. The imprint on the leaflet reads "Imprenta Sandino, México D.F." but Argüello Montiel believed that it was printed clandestinely in San José. Alejandro Argüello Montiel to ASG, San José, Costa Rica, 8 May 1950, Fondo Salvadora de Somoza, no. 8, AN.

71. *Revolución*, August 1953.

72. Unión Revolucionaria Democrática, *La lucha contra Somoza*, pp. 16–24 (quotation, p. 18).

73. *Revolución*, March 1954.

74. *Revolución*, March 1955.

75. *Revolución*, September 1954.

76. Unión Revolucionaria Democrática, *La lucha contra Somoza*, pp. 34–36, 57.

77. Ibid., p. 25.

78. Ibid., pp. 25–27, 40–41.

79. Ibid., pp. 41–42.

80. In mid-1949, at least twenty-three ex-Guardia officers who were active in

opposition politics lived in Costa Rica. See Odio to Minister of Public Safety of Costa Rica cited in n. 68.

81. The account of the 1954 plot is based largely on information provided by Julián Salaverry, one of the participants in the event. Salaverry, interviews with author, Managua, 26 June, 1 July 1985.

82. Nicaragua, Decreto de suspensión de garantías a raíz del complot armado, *LG/DO* (5 April 1954). See Fondo Salvadora de Somoza, no. 4, AN, for a poster announcing the rewards.

83. *La Prensa*, 6, 11 April 1954.

84. *La Prensa*, 7 May 1954.

85. *La Prensa*, 25, 29, 30 April 1954, 2 February 1955, 11 May 1956.

86. *La Prensa*, 12 February 1955, 5 May 1956.

87. Nicaragua, Decreto derogando restricción de garantías constitucionales en todo el país menos Managua y Carazo, *LG/DO* 58,159 (17 July 1954); and Decreto derogando restricción de garantías constitucionales en todo el país, *LG/DO* 59,82 (16 April 1955).

88. *La Prensa*, 15 February 1956.

89. *La Prensa*, 3 March 1956. In August of the same year the FDR repeated its decision to abstain, especially in view of the fact that the new president of the Consejo Nacional de Elecciones, Modesto Salmerón, was an unconditional supporter of Somoza who had presided over the 1947 electoral fiasco. The FDR also expressed its concern over the appointment of Anastasio Somoza Debayle, ASG's younger son, as acting Jefe Director of the Guardia Nacional while ASG campaigned, an appointment that they claimed violated military hierarchy, tended toward dynastic rule, and placed enormous power in the hands of "a person of arbitrary spirit and violent temperament." *La Prensa*, 4 August 1956.

90. *La Prensa*, 9, 11, 12 September 1956.

91. *La Prensa*, 17 July 1956.

92. *La Prensa*, 16 August 1956. On this occasion, Tomás Borge was jailed along with the Conservatives while covering the event for *La Prensa*.

93. Eduardo Conrado Vado, interview with author, Managua, 9 May 1984. The PLI consistently has claimed Rigoberto López Pérez as one of its own; see PLI, "Breve historia del Partido Liberal Independiente" (N.p., n.d., mimeograph), p. 16.

94. Enrique Alvarado, interview with author, Managua, 13 May 1985. See *La Prensa* 6 October–13 November and 21 November–11 December 1956 for transcripts of the testimony of those accused before the courts martial. The list reads like a who's who of Nicaraguan antisomocismo: Enoc Aguado, Pedro Joaquín Chamorro, R. A. Tefel, Emiliano Chamorro, Tomás Borge, Clemente Guido, Pablo Antonio Cuadra, and Diego Manuel Chamorro, among others. See also Millett, *Guardians of the Dynasty*, pp. 223–24, for a detailed account of the repression following Somoza's death. Clemente Guido, in his *Noches de tortura*, describes how he was arrested, tortured, and forced to sign a false statement implicating Pedro Joaquín Chamorro and Enoc Aguado in Somoza's death.

95. See *LG/DO* 54,177 (28 August 1950); 55,72 (10 April 1951); 60,222 (1 October 1956); 60,271 (28 November 1945); and 60,277 (5 December 1956).

96. See *LG/DO* 51,141 (3 July 1947); 54,165 (9 August 1950); and 60,177 (6 August 1956).

97. See *Guardia Nacional*, no. 286–287 (September–October 1956), for photos and descriptions of Somoza's funeral. This publication states that 140,000 people were present at the event.

Conclusion

1. For the European experience on the protection that states provided their inhabitants and particularly their wealthier ones, see Tilly, "War Making and State Making as Organized Crime."

2. *La Prensa*, 8 September 1956.

3. For a detailed analysis of this approach to the problem, see Torres Rivas, "El estado contra la sociedad."

BIBLIOGRAPHY

• • • • • • • • • • • • • •

Manuscript Sources

Archivo Nacional de Nicaragua

Documents consulted in the AN are located in one of the following collections: the papers of the executive branch of government (referred to as simply AN in the text); the Fondo Salvadora de Somoza (a number of bundles of documents found in 1980 in the home of Somoza's widow in Managua); the Fondo Felipe Rodríguez Serrano (private secretary to Anastasio Somoza García); and a collection of unclassified documents for the period after 1948 still in packing crates (referred to as AN[A]). When a document of the AN is found in a folder with a specific heading, the heading is cited; otherwise, the document is identified only by the number of the document box. Documents from the Fondo Salvadora de Somoza are identified by the bundle number only.

Instituto Histórico Centroamericano, Managua

Documents from IHCA are cited according to the Instituto's filing scheme.

Official Publications

Population Censuses, Statistics, and Economic Indicators

Nicaraguan Sources

Consejo Nacional de Economía. *Análisis del desarrollo económico y social de Nicaragua, 1950–1962.* Managua: N.p., 1964.
———. *Estudio de la salud pública en Nicaragua, 1950–1962.* Managua: N.p., 1964.
———. *Estructura del sector público de Nicaragua.* Managua: N.p., 1965.
———. *Estudio del desarrollo industrial de Nicaragua, 1950–1962.* Managua: N.p., 1965.
———. *Estudio de los servicios de transporte de Nicaragua, 1950–1962.* Managua: N.p., 1965.

————. *Estudio del comercio exterior y de la balanza de pagos de Nicaragua, 1950–1964*. Managua: n.p., 1966.

————. *Estudio de la energía eléctrica en Nicaragua, 1950–1964*. Managua: N.p., 1966.

Dirección General de Estadística y Censos. *Anuario estadístico general*. Managua: Talleres Nacionales. (Issued yearly between 1938 and 1947.)

————. *Boletín mensual de estadística*. (Issued every two or three months between 1944 and 1959.)

————. *Resumen estadístico de Nicaragua, 1935–1948*. Managua: N.p., 1949.

————. *Censo general de población de la República de Nicaragua, 1950*. Managua: Talleres Nacionales, 1951.

————. *Boletín de estadística*. III época. (Appeared irregularly between 1956 and 1960.)

————. *Resumen estadístico, 1950–1960*. Managua: N.p., 1961.

Instituto de Fomento Nacional. *Balances condensados y estadística*. Managua: N.p., n.d.

————. *Realizaciones*. Managua: Editorial Hospicio, n.d.

Instituto Nacional de Estadística y Censos. *Población de Nicaragua: Compendio de las cifras censales y proyecciones por departamentos y municipios*. Managua: July 1977.

————. *Boletín demográfico* 1 (November 1980): 1–53.

Ministerios de Economía y Trabajo. *Antecedentes del Seguro Social en Nicaragua, capítulo V*. Managua: N.p., 1955.

Ministerio de Hacienda y Crédito Público. *Presupuesto general de ingresos y egresos de la República de Nicaragua*. (Issued yearly.)

Oficina Central del Censo. *Censo general de 1920*. Managua: Tipografía Nacional, 1920.

Oficina Ejecutiva de Encuestas y Censos. *Boletín demográfico no. 4 y 5* (December 1978).

Other Sources

United Nations. Comisión Económica para América Latina (CEPAL). *Análisis y proyeccines de desarrollo económico*. Vol. 9, *El desarrollo económico de Nicaragua*. E/CN.12/742/Rev. 1. Mexico: United Nations, 1967.

U.S. Department of Commerce. International Reference Service. *Country Economic Reviews*, vol. 1, no. 44 (July 1944), "Economic Conditions in Nicaragua in 1940"; vol. 3, no. 33 (August 1946), "Nicaragua"; vol. 4, no. 33 (July 1947), "Economic Situation in 1946"; and vol. 5, no. 32 (May 1948), "Economic Review of Nicaragua in 1947."

U.S. Department of State. *A Brief History of the Relations between the United States and Nicaragua, 1909–1928*. Washington, D.C.: Government Printing Office, 1928.

————. *Foreign Relations of the United States*. Washington, D.C.: Government Printing Office. Published yearly.

Ministerial Documents

Consejo Nacional de Elecciones. *La verdad electoral de 1936*. Managua: Talleres Nacionales, 1937.

———. *El juicio electoral de 1950*. Managua: Talleres Nacionales, 1956.

Ministerio de Agricultura y Trabajo. *Memoria*. Managua: Talleres Nacionales. (These and the following *Memorias* were issued yearly with some gaps; they were all printed at the government's printing installation, the Talleres Nacionales.)

Ministerio de Economía. *Memorias*. (Issued yearly after the creation of this ministry in 1950.)

Ministerio de Educación. *Memoria*. (This ministry was originally designated "Instrucción Pública.")

Ministerio de Fomento y Obras Públicas. *Memoria*. (This ministry's name varied over time: Fomento y Anexos, Fomento y Obras Públicas, and finally simply Obras Públicas.)

Ministerio de Gobernación y Anexos. *Anales del primer congreso de municipalidades de Nicaragua*. Managua: Talleres Nacionales, 1939.

———. *Gobierno municipal de Nicaragua*. Managua: Talleres Nacionales, 1940.

———. *Programa del segundo congreso de municipalidades de Nicaragua*. Managua: N.p., 1942.

———. *Memoria*.

Ministerio de Guerra, Marina y Aviación. *Memoria*.

Ministerio de Hacienda y Crédito Público. *Memoria*.

Ministerio de Relaciones Exteriores. *Realidad política de Nicaragua*. Managua: Talleres Nacionales, 1948.

Ministerio de Trabajo. *Memoria*.

Presidencia de la República. *Mensaje del Presidente de la República al honorable Congreso Nacional*. (These were of three types: when the president assumed his office, when the Congress opened its sessions, and when the president presented his annual report to the nation.)

Recaudación General de Aduanas. *Memoria*. (Also known during some years as Oficina del Recaudador General de Aduanas y Alta Comisión.)

Party Documents

Argüello, Leonardo. *Plataforma política para el período presidencial 1947–1953*. Managua: Editorial Novedades, 1947.

Argüello B., Horacio, et al. *Interpretación de las propuestas que la Junta Directiva Nacional y Legal del Partido Conservador ha presentado a la Junta Directiva Nacional y Legal del Partido Liberal Nacionalista*. Managua: N.p., 1936.

Chamorro, Emiliano. *Declaración del General Emiliano Chamorro*. Guatemala: N.p., 1948.

Comité Revolucionario Nicaragüense. *Programa de acción*. Mexico: N.p., 1938.

Cordero Reyes, Manuel, Carlos Castro Wassmer, and Carlos Pasos. *Nicaragua bajo el régimen de Somoza: A los gobiernos y pueblos de América*. San Salvador: Imprenta Funes, 1944.

Coronel Urtecho, José. *Carta política del señor José Coronel Urtecho al General Emiliano Chamorro*. Managua: Editorial San Carlos, 1938.

Cuadra Pasos, Carlos. *Posibilidades de existencia del comunismo en Nicaragua*. Granada: Tipografía El Centro Americano, 1937.

―――. *Mensaje a los Conservadores de Nicaragua*. Managua: Editorial La Prensa, 1950.

Espinoza, Horacio. *El liberalismo debe renovar su ideología y su actuación*. Managua: Tipografía Alemana de Carlos Heuberger, 1935.

Frente Nacional pro Libertad de Nicaragua. *La verdadera realidad política de Nicaragua*. Bogotá: Tipografía Voluntad, 1948.

Grupo Conservador Civilista. *Manifiesto*. Managua: Editorial La Prensa, 1949.

Juventud Liberal Nicaragüense. *Recopilación de la Asamblea General de Juventud Liberal Nacionalista del 2 de febrero de 1952*. Managua: Tipografía Progreso, 1952.

Lacayo L., Chester. *590 días de acción estudiantil*. N.p., 1938.

Paniagua Rivas, Rafael. *Los principios fundamentales del conservatismo*. Managua: Editorial La Prensa, 1950.

Partido Conservador de Nicaragua. *Documentos y resoluciones del Partido Conservador de Nicaragua*. Managua: Editorial San Rafael, 1955.

Partido Liberal Independiente. "Breve historia del Partido Liberal Independiente." N.P., n.d. Mimeo.

Partido Liberal Nacionalista. *Estatuto constitutivo, programa y declaración de principios del Partido Liberal Nacionalista de Nicaragua de 1913. Reformas de 1920, 1923, 1928*. Managua: Tipografía del Partido Liberal, 1932.

―――. *Política liberal concerniente a los convenios de conciliación*. Managua: Tipografía Roja, 1935.

―――. *Informe de las actividades desplegadas por el Comité Departamental de Propaganda del PLN del Departamento de León durante la campaña electoral de 1936*. N.p., n.d.

―――. *Declaración de principios; estatutos del Partido Liberal Nacionalista; y reglamento de la Casa del Partido Liberal Nacionalista*. Managua: Tipografía Gurdián, 1944.

―――. *Informe que rinde la Junta Directiva Nacional y Legal del Partido Liberal Nacionalista a la Gran Convención*. León: N.p., 20 January 1946.

―――. *Plataforma de gobierno que el General Anastasio Somoza presenta a la Gran Convención del Partido Liberal Nacionalista al ser proclamado su candidato presidencial para el período 1957–1963*. Managua: Editorial Novedades, 1956.

Salvatierra, Sofonías, ed. *Conciliación democrática de los partidos políticos de Nicaragua: Convenios sobre representación de las minorías celebrados en 1932*. Managua: Tipografía Progreso, 1944(?).

Sánchez, Rodrigo, ed. *La vieja guardia*. Managua: N.p., 1936.

Selva, Adán. *Cero política*. Managua: Editorial Asel, 1961.

————. *Política del Partido Liberal Independiente. En defensa del pueblo y contra la dictadura*. Managua: Editorial Asel, 1961.

Solórzano, Carlos José. *La ideología que debe sustentar el Partido Conservador de Nicaragua*. Managua: Editorial Nuevos Horizontes, 1947.

Unión Revolucionaria Democrática. *La lucha contra Somoza: Crítica interna y programa*. Mexico: N.p., 1954.

Valle Rios, Julio, ed. *Por qué los obreros y los campesinos estan con Somoza*. Managua: Editorial Novedades, 1955.

Newspapers and Journals

Boletín de la Cámara Nacional de Comercio e Industrias de Managua. (Cited as *Boletín*.)

Elite. Managua. (Monthly photo magazine.)

La Gaceta/Diario Oficial. (Nicaraguan government journal published daily; contains laws, executive decrees, congressional debates, and varied official data.)

Guardia Nacional. (Official publication of the Guardia Nacional de Nicaragua; invariably a Somoza was the editor.)

Mercurio. (Journal of the Cámara de Comercio, Industria y Agricultura de León.)

La Prensa. Managua.

Revolución. (Monthly paper of the Partido Revolucionario Nicaragüense published in Costa Rica.)

Books and Articles

Amador, Armando. *Origen, auge y crisis de una dictadura*. Guatemala: N.p., 1949.

Anderson, Charles W. "Nicaragua: The Somoza Dynasty." In Needler.

Anderson, Perry. *Lineages of the Absolutist State*. London: Verso Editions, 1974.

Armijo Mejía, Modesto. *Ideas sobre la organización del ejecutivo en los países pequeños*. Managua: N.p., 1956.

Barahona Portocarrero, Amaru. "Estudio sobre la historia contemporanea de Nicaragua." *Revista del Pensamiento Centroamericano* 22, no. 157 (October–December 1977): 32–49.

Barreto, Pablo Emilio. *44 años de dictadura somocista*. Managua: N.p., n.d.

Belli, Humberto. "Un ensayo de interpretación sobre las luchas políticas nicaragüenses (de la independencia hasta la revolución cubana)." *Revista del Pensamiento Centroamericano* 22, no. 157 (October–December 1977): 50–59.

Belli, Pedro. "Prolegómeno para una historia económica de Nicaragua de 1905 a 1966." *Revista del Pensamiento Centroamericano* 30, no. 146 (January–March 1965): 2–30.

Black, George. *Triumph of the People: The Sandinista Revolution in Nicaragua*. London: Zed Press, 1981.

Callcott, Wilfrid Hardy. *The Caribbean Policy of the United States, 1890–1920*. Baltimore: Johns Hopkins Press, 1942.

Cantarero, Luis Augusto. "The Economic Development of Nicaragua, 1920–1947." Ph.D. dissertation, State University of Iowa, 1948.

Castro Silva, Juan María. *Nicaragua económica*. Managua: Talleres Nacionales, 1949.

Chamorro, Emiliano. *Autobiografía*. Reprinted in *Revista Conservadora del Pensamiento Centroamericano* 14 (April 1966).

Chapman, Charles E. "The Age of the Caudillo." *Hispanic American Historical Review* 12 (August 1932): 281–300.

Cox, Isaac Joslin. *Nicaragua and the United States, 1909–1927*. Boston: World Peace Foundation Pamphlets, 1927.

Cuadra Pasos, Carlos. *Historia de medio siglo*. Managua: Ediciones El Pez y la Serpiente, 1964.

―――. *Obras*. Vol. 1, *Historia de medio siglo*. Managua: Colección Cultural del Banco de América, 1976.

Cumberland, W. W. *Nicaragua: An Economic and Financial Survey*. Washington, D.C.: Government Printing Office, 1928.

Dodd, Thomas Joseph. "United States in Nicaraguan Politics: Supervised Elections, 1923–1932." Ph.D. dissertation, George Washington University, 1966.

Dodds, Harold W. "American Supervision of Nicaraguan Elections." *Foreign Affairs* 7 (April 1929): 488–96.

Douglas, Charles A., and John V. Morgan. *Nicaragua and the United States*. Washington, D.C.: N.p., 1936.

Espinoza Sotomayor, Enrique. *Partidos políticos*. Managua: Tipografía Progreso, 1940.

Evans, Peter, Dietrich Rueschemeyer, and Theda Skocpol, eds. *Bringing the State Back In*. Cambridge University Press, 1986.

Findling, John Ellis. "The United States and Zelaya: A Study in the Diplomacy of Expediency." Ph.D. dissertation, University of Texas at Austin, 1971.

Frazier, Charles A. "The Dawn of Nationalism and Its Consequences in Nicaragua." Ph.D. dissertation, University of Texas at Austin, 1968.

Gallardo, Ricardo. *Las constituciones de la República Federal de Centroamérica*, 2 vols. Madrid: Instituto de Estudios Políticos, 1958.

Gould, Jeffrey. "The Nicaraguan Labor Movement and the Somoza Regime, 1944–1946." Unpublished paper.

Grieb, Kenneth J. *Guatemalan Caudillo: The Regime of Jorge Ubico: Guatemala, 1931–1944*. Athens: Ohio University Press, 1979.

Guido, Clemente. *Noches de tortura*. Managua: Ediciones Nicarao, 1980.

Gutiérrez Mayorga, Gustavo. "Dos etapas en la historia del movimiento obrero de Nicaragua." Tesis de grado: Universidad de Costa Rica, 1977.

―――. "El reformismo artesanal en el movimiento obrero nicaragüense (1913–1960)." *Revista del Pensamiento Centroamericano* 23, no. 159 (April–June 1978): 2–21.

Hamilton, Nora. *The Limits of State Autonomy: Post Revolutionary Mexico*. Princeton, N.J.: Princeton University Press, 1982.

Held, David. "Central Perspectives on the Modern State." In Held, pp. 1–55.

———, ed. *State and Societies*. New York: New York University Press, 1983.

Herrera Zúniga, René. "Nicaragua: El desarrollo capitalista dependiente y la crisis de la dominación burguesa, 1950–1980." *Foro Internacional* 80 (April–June 1980): 612–45.

Hill, Roscoe. *Fiscal Intervention in Nicaragua*. New York: N.p., 1933.

International Bank for Reconstruction and Development (IBRD). Mission to Nicaragua. *The Fiscal System of Nicaragua: A Report of the Semestre on Public Finance*. 1952. Mimeograph.

———. *The Economic Development of Nicaragua*. Baltimore: Johns Hopkins University Press, 1953.

Kamman, William. *A Search for Stability: United States Diplomacy towards Nicaragua, 1925–1933*. Notre Dame, Ind.: University of Notre Dame Press, 1968.

Kaplan, Marcos. *Formación del estado nacional en América Latina*. Santiago de Chile: Editorial Universitaria, 1969.

Karnes, Thomas. *The Failure of Union: Central America, 1824–1960*. Chapel Hill.: University of North Carolina Press, 1961.

Krehm, William. *Democracias y tiranías en el Caribe*. Buenos Aires: Editorial Parnaso, 1957.

LaFeber, Walter. *Inevitable Revolutions: The United States in Central America*. New York: Norton, 1984.

Langley, Lester D. *The United States and the Caribbean, 1900–1970*. Atlanta: University of Georgia Press, 1980.

Lanuza, Alberto. "La formación del estado nacional en Nicaragua." In Lanuza et al., pp. 7–138.

Lanuza, Alberto, Juan Luis Vásquez, Amaru Barahona, and Amalia Chamorro. *Economía y sociedad en la construcción del estado en Nicaragua*. San José, Costa Rica: ICAP, 1983.

Laski, Harold. *The State in Theory and Practice*. New York: Viking Press, 1935.

Lewis, Paul H. *Paraguay under Stroessner*. Chapel Hill: University of North Carolina Press, 1980.

Macaulay, Neill. *The Sandino Affair*. Chicago: Quadrangle Books, 1971.

MacLeod, Murdo J. *Spanish Central America: A Socioeconomic History, 1520–1720*. Berkeley: University of California Press, 1973.

Mariscal, Nicolás, Rubén Zamora, and Edgar Jiménez Cabrera, eds. *El Estado*. San Salvador: UCA Editores, 1979.

Meléndez, Carlos, ed. *Textos fundamentales de la independencia centroamericana*. San José, Costa Rica: Editorial Universitaria Centroamericana, 1971.

Millett, Richard. "Anastasio Somoza García: A Brief History of Nicaragua's 'Enduring' Dictator." *Revista/Review Interamericana* 7, no. 3 (Fall 1977): 486–508.

———. *Guardians of the Dynasty: A History of the U.S. Created Guardia Nacional of Nicaragua and the Somoza Family*. Maryknoll, N.Y.: Orbis Books, 1977.

Munro, Dana G. *The United States and the Caribbean Republics, 1921–1933*. Princeton, N.J.: Princeton University Press, 1974.

Needler, Martin, ed. *Political Systems of Latin America*. Princeton, N.J.: Princeton University Press, 1964.

Nicaragua Sugar Estates, Ltd. *Ingenio San Antonio*. Granada: N.p., 1953.

North, Douglass C., and Robert Paul Thomas. *The Rise of the Western World: A New Economic History*. Cambridge University Press, 1975.

O'Donnell, Guillermo. "Apuntes para una teoría del estado." In Mariscal et al., pp. 194–237.

Oszlak, Oscar. "The Historical Formation of the State in Latin America: Some Theoretical and Methodological Guidelines for Its Study." *Latin American Research Review* 16, no. 2 (1981): 3–32.

———. *La formación del estado argentino*. Buenos Aires: Editorial de Belgrano, 1985.

Pérez Bermúdez, Carlos, and Onofre Guevara López. *El movimiento obrero en Nicaragua: Primera parte*. Managua: Editorial El Amanecer, n.d.

———. *El movimiento obrero en Nicaragua, fascículos 5 y 6*. Managua: Ediciones Avila Bolaños, 1981.

Playter, Harold. *Nicaragua: a Commercial and Economic Survey*. Washington, D.C.: Government Printing Office, 1927.

Radell, David Richard. "An Historical Geography of Western Nicaragua: The Spheres of Influence of León, Granada, and Managua, 1519–1965." Ph.D. Dissertation, University of California at Berkeley, 1969.

Ramírez, Sergio, ed. *Augusto C. Sandino: El pensamiento vivo*. Managua: Editorial Nueva Nicaragua, 1984.

Sacasa, Juan Bautista. *Cómo y por qué caí del poder*. León, Nicaragua: N.p., 1946. Reprinted in *Revista del Pensamiento Centroamericano* 23, no. 161 (October–December 1978): 2–32.

Selser, Gregorio. *Sandino: General de hombres libres*. San José, Costa Rica: Editorial Universitaria Centroamericana, 1974.

Skocpol, Theda. *States and Social Revolutions*. Cambridge University Press, 1979.

———. "Bringing the State Back In: Strategies of Analysis in Current Research." In Evans, Rueschmeyer, and Skocpol, pp. 3–37.

Stansifer, Charles L. "Una nueva interpretación de José Santos Zelaya, dictador de Nicaragua, 1893–1909." *Anuario de Estudios Centroamericanos*, no. 1 (1974): 47–59.

Stepan, Alfred. *The State and Society: Peru in Comparative Perspective*. Princeton, N.J.: Princeton University Press, 1978.

Stimson, Henry Lewis. *American Policy in Nicaragua*. New York: Charles Scribner's Sons, 1927. Reprint. New York: Arno Press and New York Times, 1970.

Teplitz, Benjamin I. "The Political and Economic Foundations of Modernization in Nicaragua: The Administration of José Santos Zelaya, 1893–1909." Ph.D dissertation, Howard University, 1973.

Tilly, Charles, ed. *The Formation of National States in Western Europe*. Princeton, N.J.: Princeton University Press, 1975.

———. "War Making and State Making as Organized Crime." In Evans, Rueschemeyer, and Skocpol, pp. 169–91.

Tirado, Manlio. *Conversando con José Coronel Urtecho.* Managua: Editorial Nueva Nicaragua, 1983.

Torres Rivas, Edelberto. "Poder nacional y sociedad dependiente: Las clases y el estado en Centroamérica." In Mariscal et al., pp. 157–93.

———. "La formación del Estado y el sector público en Centroamérica y Panamá." *Revista Mexicana de Sociología* 42, no. 2 (April–June 1980):561–89.

———. El estado contra la sociedad: las raíces de la revolución nicaragüense." *Estudios Sociales Centroamericanos* 9, no. 27 (September–December 1980): 79–96.

Tulchin, Joseph S. *The Aftermath of War: World War I and U.S. Policy towards Latin America.* New York: New York University Press, 1971.

U.S. Department of State. *The United States and Nicaragua: A Survey of the Relations from 1909 to 1932.* Washington, D.C.: Government Printing Office, 1932.

———. *Foreign Relations of the United States.* Washington, D.C.: Government Printing Office.

Valle Martínez, Marco Antonio. "Desarrollo económico y político de Nicaragua, 1912–1947." Tesis de grado: Consejo Superior Universitario Centroamericano. San José, Costa Rica, 1976.

Velásquez, José Luis. "La incidencia de la formación de la economía agroexportadora en el intento de formación del estado nacional en Nicaragua, 1860–1930." *Revista del Pensamiento Centroamericano* 32, no. 157 (October–December 1977): 11–31.

Walker, Thomas. *The Christian Democratic Movement in Nicaragua.* Tucson: University of Arizona Press, 1970.

Wallerstein, Immanuel. *The Modern World System I.* New York: Academic Press, 1974.

Wheelock Román, Jaime. *Imperialismo y dictadura: Crisis de una formación social.* Mexico: Siglo Veintiuno Editores, 1975.

Woodward, Ralph Lee. *Central America: A Nation Divided.* New York: Oxford University Press, 1976.

Wortman, Miles L. *Government and Society in Central America, 1680–1840.* New York: Columbia University Press, 1982.

INDEX

· · · · · · · · · · · · ·